From Vice to Nice

From Vice to Nice

Midwestern Politics and the Gentrification of AIDS

....

RENÉ ESPARZA

The University of North Carolina Press Chapel Hill

© 2025 The University of North Carolina Press
All rights reserved
Set in Charis and Lato by Westchester Publishing Services
Manufactured in the United States of America

Library of Congress Cataloging-in-Publication Data
Names: Esparza, René, 1986– author.
Title: From vice to nice : Midwestern politics and the gentrification of AIDS / René Esparza.
Description: Chapel Hill : The University of North Carolina Press, [2025] | Includes bibliographical references and index.
Identifiers: LCCN 2025015183 | ISBN 9781469690384 (cloth) | ISBN 9781469690391 (paperback) | ISBN 9781469683225 (epub) | ISBN 9781469690407 (pdf)
Subjects: LCSH: LGBT activism—Minnesota—Minneapolis Metropolitan Area—History—20th century. | Gay men, White—Political activity—Minnesota—Minneapolis Metropolitan Area. | AIDS (Disease)—Prevention—Government policy—Minnesota—Minneapolis Metropolitan Area. | Gentrification—Minnesota—Minneapolis Metropolitan Area—History—20th century. | Sexual minorities—Minnesota—Minneapolis Metropolitan Area—Social conditions. | Race discrimination—Minnesota—Minneapolis Metropolitan Area—History—20th century. | BISAC: SOCIAL SCIENCE / Gender Studies | SOCIAL SCIENCE /Sociology / Urban
Classification: LCC HQ73.73.U6 E77 2025 | DDC 362.19697/ 9200977657909048—dc23/eng/20250512
LC record available at https://lccn.loc.gov/2025015183

Cover art: *The Light Borrower*, by R. F. Alvarez. Courtesy of R. F. Alvarez.

For product safety concerns under the European Union's General Product Safety Regulation (EU GPSR), please contact gpsr@mare-nostrum.co.uk or write to the University of North Carolina Press and Mare Nostrum Group B.V., Mauritskade 21D, 1091 GC Amsterdam, The Netherlands.

para mi mamá y papá

Contents

List of Illustrations, ix

Acknowledgments, xi

Introduction, 1
Making Sense of the "New" Gay

1 Gay Minnesota Comes Out, 28

2 Privacy in a Time of AIDS, 63

3 From Persecuted to Protected, 92

4 The Carrier as Criminal, 124

5 Minneapolis "Matures" Past Bathhouses, 153

6 Cruising All the Way Home, 189

Epilogue, 232
What Space Can Be

Notes, 241

Bibliography, 291

Index, 307

Illustrations

Figures

0.1 "The New Gay" segment in *The Daily Show*, 2011, 2
1.1 Jack Baker's student body president campaign poster, 1970, 30
1.2 Brian J. Coyle, 1980s, 51
3.1 "Play It Safe" antiviolence flyer, 1986, 94
3.2 "Play It Safe" HIV-prevention poster, 1986, 110
3.3 "Safe Sex Is More Than Just Wearing a Condom" PSA, 1986, 113
3.4 "Be Safe!" PSA, 1986, 115
3.5 "Be Careful!" PSA, 1986, 116
4.1 Fabian Bridges, 1986, 143
5.1 Dick Brown outside the 315 Health Club bathhouse, 1987, 154
5.2 Clint Heim outside the 315 Health Club bathhouse, 1987, 157
5.3 HIV prevention PSA, 1987, 159
5.4 Dick Hanson and Bert Henningson, 1987, 164
5.5 The 315 Health Club, 1984, 180
6.1 Booth Manor Condos and Greenway Gables Townhomes, 1980, 194
6.2 Two men in Loring Park, 1989, 198
6.3 F.A.G.S. flyer, 1989, 202
6.4 F.A.G.S. at council hearing, 1989, 206
6.5 Condom bucket and antiviolence message at "Bare Ass Beach," 1991, 212
6.6 Reward flyer, 1991, 213
6.7 LGBTQ protesters at City Hall, 1991, 214
6.8 Downtown Minneapolis skyline and Loring Park, 1995, 229

Map

0.1 Map of downtown Minneapolis and Loring Park, xviii

Acknowledgments

The questions at the heart of this book stem from witnessing the gentrification of my childhood neighborhood, West Town, in Chicago during the 1990s. Lacking the language to understand these shifts, I assumed neighborhood change was inevitable—people simply came and went. And that some of us, those who appeared straight and had families and money, were somehow more deserving of housing. It was not until my journey from high school to undergraduate and graduate school that I found the words to understand these changes, to see my life mirrored in the stories of others, and to make sense of how power moves through neighborhoods like mine. For teaching me that language, I am deeply indebted to the mentors, educators, colleagues, friends, and family who follow.

I want to begin by expressing my heartfelt gratitude to my interlocutors, whose generosity and willingness to share their stories lie at the core of this work. Thank you to Roxanne "Rox" Anderson, Dean Asmundson, Ken Darling, Scott Dibble, Dallas Drake, Jerry Fladmark, Edd Lee, Nicholas Metcalf, Jim St. George, Richard Simon, and Thomas Trisko. Your insights, experiences, and courage have shaped this book in profound ways. I hope it reflects the depth and complexity of what you entrusted to me.

This book began as a doctoral project at the University of Minnesota, Twin Cities, where I was fortunate to have the guidance of exceptional advisors. Roderick A. Ferguson's sharp intellect and thoughtful mentorship challenged me to refine my arguments and deepen my analysis. His book *Aberrations in Black* changed my life; you think you are alone in the world, that the pain is yours alone, and then you read, and suddenly, you see yourself reflected, understood, and connected to something larger. Roderick's commitment to rigorous scholarship and transformative mentorship remains a guiding force in my life. Kevin P. Murphy read every draft with care, offering feedback that was both precise and insightful. His steadfast support and enthusiasm for my research shaped this book and have profoundly influenced the scholar I am today. Edén Torres offered constant encouragement, her belief in my work a source of motivation throughout graduate school. Lorena Muñoz pushed me to approach my analysis from new perspectives, broadening the scope of my research in meaningful ways. Sandra Soto provided unwavering support and thoughtful engagement with my work, for which I am deeply grateful. Martin F. Manalansan's insights have been invaluable, strengthening this project at every stage. From my undergraduate thesis to this book, Martin has been a mentor whose generosity and intellectual rigor have profoundly shaped my understanding of what scholarship can be. I am deeply thankful to each of you for your guidance and support, which have left a lasting imprint on this work.

So many people in the Twin Cities and at the University of Minnesota helped this book take shape. Rodolfo Aguilar, Irina Barrera, Akikwe Cornell, Idalia R. De Léon, Courtney Gildersleeve, Vanessa Guzman, Mingwei Huang, Rita Kompelmakher, Brittany Lewis, Joanna Nuñez, Mario Obando, Karla Padrón, Soham Patel, Kong Pha, Reina Rodríguez, José Manuel Santillana, Gabriela Spears-Rico, Robert Stewart, Daniel Topete, and Naimah Zulmadelle Petigny—thank you for your friendship and your words. You made me laugh when I needed it most, and you made me think when the words would not come. To Noro Andriamanalina, Rose Brewer, Bianet Castellanos, Paul Ching, Jigna Desai, Tracy Ann Deutsch, Kale B. Fajardo, Karen Ho, David Karjanen, Brenda Kayzar, Regina Kunzel, Erika Lee, Katie Levin, Jennifer Pierce, Elliott Powell, Catherine Squires, Jasmine Tang, and David Valentine—thank you for your guidance, encouragement, and thought-provoking conversations. Whether in classrooms, seminars, or casual moments, your insights and support shaped this project in profound ways.

My intellectual journey began at the University of Illinois, Urbana-Champaign, under the transformative mentorship of Lisa M. Cacho. Her Intro to Latina/o Studies course during my freshman year was more than an introduction to a field—it was an introduction to myself. Through her teaching, I gained the tools to embrace my intersecting identities and reconcile parts of myself I had been told were incompatible. Lisa held my hand at a time when I needed it most, guiding me with compassion and conviction and showing me that it was not only possible but necessary to undertake this journey of self-discovery and healing. Her belief in me and my voice was life-changing, giving me the courage to chart a path I had not dared imagine. Thank you, Lisa, for helping me see and trust myself in ways that continue to shape me. I am also deeply grateful to Richard T. Rodríguez, who nurtured my interest in queer of color critique and encouraged me to think critically and expansively. To the McNair Scholars Program, led by Priscilla Henderson Fortier and Michael L. Jeffries Sr., thank you for cultivating my love of research and preparing me for graduate school. Your support made me feel capable of pursuing this work and finding a place within it.

I am deeply grateful to the many people who read this manuscript at various stages and offered invaluable feedback. Andrea Friedman, thank you for your thoughtful suggestions and unwavering support; your mentorship continues to guide and inspire my academic journey. Jennifer Brier, your invaluable insights and willingness to read the manuscript multiple times were instrumental. Thank you for pioneering this field and mentoring a new generation of scholars. Nayan Shah, your expertise and thoughtful feedback helped refine this project in crucial ways. Your scholarship continues to illuminate how queer of color critique can be powerfully grounded in historical method. Lisa Duggan, your generous comments allowed me to articulate my central arguments with greater clarity and precision. Jonathan Bell, your advice brought clarity and focus to the manuscript, improving it at critical moments. Paul Renfro, your input pushed me to strengthen the work where it needed it most. Peter Hohn, my developmental editor, played an essential role in shaping this book. Your guidance made a daunting process manageable, and I am grateful for your care and skill. To the readers for the University of North Carolina Press, thank you for your thoughtful and constructive critiques. I owe a special debt to my editor, Andreína Fernández, whose sharp eye and editorial insight have strengthened this work immensely. Your expertise and patience have been vital to this process. I am also thankful to the scholars whose work and feedback have shaped this project—Julio Capó Jr., Christina B. Hanhardt, Theodore Kerr, David Román, Timothy Stewart-Winter, Phil Tiemeyer, and Stephen Vider. Each of you has contributed to refining my thinking and this manuscript in meaningful ways. To my colleagues and friends in the field— Christina Jessica Carney, Nic Flores, Eric Gonzaba, Kris Klein Hernández, Natalie Lira, Dan Royles, and Nick Syrett—thank you for your camaraderie, your encouragement, and the many ways you have supported this work and my growth as a scholar. To my students, past and present, including Abbigail Matthews and Marc Ridgell, your curiosity, engagement, and critical perspectives have been a constant source of inspiration. To Marika Cifor and Jan Huebenthal, our informal AIDS writing group was an invaluable space for exchange and support. Thank you for reading portions of this manuscript and offering feedback that has strengthened this work in countless ways.

I am grateful for several forms of institutional support that provided the time and resources necessary to complete this manuscript. The Ford

Postdoctoral Fellowship through the Ford Foundation offered critical funding to advance my research. The First Book Faculty Fellowship through the Center for the Humanities at Washington University in St. Louis supported the refinement and development of my ideas. I am deeply grateful to Jean Allman for her generous mentorship and to my fellow cohort members, including Paige McGinley, for their helpful recommendations. The LGBTQ Research Fellowship at the ONE National Gay and Lesbian Archives gave me access to invaluable archival materials that shaped this work. At the University of Maryland, Baltimore County, the Postdoctoral Fellowship in the Department of American Studies offered a space to deepen my research, and I am especially grateful to Nicole King for her thoughtful mentorship and the department's faculty for their support. Additionally, the Center for Black, Brown, and Queer Studies, under the leadership of Ahmed Ragab, provided a collaborative space where I could workshop ideas and expand my thinking alongside a supportive cohort of fellows. These institutions and individuals were instrumental in bringing this project to fruition, and I am deeply appreciative of their contributions.

Thank you to my current and former colleagues in the Department of Women, Gender, and Sexuality Studies at Washington University in St. Louis: Marlon Bailey, Cynthia Barounis, Barbara Baumgartner, Heather Berg, Rachel Brown, Ivan Bujan, Shefali Chandra, Amy Cislo, Adrienne Davis, Mary Ann Dzuback, Andrea Friedman, Tamsin Kimoto, Jeffrey McCune, Bahia Munem, Allison Reed, Trevor Sangrey, and Kimberly Soriano. Your wisdom, kindness, and encouragement have been invaluable. Special thanks to Rebecca Wanzo for her unwavering support, her inspiring model of professorial excellence, her deep appreciation of my work, and her encouragement when I needed it most. Thank you to Donna Kepley and Crystal Odelle for the support that keeps everything moving forward. To Christina Madrazo, Diana Montaño, and Miguel Valerio—your friendship has been a blessing. Together, we have shared laughter, warmth, and moments that have made St. Louis feel just a little bit more like home. I look forward to many more cherished memories together.

This book owes much to the librarians and archivists who preserve the histories essential to telling these stories. I am deeply grateful to Aiden Bettine and Lisa Vecoli at the Tretter Collection in GLBT Studies at the University of Minnesota, Twin Cities, for their invaluable support. Thank you to Ted Hathaway and the archivists at the Hennepin County Library Special Collections, as well as those at the Minnesota Historical Society, for their guidance and assistance in uncovering critical materials. I extend my appreciation to Kevin Ehrman-Solberg, Ashley Halbach, Claude Peck, and Stewart Van Cleve for their help in locating sources and for the enriching conversations that deepened my understanding of the Twin Cities' history.

Completing this book would not have been possible without the love and support of my friends. James Flowers, Claudia Marosz Miranda, David Otero, Colin Peterson, and Jason Yorek—thank you for your generosity, encouragement, and steady humor. The moments we shared throughout this journey kept me grounded and reminded me of the strength found in community. I am profoundly grateful for the communal intimacies we have built together and look forward to many more moments of shared laughter and connection.

My deepest gratitude goes to my family. This book reflects your love and support as much as the intellectual communities that have shaped me. I am grateful to my aunts, uncles, cousins, and grandparents, especially my Tía Mariela Chavarria, Tío José Contreras, Tío Jesús Vargas, and Blanca Fonseca, for their support throughout my education. To my immediate family, you have been my constant source of motivation since the day I left for Minneapolis. On difficult days, I thought of your faith in me, and it gave me the strength to keep going. To Lizbeth, Melanie, and Ian Bautista—my nieces and nephew—thank you for your unconditional love. Your curiosity, humor, and energy remind me why the work of building a more just world matters. To my "baby" brother, Christian Esparza, you have taught me the importance of persistence, of continuing forward no matter the obstacles. Your example inspires me to approach life with an open heart and determination. And to my sister, Jetzabel Karime Esparza, your resilience is extraordinary. I admire everything you have accomplished and the way you approach challenges with strength and resolve. I am honored to have you as my sister.

Finalmente, mis padres. Para mi papá, René Esparza, quien cargó el peso del mundo sobre sus hombros, entregando su juventud para darnos de comer, vestirnos, y mantenernos a salvo. Un hombre que enfrentó el ardor de miradas racistas, que caminó kilómetros cuando no había para el camión, y cuyo acento grueso fue motivo de burlas de aquellos que jamás comprenderían su historia. Él enfrentó un mundo que intentó hacerlo sentir ajeno en su propia piel. Luchó contra fuerzas más grandes que él: el racismo, la pobreza, y todo lo que quiso detenerlo. Y sí, tropezó, buscó consuelo en cosas que lo lastimaban, en lugares donde no podía sanar. Pero siguió adelante, paso a paso, porque nosotros lo esperábamos en casa. De niño, no comprendía todo lo que él cargaba. Pero ahora, como adulto, veo las barreras que enfrentó, las formas en que luchó, y las maneras en que nos amó. En su último aliento, me dijo: "Sé alguien." Y pienso en él todos los días, en todo lo que me enseñó sobre empatía y perdón. Por todas las veces que me mostró amor sin necesidad de palabras. Este libro es para ti, Apá, por todas las formas en que moldeaste mi vida con tu fortaleza, tus sacrificios, y tu enorme corazón.

Y para mi mamá, Sonia Esparza, quien cruzó ríos, desiertos y fronteras con nada más que sus sueños y sus manos como guía. Una joven con una valentía demasiado grande para cualquier pueblito o para un mundo de mentes estrechas, que nos llevó a mi hermana y a mí cruzando una línea para que pudiéramos tener un futuro más amplio que el horizonte que conocía. Enfrentó palabras tan filosas como cuchillos, manos que desconocían la ternura, y un mundo que le decía: "Aquí no perteneces." Y ella respondió: "Pues mírenme." Gracias, mamá, por cada amanecer en que trabajaste a pesar del cansancio para poner comida en nuestra mesa, por mantenerte firme cuando otros querían hacerte pequeña. Y por los viajes a la biblioteca, por alzarme sobre tus hombros y dejarme alcanzar más alto que cualquier muro o frontera. Me enseñaste que las historias podían llevarme a cualquier lugar, que los libros no eran solo palabras, sino alas. Tú, Amá, me enseñaste que este mundo podía ser nuestro, que podíamos escribirnos en él. Este libro es para ti, porque en cada página late lo que me enseñaste: que la justicia siempre merece ser buscada, incluso cuando la voz tiembla o parece apagarse, y que en esos momentos de incertidumbre es el amor lo que nos impulsa a seguir adelante.

To those who lost their lives to a pandemic that was allowed to spread unchecked: I hope this book contributes, in some small way, to the justice you were owed. And to everyone who has walked alongside me on this journey: Thank you. This book exists because of you.

From Vice to Nice

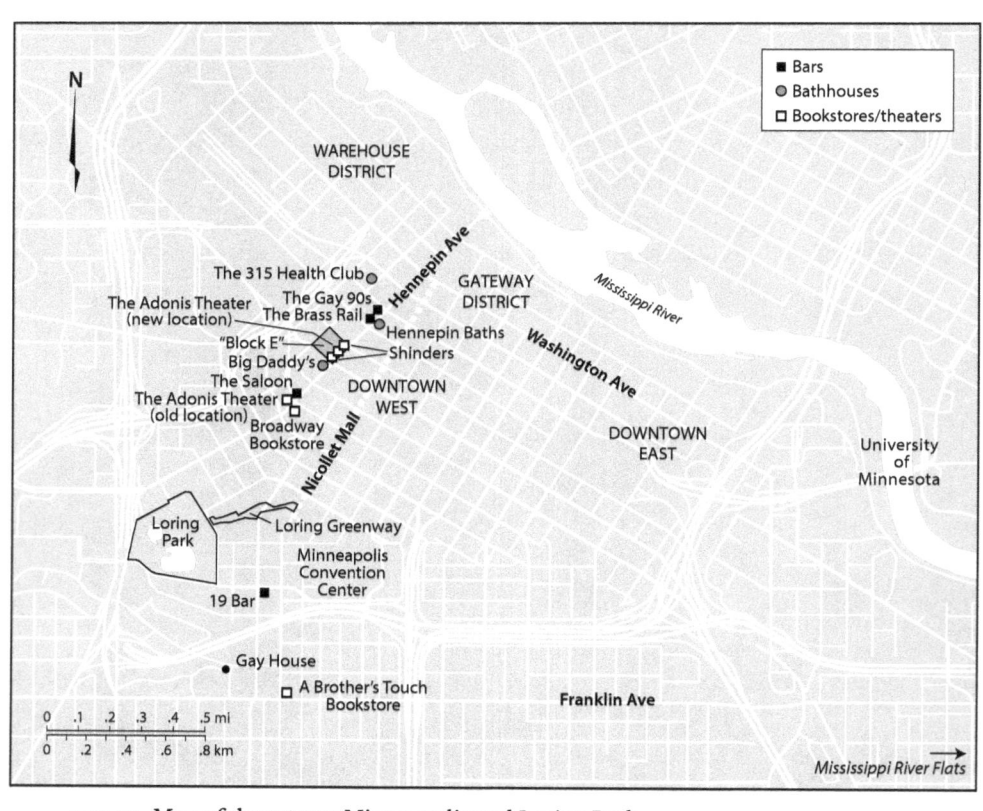

MAP 0.1 Map of downtown Minneapolis and Loring Park.

Introduction
Making Sense of the "New" Gay

· ·

America's Gayest City

What does it mean to be a gay American? By 2011, this was an open question, for that year *The Advocate*, the national LGBTQ magazine, announced an unexpected finding: Minneapolis, it declared, was America's gayest city—surpassing San Francisco, which did not even crack the top ten.[1] The announcement caught many off guard, earning national media coverage and, more importantly in 2011, the attention of Comedy Central's news satire program, *The Daily Show with Jon Stewart*. The show sent correspondent Jason Jones to both cities to compare the "old gay" of San Francisco—characterized by boas, dildos, and parades—against the "new gay" of Minneapolis, marked by bikes, boutiques, and artisanal bakeries. In San Francisco, Jones interviewed "leather daddies" and visited sex shops where, decked in fetish gear, he was strapped to a bondage wheel. After strolling through the Castro neighborhood with local gay activist Tim Seelig and attending a performance by the San Francisco Gay Men's Chorus, Jones jetted off to Minneapolis, dismissing what he perceived as San Francisco gay men "reenacting" an outdated gay lifestyle.[2]

In Minneapolis, Jones reveled in the exoticism of the "hot," "hardcore," "new" gay—the joke being that there was nothing exotic, hot, or hardcore about it. Unlike the alleged nonstop sexual frolicking and in-your-face queerness of gay life in San Francisco, in Minneapolis, a younger, white-presenting gay couple explained (to an oohing and aahing Jones) how their life together consisted of baking banana bread, playing Scrabble, and shopping the aisles of Minneapolis-based Target (the new cruising, according to Jones) (fig. 0.1). This "new" gay no longer prioritized bars, bathhouses, and sex shops—establishments associated with crime, lowered property values, and HIV/AIDS. If the new gay in Minneapolis was coupled, consumer-driven, and home-based, then the old gay that Seelig embodied was single, middle-aged, and sexually unhinged—the relic of a bygone, immunocompromised era. The young gay couple featured on *The Daily Show* embraced, even

FIGURE 0.1 Jason Jones, correspondent for *The Daily Show*, interviews a "new gay" couple at a Minneapolis Target in 2011.

celebrated, stereotypes associated with middle America and offered these "comforting fictions" about life in the Midwest as the new aspirational politics for *all* LGBTQ Americans.[3]

The Advocate's ranking was far from scientific, and *The Daily Show* sought laughs as much as information, but the issues behind the ranking and segment were certainly real and no joke. This version of gay life reflects what Lisa Duggan terms the "new homonormativity." Emerging out of neoliberalism, homonormativity is a "politics that does not contest dominant heteronormative assumptions and institutions, but upholds and sustains them, while promising the possibility of a demobilized gay constituency and a privatized, depoliticized gay culture anchored in domesticity and consumption."[4] Rather than building a broad, progressive movement, this narrow, formal, and non-redistributive approach to "equality," as Martin Manalansan argues, has "a depoliticizing effect on queer communities as it rhetorically remaps and recodes freedom and liberation in terms of privacy, domesticity, and consumption."[5] Homonormativity, in other words, shifts the pursuit of freedom from the collective public sphere to the more restrictive private sphere, where freedom has less room to operate and gain visibility, ultimately reinforcing heteronormative conventions and deepening economic inequalities.[6]

The humor in *The Daily Show* segment arose from an incongruity in popular notions about gay life in the Midwest. Minneapolis is not typically thought of as a "gay mecca"—that label is usually reserved for cities like Los Angeles, San Francisco, or New York City. LGBTQ people supposedly flee from Midwestern cities toward coastal metropolises, and those who cannot, so the assumption goes, live cursed lives in largely homophobic environments. But the history of LGBTQ people in the upper Midwest defies this simple story. Like all gay men, those living in Minneapolis faced challenges, but they responded in unique ways. *From Vice to Nice* illustrates how this community carved out its own space during the crucial years from the mid-1970s to the late 1990s—a period when AIDS ravaged their health, economic changes threatened their neighborhoods, and politicians targeted their rights. Despite these challenges, the community emerged resilient. This is a story that is uniquely upper Midwestern, yet, as *The Advocate*'s report and *The Daily Show* segment highlight, it was and remains quintessentially American. It is a story of accommodationists versus radicals, of compromises and conflicts, of invigorating optimism and crushing doubt. In that respect, this story could be told of many LGBTQ communities across the nation—and has been—but here the alchemy of LGBTQ activism differs.[7]

In Minneapolis, unlike the well-known gay hubs of San Francisco or New York City, the dynamics of same-sex desire and gender nonconformity developed not in opposition to but in alignment with prevailing notions of home and community life. A distinct "middleness" prevailed, where certain expressions of same-sex intimacy found acceptance, though only within the confines of privacy and in harmony with neoliberal values— economic and social policies emphasizing individualism, privatization, and market-driven principles that prioritize personal responsibility and economic self-sufficiency over collective social change. Those who fell outside these parameters remained as excluded and opposed as ever. Despite its size as a city, the dominant trend in LGBTQ activism in Minneapolis— while not the only one—was more in line with the sensibilities of a smaller town. This makes it a more accurate reflection of the sexual politics of homonormativity across the country than the histories of larger, more famous gay urban centers. While those cities have rightly garnered extensive scholarship due to their significance in LGBTQ history, Minneapolis offers a uniquely insightful perspective for understanding how, by 2011, the popular media could be discussing an emerging "new" gay identity characterized by married couples, children, and suburban homes.

Informed by HIV/AIDS historiography, queer of color critique, and urban studies, *From Vice to Nice* diverges from an LGBTQ historiographical tradition centered on coastal narratives of LGBTQ emancipation. Instead, it presents an alternative retelling of the US AIDS epidemic, shining a spotlight on middle America to illuminate how public health constructions of normative gender, sexuality, and domestic space, when mixed with the catalyst of private development, sparked a chain reaction with which Minneapolis still grapples. Via queer and feminist theorizing, *From Vice to Nice* elucidates how public health and the private housing market came together to recast a postindustrial Midwestern terrain as a hub of commerce, tourism, and liberal values.[8] This gentrification did not simply change *where* some gay men lived—given their newfound ability to purchase newly constructed townhouses or renovated lofts in "up-and-coming" areas—but *how* they lived and what type of a community they would be.[9] Faced with the devastation of AIDS, the LGBTQ community, particularly gay men, had to grapple with difficult decisions. Would the community's predominantly white identity drive it to prioritize racial privilege over social change? Would older, wealthier leaders force the community to embrace security over justice? Would the liberatory potential of sex see its full blossoming, or would the fear of AIDS smother it? These probing questions were not unique to the upper Midwest, but there, people arrived at answers that signaled a "new," less radical, less angry, and more comfortable gay identity was taking shape.

From Homonormativity to Middleness

The Daily Show's portrayal of the Midwest challenged cultural stereotypes of the region as backward, homophobic, and an unwelcoming place for LGBTQ people. Contrary to its reputation as a "flyover" area with little cultural significance, this part of the country had become an important center of LGBTQ life in the years leading up to *The Advocate*'s study. For the purposes of this book, the "Midwest" refers to the northern central expanse of the United States, including Illinois, Indiana, Iowa, Kansas, Michigan, Minnesota, Missouri, Nebraska, North Dakota, Ohio, South Dakota, and Wisconsin. Within this broad region lies the "upper Midwest," consisting of Iowa, Michigan, Minnesota, North Dakota, South Dakota, and Wisconsin. At the heart of this area lie the Twin Cities—Minneapolis and St. Paul, Minnesota's capital—which serve as the state's cultural, economic, and political nucleus. As the largest metropolitan center between Chicago and Denver, the

Twin Cities have long attracted LGBTQ individuals from across the region. In 2011, the same year of *The Advocate's* ranking, Minneapolis boasted the fourth-highest percentage of gay, lesbian, and bisexual adults in the United States, behind only San Francisco, Seattle, and Atlanta. A 2010 census study also found Minneapolis had the fourth-highest number of same-sex couples in the country.[10] That year, Minnesota's voters blocked a proposed constitutional amendment to ban same-sex marriage.[11] Two years later, the state became the second in the Midwest—after Iowa—to legalize same-sex marriage, prompting then-Minneapolis Mayor R. T. Rybak to actively encourage couples from neighboring states to come to Minneapolis to marry.[12] Over the following decade, LGBTQ acceptance spread across the state, and by 2019, both Minneapolis and St. Paul earned perfect scores of 100 on the Human Rights Campaign's Municipal Equality Index (MEI), reflecting their commitment to inclusive laws, policies, and services for LGBTQ residents.[13] These achievements did not happen in isolation, yet narratives of the Great Gay Migration in the 1970s—when LGBTQ people flocked to major US cities seeking community—have not, until recently, made space for places like Minneapolis, let alone the upper Midwest.[14]

While the dominant narrative of the Great Gay Migration tells of gay men and lesbians leaving small towns—places marked by "suspicion, persecution, and secrecy"—for the perceived "tolerance" of large metropolitan areas, a pattern Jack Halberstam calls "metronormativity," another perspective emphasizes the contrast between the coasts and the Midwest.[15] According to this alternative account, gay men and lesbians specifically fled the "persecution" they experienced in the Midwest to find the greater "tolerance" offered by coastal cities. Thousands of gay men and lesbians certainly gravitated toward the coastal trifecta of Los Angeles, San Francisco, and New York City, but countless others, by choice or circumstance, remained rooted in the Midwest. Finn Enke critiques this coastal-centric focus in the history of American sexuality, calling it "bicoastal-normativity," arguing that it reduces the entire Midwest to a mere hinterland.[16] Metronormative *and* bicoastal narratives tend to overlook the rich and complex histories of LGBTQ communities residing in less dominant locales. Consequently, when distinct forms of LGBTQ personhood emerge from the Midwest, they are often dismissed as "flawed" rather than recognized as authentic regional expressions with significant influence on national LGBTQ politics.[17]

Compared to the cosmopolitan allure of larger coastal cities, the Twin Cities have historically drawn people from the surrounding region, cultivating a more localized appeal. As LGBTQ individuals "escaped" to Minneapolis, they collectively brought with them the norms and attitudes of small-town life, along with an unexamined "whiteness" that might have faced more scrutiny in more diverse urban settings. Unlike those who moved far away and severed ties, many in the region often maintained closer family connections, which reinforced the cultural values and attitudes with which they grew up. Eduardo Bonilla-Silva's concept of "white habitus" proves useful here, as it describes the social environments that shape white people's worldviews, interactions, and attitudes in a racially segregated society, fostering "a sense of group belonging (a white culture of solidarity) and negative views about non-whites."[18] If a white habitus similarly shapes the mindset of white LGBTQ individuals, it could help explain in part the racial segregation in LGBTQ spaces, from bars to neighborhoods, as well as racial biases in dating preferences, social networks, and organizational leadership. LGBTQ personhood in the upper Midwest, then, is deeply rooted—and not separate from—the rural and small-town influences that permeate the region's culture and its unique politics of sexual discretion.

The only region outside the coastal metropolises that has drawn significant scholarly attention is the South. Here, as in the Midwest, rural and small-town culture plays a key role, but the dynamics are different. While both regions are deeply religious, in the upper Midwest, religiosity tends to be more moderate and less fundamentalist, which is said to foster greater equality and tolerance for LGBTQ individuals. By contrast, the rural South's more conservative and fundamentalist religious landscape has encouraged a broader spectrum of responses to LGBTQ identities, from outright hostility to ambivalent support. John Howard challenges the assumption that the South is universally hostile to homosexuality, showing how gay men in Mississippi from 1945 to 1985 pursued same-sex relationships within local institutions like the home, church, school, and workplace. Rather than relying on urban anonymity, these men adapted their relationships to familiar community structures, with spaces like the church—despite its conservative teachings—offering unexpected opportunities for queer intimacy. Yet racial divisions shaped markedly different experiences across LGBTQ communities in the South.[19]

In both the South and Midwest, white supremacy exists, but it is also perceived differently. In the Midwest, it is often viewed as a demographic fact, whereas in the South, it is seen as a historical reality, deeply intertwined with the legacies of enslavement, racial segregation, and Jim Crow. This notion of "Southern exceptionalism," as described by Matthew D. Lassiter and

Joseph Crespino, confines racism and racial violence to the South, portraying similar incidents elsewhere as anomalies.[20] This narrative of northern white innocence shields the upper Midwest from the same level of scrutiny. As a result, when white Americans imagine the heart of the nation—the repository of its values—they often think of the Midwest, which appears less problematic. This perception extends to sexuality as well. In a special *GLQ* issue on the queer Midwest, Martin Manalansan, Chantal Nadeau, Richard T. Rodriguez, and Siobhan Somerville argue that the Midwest, compared to other regions, serves as "the 'norm,' the uncontested site of middle-class white American heteronormativity."[21] Thus, the Midwest holds meaning beyond its geography; it stands as "a symbol, an expression of collective identity, an *idea*."[22] Kristin L. Hoganson calls this view of the Midwest the "heartland myth"—a national narrative portraying the Midwest as the "quintessential home" referenced by terms like "homeland security," the foundation of the nation in an era of mobility and globalization, and the embodiment of "America First."[23]

Building on these insights, I refine the idea that the upper Midwest represents a white "norm" by arguing that it fosters a cultural and social practice of "middleness"—a pervasive drive for conformity, moderation, and assimilation into mainstream society. This concept includes behaviors, attitudes, and values that prioritize uniformity and social harmony over the interrogation or subversion of dominant cultural norms. Middleness is characterized by three key aspects: (1) its geographic location at the "middle" of the country, symbolically seen as the nation's heart; (2) a middle-class identity focused on consumerism, patriotism, and private family life; and (3) a tendency to seek a "middle ground" in political debates, especially on contentious issues like abortion, affirmative action, and LGBTQ rights. In a context where moderation and an imagined—or, as we will see, media-constructed—notion of the "norm" holds sway, middleness signals alignment with "Midwestern," and therefore centrist, values such as industriousness, familial bonds, and community cohesion while rejecting identities or behaviors seen as radical, disruptive, or violent. While both homonormativity and middleness promote conformity and assimilation, they differ in focus. Homonormativity centers on the mainstreaming of LGBTQ identities through the adoption of traditional heterosexual norms. In contrast, middleness encompasses a wider range of identities and social dynamics within regional cultural norms, touching on factors like race, class, religion, and political ideology, beyond just sexuality or gender identity.

While homonormativity is specific to the LGBTQ community, middleness is indifferent to difference—including sexuality—except in those few, but profound, instances where it matters crucially.

The middleness of the upper Midwest is, in many respects, the most distilled example of "Minnesota Nice," a constellation of values and kinship networks, as Annette Atkins describes it, that includes polite friendliness, avoidance of confrontation, understatement, emotional restraint, self-deprecation, and a reluctance to stand out.[24] The narrative of Minnesota Nice paints the people of the upper Midwest as pious, modest, wholesome, and welcoming to those who share these traits. That same sense of modesty—of studiously not making others uncomfortable—extends to all expressions of sexuality, particularly for LGBTQ individuals. Whereas elsewhere, in the supposed "meccas," sexual identity helped bind the community together—making, for example, gay men into a recognizable group—here, it was not to be flaunted and no excessive pride or explicit pleasure was to be taken in sexual expression. Instead, gay men and lesbians are to be unexceptional, or, rather, to be exceptional in their efforts at being platonic friends, neighbors, and family members.

When gay men and lesbians did not adhere to the dictates of middleness—by celebrating sex publicly or protesting intolerance in ways that made others uncomfortable—they arguably stood out even more. While these actions might have been unremarkable in other regions, in the Midwest, they drew attention. In the same fashion that even the most radical LGBTQ communities on the coasts included moderate and even conservative elements since the homophile movement of the 1950s, Midwest LGBTQ communities also exhibited diversity in their ranks. Coming off the socially turbulent decade of the 1960s, LGBTQ individuals in the 1970s faced not only the challenge of how to bring about change but also the fundamental question of what changes to pursue. Some favored a more accommodationist approach—"integrationists," who worked within established legal frameworks to ensure mainstream acceptance—while others pushed for a more radical stance—"liberationists," who promoted confrontational strategies to overthrow oppressive systems. For these liberationists in the Midwest, and particularly in the upper Midwest, middleness was a double-edged sword: On the one hand, it encouraged adherence to a status quo that they had to fight against, but, on the other hand, because the scope of radical activism was so limited, when they spoke, they were all that much more noticeable.

One reason radical activism remained comparatively limited in the region arises from its overwhelming whiteness.[25] LGBTQ people there had fewer opportunities to forge cross-racial coalitions and develop an awareness of the intersections between race and sexuality. In contrast, cities like Los Angeles, San Francisco, and New York City saw LGBTQ groups collaborate with social movements like the Black Panther Party, the Young Lords, and the United Farm Workers.[26] Even in "mid-tier" urban centers, gay men and lesbians formed cross-racial alliances. Marc Stein highlights Philadelphia as an example, where a diverse and tolerant atmosphere encouraged cross-gender and multiracial organizing, including African American lesbian feminism and multiracial gay liberation.[27] In contrast, Minneapolis saw divisions, such as disagreements over the role of pornography in gay liberation, which hindered unity between gay men and lesbian feminists. In Chicago, the Midwest's largest city, LGBTQ activists collaborated with African American leaders to combat police harassment, building on Black-led police reform efforts. Timothy Stewart-Winter notes that Chicago's LGBTQ communities, drawing on civil rights strategies, achieved legal protections and expanded political influence through alliances with Black leaders and progressive white allies. However, by the 1990s, neoliberal policies and racial divides within LGBTQ spaces weakened these coalitions, reinforcing perceptions of LGBTQ identity as predominantly white.[28] In the upper Midwest, where racial and ethnic diversity was less prominent, many LGBTQ communities were often less likely to interrogate normative assumptions about race. Instead, some would come to support institutions like law enforcement that disproportionately inflicted racialized punishment. Their proximity to whiteness—shaped in part by staying closer to their hometowns—pushed segments of mainstream LGBTQ politics in the region toward reinforcing the status quo, with a focus on domesticity, privacy, and respectability.

For integrationists in the 1970s striving for social acceptance, the couple featured in *The Daily Show* segment represented their ultimate goal: two gay men presenting a sanitized, bourgeois version of same-sex desire that appeared at ease, nonthreatening, and unremarkable—even "vanilla." As early as the 1970s, years before AIDS would erupt, Minnesota integrationists clashed with liberationists over how to steer the gay rights movement. They argued for more "respectable" approaches to key civic issues like repealing sodomy laws, preventing police entrapment, and curbing antigay violence. With the arrival of AIDS in the early 1980s, coinciding with city planners' efforts to revitalize a deindustrialized Minneapolis, it would be the integrationists, with their "middleness," who would enlist gay identity to help consolidate whiteness for the cause of urban renewal. For them, positioning gay identity as a tool for urban renewal became a strategy to secure the domestic privacy they needed to assert their belonging within the region's social fabric.

Undoubtedly, echoes of middleness appear in the rhetoric and actions of integrationists across various locales. Elizabeth Armstrong charts the evolution of gay identity and politics in San Francisco from the 1950s to the 1990s, identifying three phases: interest group organizing, redistributive politics, and identity-based advocacy. In the 1950s and 1960s, conservative homophile groups prioritized gradual reform and assimilation over structural change. This shifted in the late 1960s with gay liberationists advocating for visibility and social revolution in solidarity with New Left movements. By the 1970s, the movement embraced identity-based advocacy, cultivating a vibrant LGBTQ cultural and commercial scene that celebrated diversity and self-expression.[29] Clayton Howard notes that many San Francisco gay activists adopted a discourse of sexual privacy, leveraging middle-class respectability to build alliances with straight voters and policymakers. However, this strategy often reinforced social hierarchies, privileging middle-class, white gay activists while sidelining poorer, gender nonconforming individuals, such as sex workers or unhoused queer people.[30] In contrast, Minneapolis, with its smaller size, fewer LGBTQ alliances, and more conservative social environment, fostered a culture of discretion among LGBTQ individuals, curbing visibility and inhibiting organized political movements.

In today's world, where LGBTQ integration and accommodation have become more common, it is crucial to revisit and critically assess the successes of this privacy-oriented approach, especially to understand its limitations. *From Vice to Nice* traces the trajectory toward homonormativity, connecting regional developments in the upper Midwest to broader national dynamics. This book reveals that while the upper Midwest views itself as distinct—championing white virtue and social welfare—it is deeply enmeshed in the larger national histories of whiteness, neoliberalism, and LGBTQ politics.

Yet middleness, as an analytical tool, must extend beyond the upper Midwest, for it is also a call to avoid oversimplified dichotomies—such as reformist versus revolutionary or coastal versus inland—and to appreciate the uniqueness of each locale in LGBTQ history. Queer urban studies can benefit from examining the cultural and symbolic meanings tied to specific regions, particularly the forces shaping LGBTQ communities. In the Midwest, this symbolic "heartland" complicates queer experiences and political movements, as these narratives are shaped not only by urban dynamics but also by the region's unique racial and moral geographies. Middleness encourages us to see that while efforts like repealing sodomy laws, diversifying police forces, and securing same-sex marriage took place across the country, the ways these efforts unfolded—and the different goals to which they were aligned—highlight the diverse experiences and struggles within the LGBTQ community.

Middleness in an Age of Neoliberalism

The Daily Show's portrayal of a new, more wholesome gay identity in the American heartland, contrasting with the older, more sexually liberated image of coastal cities like San Francisco, subtly reflects the different responses to the AIDS crisis. In San Francisco, Seelig flirts with the correspondent in a sex shop before taking him to the San Francisco Gay Men's Chorus, an organization that raised funds for AIDS research and prevention throughout the 1980s and 1990s.[31] On the other hand, because there is no mention of sex by the Minneapolis gay couple interviewed in *The Daily Show* segment, AIDS disappears. Though unintended, this erasure unwittingly underscores the divergent ways Midwestern LGBTQ communities responded to the AIDS crisis compared with their coastal counterparts, at both the grassroots and institutional levels. The aversion to uncomfortable topics or confrontation, a hallmark of Minnesota Nice, may have contributed to delayed public discussions of AIDS, potentially slowing the public health response and limiting the dissemination of accurate information about the disease and its transmission. This middleness certainly constrained the forms of activism that LGBTQ people in Minnesota felt comfortable pursuing. Dallas Drake, a leader in ACT UP/Minnesota, lamented the low turnout at local chapter meetings, noting, "It was hard to get anybody to show up for anything . . . People were scared of being outed . . . and people finding out that they were at a protest."[32] In the context of Minnesota Nice, being seen at a protest could be as nerve-racking as being outed as gay.

But AIDS was just as real in Minneapolis as anywhere else. One key aspect of the region's middleness is that the urban–rural divide, prominent in much of the United States, breaks down in the upper Midwest—especially in Minneapolis, a city blending urban density with a cultural character often linked to rural areas. Using an urban studies framework helps us grasp how AIDS reshaped LGBTQ life in this region. While scholars have explored

LGBTQ-rights and urban politics, the impact of AIDS on these narratives remains underexamined.[33] Early AIDS historiography focused on activist, medical, and institutional perspectives, but by the 1990s, LGBTQ studies—especially those employing a queer of color critique—highlighted race and health disparities to challenge dominant biomedical narratives.[34] Jennifer Brier's 2009 book *Infectious Ideas* reshaped the field by linking health, civil society, and state governance, emphasizing marginalized voices such as women, queer people of color, and those in the Global South.[35] Recent interdisciplinary work continues to examine how HIV/AIDS intersects with colonialism, capitalism, poverty, drug policy, and other forms of structural violence.[36] *From Vice to Nice* builds on this scholarship by using spatial analysis to rethink the AIDS epidemic, providing alternatives to the dominant medical and social movement perspectives typically centered on the coasts.

We need to explore the unique ways AIDS manifested across regions because its impact varied significantly by location. In the Midwest, AIDS arrived later and on a smaller scale than in coastal cities, prompting a different kind of response. Writing about St. Louis, Katie Batza argues that the region's smaller openly gay population and limited political and social service infrastructure required collaboration with unexpected allies, such as religious institutions.[37] Whereas LGBTQ communities in coastal cities often responded through direct action and expansive public health initiatives, in the heartland, some of the most intense battles against the epidemic took place within the home. Here, LGBTQ individuals and their allies navigated caregiving amid fewer institutional resources and smaller social networks. By leveraging domestic space, they fostered community, redefined family, and pioneered novel forms of medical and emotional support. Drawing on Stephen Vider's work, this politicization of the private sphere can be understood as a form of "domestic activism."[38] In the absence of adequate social services and medical infrastructure, the home became a hub for innovative caregiving practices like meal delivery programs, "buddy" support systems, and adult foster care. Domestic activism, however, sprang beyond mutual aid; it also participated in a broader cultural shift that reframed gay male sexuality as private, monogamous, and couple-bound—essentially, "nice." While this alignment with heterosexual norms was often a strategic means of securing protections and respectability, it also marked a departure from earlier models of public, communal eroticism. Coastal narratives that emphasize a linear progression from state abandonment to direct action, while vital, can inadvertently obscure regional responses that developed under different conditions—responses less rooted in confrontation and visibility, and more in improvised forms of care shaped by domestic labor and kinship.[39]

That domestic activism arose so prominently in the region is not simply a consequence of middleness, but also a response to the broader neoliberal revolution sweeping the nation. As David Harvey explains, the 1970s saw economic and political elites restructure government policies to prioritize capitalist interests, including deregulating markets, weakening unions, imposing austerity, cutting taxes, and privatizing education, housing, and social services. These changes disproportionately harmed marginalized communities, dismantling social safety nets, fueling mass incarceration, and targeting people of color under the guise of combating crime, drugs, and poverty. While Harvey situates this shift after the global economic shocks of 1973, Gary Gerstle argues it began earlier, during the New Deal order of the 1930s.[40] Similarly, Mary Pattillo notes that even at its most liberal, the American welfare state primarily prioritized big business and the white middle class, leaving the poor behind.[41] Following Gerstle and Patillo, I recognize that the policing tied to 1970s gentrification has roots in earlier urban policing practices focused on gender and sexuality.[42]

Neoliberalism, nonetheless, remains a critical framework for understanding the gentrification of AIDS, given its profound impact on urban landscapes and public health policies. In urban development, neoliberalism favors market-driven approaches that often marginalize vulnerable groups, including those affected by HIV/AIDS.[43] In health, it prioritizes profit over comprehensive care, shaping resource allocation, healthcare access, and responses to HIV/AIDS. Neoliberal ideologies also intersect with cultural narratives of individualism and self-sufficiency, exacerbating disparities in access to health care, housing, and support services for people with HIV/AIDS. As the welfare state shrank and became increasingly intertwined with the carceral state, domestic activism deputized the family as the primary site of affective and economic care. This shift inadvertently reinforced a core tenet of neoliberalism: reliance on individual and market-based remedies to social ills. In the upper Midwest, the neoliberal revolution simulated the innate politics of middleness. Consequently, it did not provoke significant cultural upheaval, as residents—despite benefiting from government support through crop subsidies, insurance programs, and homeownership assistance—did not view themselves as dependent on welfare.[44]

Home-based approaches to the health crisis emerged as a spatial technology of neoliberalism—what I term a "neoliberal spatial fix." Drawing on David Harvey's formulation of the "spatial fix"—which originally described capitalism's tendency to resolve crises of overaccumulation by shifting or reorganizing economic activity across geographic space, often from the Global North to the Global South—I adapt the term to describe a different but related phenomenon within late capitalist urban regimes in the Global North. In this context, the neoliberal spatial fix refers not to external expansion but to the internal reorganization of space through privatization, moral regulation, and homonormative redevelopment.⁴⁵ Rather than merely relocating capital, neoliberalism opens new markets within previously non-commercialized domains, such as the home or the intimate lives of marginalized subjects. The homonormative couple featured on *The Daily Show* represents the ideal consumer subject within this neoliberal landscape. Yet, much like its classical counterpart, the neoliberal spatial fix ultimately prioritizes profit over collective well-being, leading to the commodification of urban space and the displacement of vulnerable populations.

This spatial strategy rests on the premise that built environments shape behavior—promoting spatial interventions as solutions to economic and moral crises. In the case of the AIDS epidemic, city officials, gay politicians, and health authorities encouraged gay men to adopt monogamous domestic arrangements—a spatial prophylactic, of sorts—to curb the spread of HIV. But this homeward turn also coincided with a broader effort to remake cities in line with neoliberal principles. Homonormative-inflected gentrification did not just operate as a barrier against HIV; it also facilitated urban redevelopment by eliminating spaces deemed undesirable, such as public cruising spots and commercial sex establishments like adult bookstores, theaters, and bathhouses.⁴⁶ Understanding how the dictates of homonormativity and neoliberal political economy worked together—how "solving" AIDS solved "urban problems"—gets at the growing dominance of homonormativity.

Being in the "Middle" by Casting Others Out

While Minnesota Nice is often characterized by outward displays of friendliness and hospitality, it can sometimes mask underlying tensions or inequalities. Beneath the surface of this narrative—despite the supposed tameness and wariness of conflict exhibited by Minnesotans—lies a story of fear, suspicion of others, and reluctance to confront uncomfortable truths or hold institutions accountable. Middleness *necessarily* excludes. The easiest way to define what connects two people is by identifying a third who is categorically different. Once that difference has been established, exclusion invites various forms of violence, including segregation, criminalization, impoverishment, and vulnerability to illness and premature death.

How, then, can a discourse rooted in distrust of others also embrace some gay men and lesbians? One answer lies in race. Britt E. Halverson and Joshua O. Reno argue that the seeming ordinariness of the Midwest as plain, average, and homogenous has historically enabled "exclusionary national narratives of race and belonging."[47] The heartland myth, as Kristin L. Hoganson notes, functions as a political tool to unify the nation and advance shared interests "in the vortex of an unruly world."[48] At the core of this myth is the belief that the nation's essence is under constant threat from external forces and must be safeguarded through strict control and isolation. Unlike the South, with its overt Jim Crow laws and violence, the Midwest is, supposedly, harmless, yet it sustains what Jasbir Puar, drawing from Rey Chow's formulation, calls "the ascendancy of whiteness," wherein racial domination is maintained not through spectacle but through idealized images of dignified, decent property-bearing white Midwestern farmers. These men (typically) embody independence, hard work, and masculinity, in contrast to the supposed moral decay of urban America.[49] Given the importance of race to the regional concept of the heartland Midwest, middleness exemplifies the ways through which white gay and lesbian Minnesotans have downplayed their gender and sexual differences by aligning themselves with the racial and class ideals of an imagined white middle America. While gay and lesbian communities in cities like Los Angeles, San Francisco, and New York City openly politicized their identities during the 1960s and 1970s, key figures in the upper Midwest were more reluctant, choosing instead to present themselves as rightful participants in the (white) consensus values of the heartland.

The narrative of Minnesota Nice, with its emphasis on consensus and conflict avoidance, masks a history of exclusions and violence, particularly against the racialized poor and queer gender and sexual dissidents. This tension is encapsulated in what Samuel L. Myers calls the "Minnesota Paradox." Despite Minneapolis—and Minnesota as a whole—being celebrated as one of the most livable places in the country, with good schools, abundant green spaces, well-paying jobs, and a low cost of living, it also harbors some of the nation's starkest racial disparities in education, housing, and income.[50] This state of affairs was not inevitable. In 1973, *Time* magazine featured a now-iconic and often-parodied cover of a beaming Minnesota Governor Wendell Anderson, clad in flannel, hoisting an 18-inch northern pike, next to the headline "The Good Life in Minnesota." The article praised Minnesota as a "state that works," citing its strong work ethic, honest politics, and commitment to the common good. Two years earlier, Anderson had implemented several measures known as the Minnesota Miracle, which required communities in the Twin Cities metro area to share their commercial and industrial tax base, seemingly eliminating pockets of poverty and inequality observed in other cities.[51] While many Rust Belt cities in the Northeast and Midwest struggled with what Thomas J. Sugrue describes as an "urban crisis"—marked by aging housing, shrinking budgets, declining industries, and rising welfare rolls—the Twin Cities thrived. Once the nation's capital for timber and flour milling, the region transitioned to a diversified economy in electronics, medical products, machinery, and food processing, generating tens of thousands of jobs and avoiding the economic decline seen elsewhere.[52]

Time magazine overlooked a crucial detail: The so-called Minnesota Miracle occurred when the state's population was overwhelmingly white—99 percent, to be exact. Since then, Minneapolis's non-white population has grown, bringing with it challenges similar to those faced by other large American cities.[53] As the percentage of white residents in the Twin Cities metro area declined during the 1980s, politicians attributed rising homicides, increasing welfare caseloads, and widening educational disparities to Black urban migrants arriving from other Midwest Rust Belt cities—such as Chicago, Detroit, Milwaukee, St. Louis, and Gary, Indiana—as well as Afro-Cuban refugees from the 1980 Mariel boatlift. Instead of finding better opportunities, these migrants encountered hostility from policymakers who blamed them for overburdening the welfare system. The racial underclass in Minnesota was not a home-based problem, these politicians insisted; it was an imported problem that warranted some kind of punitive embargo. In this context, gay elected officials—all white—and their constituents in the Twin Cities, many of whom might have found common cause with communities of color, often endorsed and amplified this narrative, whether through explicit rhetoric or tacit alignment with broader efforts to assert respectability, responsibility, and belonging within the state's racialized moral order.[54]

The ethos of Minnesota Nice and middleness that has granted some white gay and lesbian Minnesotans symbolic inclusion within the culture and customs of the upper Midwest has, until recently, stifled discussions about race—a conversation urgently needed.[55] By 2021, Minneapolis was about 60 percent white, 19 percent Black, 10 percent Latinx, 6 percent Asian, and 1 percent American Indian.[56] St. Paul, just across the Mississippi River, was even more diverse, with a population that was 51 percent white, 16 percent Black, 9 percent Latinx, 19 percent Asian, and 1 percent American Indian.[57]

Despite this growing diversity, resource distribution remained inequitable, especially for Black residents. In the Twin Cities, Black people experience poverty at four times the rate of white people and unemployment at more than three times the rate.[58] They also endure greater health disparities, shorter life expectancy, educational barriers, and disproportionate incarceration rates.[59] Only as the state's demographics shifted away from being predominately white did white heterosexual Minnesotans begin aligning more closely with homonormative white gay men and lesbians, focusing on what they shared—their racial identity—rather than what they did not—their sexual identity.

Creating this bond required a major shift in Minnesota's racial history. Starting with the 1862 Homestead Act, which allowed settlers to seize Dakota and Anishinaabe lands and forced Indigenous people onto reservations controlled by the Bureau of Indian Affairs, Minnesota was envisioned as exclusively white.[60] Although few Indigenous people lived in the Twin Cities during the early twentieth century, World War II marked a turning point. Over 25,000 Indigenous people enlisted in the military (the highest participation rate of any group), and another 40,000 worked in wartime industries.[61] After the war, the federal government pushed assimilation policies through the 1956 Indian Relocation Act, aiming to transition reservation residents into wage economies. Between 1952 and 1972, over 100,000 Indigenous people relocated to urban centers.[62] In the Twin Cities, the Indigenous population grew from a few hundred before the war to over 6,000 by its end. By the late 1960s, about 10,000 Indigenous people lived in the Twin Cities, many concentrated in the Phillips neighborhood of south Minneapolis.[63]

Federal policies simultaneously confined Black and brown communities to specific inner-city neighborhoods.[64] During the New Deal and World War II, white Minnesotans gained access to Federal Housing Administration (FHA) and Veterans Affairs programs that offered low-interest mortgage loans for suburban homes, while people of color—especially Black Minnesotans—were excluded from homeownership through racial covenants. These legal clauses, in effect from 1910 to 1950, barred home sales to non-white buyers and covered 40 percent of Minneapolis at their peak.[65] Racial covenants preserved racial homogeneity and fueled housing and wealth disparities, laying the groundwork for the Minnesota Paradox. Practices like redlining—the FHA's refusal to insure mortgages in Black neighborhoods—and limited job opportunities further entrenched racial inequality. Although the 1968 Fair Housing Act banned racial covenants, housing segregation persisted through other mechanisms.

Just as the region's middleness concealed the truth of the Minnesota Paradox behind the allure of the Minnesota Miracle, it also masked the racial and sexual realities underlying Minneapolis's much-touted "urban renewal" programs of the 1950s. After World War II, while the federal government promoted suburban homeownership for white Americans, it also funded urban revitalization to counter the decline of cities during the Great Depression and suburban migration. The Housing Acts of 1949 and 1954 formalized the "urban renewal" program, channeling resources into inner-city redevelopment. In Minneapolis, the Gateway Urban Renewal Plan replaced 40 percent of the city's downtown, transforming what were labeled as "blighted" areas with offices, commercial spaces, and upscale housing.[66] This renewal, along with federal highway construction like Interstate 94 through St. Paul's Rondo neighborhood, fractured communities—displacing primarily working-class residents and people of color, lowering property values, and eroding social support networks.[67] By the 1970s, Minneapolis leveraged the Minnesota Miracle for economic growth while bulldozing "ghettos" and displacing residents under the "Metro Center '85" redevelopment plan, designed to attract wealthier residents and expand the tax base.[68] As a result of these policies, Black homeownership in Minnesota remains among the lowest in the nation. In 2019, white Minnesotans had a homeownership rate of 76.9 percent, followed by Asian residents at 60 percent and Latinx and Indigenous residents at around 49.5 and 48.6 percent, respectively. At the bottom, Black Minnesotans had a homeownership rate of just 25.3 percent—the third largest gap in the United States.[69]

Despite the harm to Black homeownership, wealth, and civic health, Minneapolis earned recognition for its urban renewal efforts during the 1960s and 1970s, largely due to the perceived success of the Gateway Urban Renewal Plan.[70] In this regard, the city reflected broader trends analyzed in recent urban histories that critically explore the roots of neoliberal urban restructuring. Yet Minneapolis often remains overlooked in these accounts.[71] This neglect arises from the city's perceived middleness, which obscures the racial conflicts embedded in neoliberal policies, creating an illusion of consensus and harmony. Recent works, such as the essays in *Neoliberal Cities*, challenge the dominant narrative by showing that neoliberal urban policies did not abruptly emerge in the 1970s but developed gradually and unevenly throughout the twentieth century.[72] While these studies illuminate the interplay between race and neoliberalism, they often sideline discussions of sexuality, particularly the intersections of race *and* sexuality—a gap that *From Vice to Nice* seeks to address.

Building on recent studies of sexuality in historical contexts—and on work by scholars like Damon Scott, who argues that urban redevelopment, framed by racialized and heterosexist notions of "blight," eradicated "queer land uses" increasingly seen as threats to modernization—this book reveals how urban renewal initiatives sought to rectify the perceived moral decay of downtown areas by not only acquiring land but also implementing innovative policing strategies targeting racial and sexual "undesirables."[73] The bitter irony of Minnesota's middleness is that white gay men and lesbians had, not too long before, been excluded from the very structures of belonging they would later seek to join. Postwar policies overwhelmingly favored white, heterosexual families, effectively shutting out sexual minorities from suburban spaces. The Federal Housing Administration's 1938 Underwriting Manual, which set the criteria for FHA-insured mortgages, included "character" as a key requirement, defining it as "the sum of the traits and habits that constitute a person's mental and moral being."[74] Because the law criminalized sodomy and the medical profession diagnosed homosexuality as a mental illness, those accused of homosexuality were essentially barred from FHA-insured mortgages on the basis of their "character." Additionally, the FHA appraiser's manual penalized households unrelated by blood or marriage with a low rating, further excluding LGBTQ people from suburban homeownership.[75] LGBTQ individuals likewise lost access to GI Bill benefits if discharged for homosexual activity, denying them education, mortgages, and business loans. These federal policies entrenched the white, heterosexual family as the standard for citizenship, a dynamic Margot Canaday describes as the "Straight State."[76] As Adam M. Geary observes, this exclusion pushed many LGBTQ individuals—particularly white gay men—into inner-city neighborhoods where racialized poverty and sexual nonconformity coexisted in uneasy proximity.[77] In Minneapolis, the Loring Park neighborhood became a hub for LGBTQ individuals, drawn by its affordable tenement-style housing and proximity to gay bars along Hennepin Avenue. Although many were white and some middle-class, LGBTQ residents of Loring Park, like the Black, brown, and Indigenous families in the city's north and south disinvested neighborhoods, were seen as sexually deviating from the postwar ideal of white, middle-class Minnesota. A central focus of *From Vice to Nice* is to understand how, over time, some white gay men moved to distance themselves from potential allies—those who might have helped challenge the very systems that upheld both homophobia and racism—in order to gain proximity to mainstream respectability. This shift did not erase their earlier marginalization but reshaped it, channeling the fight for rights into modes of accommodation rather than collective resistance. It is a story that intertwines sexual politics with urban renewal and public health with the racialized policing of space. It is, in many ways, a story of postwar America.

Minnesota Nice Tested in a Vicious Time

As gentrification intensified, the relationship between LGBTQ people and communities of color shifted despite shared histories of urban abandonment and suburban exclusion. By the 1970s, efforts to destigmatize homosexuality—initiated by homophile groups in earlier decades—were already in motion. However, these efforts took on greater urgency during the AIDS crisis, as the public, government, and medical establishment largely ignored a disease affecting marginalized populations. In the midst of this indifference, the LGBTQ community faced a critical juncture, one in which the potential for solidarity with communities of color was complicated by the pull of middleness.

Although the role of HIV/AIDS in post-1960s urbanization and suburbanization is often overlooked, health geographers have shown how spatial processes like segregation and exclusion heightened vulnerability to the virus.[78] Roderick Wallace argued that cities have a hierarchical structure of safety and health, with poor Black and brown communities at the bottom and wealthier white ones at the top, and that HIV moved through urban areas from the bottom up, with the "lower" rungs absorbing the worst of the shock. Like pylons, they bore the brunt of the storm, lifting the upper echelons to safety. The trajectory of the disease through space and time—what health geographers call "disease diffusion"—followed pathways laid down by both social organization and economic inequality.[79] Sarah M. Schulman linked AIDS-related deaths in 1980s New York City to the rapid turnover of rental properties, unveiling the broader undercurrents of gentrification and displacement.[80] Similarly, Adam M. Geary highlighted how urban ghetto formation—both racial and LGBTQ-defined—created the human landscape for AIDS to take hold as a national crisis.[81] Rather than individual or communal "high-risk" behaviors, it was the economic and social isolation caused by residential segregation that ensured gay men and the racialized poor bore the epidemic's heaviest burdens.

In the upper Midwest, AIDS arrived with more of a slow-building moan than a ferocious roar. Bruce Brockway, a prominent gay activist and publisher of the Twin Cities' first gay newspaper, *Northland Companion*, marked the region's first official case in 1982. By the close of 1987, Minnesota had recorded 302 cases, with 125 new diagnoses that year alone. Public health data attributed 82 percent of cases to transmission among homosexual/bisexual males, 4 percent to intravenous drug use, 3 percent to hemophilia, and 2 percent to heterosexual transmission. Although 87 percent of cases were among white individuals, Black people, who comprised less than 2 percent of the state's population, accounted for 9 percent of cases, while Latinx people, just 1 percent of the population, represented 3 percent—highlighting significant racial disparities.[82]

Before AIDS struck, middleness for LGBTQ people manifested itself as an attitude or sense of personal comportment, one of many ways of being LGBTQ along a spectrum that had integrationists on one end and liberationists on another. While the region likely harbored, proportionally, more integrationists than elsewhere, they did not necessarily dominate the often-heady and occasionally loud debates erupting within the local LGBTQ community. The arrival of AIDS changed that dynamic. More and more people gravitated toward middleness, and activists and leaders embraced it in far more tangible ways—not least in where they lived and socialized and how they regulated those spaces. Mirroring trends elsewhere, the outbreak accelerated what Stathis Yeros calls the "desexualization" of urban space, leading to the closure of adult bookstores, bathhouses, and X-rated theaters, as well as crackdowns on public sexual cultures.[83] In the Twin Cities, these measures—framed as HIV prevention—effectively criminalized nonnormative gender and sexual expressions happening outside the home—metaphorically speaking, those outside the middle.

The policies of middleness, whether intentional or not, commonly undermined and, in some cases, eradicated spaces where LGBTQ people gathered. This impact was recognized even at the time. In 1983, amid the unfolding AIDS epidemic, openly gay San Francisco Board Supervisor Harry Britt told geographer Manuel Castells, "When gays are spatially scattered, they are not gay, because they are invisible."[84] Implicit in this assertion was the recognition that the closure of gay bathhouses and other commercial sex establishments contributed to the dispersal of gay men, depriving them of essential safe spaces. At a time when homosexuality was highly stigmatized, gay bathhouses had served as crucial hubs for socialization, support networks, and the forging of acceptance. While policymakers and public health officials justified shutting them down as a measure to curb HIV transmission, safer-sex advocates argued that these spaces could have been instrumental in distributing information to hard-to-reach populations. Instead, integrationists, lionizing the sanctity of the private sphere, supported the closures, erasing sex and sexuality from public life. By helping cement the arbitrary distinction between public and private, integrationists inadvertently made nonnormative sexual practices more visible and vulnerable to criminalization. Though some gay leaders believed these closures would benefit the LGBTQ community in the long run, the immediate beneficiaries were commercial real estate developers and local officials eager to advance gentrification.

In addition to facing the threat of displacement, LGBTQ people, during the peak of the AIDS epidemic, grappled with the social stigma associated with illness and particular sexual practices. As job loss, medical expenses, rent regulations, and insurance barriers mounted, people with AIDS found themselves denied sufficient care and stable housing. In major cities, these challenges fueled direct-action AIDS activism. Amid the Reagan administration's shrinking welfare state and the homophobia of the New Right, LGBTQ activists transformed the AIDS crisis into a powerful political movement. As Jennifer Brier notes, these activists became some of the most vocal critics of 1980s neoconservatism and neoliberalism.[85] Their efforts extended beyond mere protest; they provided services to those affected by the virus, educated the community on prevention, and condemned governmental agencies, medical institutions, and pharmaceutical companies profiting from the inadequate response. Consequently, much of the historiography of the AIDS epidemic has focused on the organized political response in urban areas.

Beyond memoirs, little attention has been given to the private, everyday caregiving performed by friends, lovers, and family members behind closed doors—and hardly any in middle America. These domestic spaces represent the very spaces where middleness spurred action, yet because people have still to fully appreciate its impact, the history of the AIDS epidemic rarely includes the Midwest. While direct-action AIDS activism in Los Angeles, San Francisco, and New York City dominates the narrative, it was the exception rather than the norm. In homes across the country, including small Midwestern towns, people cared for loved ones dying of AIDS, often because resources were scarce but also because people considered an HIV diagnosis a private, family affair in keeping with Minnesota Nice and its emphasis on politeness and avoidance of conflict. This domestic activism starkly illustrates the neoliberal shift that placed the nuclear family at the center of caregiving and material support. As Wendy Brown argues, while economic privatization is the most visible face of neoliberalism, it masks the equally significant privatization of social welfare through the family. This expansion of the private sphere complements economic privatization insofar as both fronts work together to delegitimize the concept of social welfare provision.[86] The pro-business movement of the 1980s—with its tax cuts, welfare rollbacks, and deregulation—further reinforced the nuclear family as the primary locus of economic security.[87] As social welfare responsibility shifted from corporations and the state to families, the white nuclear family reemerged as a central organizing site of the post-Keynesian economy, a development that even resonated within LGBTQ communities in the upper Midwest.[88]

Embracing the white, suburban, nuclear home might seem like a pragmatic response for a group under siege—a necessary concession that harmed no one. However, a queer of color critique reveals how this alignment with dominant institutions had deeper consequences. As some white middle-class gay men assimilated into prevailing norms, they helped redirect white anxieties about perverse spaces, nontraditional gender roles, and deviant sexualities onto the racialized poor. Some even touted the moral rectitude of the LGBTQ community in contrast. Investing in homonormativity greatly weakened coalitional politics with other marginalized groups, leading to a situation where, by the end of the twentieth century, LGBTQ Minnesotans celebrated victories, like the repeal of sodomy laws and the legalization of same-sex marriage, while communities of color remained at the bottom of the state's social hierarchy. This disparity came into sharp relief in 2016 when police fatally shot Philando Castile, a Black man, during a routine traffic stop in a St. Paul suburb. After the officer's acquittal, Twin Cities Pride initially banned uniformed police from marching in that year's parade but reversed course after criticism from Minneapolis Police Chief Janeé Harteau, the city's first openly LGBTQ chief, who called the ban "divisive" and stressed that "police officers are . . . human beings with families who are also part of this community."[89] Fast-forward to Memorial Day in 2020, amid the COVID-19 pandemic, when Minneapolis police arrested George Floyd for allegedly using a counterfeit bill. Less than twenty minutes later, Floyd was dead, a knee pressed against his neck in a shocking display of police brutality. The ensuing uprising engulfed the Twin Cities, with images of charred Target stores, like the one featured in *The Daily Show*, broadcast worldwide.

By aligning with middleness, segments of the LGBTQ community in the Twin Cities distanced themselves from more radical critiques and structural analyses of inequality. As some gay men accepted the dominant narrative that it was their "risky behavior"—rather than structural vulnerabilities—

that fueled the AIDS crisis and they acted to reduce the opportunity for those behaviors, it left—at least in the public's imagination—only the racialized poor and their "risky behaviors" (drug use and supposed untamable sexual impulses) as the primary drivers of the epidemic. Within this context, domestic activism functioned as a neoliberal spatial fix. While it appeared to challenge heteronormative paradigms by reimagining the home as a site of queer care, it also aligned with the state's withdrawal from public services by reinforcing advocacy grounded in privacy and respectability. This retreat further marginalized the racialized poor, leaving them vulnerable to widening health disparities, housing displacement, and increased surveillance and criminalization—dynamics that help explain the disproportionate impact of COVID-19 on Black and brown communities.[90] By the end of the period covered in this book, the idea that AIDS was ever even considered a specifically "gay cancer" would seem like an archaic fact; AIDS would become a problem of unregulated (and unregulatable) Black and brown bodies.

Chapter Outline

From Vice to Nice traces how segments of the LGBTQ community in the upper Midwest transitioned from being vilified as a medical menace to celebrated as a model minority for the twenty-first century—what Richard Florida calls "canaries of the creative economy"—and how that transformation was deeply tied to the private housing market.[91] This book examines how privacy-centered approaches to sodomy repeal, anti-LGBTQ violence, domestic partnerships, and the AIDS epidemic intersected with policies aimed at "cleaning up" low-income neighborhoods and vice districts, targeting racial denizens such as single Black mothers and Native American transgender sex workers in Minneapolis and St. Paul. Rather than centering individual gay leaders or assigning moral culpability, this study foregrounds the entangled relationships between marginalized communities and the state, legal, and market forces—emphasizing how structural constraints shape the range of possibilities for political recognition, material survival, and spatial belonging.

Chapter 1, "Gay Minnesota Comes Out," chronicles the emergence of politicized queer social formations in the upper Midwest, beginning in the 1970s after the Stonewall Uprisings with the establishment of the region's first gay rights groups. Out of efforts to secure gay rights ordinances during this period emerged two often-competing local factions: integrationists and liberationists. Understanding their emergence and symbiotic relationship helps explain how integrationists harnessed the culture and politics of middleness to their advantage. The chapter also lays the groundwork for later confrontations between gay men and the Minneapolis Police Department, outlining the vice unit's policing of gay male sexuality in commercial sex establishments and its role in fostering antigay violence.

In chapter 2, "Privacy in a Time of AIDS," the focus shifts to how gay leaders seized the AIDS epidemic as a catalyst for white normative recovery. By charting the genesis of the "consenting adults in private" legal framework and examining the aftermath of the 1986 Supreme Court decision in *Bowers v. Hardwick*, the chapter shows how Minnesota's gay elected officials strategically tied efforts to decriminalize private homosexual acts to increased policing of public sexual activities. It recounts the campaign to repeal sodomy in Minnesota and legal battles involving men convicted of soliciting underage male sex workers. Framed as HIV prevention, this privacy-centered approach channeled benefits to middle-class, same-sex households that conformed to homonormative ideals while disregarding those who challenged or fell outside this framework.

Chapter 3, "From Persecuted to Protected," considers how gay activists fighting antigay violence adapted the HIV prevention rhetoric discussed in chapter 2 to promote monogamy as a spatial fix against bias-motivated violence. Using public service announcements and antiviolence campaign materials from 1980s Minneapolis, the chapter reveals how activists repurposed HIV prevention messaging to advance hate crime prevention strategies. These efforts aligned with the goals of those hoping to gentrify formerly gay communities in Minneapolis, forging new and, for affluent gay men, profitable alliances with the police. However, while the AIDS epidemic encouraged privatization and pro–law enforcement imperatives, these measures did little to actually reduce antigay violence.

Expanding on the premise in chapter 3 that the AIDS epidemic amplified deep-seated anxieties of racial contagion, chapter 4, "The Carrier as Criminal," illustrates how the moral panic surrounding HIV-positive sex workers of color reflected broader fears of white injury amid the upper Midwest's shifting political economy. This chapter considers the cultural paranoia about race and sex that escalated in response to the urban social and economic upheavals of the 1980s. It argues that the moral panic over AIDS—sometimes reinforced, explicitly or implicitly, by segments of the white gay activist community—served racial and political interests, using the specter of non-white carriers infecting white communities to justify an increasingly punitive approach to disease control.

Chapter 5, "Minneapolis 'Matures' Past Bathhouses," unveils how city officials, public health authorities, and gay elected officials weaponized urban planning, health reforms, and environmental modification to target commercial sex establishments. It details the passage of an ordinance, supported by public health officials, private developers, and gay Minneapolis leaders, to shut down the city's last bathhouse, the 315 Health Club. Viewing sex-oriented businesses as obstacles to postindustrial economic growth in the downtown core, the city leveraged the AIDS epidemic to justify closing, restricting, or evicting businesses associated with sexually explicit material or public sexual cultures.

Emboldened by the closure of the bathhouse, city officials—backed by some gay residents—moved to crack down on public sex in Loring Park, the city's central hub for male cruising. In chapter 6, "Cruising All the Way Home," the focus shifts to a proposed anticruising ordinance aimed at enhancing police surveillance in the city's public parks. Like the earlier antibathhouse ordinance, this measure sought to reshape public spaces by discouraging "high risk" sexual conduct and ostensibly reducing HIV transmission. Although grassroots queer activists resisted these efforts to privatize both sexual expression and public spaces, this form of gay moralism, which supported crackdowns on public sex and promoted monogamous marriage, ultimately narrowed the public sphere. This shift, in turn, laid the groundwork for a homonormative politics centered on domestic privacy, further accelerating gentrification.

The epilogue, "What Space Can Be," ventures beyond domestic activism to explore an alternative paradigm of AIDS caretaking, one proffered by queer and feminist collectives of color in the 1990s. It highlights Twin Cities–based groups like the Minnesota American Indian AIDS Task Force and Minnesota Men of Color, whose approach to "radical care" prioritized intimate, communal, and culturally rooted support rather than the legal and policy-focused agendas often pursued by white gay officials, such as sodomy repeal and domestic partner benefits. These activists sought to liberate the concept of home and family from the confines of the private housing market and the nuclear family ideal. In contrast to mainstream approaches, these practitioners of radical care understood that physical well-being, at both an individual and community level, served as the foundation on which challenges to systemic issues such as racism, poverty, and settler colonialism could be mounted. The epilogue contends that this grassroots model of radical care offers what Juana María Rodríguez calls a "cartography of insurgency," illuminating a pathway of personal and collective regeneration amid the enduring health disparities wrought by HIV/AIDS and, more recently, COVID-19.[92]

From Vice to Nice tells a story of people, the spaces they occupied, and how they imagined those spaces might function—what they could hold, whom they could welcome, and what behaviors they might encourage. In particular, it speaks to how select LGBTQ community members helped reconfigure and regulate spaces in a way to garner power, often at the expense of other marginalized groups. Mapping the relationship between power and spatial dynamics reveals the biopolitical forces that shape and sustain homonormativity. Without interrogating how domestic spaces in the United States have long served as sites for defining race, conferring citizenship, and accumulating wealth, we risk obscuring privacy's complicity with neoliberalism and white supremacy. What does it mean when strategies of survival and resistance for some simultaneously produce sites of exclusion, oppression, or even death for others? It is a question only a history of the "new" gay can answer.

1 Gay Minnesota Comes Out

The Hope of Freedom

In his travels through the late 1970s, author Edmund White ventured into the heart of Minneapolis, where he encountered a gay community steeped in what he deemed a curious state of complacency. "For generations, homosexuals and lesbians have led furtive, self-hating lives in the Midwest—static, dreary lives," White wrote. In Minneapolis, however, he detected a mix of "old self-oppression" alongside "something new, fresh, pure." Reflecting on the city's potential, White mused, "Since Minnesota is at the source of our greatest river, perhaps this new spirit will someday flood the entire region, wash clean an area that seems, more than anything else, complacent. No place else in America has lived with the status quo for so long."[1] White depicted a community marked by innocence, set against the backdrop of a rapidly evolving national landscape. He argued that "only in the Midwest has so little changed over such a long period," contrasting its enduring wholesomeness with the "faddish and rootless" West Coast and "class-conscious and pretentious" East Coast. This stability, he suggested, shaped a distinctive politics—one of middleness—that fits neatly into the existing social fabric. "Many gays, especially gay couples," White observed, "are able to fit into the work-centered, down-to-earth, conservative Midwest with ease and satisfaction."[2]

There is a certain irony in White's observation, as Minnesota's LGBTQ community—especially in Minneapolis—had just emerged from a tumultuous decade. LGBTQ historians have long discerned the tension between gay accommodationists and gay radicals, and Minnesota was no exception. Like in San Francisco and New York City, "homophile" organizations of the 1950s and 1960s had begun advocating for the rights of homosexuals as a distinct group. In Minneapolis, these efforts initially took a diffuse, intangible form. But as was the case nationally, beginning in 1969, the radical politics of the New Left ignited a shift, with some older members of homophile groups and many young, newly out LGBTQ individuals embracing "gay liberation." One of the first expressions of this movement in Minneapolis occurred in the spring of 1969 at the University of Minnesota, Twin Cities—weeks before the Stonewall Uprisings—when students founded Fight Repression of Erotic Expression (FREE). Influenced by the Black Panthers, FREE became the Midwest's first LGBTQ campus group and the second in the nation, after Columbia University. Declaring itself "militant," FREE engaged in protests, pickets of discriminatory employers, consciousness-raising sessions, and "integrated dances." Its efforts culminated in October 1970 with the Midwest's first gay convention, drawing speakers from the region and as far as New York City.[3]

Out of this ferment, Jack Baker, president of FREE and a US Air Force veteran discharged for being gay, ran for president of the Minnesota Student Association. A committed liberationist, Baker used camp, gender nonconformity, and confrontational tactics throughout his campaign. One memorable poster featured him seated on the floor in a button-down shirt, tie, and jeans, seemingly clean-cut and respectable—except for the prominent women's high-heeled shoes he wore. The caption read: "Put Yourself in Jack Baker's Shoes" (fig. 1.1). On April 8, 1970, CBS News anchor Walter Cronkite announced: "In Minneapolis, an admitted homosexual, Jack Baker, has been elected president of the University of Minnesota Student Association"—making Baker the first publicly gay student body president of a major US university.[4] During his presidency, Baker secured a student seat on the Board of Regents and helped establish a student-owned corporation to develop affordable housing for students.[5]

Paradoxically, despite being seen as a "radical" figure of gay liberation in the region—a prophet of radical vision and instigator of momentous firsts—Baker also embodied elements of integrationist politics. In 1971, Baker and his partner, Michael McConnell, a librarian at the University of Minnesota, applied for a marriage license in Hennepin County, Minnesota's largest county, which includes Minneapolis. Predictably, the Hennepin County District Court denied their application. After both the Minnesota Supreme Court and the US Supreme Court dismissed the case, the couple tried again, this time using gender-neutral aliases. They succeeded in obtaining a license, later sanctified by a sympathetic Methodist minister, thrusting them into the national spotlight. A 1971 special issue of *Look* magazine on "The American Family" featured Baker and McConnell as "the homosexual couple," portraying them at home and noting, "Not all homosexual life is a series of one-night stands in bathhouses, public toilets or gay bars . . . Some homosexuals—a minority—live together in stable, often long-lasting relationships, like Baker's and McConnell's."[6]

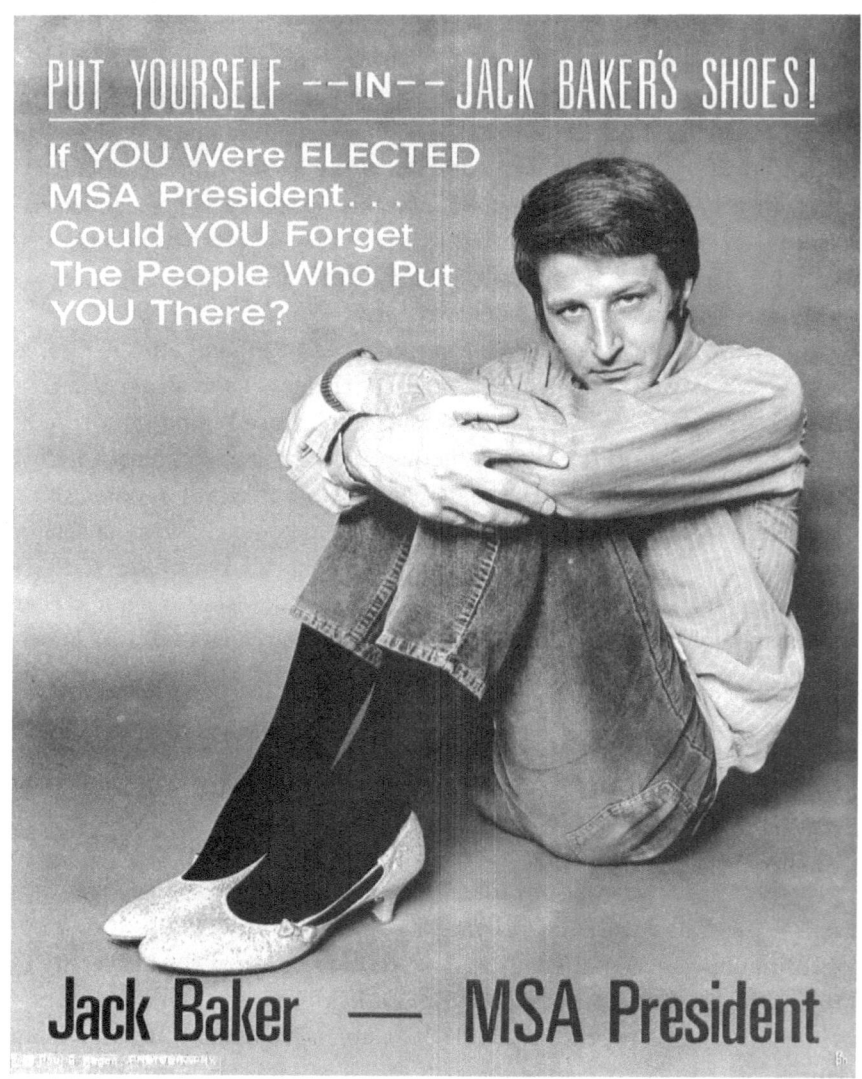

FIGURE 1.1 Jack Baker's campaign poster for president of the Minnesota Student Association, 1970. Photo by Paul Hagen. From the Michael McConnell Files, Box 39, Folder Photos 03: Gay Rights Activism. Courtesy of the Tretter Collection in GLBT Studies, University of Minnesota, Twin Cities.

While Baker and McConnell were key figures in Minnesota during this period, the real political force in the LGBTQ community over the decade, shaping its goals and policies most decisively, was Steve Endean. Ironically, Endean owed his start in gay activism to Baker and McConnell. In 1970, while working as an aide on Wendell Anderson's gubernatorial campaign, Endean realized he was gay. A middle-class Catholic from Minneapolis, Endean had no idea where to turn until a phone operator directed him to Gay House, one of the country's first gay community centers. There, Endean met Baker and McConnell, who, along with John Preston (a future editor for *The Advocate*), had used a $2,000 grant from Protestant denominations to establish Gay House in response to the lack of social services for the Twin Cities' LGBTQ community. Given the challenges of being disowned by family and facing widespread discrimination, Gay House addressed critical needs like housing, job counseling, and food. For nearly a decade, Gay House hosted a full slate of events, including political action meetings, yoga and sewing classes, sports matches, movie nights, informal "rap" discussion sessions, and addiction counseling. Committed to coalition building, it collaborated with organizations like Lutheran Social Services and Vietnam Veterans Against the War.[7] At Gay House, Endean was exposed to gay liberation politics, direct-action street protests, and a more flexible understanding of family beyond the traditional nuclear model. But Endean never became a convert to radicalism at Gay House, later recalling how he met "outrageous counterculture queens" who personified for him pernicious stereotypes associated with gay men.[8]

Coming from the straitlaced world of electoral politics, Endean observed that many involved in the early LGBTQ movement had "little to lose." As a white, middle-class man, his background set him apart. His time at Gay House, combined with his work for the Democratic-Farmer-Labor Party (DFL)—the political machine that dominated Minneapolis City Hall—made him skeptical of sweeping, revolutionary change. He came to believe that lasting progress would come through "within-the-system lobbying." Rejecting the term "gay liberation," Endean preferred "gay civil rights," viewing success as integrating LGBTQ issues into the mainstream rather than challenging it. To him, "liberation" suggested a needless critique of the establishment, while "civil rights" implied a desire to work within it. In his memoirs, Endean dismissed liberationists as seeking "instant gratification" through performative protests rather than pursuing thoughtful, strategic action.[9] A child of Minnesota, Endean deeply believed that bold demonstrations flaunting gender or sexual difference hindered the broader goal of quiet accommodation. If securing gay civil rights meant downplaying aspects of gay identity that the mainstream found uncomfortable, Endean was willing to do so, for, in his formulation, his sexuality was a mere aspect of his identity and not his *entirety.*

Unlike FREE and its public protests, Endean took a more establishment-oriented approach, becoming a full-time lobbyist at the Minnesota State Capitol. In 1972, he and a group of like-minded middle-class, white gay men founded the Gay Rights Legislative Committee (GRLC), focused on repealing the state's century-old sodomy law and securing antidiscrimination protections for gay men and lesbians. Central to this strategy, as Endean explained, was "capturing the middle" of legislators.[10] Thus, when he met with a junior state representative to discuss gay civil rights, Endean wanted him to know "we were serious, mainstream, and respectable, and I wanted him to think of gays in general and me in particular as more than just 'sexual' beings."[11]

Capturing the middle was as much about appealing to moderates as it was about conforming to traditional gender norms. Between 1973 and 1975, while lobbying the state legislature by day, Endean worked nights as a coat checker at Sutton's, a gay bar in downtown Minneapolis. There, he found comfort in the absence of the "screaming queens [that] I had been taught gay people were."[12] While it might be tempting to view his personal unease with "screaming queens" as a remnant of his time in the closet, he never shook off the sentiment, and it remained his lodestar up until his death from AIDS-related complications in 1993. To Endean, one of the greatest barriers preventing gay men and lesbians from entering the mainstream was their refusal to conform. If gay activists sought to craft a wider, more radical movement that purposefully challenged and even alienated the American mainstream—for example, by embracing transgender rights—Endean feared they would succeed but to the detriment of all gay men and lesbians. His discomfort with "queens" would inform his disagreements with gay liberationists, including Baker, regarding the inclusion of gender nonconforming people in gay rights legislation.

By the early 1970s, Endean's accommodationist politics gained purchase as the GRLC spearheaded efforts for the nation's first statewide gay rights bill. The GRLC evolved into the Minnesota Committee on Gay Rights (MCGR), expanding to 300 dues-paying members with a statewide board of directors and Endean as coordinator.[13] Acting as a single-issue interest group, the MCGR thrived on its clear focus and commitment to working within the existing political system through lobbying and electoral strategies. It aimed to influence elections by establishing a gay voting bloc and believed that progress was best achieved through top-down legislative efforts.

The MCGR also punched above its weight because of the talents of those it recruited, and few were so singularly important to the organization's efforts as Allan H. Spear. In 1972, Spear, who grew up Jewish in a small Indiana town and later became an associate professor of history at the University of Minnesota—Twin Cities, was elected to the Minnesota Senate. Two years later, he made national headlines by coming out in a front-page interview in *The Minneapolis Star*, becoming the first openly gay man to serve as state legislator.[14] However, Spear was not the voice of gay liberation for which many hoped. Like Endean, Spear criticized Baker's "dramatic, publicity-generating actions," calling them ineffective and alienating.[15] Instead, the gay movement needed to mature and distance itself from the "1960s-style radicalism and enter the mainstream" by "winning a place at the table, electing gay people to office, changing the laws, and gaining acceptance for gay rights as a legitimate civil rights movement."[16] Spear believed the MCGR could embody this maturity, pointing to its membership of middle- and upper-class professionals. In a letter to Howard Brown, chairman of the National Gay Task Force, Spear highlighted the MCGR's inclusion of "two public officials . . . three university professors and several teachers, lawyers and social workers," contrasting it with Minnesota's "student-oriented" gay rights groups.[17] Spear saw Baker and his fellow liberationists—many of whom were younger, working-class, or employed at adult bookstores and bathhouses—as out of step with the times, for by the mid-1970s the New Left had faded and a new, more sustainable politics needed to arise.

At first, Endean and Spear's strategy seemed promising. In 1974, the MCGR scored a major victory when the Minneapolis City Council amended its civil rights ordinance to prohibit discrimination based on "affectional or sexual preference," making Minneapolis the third major US city, after Washington, DC, and Seattle, to offer such protections.[18] (Notably, the law excluded the Minneapolis Police Department, which had been exempt from the city's civil rights ordinance since 1972.[19]) Part of the ordinance's success lay in Endean and Baker putting aside their differences and collaborating. While Endean secured city council sponsors, Baker crafted the ordinance's language. Earlier, they had abandoned a statewide bill due to disagreements over the word "homosexual," with Baker arguing that it focused too much on sexual acts rather than emotional bonds. Determined to avoid another setback, Endean accepted Baker's "affectional or sexual preference" phrasing. He was wise to do so, for once Minneapolis passed the ordinance, a year later, in 1974, St. Paul followed suit.[20] Although tensions between integrationists and liberationists were already brewing in 1974, they would not fully surface until the following year, when gay activists set their sights on something even larger—a statewide gay rights bill.

Gay liberationists like Baker diverged sharply from integrationists like Endean and Spear, envisioning "equality" as part of a broader fight for racial, economic, and gender justice. To that end, they explicitly included transgender people in their advocacy. Among the liberationists was Tim Campbell, a Texas transplant with an Irish Catholic background who had been a seminary student before becoming a certified chemical dependency counselor. Campbell ran as an openly gay candidate for mayor of Minneapolis in 1980 with the slogan "Decriminalize Fun and Lovemaking," a play on "DFL."[21] He also published the influential local gay newspaper, the *GLC Voice* (1979–1992). Together, Baker and Campbell championed a statewide gay rights bill that included protections for "transvestites" and "transsexuals" and extended rights to same-sex marriage and adoption. As Endean recalled, Baker and Campbell were "furious" when the bill excluded a provision allowing "transvestites to go to work in drag."[22] Seeing no reason to antagonize its political enemies or alienate potential allies, the MCGR rebuffed Baker and Campbell's demands, arguing that no bill would pass with the "additional political weight."[23] Spear later recounted asking Campbell and his allies to help pass the gay rights bill first and "then, I promised, I would come back in another year or two to try to make the bill more inclusive." Campbell and his liberationist allies refused, doubting Spear's commitment and suspecting that when the inevitable pushback came to his hypothetical future bill, he would fold, content with the rights he had secured for those most like himself. In response, liberationists formed the Coalition of Concerned Gays, working with local transgender organizations like Twin Cities Transsexuals and the Minnesota Gender Identity Association. They criticized the bill for only protecting what they called "straight-looking gays" and warned, "Obvious Gays must be protected or no one is safe."[24]

When the nondiscrimination bill reached the House Judiciary Subcommittee, Campbell and Thom Higgins, another outspoken gay liberationist and former member of FREE, testified that including "public services" and "public accommodations" would pave the way for same-sex marriage and adoption. This testimony raised concerns among subcommittee members, prompting them to table the vote. Frustrated by what he saw as liberationist missteps, Endean used this delay to rally the *right* kind of supporters for the next hearing. He circulated flyers in gay bars urging people to come but not to "be so flamboyant as to alienate possible supporters." Endean emphasized, "We know that Gay people don't fit those tired stereotypes that some straights label us with," and, to make his point explicit, he encouraged attendees to "dress respectably."[25] As Spear noted, Endean "didn't want guys over there with dresses and mascara."[26]

Campbell, however, was not about to allow gay identity to be put into a three-piece suit straitjacket. Enraged by Endean and Spear's exclusion of "cross-dressers," Campbell staged a now-infamous press conference in the men's restroom of the Minnesota State Capitol, flanked by "transvestites" and "transsexuals." To Endean's dismay, Campbell also led "transvestite parades" through the legislative halls and encouraged those identifying as women to use women's restrooms.[27] These shock tactics—Campbell also went on a hunger strike—served a purpose. "We wanted a bill to include affectional preference in gender identity," Campbell later explained. "It was meant to be broad enough to include a sissy boy, a butch girl, a cross dresser, or a transsexual."[28] For Campbell and other gay liberationists, the power of what would later be known as the LGBTQ community lay in its solidarity. If he had to sabotage a milquetoast piece of legislation to secure and maintain that solidarity, it was a risk he was willing to take. Waiting for real, monumental change was far better than being bought off with token gestures and empty promises for the future.

Endean, who prided himself on leading a "low-key, dignified lobbying effort," felt that the "outrageous antics" of Baker and Campbell "managed to turn an issue we'd worked hard to make serious and respectable into a joke."[29] To Endean and Spear, these tactics confirmed that the gay liberationists lacked a practical vision. They would rather cling to an almost abstract sense of moral purity—a dream that all people could be free at once—than confront the tougher reality that victory came in stages and with sacrifices. Those who could advance the furthest should so that others could follow in their path.

At the time—and even years later—Endean portrayed himself as a moderate, open to compromise on his 1975 gay rights bill. He was willing to compromise in many ways, but never with gay liberationists. Liberationists, for all practical purposes, proved as much a roadblock as archconservative, antigay groups, and Endean was willing to use them as leverage to secure the center right. To allay legislators' concerns about the bill's scope, Endean removed provisions regarding public services and accommodations, narrowing the focus to banning discrimination in housing, employment, education, credit, and real estate based on "affectional or sexual preference." Endean's maneuvering helped the bill narrowly survive the House Judiciary Committee by a vote of 12 to 10. Facing tougher odds in the full House, Endean encouraged local editorials to frame the liberationists' protests as evidence of the bill's moderation, portraying it as a reasonable measure that offered only basic rights—an approach he hoped would make it more palatable to legislators.

Ironically, Campbell largely agreed, and in protest of the watered-down version of the bill passed by the committee, he drafted a new version that included protections for gender variance. He persuaded Republican State Representative Arne Carlson, who would later become governor, to introduce it as an amendment. The revised bill broadened the definition of "affectional or sexual preference" to include individuals "having or projecting a self-image not associated with masculinity or femininity." Despite two hours of debate, the House rejected the entire gay rights bill by a vote of 68 to 50.[30] Outraged by what it saw as unreasonable demands from liberationists, a group called FAB organized a protest outside Baker's home in south Minneapolis in June 1975. In a flyer promoting the picket, FAB stated, "We, the Gay community, must publicly censure those members who insist on making the rest of us appear foolish by their unreasonable demands." FAB accused the Coalition of Concerned Gays of being a "splinter group" that failed "to recognize elementary political reality by demanding everything immediately" and condemned Campbell's inclusion of transsexuals and transvestites in the bill, saying: "To quibble over an issue like cross dressing is frivolous and irresponsible in the extreme."[31]

The bitter infighting between integrationists and liberationists attracted national attention. Boston's *Gay Community News* quoted Baker, identified as the de facto leader of the "militants," as saying, "I agree that you should take what you can get in chunks. But we are not willing to take a step backwards from what we have in the Twin Cities," referencing the local gay rights ordinances.[32] *The Advocate* took a harsher stance, condemning Minnesota's "no compromise" faction as a "lunatic fringe." Its editorial board called for "Solomon-like diplomacy and a good dose of public censure . . . before these crazies succeed in embarrassing the movement throughout the nation."[33] In response, gay liberationists seized the upcoming 1976 election season to rally voters with the slogan "Dump Allan Spear!"[34] Baker, who had supported Spear's 1972 campaign, even worked on a failed Republican effort to unseat him.[35]

After the bill's failure, religious conservatives and antigay groups seized the opportunity to target existing local gay rights ordinances. Evangelical singer and former beauty pageant contestant Anita Bryant, leading her "Save Our Children" crusade from Dade County, Florida, pledged to extend her efforts to cities with such ordinances. In 1977, a St. Paul Baptist pastor submitted a petition with 7,100 signatures to place a referendum on the ballot to repeal the city's three-year-old gay rights protections from its nondiscrimination law.[36] Supported by Bryant, Citizens Alert for Morality (CAM) used fearmongering tactics, claiming that homosexuals sought to "recruit" children. A CAM pamphlet warned that because homosexuals "can't reproduce, they must seduce" and alarmingly suggested that St. Paul's ordinance allowed for "the selection of a homosexual as a worker in your local daycare center . . . as scoutmaster of your son's or daughter's scout troop . . . as your children's' schoolteacher . . . as a 'big brother'!"[37] CAM reframed the repeal effort as a fight to protect children's "moral and spiritual values" from "homosexuals and other deviates."[38]

In response, Baker and Higgins founded the Target City Coalition (TCC), a group of fifty to eighty queer activists who embraced direct action and street theater, contrasting sharply with the MCGR's moderate approach. A key distinction between the groups was their stance on confrontational tactics. TCC sought to shame public officials, including clergy, who violated LGBTQ rights, creating a list of bigots called the "Pie File"—individuals they planned to humiliate with a pie to the face.[39] Those pied included a state senator allied with Bryant, the director of the local Big Brothers organization, and the Roman Catholic archbishop. While integrationists like Kerry Woodward, MCGR's codirector, denounced pie throwing for reinforcing "the image of gays as frivolous and violent," TCC disregarded such criticism.[40] In the fall of 1977, Higgins made national headlines by hitting Bryant with a strawberry rhubarb pie as she received the keys to the city of Des Moines. Wiping her face, Bryant famously quipped, "Well, at least, it's a fruit pie." Baker later told *The Advocate* that TCC's tactics were "designed to make a lot of people uncomfortable," adding, "They won't give us a gay rights bill, and they should feel uncomfortable."[41] Despite the boldness of these tactics, the strategy failed. On April 25, 1978, St. Paul voters repealed gay rights protections by a two-to-one margin.[42] Minneapolis's ordinance survived only because its city charter prevented repeals by referendum. Statewide, antigay sentiment remained strong; a 1977 *Minneapolis Tribune* poll found that 47 percent of Minnesotans believed LGBTQ people posed a threat to children,

56 percent viewed homosexuality as an "abnormal condition," and 46 percent considered it sinful.[43]

The repeal sparked a lasting conservative backlash against gay civil rights in Minnesota. Although the state legislature had considered antidiscrimination bills in 1973, 1975, and 1977, it remained unresponsive to Spear's proposals until the early 1990s. Despite this setback, the MCGR rebranded in 1980 as the Minnesota Committee for Gay *and Lesbian* Rights (MCGLR). By then, Baker, now a lawyer, had stepped away from LGBTQ activism, later criticizing the MCGLR as a "DFL front group" more focused on fundraising and securing votes for Democratic candidates than advancing LGBTQ rights.[44] Frustrated by Minnesota's resistance to statewide protections, Endean moved to Washington, DC, where he became the first gay rights lobbyist in Congress, leading the Gay Rights National Lobby (GRNL).

Still reeling from his defeats in Minnesota, Endean left the state but carried his politics of moderation with him to Washington, DC. His pragmatic, within-the-system approach only hardened in the nation's capital, particularly after Ronald Reagan's 1980 election and the country's rightward shift. Endean became convinced that a national political action committee for gay men and lesbians was essential to channel funds to congressional candidates and build influence on Capitol Hill. On April 14, 1982, he officially founded the Human Rights Campaign Fund (HRCF) and became its first executive director.[45] Adapting strategies honed in Minnesota, the HRCF used targeted mail campaigns to build a national donor base and hosted black-tie fundraising dinners in major cities. The principle of middleness that had guided Endean's politics in 1970s Minnesota would also shape the HRCF's approach, including its contentious history with transgender people and rights.[46]

Endean and his integrationist, homonormative politics may have lost a significant battle in Minnesota, but not the war. He foresaw a strategic shift that none of his opponents—whether gay liberationists or homophobes—fully grasped. As early as 1975, Endean noted, "If the movement is going to be successful, it's going to move towards an ongoing professional sort of thing."[47] In a conversation with Edmund White, he underscored the importance of engaging affluent, professional gay men, asserting, "Gay liberation needs middle-class gays. It's important to make gay liberation a chic cause among young gay professionals—they're the ones with the money and the energy and the influence."[48] This push for professionalization required abandoning the "radical" tactics of gay liberationists, rejecting public displays of male effeminacy, and distancing the movement from nonnormative sexual practices, which Endean dismissed as "the politics of self-indulgence."[49]

Ultimately, the professionalization and emphasis on middle-class respectability that Endean championed would contribute to the national ascendancy of homonormativity, shaping the trajectory of LGBTQ politics for decades to come.

Police, Bathhouses, and a Quiet Accommodation

In 1975, *Ciao!* magazine published a gay travelogue of the Twin Cities, calling it "a little star in the north that truly brightens the Midwest sky." But, in reality, the travelogue was less a celebration of the city and its efforts at urban renewal and more the author's account of cruising Minneapolis for the "tall, healthy-looking Scandinavian types . . . who make [Minneapolis] even more a paradise." The tour of the city's prime cruising spots began at the Hennepin Baths downtown, which the author described as "clean" but catering to "an older crowd" with "mostly hustlers and drunks." In contrast, the Locker Room was praised for being "attractively paneled and carpeted, with very sensual drawings of Greeks fucking." Its centerpiece, the "orgy room," was "where everyone crowds and glue themselves to each other until exhausted."[50]

As the first institutions to allow men the freedom to explore their same-sex desires in a safe, sex-positive, and supportive environment, bathhouses, Allan Bérubé argues, helped spur a movement for gay civil rights in the 1960s and 1970s. At a time when homosexuality was heavily stigmatized, bathhouses became "safety zones" where men could be "sexual and affectionate with each other with a minimal threat of violence, blackmail, loss of employment, arrest, imprisonment, and humiliation."[51] These safety zones, in turn, became vital hubs for the gay rights movement, hosting fundraisers, community meetings, and information-sharing networks. Building "a social world on the basis of a shared marginalized sexuality," bathhouses, George Chauncey contends, affirmed gay men's erotic desires. They provided a venue where men could shed the shame of homosexuality and engage in mutually satisfying sexual encounters with other gay men rather than servicing straight men in parks, bookstores, or public restrooms.[52] By fostering sexual expression and affirming community, bathhouses empowered gay men and fueled their advocacy for rights and legal protections.

In 1970s Minneapolis, gay men could choose from three downtown bathhouses: Hennepin Baths, a public bathing relic from 1925; Big Daddy's, a venue specifically catering to gay men; and the Locker Room, the most popular, operating since the late 1960s.[53] Situated along or near Hennepin Avenue, these bathhouses formed part of a bustling local sex economy. In 1980, the *GLC Voice* emphasized their appeal for offering anonymity, privacy, and safety, particularly for men unable to host partners at home or travel to more discreet locations. "Others live with their parents, in a college dormitory or with straights who would not be accepting of their gayness. All have to deal with the fear of being alone with a potential assailant if they go off anywhere in a car."[54]

As the vice squad's crackdown on homosexuality intensified in Minneapolis, Steve Endean's brand of accommodation and reluctance to challenge established institutions initially proved ineffective.[55] Rather, it would be the liberationists who offered a more suitable response to the institutionalized oppression facing the LGBTQ community, for even while police raids on bathhouses declined sharply nationwide during the 1970s, Minnesota remained an exception. After World War II, as police departments professionalized, they created specialized units to target specific crimes, including those related to sexual offenses. Driven by postwar anxieties, these vice squads sought to suppress public expressions of same-sex desire. Initially, they relied on vagrancy laws to arrest gay men and shut down their gathering places. However, after courts deemed vagrancy laws unconstitutional in the 1960s and early 1970s, police shifted tactics, using charges like disorderly conduct, public lewdness, and solicitation.[56] Undercover officers, typically young and attractive, patrolled bars, parks, and public bathrooms, employing covert surveillance and entrapment to apprehend unsuspecting men.[57]

Before the 1970s, the Minneapolis Police Department's (MPD) vice squad primarily targeted female prostitution, at times pornography, and some gambling. But as LGBTQ individuals began coming out and advocating for rights, the vice squad redirected its attention toward them. This antigay crackdown escalated under Charles Stenvig, a former MPD detective and police union president, who was elected mayor in 1969. Stenvig capitalized on white resentment following the 1967 uprising in north Minneapolis, where Black residents protested police brutality. Running on a law-and-order platform similar to George Wallace's 1968 presidential campaign, Stenvig vowed to "take the handcuffs off the police" and crack down on criminals, "racial militants," and student demonstrators, winning 62 percent of the vote.[58] Reelected in 1971, Stenvig lost to DFL candidate Albert Hofstede in 1973 but ran again in 1975, accusing Hofstede of being "soft" on pornography and promising to restore "decency" to the city. To bolster his campaign, Stenvig declared war on the city's "homosexual problem," opposing the 1975 Gay Pride Day amendment that celebrated Minneapolis's LGBTQ community, making it the second city to do so after Los Angeles. As mayor, Stenvig revoked the amendment, citing it as evidence of Hofstede's moral leniency. His campaign materials even implied that Hofstede's unmarried status meant he might be gay.[59]

Stenvig's tough-on-crime policies elevated the MPD to a powerful position in Minneapolis politics during the 1970s.[60] This newfound influence emboldened the police, leading gay activists to label the period a "reign of terror."[61] Even after Stenvig's final defeat by Hofstede in 1977, the MPD continued to flex its muscle. Over a nine-month period in 1979 and 1980, the MPD vice squad raided the city's bathhouses three times. The first raid occurred at 4:30 a.m. on June 28, 1979, the night before the Twin Cities Gay Pride Festival. Sgt. John Locke, head of the vice squad, along with Deputy Mayor Erv Dauphin and financier Dennis Schroeder, stormed into Big Daddy's without a warrant, police authorization, or approval from superiors. They pounded on doors, forcing thirty men to dress and leave. Despite not being officers, Dauphin and Schroeder falsely claimed they were. Affidavits from patrons described Locke and Dauphin as drunk, abusive, and homophobic, with one account recalling a clerk being slammed against lockers and customers subjected to slurs.[62] One patron called it "the scariest experience of my life."[63]

The aftermath of the raid proved as consequential as the event itself. When questioned by *The Minneapolis Star*, Locke denied being drunk but bluntly declared, "I didn't catch anybody in the act this time. But as far as I'm concerned, it's a whorehouse for men . . . we will go back and lock that place up." When reminded he had no warrant, Locke brazenly replied, "I am the head of the vice squad. I don't have to have any warrant. I can go in anywhere and inspect anything anytime I want."[64]

The raid sparked civil unrest among gay liberationists and their allies. On July 2, 1979, about twenty protesters gathered outside Mayor Al Hofstede's office, with nine, including activist and former sex worker Rebecca Rand, entering the mayor's office to demand a meeting about police harassment of gay men and sex workers. When denied, the protesters staged a sit-in, chanting and blowing whistles. Tim Campbell sat in Hofstede's chair, lit one of his cigars, and reportedly spilled coffee on the desk. With TV cameras rolling, police forcibly removed the group and charged them with interfering with public business.[65] Dubbed the "Hofstede 9," the protesters called for the vice squad to be disbanded and for Locke to be dismissed.[66]

Police Chief Elmer Nordlund rebuffed their demands, saying, "Tell them to elect their own mayor, then the rest of their people can join 'em if they want that crap."[67] The actions of the Hofstede 9 thrust the raid and the plight of sex workers into the spotlight, making front-page news across all four major Twin Cities newspapers and leading the evening TV news.[68]

Despite the unrest, little came of the raid. Intimidated by the squad cars stationed outside his establishment, the owner of Big Daddy's chose not to file a complaint.[69] A Hennepin County grand jury declined to indict Locke and Dauphin due to insufficient evidence. Locke was reassigned from the vice squad, and both men received only brief suspensions.[70] Meanwhile, businessman Schroeder, who had accompanied Locke and Dauphin, became a target of gay liberationists' direct action and street theater. In August 1979, Patrick Schwartz, one of the Hofstede 9, organized a rally outside Schroeder's home in the affluent suburb of Edina. In front of news cameras, protesters chanted, "Mrs. Schroeder, can Dennis come out and play cop?"[71] Beyond public embarrassment, Schroeder faced no consequences.

While Schwartz dismissed Schroeder as merely "playing cop," other gay activists saw his presence at Big Daddy's as part of a larger agenda. Schroeder's company, Miller-Schroeder Municipals, Inc., had secured a significant share of city development bond underwriting after making substantial contributions to DFL campaigns. Since 1970, the firm had participated in at least eight major renewal projects. Activists suspected Schroeder and DFL leaders at City Hall aimed to close establishments like Big Daddy's to facilitate downtown redevelopment. *Positively Gay* even alleged that bonding and development companies had specifically targeted the north side of Hennepin Avenue, linking the raid at Big Daddy's to the 1979 closure of Hennepin Baths.[72] Tim Campbell, writing in the *GLC Voice*, suggested that private real estate interests drove the bathhouse raids. He questioned why Schroeder, the president of a municipal bonding firm, had participated in a bathhouse raid and why former City Council President Lou DeMars joined the same firm after resigning.[73] Campbell argued that the Minneapolis Planning Commission sought to replace lower-income downtown residents with wealthier families, noting that arrests at other commercial sex establishments often occurred on properties the city was considering selling or leasing.[74] He suspected the city wanted to shutter these businesses, acquire the properties, and strengthen its bargaining power with private developers.[75] To Campbell and other liberationists, this pattern revealed a clear collusion between capitalism and "moral policing."[76] In contrast, moderate integrationists, many of whom wanted to leverage the political and economic power of wealthy elites, responded weakly to these allegations. Their silence on the raids underscored their unwillingness to challenge the suspicious overlaps between urban redevelopment and LGBTQ repression.

The raid backfired on the vice squad, occurring as the MPD faced mounting accusations of corruption, including bribery and selective enforcement, all tied to its entrenched "boys club" culture. The situation worsened when Police Chief Nordlund abruptly resigned a week after the raid. In response, Mayor Hofstede appointed Donald Dwyer, a former police chief with a reputation for tough law enforcement. Although Dwyer claimed to bring change, LGBTQ and sex worker activists saw his efforts as little more than a reorganization of the same police force that had terrorized them. Public frustration with the MPD reached a tipping point. In November 1979, voters elected Donald Fraser as mayor. Declining the police federation's endorsement, Fraser positioned himself as a vocal critic of the scandal-plagued department. He pledged to "eradicate politics from and restore professionalism to the department" by prioritizing merit over loyalty in leadership.[77] Widely expected to appoint an outsider as police chief, Fraser aimed to dismantle the internal corruption that had long defined the MPD.

Anticipating limited time to act before Fraser assumed office, the MPD ramped up its crackdown on commercial sex establishments, increasing surveillance and enforcement efforts. Following Fraser's victory, vice officers raided a massage parlor and several adult bookstores, harassing customers and assaulting employees. However, this was merely a prelude to a larger operation planned for the early morning of December 1, 1979: a raid on the Locker Room, Minneapolis's last untouched bathhouse. Opening in 1969, the Locker Room served as a central hub of gay male sexuality in the upper Midwest.[78] Nestled in the Warehouse District, near the gay bars on Hennepin Avenue, the bathhouse boasted a whirlpool, a sauna, a steam room, an "orgy room," a disco dance floor, a lounge area, a movie theater, fifty-four sleeping rooms, and even a free venereal disease clinic. Unlike its counterparts, the Locker Room provided superior facilities, tolerated more flagrant sexual activity, and attracted a younger, more athletic clientele, making it the premier bathhouse in the region. Operating twenty-four hours a day, seven days a week, 365 days a year, the Locker Room, drew approximately two thousand men weekly and generated over $500,000 annually, far surpassing competitors like Hennepin Baths and Big Daddy's.[79] Men from across the five-state upper Midwest—North and South Dakota, Minnesota, Iowa, and Wisconsin—flocked to the venue, particularly after the 2 a.m. closure of local gay bars.

At 12:45 a.m. on December 1, 1979, two plainclothes police officers entered the Locker Room bathhouse in downtown Minneapolis, paying the $5 admission fee and gaining access into the second-floor locker room area where they disrobed to their underwear. As they cased the bathhouse, one officer came across a scene of one soon-to-be defendant with "his erected penis in [another defendant's] rectum and . . . pumping up and down." After about five to ten minutes, the officers called in backup: twenty police officers, including the canine unit, and ten vehicles, including the "Street Crimes Van."[80] Having secured the entrance, one of the initial officers announced his presence and commanded everyone present to line up with their IDs.[81] In a panic, some men attempted to flee but were thwarted by the canine unit at the door. Others complied and even sought legal advice from the officers.[82] At least three people managed to elude the police. One man, tenaciously avoiding arrest, hid for two hours in a locker.[83]

During the raid, officers confiscated various items, including a bottle of "poppers" (a recreational drug inhaled for its muscle-relaxing effects) and "a baggie of suspected marijuana." They also photographed cubicles containing "bondage type leather paraphenalia [sic], whips, chain, cans of suspecting shortening [Crisco] and grease type guns used to lubricate the anal canal."[84] Notably, police also seized a twelve-foot papier-mâché penis with an attached scrotum that hung from the lounge ceiling. Unable to fit it inside the police wagon, officers mounted it on top and drove it through town to headquarters. All these mementos would later be paraded in court as evidence.

In what became arguably the largest bathhouse raid in US history, police issued citations to 116 men for "participating in a disorderly house" and arrested nine others on sodomy charges. The operation dragged on long enough for a crowd of about twenty-five onlookers, including journalists and disgruntled gay men, to gather outside. As officers escorted the nine "accused sodomites" in a chain of handcuffs, some spectators shouted, "Fuck the pigs!" while others urged those arrested to remain silent.[85]

The morning after the raid, condemnation came swiftly from various levels of government. Mayor-elect Don Fraser rebuked the police, emphasizing that their foremost duty should have been ensuring public safety on the streets. A group of fifteen city and state officials, led by Spear, issued a joint statement denouncing the raid as "deplorable."[86] The Minneapolis Commission on Civil Rights joined in the criticism, describing the operation as a "wasteful misallocation of scarce police resources" and urging law enforcement to prioritize preventing assaults rather than policing the consensual behavior of adults in private. Hennepin County Attorney Thomas L. Johnson further inflamed tensions with MPD leadership by refusing to prosecute the nine sodomy cases, arguing that the penalties would "be disproportionate to the nature of the act." Johnson underscored the consensual nature of the activities and the absence of financial transactions.[87] These responses demonstrated the limits of Minnesota's homophobia. Though the *idea* of gay sex and identity unsettled many—sodomy laws remained in place, and St. Paul had recently repealed its gay rights ordinance—Minnesotans did not think that their tax dollars should go to suppressing gay men and the consensual sex they privately enjoyed.

Chief Dwyer defended what he insisted be called an "inspection," claiming the police were not "legislating morality" but merely enforcing the law. When a reporter suggested that arresting people for sodomy seemed "archaic," Dwyer countered, "No, there are some people . . . within our community, probably the vast majority of 'em who don't condone this." At the press conference, he dismissed the Locker Room's classification as a health club, sarcastically noting, "There was no bathtub open last night." Dwyer added that during the "inspection," a registered nurse—cited for "participating in a disorderly house"—had been drawing blood from patrons. According to Dwyer, the nurse explained, "We get a lot of [venereal disease] around here." Concluding his remarks, Dwyer declared, "I think it's a health problem. I think it's a crime problem."[88] By 1980, Dwyer's perspective was increasingly out of step with city officials, but the emergence of AIDS would soon bring such views back into focus.

Most men arrested at bathhouses, bookstores, restrooms, or outdoor locations typically preferred to avoid public scrutiny and resolve charges quickly. Within a week, the 116 bathhouse patrons and employees cited during the Locker Room raid began paying their $25 fines, roughly $103 in 2024 dollars. Of the nine men charged with sodomy, six accepted plea deals, pleading guilty to the lesser misdemeanor of "participating in a disorderly house" and paying fines.[89] As was customary, the *Minneapolis Tribune*, the city's newspaper of record, published the names and home addresses of those arrested. Among them was a high school teacher from a northern Minneapolis suburb, who pleaded guilty and paid the fine, only to be fired by the school board.[90] Tragically, one week after the raid, another of the arrestees took his own life.[91]

Only one of the nine arrestees, Douglas Victor, dared to contest the charges, defiantly pleading not guilty to one count of "participating in a disorderly house" and three counts of "indecent conduct." Speaking to the press, Victor defended his actions, "My personal sexual behavior with another consenting adult behind a locked door is private."[92] His stance found backing from the Minnesota Gay Defense Fund Inc., a liberationist group that financed legal defenses for gay men ensnared in police raids.[93] Yet Victor's confidence in the solidarity of the LGBTQ community wavered, as he expressed feeling ostracized by certain quarters. This led Tim Campbell to sarcastically refer to the MCGR as the "Minnesota Closets for Gay Rights."[94] At the post-raid press conference, Police Chief Dwyer disclosed that before the raid, MCGR leaders had privately told him they disapproved of gay men frequenting bathhouses. "They said," Dwyer recounted, "'[gay men] have no business being in any of these public places.'"[95] Dennis Miller, MCGR cochair, confirmed the exchange, acknowledging that the bathhouse issue was "divisive" and admitting that at least one MCGR board member "had no sympathy for people who go to the baths."[96]

When Victor contested his citations, he did not dispute the facts, candidly stating, "I was sucking cock at the Locker Room."[97] Instead, he argued that the ordinances violated his fundamental right to privacy. The Hennepin County District Court disagreed. While recognizing the existence of "zones of privacy" impervious to government intrusion, the judge ruled that not all "private" conduct was immune to regulation. The ordinance against "participating in a disorderly house," the court argued, targeted "unlawful activities" rather than the "privacies" of personal relationships. The court further deemed the bathhouse a public space, rendering the private cubicle where Victor was found irrelevant to the question of constitutional protection for consensual sodomy.[98]

Despite the fallout from the December raid, which forced the Locker Room to rebrand as a "private club" requiring annual memberships and disclaimers about its activities, the vice squad was not done with the establishment. At 1:00 a.m. on Sunday, February 10, 1980, officers conducted another raid, issuing 102 citations.[99] *The Advocate* called it a "last-chance raid," with three cited for "indecent conduct" and the rest for "participating in a disorderly house."[100] After Hennepin County Attorney Johnson announced he would no longer prosecute sodomy cases, the vice squad shifted to charging "indecent conduct" for public acts.[101] Among those ticketed were two members of the DFL State Executive Committee, including none other than Dennis Miller, cochair of the MCGR, who had reluctantly supported Victor in the press.[102] The search warrant, hastily signed late at night on the grounds of alleged juvenile male sex workers being present, proved unfounded—all those cited were of legal age.[103] A bathhouse employee scoffed at the notion of sex work there, asking "Who's going to hire a prostitute if it's all free?"[104] But the Locker Room was not the vice squad's real target; Mayor Fraser and incoming Minneapolis Police Chief Anthony Bouza were. Timed one day before Bouza's inauguration, the raid sent a clear message that the MPD would not be intimidated.

Fraser and Bouza found themselves at odds with MPD leadership, largely due to their outspoken stance against policing private behaviors between consenting adults—regardless of sexual orientation. Bouza, in particular, was unpopular within the department for several reasons. A Bronx native of Spanish heritage, Bouza stood out with his fluency in Spanish and authorship of six books, including two novels. During New York City's 1976 fiscal crisis, during which 5,000 officers were dismissed, Bouza drew ire by advocating for even deeper cuts, targeting what he described as the "psychos, criminals, and the unfit" in the NYPD.[105] In essence, he was the quintessential outsider, both geographically and culturally. With a resolve to overhaul a department that saw a revolving door of eleven police chiefs in as many years, Bouza championed sweeping changes, chief among them a minority recruitment initiative. This groundbreaking program not only aimed to diversify the force but also included provisions for the recruitment of gay men and lesbians, alongside mandatory police sensitivity training.[106]

The MPD rank and file viewed Bouza as an interloper, a sentiment fueled by the Minneapolis Police Federation's "Dump Bouza" campaign, which disparagingly labeled him a "carpetbagger" and a "faggot."[107] While Bouza actively sought to engage with the city's growing and influential LGBTQ community, the police leadership exhibited blatant homophobia. One officer complained, "Homosexuals are in our schools, in our community agencies, in programs like the Boy Scouts. They are trying to give themselves a cloak of respectability, when they are sick, perverted people. Because they are a voting bloc does not give them equal rights to be a pervert." Another officer lamented that politicians "catered to homosexuals," claiming that such leniency encouraged gay men to "show up in the bathrooms at places like Powers and Penny's [department stores]," adding, "The sick part is that they are involving young kids."[108]

If Bouza and Fraser purported to champion LGBTQ interests, their efforts left much to be desired. The day after the Locker Room raid, during Bouza's swearing-in, he declared, "The honeymoon is over," regarding the vice squad.[109] This proclamation failed to placate the seventy-five angry gay protesters and allies who confronted him.[110] Their demands were clear: disband the vice squad and oust its commander.[111] In a dramatic display of defiance, Patrick Schwartz, one of the Hofstede 9, and Douglas Victor, cited at both raids, incinerated their summonses in full view of the mayor, police chief, and assembled media.[112] Despite the protesters' fervor, Bouza balked at their demands, opting instead for a compromise. He pledged to meet with the demonstrators and implement a new vice policy.[113] True to his word, on his second day in office, Bouza reassigned two of the unit's highest-ranking officers, defying police union objections. Bouza's motivations, however, seemed driven more by pragmatism than a genuine commitment to LGBTQ justice.[114] He admitted, "I do not support what goes on inside a gay bathhouse," describing them as "dirty and disgusting," though he also dismissed vice squad raids on bathhouses as ineffective due to their low conviction rates.[115]

The three bathhouse raids of 1979 and 1980 profoundly reshaped the boundaries of permissible sexual conduct in these establishments. At Big Daddy's, sex in common areas—a focal point of vice officers' ire—was no longer allowed. Former Chief Donald Dwyer, describing the first Locker Room raid, painted a vivid picture of the scene: "These acts of sodomy were being committed in plain view . . . like [a] Roman circus where the audience urges on the combatants." For Dwyer, as well as other authorities, the communal and overtly public nature of these sexual exchanges, coupled with their same-sex participants, marked them as deviant and deserving of regulation. Not only was sex taking place outside the home, but it involved multiple participants engaged in the collective pursuit of pleasure, a subversive act that violated the modest sensibilities of Minnesota's middleness. No authority made an official announcement, but gay men read between the lines of what Dwyer, Bouza, and others said and an unspoken policy emerged: sex in public areas of the bathhouses was strictly prohibited; sex in private cubicles was more permissible. After all, Bouza himself had clarified that as long as sexual acts took place in private rooms without monetary exchange or the involvement of minors, the police would not intervene. By targeting only *public* sexual activity, the vice squad signaled a tacit tolerance of private bathhouse encounters.[116] This marked the end of large-scale raids, as the LGBTQ community adapted to a more discreet framework for sexual expression in bathhouses. While some liberationists defended the right to enjoy sex in any space or form, many gay men in Minneapolis made a pragmatic compromise, aligning their practices with the culture of middleness. Integrationists, who had largely remained silent during this fight, took note of this practical accommodation. The episode would inspire them to champion similar compromises in future battles, solidifying the growing influence of middleness in shaping the city's LGBTQ politics.

Integrationists Find Their Voice

In the early 1980s, pornography brought together unlikely allies. In several cities, socially conservative Christians and radical feminists united to fuel a powerful antipornography movement. They pressured police to crack down on commercial sex establishments like saunas, X-rated theaters, and adult bookstores. In Minneapolis, this alliance led to the controversial 1983 passage of an antipornography ordinance authored by Andrea Dworkin and Catherine MacKinnon, which defined pornography as a violation of women's civil rights. While Christian opposition to pornography was long-established, the emergence of grassroots feminist groups—women blending feminist theory with urban renewal—was a new force. These women staged protests through street theater and direct action, even confronting men inside adult bookstores.[117]

Feminist groups often portrayed the patrons of sex establishments as wealthy, suburban heterosexual men seeking sex with women. In reality, many were men seeking sex with other men. While the antipornography movement pushed for increased police regulation of these venues, the MPD already had a long history of monitoring such spaces, partly driven by fears of straight men engaging in sex with gay men. Police Chief Bouza initially appeared open to reducing vice squad activity in bathhouses, asserting that private sexual acts in cubicles were not a public concern. However, this leniency did not extend to adult bookstores. Unlike bathhouses, which catered primarily to a gay clientele, adult bookstores attracted both gay and straight men, creating opportunities for sexual encounters that pushed beyond societal norms associated with middleness. The prospect of straight men engaging in public sexual acts with gay men caught the attention of the vice squad, prompting continued surveillance of these venues.

During Bouza's first three years in office, the vice squad made around seven thousand arrests, with gay men accounting for a third of those detained.[118] By August 1980, an adult bookstore clerk on Fourth and Lake Streets reported vice officers visiting four or five times a week.[119] Two months later, St. Paul attorney Ken Keate received five calls in two weeks from men seeking legal defense against vice squad arrests, highlighting a growing caseload.[120] As the summer of 1982 neared—a time when Bouza's promised reforms should have been taking effect—the Police-Community Relations Task Force of the newly renamed MCGLR revealed a record number of calls from gay men "reporting violent actions on the part of the police."[121] These incidents often followed a pattern: police decoys—typically attractive men procured from the Minneapolis Police Academy or paid criminal justice students earning $8 to $10 an hour (well above the $3.10 state minimum wage)—would entice men into engagement.[122] Once entrapped, arrestees reported rough treatment, verbal abuse, and even physical assault.[123] Unlike the widely publicized bathhouse raids, these isolated arrests at bookstores received little media attention, leaving victims largely unsupported and alone.[124]

This campaign escalated so intensely that by the fall of 1980, operators of commercial sex establishments took an unprecedented step: they united to sue the MPD. In one lawsuit, three sauna owners sought over $200,000 in damages, accusing the MPD of using force, intimidation, and threats of harm. They obtained a temporary restraining order limiting the MPD's ability to threaten closure, harass patrons, or unlawfully enter the premises without meeting specific conditions. In another lawsuit, a dozen adult bookstore clerks petitioned the court to bar police from entering the stores or adjacent parking lots. The clerks accused the MPD of waging a "campaign against homosexuals" at the bookstores in Minneapolis, which included hurling slurs like "queers" and "faggots" and using loudspeakers to harass patrons as they exited. The clerks also claimed police recorded license plates, demanded identification, and peered into private movie booth doors—sometimes even breaking down the doors.[125] One report described canine units prowling the aisles to intimidate customers.[126] Although the plaintiffs secured a restraining order, offering temporary relief, the judge ultimately deferred to the police to rein in their aggressive tactics.[127]

With minimal repercussions, the vice squad continued to run rampant, terrorizing patrons at commercial sex establishments. This escalating situation forced alliances unimaginable to integrationists like Endean and Spear, who had hoped to capitalize on the public image of respectable gay identities. In 1985, Campbell partnered with Ferris Alexander, a notorious porn magnate and frequent target of city officials and antipornography feminists. Described by one local paper as presiding over an "empire of smut," Alexander owned two adult bookstores and an X-rated theater.[128] On February 19, 1985, Campbell and Alexander filed a lawsuit against the city of Minneapolis, accusing the police of harassment and entrapment in violation of the First Amendment. They demanded an injunction to prevent po-

FIGURE 1.2 Brian J. Coyle outside Minneapolis City Hall, circa 1980s. From the Brian J. Coyle Papers, Box 12, Folder Vol. 4, 1984–1986. Courtesy of the Minnesota Historical Society.

lice from making false arrests through enticement and aimed to certify their case as a class action representing all gay men in the Twin Cities.[129]

The legal standoff between commercial sex establishments and the vice squad ended in a stalemate, with no clear victor on either side. It would take more politically influential allies to redirect the vice squad's attention away from gay men. By 1984, Brian J. Coyle (fig. 1.2) had emerged as a pivotal figure, becoming the first openly gay member of the Minneapolis City Council. However, like Spear before him, Coyle did not see himself as a "gay politician" but rather as a politician who simply happened to be gay. This distinction reflected his alignment with a politics of middleness that prioritized integration into mainstream political norms over the explicit centering of marginalized identities. Coyle's journey began in his Republican household in rural Minnesota, where he founded the group 125 Students for Nixon in high school. His political views shifted radically to the left in

Gay Minnesota Comes Out 51

college during the Vietnam War, leading him to leadership roles in the Student Peace Union and two federal indictments for draft dodging. In 1974, he even traveled to North Vietnam. After college, Coyle joined farmers protesting power line construction through their land, resulting in being arrested twice. In Minneapolis, he became involved in grassroots organizing, including advocating for citywide rent control. Despite attempts to discredit him for being gay, Coyle won the Sixth Ward seat on the Minneapolis City Council in 1983.[130] Although Coyle had a history of radical activism, once on the city council, he faced criticism from progressives for becoming more moderate.

Whatever his political stances on other issues, when it came to LGBTQ rights, Coyle was an integrationist in the vein of Endean and Spear, leading the gay community through the next phase of its struggles with the police. As Minneapolis's highest-ranking openly gay politician, Coyle fielded numerous complaints from gay men about excessive police force. Though he expressed mixed feelings about the arrests for public sex in parks—remarking, "My impression is that there is increased public sex activity and it's hard to argue that [gay men] shouldn't get busted"—he adamantly opposed vice squad entrapment and police brutality.[131] While liberationists fought the police publicly through the courts, Coyle worked behind the scenes with Spear and openly lesbian State Rep. Karen Clark to press Mayor Don Fraser and Police Chief Tony Bouza for policy changes. In a letter to Spear, Coyle made his stance clear: "While many will find the notion of anonymous sex in the back room of a porn shop distasteful, it is unclear what harm is done to society by this behavior . . . What goes on in a movie booth, closed from floor to ceiling on all four walls, should not be in the city's business."[132] Coyle argued to Fraser and Bouza that entrapping men at adult bookstores was, as an aide put it, a "lousy use of police resources" and "awful to the people who are getting arrested" and ultimately "serves no good interest."[133] With Coyle's support, Spear's office organized a critical meeting on February 19, 1985, with Fraser, Bouza, Clark, and a coalition of gay leaders and straight allies from city and state government. The meeting aimed to push for policy reforms and address systemic issues in law enforcement's treatment of LGBTQ individuals.

At the meeting, Bouza denied the allegations of ongoing vice squad patrols at adult bookstores, claiming the raids had ceased months earlier. However, Spear's aide recounted a recent case of police entrapment at an adult bookstore, leaving Bouza "red-faced" and unprepared in front of Mayor Fraser, a known supporter of the LGBTQ community. State Rep. Phyllis Kahn questioned the MPD's multimillion-dollar budget, criticizing the use of resources to target consensual activities in semi-private spaces. According to Jerry Fladmark, Spear's aide, the threat of reduced funding from Kahn and other lawmakers ultimately pressured the MPD to change course.[134] By the meeting's conclusion, gay leaders secured an informal agreement with police officials: officers would refrain from patrolling adult bookstores and X-rated theaters, provided any sexual activity occurred behind closed, locked doors.[135] While gay liberationists may have achieved less tangible progress due to their refusal to compromise, their principled stance reflected a commitment to justice that stood in contrast to the pragmatic, institution-focused strategy of integrationists and their allies.

Karen Clark navigated a difficult political landscape, balancing the opposition of lesbian feminists to adult bookstores with the concerns of gay men who frequented them. A former nurse from rural southeastern Minnesota, Clark entered politics through feminist and neighborhood organizing. She cofounded the Lesbian Feminist Organizing Committee (LFOC), a separatist group in the Powderhorn neighborhood, which became instrumental in her successful 1980 campaign for the Minnesota House of Representatives. Building a broad electoral coalition that included senior citizens, single mothers, renters, and both gay men and lesbians, she won her seat by a two-to-one margin.[136] While many lesbians condoned the vice squad's arrests of men in cubicles, labeling adult bookstores as public spaces, Clark held a more nuanced view. Speaking at an MCGLR forum in October 1980, she stated: "The issue is complicated but one thing is clear—it is not appropriate at all that Gay [sic] men be arrested." Acknowledging concerns about the negative impact of adult bookstores on neighborhoods and expressing her personal opposition to violent pornography, she nonetheless maintained her firm stance against both arrests and censorship.[137]

Facing lawsuits, the threat of reduced funding, and the growing political clout of the LGBTQ community, Bouza directed the vice squad on February 21, 1985, to "radically deemphasize" patrols of adult bookstores and X-rated theaters.[138] However, Bouza maintained to the *Star Tribune* that "anything that spills into the public won't be tolerated if it's indecent conduct. It won't be tolerated in Loring Park, if children are involved or if there's any public element to it." He urged gay men to "keep it discreet and keep it very private."[139] The directive had swift effects despite backlash and warnings of a "homosexual takeover."[140] Between February 17 and April 20, 1985, the vice squad arrested twenty-seven men at sex-oriented bookstores and theaters in Minneapolis, a sharp drop from the 157 arrests during the same period in 1984. Reports of police harassment at these venues plummeted to "literally down to zero," according to Coyle's office. Vice squad head Lt. Lyle Goodspeed confirmed the shift, telling the *Tribune*: "Arresting the gays in the bookstores is not a priority issue with us," noting the squad's new focus on street prostitution.[141] The vice squad shifted its attention from consensual activities in commercial sex establishments to public sex in popular cruising spots and street prostitution, influenced by both the escalating AIDS crisis—which linked public sex to high-risk behavior—and the city's ongoing downtown redevelopment efforts.

Not everyone welcomed the compromise over bookstores and bathhouses. Dan Cohen, president of the Minneapolis Planning Commission, warned that tolerating the "icky" sex in these venues would turn Minneapolis into a greater "haven" for LGBTQ people, bringing vice and drugs in its wake. City Council President Alice Rainville had echoed this sentiment, cautioning that the city risked becoming "the San Francisco of the Wheat Belt."[142] Liberationists like Campbell begrudgingly accepted the arrangement, frustrated that gay men lacked a stronger constitutional basis for the rights he believed they deserved. Meanwhile, moderate integrationists like Coyle, Spear, and Clark celebrated the compromise as a tangible victory—not for the entire LGBTQ community but at least for the gay men who sought pleasure at bookstores and bathhouses. Their efforts had achieved real progress, but while they were willing to make significant concessions, straight Minnesotans had firm limits on how far they would accommodate gay men—respectable or not.

"Queerbashing" and the Limits of Accommodation

In the Twin Cities, as in many urban areas across the United States, LGBTQ people endured persistent harassment and violence, exacerbated by the secrecy surrounding same-sex desire and a reluctance to report assaults. Closeted gay men, particularly those cruising parks at night, were especially vulnerable, often becoming easy targets for assailants. As the LGBTQ movement gained momentum, so did awareness of this violence and the need for community-led action, given law enforcement's frequent indifference—or outright complicity. In September 1974, two members of the short-lived Minnesota Mattachine Society held a press conference condemning police inaction after assaults in Minneapolis and St. Paul. One had been robbed and beaten, while the other reported being threatened at gunpoint by teenage "fag-baiters" in Loring Park. Drawing inspiration from local community patrols organized by Black and Indigenous groups like Soul Force and the American Indian Movement (AIM), the men announced the creation of the Lambda Squad, a gay street patrol dedicated to safety. Unlike the more assimilationist stance of many Mattachine chapters, the Lambda Squad adopted a confrontational approach, arming themselves with handcuffs, chemical mace, and an infrared camera to document incidents and shame authorities into action. "We've tried to talk to the police. We've tried to talk to our alderman. We've tried everything else; now we'll use force if we have to," one member declared.[143] Despite their determination, the police refused to cooperate, and public pressure failed to spur change. The Lambda Squad disbanded, leaving LGBTQ individuals vulnerable as violence continued to escalate throughout the 1970s.[144]

With law enforcement failing to treat bias-motivated crimes as a distinct category, the task of documenting antigay violence fell to the LGBTQ community. In its September 1975 newsletter, Gay House encouraged readers to report assaults and provided guidance on gathering key details, such as license plate numbers and physical descriptions.[145] While the data collected was incomplete, it painted a disturbing picture: fifty-two beatings, rapes, and other assaults against LGBTQ individuals were reported in 1976 alone.[146] After St. Paul repealed its gay rights ordinance in 1978, activists noted an increase in assaults and robberies targeting LGBTQ people, linking the spike to the loss of legal protections. Kerry Woodward of the MCGR told *The Minneapolis Star* that the rollback had effectively given "permission to a number of adolescent boys to assault any person they think might be gay in order to prove their masculinity."[147]

In response to rising violence, the MCGR established the No More Assault Project (NMAP) the summer after the ordinance repeal. NMAP provided crisis intervention, advocacy, and support services, including counseling and medical care.[148] It encouraged victims of "queerbashing" to report incidents to establish a clear pattern of assaults, distributing standardized reporting forms through LGBTQ organizations and operating a hotline for those wary of contacting the police. Reflecting the MCGR's cautious and accommodating sentiments, NMAP advised men to avoid walking alone at night, remain vigilant in "bars, parks, and beaches," and even consider steering clear of these areas altogether.[149] Despite these efforts, police response remained minimal. It was not until a series of deadly assaults on gay men in the late 1970s—coinciding with increased vice squad raids on public and semi-public sexual spaces—that LGBTQ people pressured the police to take action and offer protection.

On June 6, 1979, Terry Knudsen, a thirty-three-year-old maître d' at the Minneapolis Athletic Club, was brutally attacked by three young men wielding a three-foot metal rod as he walked through Loring Park at 1:00 a.m. The assault left Knudsen with a traumatic brain injury, the loss of his right eye, and in a coma. Friends described Knudsen as a quiet, reserved man who did not "flaunt" his sexuality, insisting he was not the type to seek sexual partners in Loring Park. This portrayal was an attempt to distance him from cruising, suggesting he was undeserving of such a violent attack.[150] However, when asked if Knudsen had been cruising, Tim Campbell remarked that it would be "naïve to think [Knudsen] was [at Loring Park] for any other reason than the same reason everybody else is."[151] Regardless of the circumstances, the LGBTQ community and its allies saw Knudsen as a victim of the homophobic violence that continued to plague the Twin Cities.

In response, on June 12, 1979, approximately 1,000 people marched to Loring Park from nearby Plymouth Church, holding candles and chanting in solidarity. The event followed a community forum hosted by the NMAP, which raised over $5,000 (about $21,700 in 2024) to fund a reward for information leading to the assailants' arrest.[152] The day before, Mayor Hofstede and Police Chief Nordlund announced that they were "beefing up" police patrols in Loring Park, including plainclothes foot patrols.[153] However, many at the protest voiced concerns that these measures might lead to further police harassment and entrapment of LGBTQ individuals. Terry Couch of Gay Community Services predicted: "If the role of the police is to entrap gay men, or if the police are going to be there to hassle the hustlers," then the LGBTQ community would strongly resent it. One protester garnered thunderous applause for declaring: "We need to come up with a mass program of how we're going to deal with the Minneapolis police!"[154] The prevailing sentiment at the protest was clear: The police were part of the problem, with their inaction bordering on complicity in the violence.

Yet the more accommodationist MCGR took a different approach, seeing in the moment an opportunity to build an alliance with the police. The organization's Police-Community Relations Committee sent a letter to Mayor Hofstede "respectfully insist[ing]" that he take steps to improve relations with the LGBTQ community. These included ending police harassment of gay and lesbian establishments, recruiting LGBTQ individuals into the police force, and creating a position of police liaison for the LGBTQ community.[155] MCGR believed these measures could reduce bias within the force and improve relations with the LGBTQ community.[156] However, both

Hofstede and Police Chief Nordlund declined to attend a conference convened by NMAP to address the violence.[157] Tragically, on June 14, 1979, just eight days after the attack, Knudsen succumbed to his injuries.

A week after Knudsen's attack, the LGBTQ community faced another devastating loss with the death of thirty-one-year-old Les Benscoter in St. Paul. Benscoter was discovered in his apartment after failing to show up to work. Despite the chilling message "Fags will die" scrawled in toothpaste on a piece of furniture, St. Paul police refused to classify the death as a homicide, instead treating it as an "adult crib death."[158] With no clear cause of death identified by the coroner, police entertained the possibility that Benscoter had written the message as a crude suicide note and sold off his missing belongings.[159] To his friends, this theory was asinine—he had been in good spirits and appeared healthy.[160] Instead, they believed Benscoter likely met his attacker while hitchhiking home from a gay bar and the two presumably returned to Benscoter's apartment, where the fatal encounter occurred.

In response to Benscoter's death, around two hundred LGBTQ protesters marched from St. Paul City Hall to police headquarters, where organizers threatened to "burn a male chauvinist pig cop and . . . pig judge in effigy."[161] Despite assurances from the head of the homicide division that the case had been investigated "as thoroughly as possible," friends and activists argued otherwise. Facing mounting pressure, investigators revised their theory, but only slightly, now suggesting that Benscoter died of natural causes and that "an opportunist" simply entered his apartment afterward, stole his stereo and television, and wrote the ominous message.[162] The LGBTQ community's demands for accountability elicited an exasperated response from Capt. Gerald Kissling of the Crimes Against Persons Unit: "It's getting so that if a homosexual, Negro, or Chicano get killed, you hear all this stuff about cops not doing their job. When a WASP gets killed nobody says nothing. I'm getting pretty damn sick of all these pressure groups."[163]

In July 1979, more than a month after Benscoter's death, Ramsey County Attorney Tom Foley announced at a press conference that Benscoter had "probably" been murdered. Foley revealed new evidence showing that Benscoter had been strangled and suffocated, but in an unexpected twist, the alleged killer, twenty-year-old Mark Miller, had died in a car accident before charges could be filed.[164] A combative Foley refused to name the suspect or share details about the accident, stating, "I see no purpose in revealing the name" and citing the need to protect Miller's family: "We have to protect the innocent families."[165] The reasons for Foley's unusual discretion remain unclear, but the *Star Tribune* hinted at a possible motive by reporting on the suspicious circumstances surrounding Miller's "accident."[166] A photograph of his fiancée was reportedly found on the passenger seat, hinting that Miller may have been pursuing a conventional heterosexual life and that his encounter with Benscoter might not have been random. Foley's reluctance to associate Miller with a gay man points to deeper societal biases. In protecting Miller's heterosexual image, Foley seemed more concerned with upholding heteronormativity than seeking justice. This highlights how, even in murder cases, the mere suggestion of a connection to a gay victim could threaten a man's reputation—exposing a broader societal discomfort with queerness and a tendency to shield heterosexual men, even when implicated in violence.

The deaths of Knudsen and Benscoter starkly reminded LGBTQ individuals in the Twin Cities of the systemic failures that left them vulnerable to violence. Dallas Drake, a leader of ACT UP/Minnesota, described this grim reality: "It was well known that if you tried to report antigay violence, the police might arrest you." Even when perpetrators were arrested, Drake noted, "They'd put them in the back of the squad car, maybe not even handcuff [them], drive for a few blocks, stop the squad car, let them get out and just say . . . 'Don't come back here.'" This indifference, he explained, reflected a broader complicity: "They kind of agreed with it . . . 'These fags are being beat up, so what?'"[167]

In response to the deaths of Knudsen and Benscoter, gay men began adopting safety measures, including carrying whistles—over two hundred were distributed at Knudsen's vigil at Loring Park—a strategy borrowed from feminist-led Take Back the Night marches.[168] The NMAP also organized self-defense classes for LGBTQ people, and some gay men informally patrolled Loring Park, with *Positively Gay* describing it as a "gay-run security patrol." Despite these efforts, the violence persisted. Just three months after Knudsen's murder, on September 6, 1979, Robert Allan Taylor, a thirty-year-old gay man from St. Paul, was killed near Loring Park.[169] Taylor had picked up eighteen-year-old David R. Houle in south Minneapolis, and the two drove to a parking lot known for furtive gay sex. There, Houle attacked Taylor.[170] In his police statement, Houle claimed he was hitchhiking when Taylor offered him a ride home but instead drove to Loring Park where he allegedly made sexual advances and offered Houle $15 to undress. Houle would later tell a psychologist that he was frightened by Taylor's sexual advances and tried to jump out of the car. When Taylor allegedly grabbed his thigh and moved his hand to Houle's genitals, Houle claimed he warned Taylor he had a knife, but when Taylor continued, Houle stabbed him in the chest with a Swiss army knife.[171]

Yet, despite the presence of a gay man's corpse, the central question for police and the broader straight public became who the real victim was. A homicide investigator, when asked about Houle's account, remarked, "We're not really sure what happened. That's the *kid's* story."[172] Referring to Houle as a "kid" reframed the entire encounter, casting him as an innocent youth—a narrative that would shape the outcome of the trial. Hennepin County Attorney Tom Johnson refused to offer Houle a plea deal, believing the evidence supported charges of second-degree murder or manslaughter. After all, Houle had confessed to killing Taylor, stating, "That fucking faggot deserved to die."[173] However, the jury was swayed by Houle's attorney, who argued that Taylor had been interrupted during sex with his partner nine hours earlier, which led to an unusual level of sexual aggressiveness. After deliberating for only three hours, including a lunch break, the jury acquitted Houle of all charges.[174] His defense relied entirely on the claim that he had acted in self-defense during a "homosexual attack." This "gay panic" defense—commonly used to justify reduced sentences or outright acquittals—blamed the victim's sexual orientation and supposed predations for the violence inflicted on them. Following the verdict, the jury foreperson told the press that there was "no doubt the *kid* was absolutely terrified."[175]

The verdict sent shockwaves through the LGBTQ community, for it effectively granted a license to target and kill LGBTQ individuals with impunity. To make matters worse, the media portrayed the perpetrators as young victims—"kids" really—of "predatory" gay men despite some of the attackers having a known history of sex work in Loring Park. Whether the verdict directly increased crime rates is unclear, as robbing gay men had long been an easy and lightly punished means of making money. Unfortunately, this ultimately proved to be the cause of Knudsen's earlier murder.

In the spring of 1981, Greg Smith, eighteen, and James Patterson, nineteen, were charged with the murder of Terry Knudsen. Patterson, who had gone to the park to make some quick cash by "hustling"—that is, through sex work—ran into Smith, who suggested they "roll some fags" for money instead. Patterson agreed, and Knudsen became their unfortunate target. As Patterson tried to remove a ring from Knudsen, Smith struck Knudsen in the head with such force that Patterson later likened the sound to "a hammer hitting a watermelon."[176] In the end, they stole only $3.27.[177] Yet the tragedy of the event was eclipsed by the fact that Patterson had been, at the time, an underage, seventeen-year-old sex worker.

Four months later, the *Star Tribune* published a salacious exposé of teenage male sex workers in Loring Park, alleging that the purpose of cruising was "homosexual prostitution." The paper described the "streetwalkers" as "teens, some as young as 15, few older than 20 . . . Most have clean faces; they appear too young to shave regularly." It justified its focus on the subject by citing the recent arrest of a teacher and a Cub Scout leader, who had been "accused of paying boys as young as 12 to perform in videotape sex shows." Neither men met their victims at Loring Park—both knew their victims well—and neither identified as gay. Yet the *Tribune* rekindled the toxic trope that gay men were pedophiles. The article claimed gay men lured these boys into the park for oral and anal sex for as little as $20, stating, "Usually, it is performed in the car. Sometimes it's preceded by small talk in a bar. Sometimes it's at an apartment."[178] By specifically mentioning Patterson, the paper had implicitly turned Knudsen from a victim of a violent crime into a suspicious perpetrator who might have deserved what came to him. It did not matter that the story lacked logic—how were boys "as young as 12" in bars without being noticed? —or that it failed to distinguish between consensual adult encounters and prostitution, whether underage or not. The message was crystal clear: a vital aspect of gay sex depended on hunting the vulnerable and taking advantage of them. And if so, according to this trope, then gay men were so reprehensible that they effectively deserved the violence inflicted on them.[179]

The police's refusal to recognize the severity of antigay violence was reflected in their failure to document such incidents or consider the sexual orientation of victims. In 1981, Police Chief Bouza dismissed the idea of a pattern of violence against LGBTQ people, even as he admitted the difficulty of sensitizing officers toward the LGBTQ community. When a proposal was made for a gay officer to speak at a training session, it was "vigorously opposed," with one officer reportedly asking, "Do you realize what those people do?"[180] Lacking clear guidance from leadership, rank-and-file cops filled the void with their biases. One officer patrolling Loring Park told the *Star Tribune* that crimes against LGBTQ people had increased but blamed the victims, claiming gay men who picked up "tricks" in the park brought violence on themselves. With cruising, he explained, "Somebody poses as a sexual partner and may be a willing participant for a while, and then commits a robbery."[181] By 1980, assaults against LGBTQ people had risen to eighty-nine.[182] These statistics confirmed the limits of "working within the system." Despite the efforts of gay integrationists to build relationships with the police, courts, and media, these institutions remained entrenched in homophobia. This institutionalized prejudice created a culture of impunity for perpetrators and constrained meaningful progress. The public's indifference to the lives of gay men, coupled with police neglect, allowed violence against them to proliferate unchecked. Only the looming AIDS epidemic would disrupt these dynamics, reshaping the political, social, and sexual landscape and forcing a reckoning with integrationist politics.

AIDS Tips the Scales

The portrayal of the upper Midwest in Edmund White's travelogue as uniquely equipped to tackle homophobic laws and policies proved more fanciful than factual. Comparing "radicals" and "moderates" in the late 1970s—integrationists and liberationists in today's terms—White discerned that each group imagined distinct futures. "Radicals," he noted, sought to transform society by overhauling national institutions, while "moderates" aimed to assimilate into the mainstream. "Whereas the radical goal is to transform society," White observed, "the moderate goal is to enter it."[183] If liberationists opted for anger and confrontation, integrationists favored persuasion and politicking. Despite the continued influence and assertiveness of liberationists, it was the integrationists who achieved measurable gains, albeit within significant constraints. As conservatism surged in the 1970s, integrationists adjusted their goals to align with the dominant political culture. Debra Minkoff explains that the "law and order" policies of the Nixon era and beyond did not suppress activism entirely but instead redirected it into institutionally sanctioned forms.[184] By prioritizing privacy, respectability, and law and order, integrationists found a strategy compatible with the political climate. With the arrival of AIDS, this emphasis would only become more compelling.

The onset of the AIDS epidemic marked a decisive turning point, shattering the stalemate between integrationists and liberationists. Confronted with the Reagan administration's homophobia, the prevalence of the closet, and stereotypes of gay men as diseased and hypersexual, integrationists, as Urvashi Vaid noted, made "a series of strategic decisions" to secure access and resources. They downplayed the sexual liberation ethos of the 1970s in favor of emphasizing monogamous relationships.[185] Reflecting on his 1980 travelogues in 2014, White agreed that the epidemic propelled "assimilation over gay exceptionalism," elevating moderates over radicals within the movement.[186] Thomas Trisko, a young gay urban professional in the Twin Cities during the 1970s, shared White's assessment. "In the 70s, practically nobody was practicing monogamy. The 70s were kind of a golden age for gay people because we were discovering one another and having sex," he recalled. By the 1980s, that changed. "For our generation, [the epidemic] pretty much shut it down, and people started to couple up," Trisko noted.[187] He and his partner, John Rittman, would later sue Minnesota successfully in 2010 over its same-sex marriage ban. The emergence of HIV, amid ongoing urban redevelopment, offered integrationists the tools to frame cruising as both a public health hazard and a safety concern. By promoting homonormativity as a spatial fix for AIDS and violence, they found a narrative that aligned with the politics of middleness dominant in the upper Midwest. The battles between integrationists and liberationists took on a new register during the epidemic, but it would be the integrationists who would thrive in this climate, leveraging respectability to secure greater institutional acceptance.

2   Privacy in a Time of AIDS

Bowers in Minnesota

Though he lived far from Minnesota, in the mid-1980s, Michael Hardwick would leave an indelible mark on the state's politics. In 1982, Hardwick, a white gay Atlanta resident, was arrested for sodomy after a police officer, serving a warrant, discovered him engaging in consensual oral sex with another man in his private bedroom. With the support of the American Civil Liberties Union (ACLU), Hardwick challenged his conviction, taking his case all the way to the US Supreme Court. However, on June 30, 1986, in *Bowers v. Hardwick*, the court upheld Georgia's sodomy law in a 5–4 decision, ruling that the Constitution did not protect consensual homosexual relations, even in private homes. The majority opinion argued that homosexual sodomy lacked historical precedent and public approval, dismissing claims of a fundamental right to privacy for gay men and lesbians as "facetious."[1] With *Bowers*, the court embraced legal moralism, departing from the court's earlier rights-based approach in sex-related cases.[2]

The *Bowers* decision reignited activists' efforts to repeal sodomy laws across the country, and nowhere was this more evident than in Minnesota. The state, which had failed to repeal its sodomy laws in the 1970s, remained an outlier in the region, surrounded by states that had already abolished such statutes. Like many LGBTQ leaders nationwide, Minnesota's activists reacted to *Bowers* with a mix of horror and anger. Their reactions could be raw, almost visceral. Gay City Councilmember Brian Coyle called the ruling "an outrageous and very political decision" that had "invade[d] the bedroom."[3] Concerned constituents flooded Coyle's office with inquiries, fearing the implications of the decision on their own lives.[4] Yet in Minnesota, the failure of the Minnesota Committee on Gay Rights (MCGR) twelve years before to secure even modest gains remained vivid in many leaders' minds. In the years since the MCGR's failed attempt, while all neighboring states had repealed sodomy laws, Minnesota stood as an inland island of legalized antigay sentiment. Now, for the first time in over a decade, momentum built to finally change that.

Part of this groundswell arose from anger. Although the ruling specifically addressed sodomy, gay activists argued that it legitimized the belief that gay men and lesbians were incapable of forming families, marriages, or intimate relationships. To them, the Supreme Court had effectively codified toxic stereotypes into law, denying the validity of love and commitment in same-sex relationships. Another source of this surge in activism was justifiable fear, as the decision further endangered the already precarious lives of LGBTQ families. Nan D. Hunter, director of the ACLU's Lesbian-Gay Rights Project, warned that labeling a gay or lesbian parent as a "habitual lawbreaker" could be used to strip them of basic civil rights.[5] Attorney Gary Rankila of the Minneapolis Commission on Civil Rights echoed these concerns, noting that *Bowers* could undermine gay and lesbian parents' ability to prove their suitability in custody cases.[6] These fears were quickly realized, as courts cited *Bowers* to justify discrimination in adoption, custody, and visitation rights. In a prominent example, the New Hampshire Supreme Court relied on *Bowers* in 1987 to uphold a law prohibiting gay men and lesbians from adopting or fostering children.[7]

Gay families also faced the court's casual comparison of consensual same-sex relations to crimes like rape and incest. Not to be outdone, Chief Justice Warren Burger went further, calling sodomy between consenting adults an "offense of deeper malignity than rape."[8] Outraged by the *Bowers* decision, the Twin Cities–based Ad-Hoc Committee on Liberty organized a protest outside the downtown Minneapolis Federal Building on July 9, 1986. The demonstration drew about 170 protesters—the largest turnout for a local gay protest in years—who marched and listened to speeches from community leaders and activists. The crowd's anger was palpable, and one woman was arrested for kicking the building's locked glass doors.[9] Addressing the demonstrators, Coyle voiced his frustration, condemning the court for equating "incest, wife battering and other outrageous acts" with "homosexual love."[10]

On that day, Coyle emphasized a pivotal issue that would dominate discussions in the weeks and months to come: privacy. Drawing from lessons learned during the bathhouse and bookstore battles, he argued that consensual sexual activity between adult homosexuals in private deserved constitutional protection. If heterosexual acts between consenting adults in private enjoyed well-established legal safeguards, then the same principle should extend to same-sex intimacy. To accomplish this, however, two simultaneous steps would be necessary. First, leaders would need to draw a clear dividing line between "homosexual love" and "outrageous acts" involving physical and sexual violence and implied coercion. Predictably, religious and conservative opponents would inevitably resist this distinction, but even within the LGBTQ community, ongoing debates swirled over the place of radical and subversive sexual identities and practices, specifically those related to the elimination of age-of-consent laws. The second move would involve grouping all these "outrageous acts" under the umbrella of "public" behavior, thus sacrificing them to the altar of continued state surveillance. At the core of gay leadership's efforts to repeal sodomy laws lay a commitment not only to the principle but also to the actual practice of transforming all acceptable sexual acts into private affairs.[11]

The 1965 *Griswold v. Connecticut* decision, a landmark in privacy rights, significantly influenced the trajectory of gay civil rights. By invalidating a Connecticut law banning contraceptive use by married couples, the Supreme Court effectively removed legal barriers to certain intimate acts within heterosexual marriages. While the Court acknowledged that the ruling did not impede a state from regulating sexual behavior, the ruling subtly destigmatized private acts of sodomy without endorsing public expressions of homosexuality.[12] Organizations like the ACLU seized upon this legal precedent, prioritizing challenges against restrictions on private conduct over efforts to defend public behavior. Consequently, by the 1970s, while opposition to the criminalization of private sodomy gained traction, advocates largely maintained support for measures aimed at regulating public sexual activity.[13]

Gay leaders and allies acknowledged the criminal justice system's role in regulating behaviors deemed "undesirable" or socially harmful, a view some of them shared with their detractors. However, they diverged from their homophobic adversaries by advocating for a new standard for acceptable, constitutionally protected sexual conduct: the "consenting adults in private" principle.[14] This idea traced back to the 1970 case *Buchanan v. Batchelor*, in which a gay man arrested for public sex attempted to overturn Texas's sodomy law. Although the man's legal efforts failed, gay activists highlighted the court's focus on the public nature of the acts, rather than the acts themselves, as the basis for criminality.[15] This prompted advocates, lawyers, and judges throughout the 1970s to wrestle with where to draw the line between public and private sexual behavior. By the 1980s, this demarcation grew sharper as activists emphasized the distinction between the illegitimate moral policing of consensual private acts and legitimate public health interventions targeting promiscuity and its associated environments.

Several weeks after Coyle's speech at the Minneapolis Federal Building, Minnesota saw the first step toward a strategy of trading public sex laws for sodomy repeal. On July 26, 1986, State Sen. Allan Spear and State Rep. Karen Clark hosted a community forum to discuss repealing Section 609.293 of the Minnesota Statutes, the state's sodomy law.[16] Spear indicated that the repeal would likely take the form of a standalone bill, separate from broader legislation. He expressed uncertainty about whether the bill should also repeal laws against adultery and fornication (sex between unmarried heterosexuals), noting that defending behaviors like "cheating" could undermine efforts to establish same-sex relationships as equal to heterosexual ones. On the other hand, Clark pointed out that strong opposition to policing fornication might help build broader support for the bill. Despite these debates, participants agreed on one key point: The repeal would focus on private, consensual adult conduct while maintaining laws against public sex.

One reason Clark and others hesitated to expand the repeal of sodomy was that including heterosexual coplaintiffs had shown little success in court. In 1984, the Minnesota Civil Liberties Union (MCLU) had challenged the state's sodomy law in federal court on behalf of Stephen McClellan, a heterosexual man with degenerative multiple sclerosis, and his wife. The law, as one ACLU attorney argued, forced McClellan to choose between "being unable to express his sexuality at all or being a criminal." People with disabilities were frequently unable to engage in heterosexual intercourse—that is, penile-vaginal sex—due to issues with physical agility or motor function as well as atrophy or paralysis of limbs and genitalia. Sodomy laws, which included oral sex, criminalized what for many of them was their only option of being sexual beings. With support from the ACLU Lesbian-Gay Rights Project, the MCLU aimed to show how the law harmed a diverse group of plaintiffs.[17] McClellan's case included a gay man and a lesbian, both citing personal and professional harm caused by the law. But, after *Bowers*, the ACLU and Lambda Legal Defense realized they lacked standing in federal court. This forced them to abandon the McClellan case and other federal challenges, redirecting their efforts to state courts and legislatures.

Despite the *Bowers* decision, the national trend was moving away from sodomy laws. In 1955, the American Law Institute (ALI) excluded sodomy from its draft Model Penal Code, arguing that states should not enforce moral or religious standards. The revised code decriminalized "all sexual practices not involving force, adult corruption of minors, or public offense," reasoning that such acts posed no threat to secular community interests when enacted privately. Notably, the ALI retained vagrancy laws targeting "lewd or dissolute" individuals, laying the groundwork for activists to emphasize the distinction between public and private homosexual conduct.[18]

In 1960, all fifty states, along with the District of Columbia and Puerto Rico, had sodomy laws. Illinois led the way in decriminalizing sodomy between consenting adults in private in 1961, followed by Connecticut in 1969. States that repealed their sodomy statutes in the intervening years typically did so indirectly while overhauling their penal codes.[19] By December 1986, only twenty-four states—including Minnesota—still retained sodomy statutes. Minnesota's sodomy law, Section 609.293 of the Minnesota Statutes, dated back to 1849 when the area was still a territory. The statute banned all anal and oral sex, with no exceptions for married couples, and defined sodomy as "carnally knowing any person by the anus or by or with the mouth." Violations were classified as gross misdemeanors, punishable by up to a year in jail and/or a $3,000 fine (approximately $8,500 in 2024).[20]

Minnesota's status as the last state in the upper Midwest with a sodomy law did not escape the notice of local gay leaders and progressives. They highlighted the contradiction between the law and Minnesota's reputation for liberalism, progress, and tolerance. During a fall 1986 visit, Thomas Stoddard, Lambda Legal's executive director, criticized this inconsistency, noting that most states with sodomy laws were in the South or Southwest—regions typically perceived as having less politically active LGBTQ communities. Nan D. Hunter, director of the ACLU's Lesbian-Gay Rights Project, viewed Minnesota's strong LGBTQ community as a promising sign for repeal efforts. Peter Fowler, cochair of the National Gay and Lesbian Task Force, agreed, citing Minnesota's openly gay elected officials as evidence of its progressiveness. "In many of these states [with sodomy laws] we don't have an infrastructure in place. Minnesota is an exception," Fowler noted.[21] The *Star Tribune*, Minneapolis's newspaper of record, echoed these sentiments, describing the sodomy law as a "legal anomaly" that lived in "uneasy coexistence" with "state and local antidiscrimination edicts and a legacy of liberalism."[22]

During the infamous police "reign of terror" in the Twin Cities from 1979 to 1985, nearly five thousand people were arrested, though almost none faced charges or convictions under Minnesota's sodomy law.[23] Instead, law enforcement arrested people for offenses like indecent conduct, solicitation of prostitution, and lewd and lascivious behavior.[24] When sodomy charges did arise, they usually involved minors, violence, or public settings.[25] In Hennepin County, the most populous county that includes Minneapolis, only fourteen gross misdemeanor sodomy charges were filed from 1980 to

1985, mostly involving public acts.[26] These included men arrested in police stings in restrooms or engaging in consensual intercourse in adult bookstores.[27] At the state level, a similar pattern emerged: Between 1983 and 1984, twenty-five men were charged with sodomy for consensual acts occurring in public places, such as adult bookstores, department store restrooms, or automobiles.[28] In rare instances where sodomy charges involved private settings, the cases always, as far back as Minnesota's first reported prosecution in 1937's *State v. Nelson*, involved sexual acts with minors. While the state largely overlooked private, consensual sexual activity between adults, it strictly enforced laws against sexual conduct involving minors or occurring in spaces where children or families might be present. Ultimately, it was always the public visibility of sodomy—or its association with minors, which inherently made it public—that drew the state's attention, underscoring how the law functioned as a tool of moral regulation in public spaces.

Courts and the Limits of Privacy

Police arrest patterns essentially aligned with the principle of "consenting adults in private," bolstering activists' confidence in their strategy. Of the three components—privacy, consent, and adulthood—only the last posed significant challenges. Activists had already demonstrated that advocating for "privacy" in Minnesota could be effective, and "consent" was generally accepted as a given (though sexual assault could still occur within the LGBTQ community). However, defining "adult" proved more contentious. Although arrests involving gay men and underage sex workers were rare, they attracted outsized attention and reinforced harmful stereotypes of gay men as sexual predators. To combat this, activists worked to dispel fears that repealing sodomy laws would lead to the exploitation of minors. For Minneapolis-based gay politicians, sex in public but especially sex with minors represented the "outrageous acts" that the US Supreme Court had conflated with "homosexual love." If gay elected officials could persuade Minnesota's courts and legislators to focus on the consensual, adult gay relationships already taking place in private, they believed they could successfully repeal the sodomy law. In doing so, they hoped to also challenge the internalized shame that supposedly kept many in the LGBTQ community closeted, which leaders believed could drive individuals toward "outrageous acts."

No doubt, gay elected officials had this sentiment in mind in the case of Hennepin County District Judge Crane Winton Jr. A graduate of Harvard

Law School, Winton had been on the bench since 1967. He was, according to *The Minneapolis Star*, "one of the most respected and experienced judges of the Hennepin District Court."[29] Thus, it came as a public shock when a grand jury charged him with four solicitation misdemeanor charges and two felony charges of having sex with a minor. The local CBS affiliate, WCCO-TV, revealed Winton's homosexuality in a report on childhood sexual abuse, based on information obtained from police sources. In a televised interview on February 11, 1982, three unidentified young male hustlers, shown in silhouette, alleged that Winton solicited them in Loring Park, brought them to his home, and paid them for sex. After one of the men featured in the segment was arrested for soliciting an undercover officer in Loring Park in 1980, police attempted to recruit the man as an informant by asking him to name any high-profile clients. He named Winton.[30] As part of a plea deal, Winton pleaded guilty to two misdemeanor charges of paying for sex and was fined $300, approximately $1,000 in 2024 dollars. At a disciplinary hearing before the Board on Judicial Standards, Winton expressed remorse for his actions, explaining that his closeted lifestyle limited his choice of sexual partners: "My decision to conceal an aspect of myself and to try to lock that part in a tight, inaccessible compartment led to years of loneliness and a sense of isolation."[31] His attorney added that Winton was now committed to pursuing more "adult" relationships. "He's willing to live his life as a mature, responsible homosexual adult. And that includes no activities with prostitutes. That does include satisfying adult relationships—intellectually, sexually, emotionally—with men."[32]

The board, nonetheless, recommended removing Winton from the bench, citing his past solicitations of male sex workers, including one as young as sixteen; the potential for future violations of Minnesota's sodomy law; and the damage to the public confidence in the judiciary.[33] In response, Spear, who did not personally know Winton but empathized with his situation as a fellow professional, white, gay man forced to come out, launched a letter-writing campaign in Winton's defense. In a letter to constituents, Spear argued that Winton's case had "broad implications for gay and lesbian civil rights in this state," claiming he was being punished for refusing to comply with "Minnesota's ludicrous consensual sex laws."[34] The National Gay Rights Advocates and the Lambda Legal Defense and Education Fund also supported Winton, filing amicus curiae briefs on his behalf.[35] During the trial, the prosecuting attorney pressed Winton on whether he intended to continue violating the sodomy law. Winton responded, "That's a difficult question . . . My life has changed. What I used to do furtively . . . has all changed. I suppose if I met a suitable person who wants a relationship that involved sexual acts, I'd probably do so. But it would be in private, behind closed doors, in such a manner that won't bring disrepute to the bench."[36] Despite assurances to act within existing legal and social boundaries, it was not enough. On May 25, 1984, the Minnesota Supreme Court unanimously upheld the Board on Judicial Standards' recommendation, removing the fifty-seven-year-old Winton from the bench, ruling that he had "exploited vulnerable young persons."[37]

For moderate, accommodating gay leaders, Winton's revelation became their own. He was not a criminal, but a lonely man pushed to "outrageous acts" by societal and internalized homophobia. Leaders supported Winton, either believing he was unaware of the sex workers' ages or choosing to overlook this detail, hoping his case could still advance sodomy repeal efforts. If Winton could engage in these acts in private, in the confines of a loving relationship—that is, a noncommercial one—with an adult man, then these acts would not bring "disrepute" upon him and his public standing. For activists, Winton's case was not a cautionary tale against repealing sodomy laws under the principle of "consenting adults in private," but rather an example of what would continue if such laws *were not* repealed and otherwise decent people had to engage in disreputable practices. Still, to embrace Winton as an LGBTQ-rights cause required ignoring uncomfortable details of his actions. By the summer of 1984, gay leaders would confront the reality that not everyone charged under sodomy laws could be seen as a "victim."

On April 18, 1984, about a month before Winton was removed from the bench, agents from the Bureau of Criminal Apprehension (BCA) charged John Clark Donahue, the forty-five-year-old founder and artistic director of the world-renowned Children's Theatre, with sexually abusing three teenage boys between April 1981 and October 1983. Donahue was one of seven men arrested and charged with either having sex with minors or failing to report suspected sexual abuse. BCA affidavits painted a picture of a sex ring of pedophiles and supplied evidence for what Paul M. Renfro identifies as the late twentieth-century "stranger danger" panic of endangered white childhood.[38] Donahue was accused of luring boys into his office with alcohol, of bribing them into sex with promises of starring roles, and of attending parties where sex between men and boys was rampant.[39] The story stirred the public into such a frenzy that in the three days after Donahue's arrest, the BCA received more than two hundred calls from concerned parents of students at the Children's Theatre and from people who claimed to have incriminating information on the arrested men.[40] Donahue eventually pleaded guilty to having sex with three fifteen-year-old boys and was sentenced to a year in the Hennepin County Workhouse along with fifteen years' probation, but the scandal had far longer-lasting implications for the local LGBTQ community.[41]

Debate about whether all gay men were sexual predators erupted with a letter to the *Star Tribune* on May 15, 1984, from Spear's nemesis, gay liberationist Tim Campbell. In it, he critiqued local reporting on Winton and Donahue for fueling what he described as the "vampire theory" of homosexuality—that is, that gay men preyed on boys. Campbell denounced the suggestion that pedophilia was inherent to gay men by reminding the public that family relatives were likelier to be the perpetrators of abuse. But he also downplayed sex as the primary culprit in "the malformation of children," claiming, "All kinds of kids have sex with adults without harmful side effects."[42] Unclear as to what he meant by "kids," whether pre- or post-pubescent, Campbell's intention to start a conversation around youth sexuality became instead interpreted as a promotion of pedophilia.[43]

Then, just a few weeks later, on June 23, David Thorstad, cofounder of the North American Man/Boy Love Association (NAMBLA) and a native of Thief River Falls, Minnesota, arrived in Minneapolis for a panel titled "Forum on Pedophilia" convened by the Minnesota Gay Defense Fund and A Brother's Touch Bookstore and held at the Hennepin County Government Center. NAMBLA, founded in 1978 in New York City, called for the abolition of age-of-consent laws.[44] Thus, it came as no surprise when at the forum, Thorstad, a former president of the Gay Activists Alliance, described "man/boy love" as "sensual" and "mutually rewarding." He insisted that boys seldom complained about such sexual contact and that police investigators pressured boys into testifying against older men. Claiming that "boy-lovers have always played a very important part in the gay liberation movement," he chastised those in the movement who distanced themselves from the issue. The audience overwhelmingly disagreed that sex between men and boys was a civil rights issue, and shouting matches and scuffles broke out. Adding to the chaos, Christian demonstrators snuck into the meeting and, while clutching Bibles, tried to convince audience members to repent. At the end of the forum, a woman denounced the crowd as "a bunch of cocksucking faggots" and stormed out of the room. Outside, she would have found a boisterous group of protesters holding picket signs, including one that read "NAMBLA promotes kiddie porn." Circulating in the mob were lesbian feminists handing out anti-NAMBLA leaflets.[45] The crowd marked the beginning of a public backlash against Thorstad's visit. The day of the forum, NAMBLA opponents held a news conference in which a board member of the American Society for the Prevention of Cruelty to Children accused gay leaders of "tacitly encouraging the rape of children" by their silence.[46] Gene Sullivan, a candidate for the Minnesota House of Representatives, used Thorstad's visit to condemn Mayor Don Fraser's proclamation of June 24 as Gay and Lesbian Pride Day, writing to the *Star Tribune*, "City officials should show more responsibility before allowing a group of lawbreakers to organize and use public facilities for these purposes."[47]

In Minnesota, like elsewhere in the country, the persistent myth of gay men as child predators dampened efforts to repeal sodomy laws. Stephen Vider notes, "The specter of the male homosexual pedophile haunted postwar American culture, threatening to corrupt boys and young men and disrupt their 'normal' development toward heterosexuality."[48] This myth positioned pedophilia as an outside-the-home threat, reinforcing the belief that gay men did not deserve the privacy protections that sodomy repeal would afford. In other words, enemies of sodomy repeal argued that decriminalizing gay sex would remove safeguards against the pedophile's threat. By the late 1970s, amid growing liberalization of some sexual norms, the Christian Right emerged as a venerable foe against the decriminalization of sodomy and, in the process, recycled tropes that conflated homosexuality with predation. During her 1977 "Save Our Children" campaign, which targeted gay rights ordinances nationwide, including in St. Paul, Minnesota, Anita Bryant famously declared, "Since homosexuals cannot reproduce, they must recruit," echoing Campbell's vampire theory of homosexuality.[49] Each high-profile case of a gay man involved with a minor further fueled the narrative that gay sex was inherently deviant and criminal. To counter these perceptions, antisodomy activists needed the "right" case to present in court—one involving consensual relations between adults in a private home, free from associations with sex work or underage individuals. Unfortunately, the first sodomy case in Minnesota after *Bowers* was anything but ideal.

Just months before the July 1986 community forum on repealing the state sodomy law, in May 1986, forty-five-year-old real estate broker Richard Gordon Gray Jr. pulled his car over near Loring Park and offered to pay a young man for sex. When Gray asked his age, the young man, who was sixteen at the time, lied and said he was eighteen, but as he later told the police, "If [Gray] was a retard he would believe that." The two drove to Gray's Shorewood, Minnesota, home, where they had oral sex. Shorewood, a second-ring suburb north of St. Paul with an estimated population of twenty thousand in the mid-1980s, was a wealthy, overwhelmingly white, family-oriented residential town.[50] The young man told the police the two had sex on two later occasions—both in Gray's house—with Gray paying him $200 in total (about $600 in 2024), but Gray disputed these claims. He insisted the two only had sex once and that he did not pay for sex. Rather, Gray claimed he merely extended a loan. When Gray suspected the young man and another unidentified adult had stolen his boat, he contacted the Shorewood Police Department, which charged the young man and the unidentified adult with theft. Upon Gray divulging details of his relationship with the young man, the police then arrested Gray, charging him with sodomy in July 1986, three weeks after the US Supreme Court's *Bowers* decision.[51]

Gray's arrest was the first in Minnesota since the US Supreme Court upheld the constitutionality of sodomy laws. Shorewood officials stated that *Bowers* resolved any doubts prosecutors had about whether the state's sodomy law violated constitutional privacy rights.[52] Before *Bowers*, prosecutors rarely invoked the sodomy law, reserving it for cases involving sexual violence, such as rape or child abuse. However, the Shorewood city attorney charged Gray solely with sodomy—not prostitution or even statutory rape despite the involvement of a minor. Confident that *Bowers* affirmed the criminality of sodomy, prosecutors felt no need to pursue additional charges. In their view, the act of gay sex itself was criminal enough. It was a striking and clear demonstration of how the Supreme Court had emboldened homophobia in the legal system.

In the fall of 1986, Gray's defense attorney filed a motion to dismiss the charges, arguing that Minnesota's sodomy law violated federal and state constitutional rights to privacy. On December 1, 1986, a Hennepin County District Court judge agreed, declaring the law unconstitutional and dismissing the charges against Gray. In the decision, the judge blasted the state's sodomy law for being overly broad and failing to distinguish between heterosexual and homosexual acts or between adults and minors. Furthermore, the judge ruled that Minnesota's Constitution guaranteed a right to privacy in matters of sexual intimacy, "so long as it involves *private* sexual activity between consenting adults."[53]

The court's decision drew both praise and criticism. Gray's defense attorney, who had also represented Winton and Donahue, hailed the ruling as a significant extension of privacy rights. The decision was "a big deal for the gay community," the attorney stated, "because now they [could] have some sort of sex without committing a crime."⁵⁴ Yet, while Gray and his defense celebrated, gay elected officials remained mute in their public support for Gray. As *The Advocate* put it, "The case on which [the judge] ruled was not one chosen by gay activists."⁵⁵ There was no letter-writing campaign on Gray's behalf. Even the MCLU, committed to repealing the sodomy law, submitted an amicus brief in *State v. Gray* not to support Gray himself but as a strategic move. When *Gray*'s case was expedited to the Minnesota Supreme Court, the MCLU quietly filed a separate lawsuit in district court on behalf of Stephen McClellan, the disabled heterosexual man, and three other plaintiffs.⁵⁶ In a letter to MCLU director Matthew Stark, staff attorneys explained, "By having filed an action, the plaintiffs as amici showed the Supreme Court that there were people without Mr. Gray's criminal record or complicating facts who were adversely affected by the law."⁵⁷ The MCLU explained that it pursued this alternative challenge, seeking to present the issue in "a neutral context."⁵⁸ One of the MCLU volunteer attorneys told the press that Gray's circumstances "may cloud the legal issue."⁵⁹ These concerns deepened when it was revealed that at the time of his arrest, Gray was on probation after pleading guilty in 1984 to criminal sexual conduct involving a thirteen-year-old boy he had met through the Big Brothers program.⁶⁰

Gray hewed uncomfortably close to the toxic stereotypes of gay men as sexual predators, prompting the MCLU to distance itself from any insinuation it condoned underage sex. In a 1984 letter to the *GLC Voice*, Robert Halfhill, a founding member of FREE, claimed that he—not McClellan—had originally initiated the MCLU lawsuit to overturn Minnesota's sodomy law. However, the MCLU allegedly dropped Halfhill as a plaintiff after learning of his association with NAMBLA.⁶¹ While the MCLU neither confirmed nor denied Halfhill's claims, the organization had a record of selecting plaintiffs with less "complicating facts."

While Gray's supporters hesitated to fully embrace his victory, his opponents wasted no time in exploiting public fears of child sexual predators. Shorewood officials, state authorities, and religious groups swiftly condemned the Hennepin County District Court's decision. The very next day, the State of Minnesota, representing Shorewood, filed an expedited appeal to the Minnesota Supreme Court. A state attorney dismissed Gray's lawyer's assertion that most Minnesotans engaged in sodomy, countering that if this were true, the legislature would have already repealed the law. Minnesota Attorney General Hubert Humphrey III pledged to overturn the ruling on appeal, emphasizing that Gray had paid an underage youth for sex.⁶²

Gray's defense strategy aimed to give the state a chance to break from the homophobic precedent set by *Bowers v. Hardwick*. During arguments before the Minnesota Supreme Court on May 7, 1987, Gray's attorney urged the court to strike down the state's "repugnant, archaic" sodomy statute by "pushing the frontiers of the state Constitution beyond those of the U.S. Constitution." In Gray's defendant reply memorandum, his attorney referenced the court's earlier recognition, drawing on *Griswold*, of a "zone of privacy" protecting all Minnesotans' sexual relations. "The essence of the zone of privacy," the attorney argued, "is that it creates a boundary around the area of private, consensual sexual relations that is not to be invaded by the state."[63] He contended that it was unconstitutional for the state to encroach upon this zone of privacy simply because officials "don't like gays."[64]

The prosecution also refined its strategy before the Minnesota Supreme Court, shifting focus to the transactional nature of the encounter and painting Gray as a sexual predator. The prosecution labeled Gray a "convicted pedophile" who sought underage partners, including, in this case, a "prostitute." But character assassination represented only one front in the prosecution's broader offensive. Instead of relying solely on traditional moral arguments to defend the sodomy law—such as its long-standing presence since the nineteenth century—the prosecution argued that Gray lacked standing to challenge the statute because he could not claim privacy rights. Although the sexual activity occurred in Gray's home, prosecutors contended that his solicitation of the young man in Loring Park, a public space, and the alleged payment for the encounter gave the case public implications. Consequently, the state concluded that unlike Michael Hardwick, who, according to Abby Rubenfeld, legal director of Lambda Legal Defense and Education Fund, was the "ideal case" because he was "in his own bedroom, not bothering anyone, and police appear[ed] at his door," Gray's actions were wholly public.[65] So "repulsive" was Gray's behavior that the state insisted it would be "offensive" to allow Gray to "champion the rights of married couples or the vast majority of gay men and women who do not prey on juveniles and do not hire juvenile prostitutes."[66]

On October 2, 1987, the Minnesota Supreme Court delivered a unanimous decision in favor of the prosecution, affirming the state's sodomy law, particularly in cases involving prostitution. The court rejected Gray's claim that the encounter qualified as "private sexual conduct" simply because it occurred in a bedroom. Instead, the court outlined its rationale for deeming Gray's actions "public": "Gray picked up the complainant, who was previously unknown to Gray, at or near a public park [Loring Park] recognized as a gathering place of young prostitutes; the sexual contacts between the two were essentially no more separate 'one night stands' (and if, as Gray stated, the two committed only one sodomous [sic] act, our perception of the contact as a one night stand is bolstered); and, most importantly, this is a case of sex for compensation." The court acknowledged a right to privacy but concluded that commercial sex, regardless of location, was not protected as a fundamental right. While Gray argued that the sexual act was private because it took place in his suburban home, the court disagreed, stating that "it is simply wrong to say that the sexual conduct in this case became private once the bedroom door was closed."[67] Closing the bedroom door, in other words, did not shield the behavior from legal scrutiny, especially when compensation or minors were involved.[68] For gay activists paying attention, even the swanky doors of Shorewood were not strong enough to guard the privacy of *all* sexual acts. The fight for privacy would also mean confronting deep-seated judgments about what kind of intimacy was deemed acceptable, even in the most private of spaces.

Like the US Supreme Court, the Minnesota Supreme Court avoided ruling on whether the sodomy law violated the right to privacy outside of prostitution. Instead, it invited future constitutional challenges to address the issue. One judge expressed interest in considering a case involving "consenting adults in private and not paying for sex," hinting at a potential willingness to recognize homosexual relationships within the privacy of the home. However, in Gray's case, the court clarified what it would *not* protect and, in so doing, implied that the only protections afforded to homosexual intercourse would be granted when it aligned with societal norms of heterosexual behavior in private.[69]

In reversing the Hennepin County District Court's ruling, the Minnesota Supreme Court reinstated the complaint against Gray and sent the case back for trial. Yet, in a surprising turn of events, the charges were quietly dropped when the prosecution failed to ensure the anonymity of its key witness, the young man involved. The Shorewood City Attorney praised the witness as a "rehabilitated" adult with "an excellent job" and "a girlfriend."[70] The case, thus, concluded not with a legal victory but with the reassurance that, despite a homosexual's attempt to "corrupt" him, the young man had been restored back to the heterosexual family ideal. This outcome underscored how legal and cultural battles over privacy and morality were shaped by deeply entrenched heteronormative ideals. As the AIDS crisis soon intensified public fears about sexuality, these debates would only grow more fraught, with privacy and moral regulation taking on even higher stakes.

Legislating Private Virtue and Public Health

Though the court invited challenges to the state's sodomy law, none arose. Instead, gay men and lesbians would wait another fifteen years before a case with the right kind of plaintiff came before the Minnesota Supreme Court. Activists and their allied politicians had not put much faith in the courts to repeal sodomy, with Sen. Allan Spear saying, "I am not overwhelmingly optimistic the state Supreme Court will see the logic of [the Hennepin County District Court's] reasoning."[71] In December 1986, five months after they called an initial community forum to address the sodomy law, he and State Rep. Karen Clark organized another community meeting to map out alternative repeal strategies. It was the first step toward a legislative solution.[72]

Spear, however, harbored little optimism that politicians of any stripe would rally to the cause of repealing sodomy, so, instead, he made a deft political calculation. Rather than repealing the law outright, his bill would replace it with a law targeting "public" sex. Strictly speaking, it was all political posturing, as public sex was already forbidden under public nuisance and indecent conduct statutes. Still, Spear believed this approach would allow legislators to claim they were ending state interference in private, consensual sexual activity while also appearing tough on crime.[73] In 1987, bowing to the realities of the *Gray* decision, gay leaders accepted the court's definition of what constituted "public" sexual practices and backed a bill criminalizing all sexual activity outside the home. This proposal signaled an uneasy compromise, as gay leaders embraced carceral frameworks and distanced themselves from more stigmatized forms of sexual expression within their community in an effort to gain broader societal acceptance.[74]

Law, rooted in notions of propriety, property, and privacy, operates spatially by regulating which behaviors are acceptable in specific areas.[75] By distinguishing the legality of sexual acts across different locations, the law creates what Phil Hubbard calls "moral geographies."[76] These geographies align with Gayle Rubin's concept of the "charmed circle," which encompasses sexual identities and practices deemed "good," "normal," and "natural" while relegating others—the "most despised sexual castes"—to the "outer limits."[77] This marginal zone includes individuals engaged in homosexual, unmarried, promiscuous, non-procreative, or commercial sexual activities, particularly in public spaces, or what Rubin described as "the bushes or the baths." But "the lowliest of all," Rubin wrote in 1984, were those whose eroticism crossed generational lines—men like Winton and Gray.[78] The boundary between the charmed circle and the outer limits also marks the division between public and private spaces, exposing individuals in the outer limits to heightened policing and structural violence. Although sexual identities and practices may transition from the outer limits to the charmed circle, the restrictive nature of the circle in the 1980s posed challenges for gay activists seeking inclusion. Unable to make gay sex procreative and heterosexual, activists focused on the most attainable quality of "moral" or "acceptable" sex: keeping it private and confined to private property.

The proposed public sex law, as such, targeted public visibility, making it a crime to engage in certain sexual activities in which there was a reasonable expectation of being observed by others. While speaking at the December 1986 forum, Spear confessed that the "trick" lay in defining public and private sex. He insisted that the public sex law would not be selectively applied against men and clarified that "public" meant exactly that. According to Spear, clandestine activities conducted behind locked cubicles or closed rooms in commercial establishments like bathhouses and adult bookstores would be deemed private and thus lawful, whereas, as he emphasized, "Public is where people can stumble upon you."[79] This definition of privacy protected patrons who could dish a few bucks to cruise behind doors, but it exposed those who cruised in public parks to continued criminalization.

As part of Spear and Clark's strategy to modify the sodomy law, they formed the ad hoc group Minnesota Coalition for Privacy.[80] Comprising various gay rights and legal advocacy organizations, the coalition aimed to safeguard the right to privacy for consenting adults across Minnesota. To avoid the perception that this was a "gay rights bill," the coalition (which intentionally omitted the word "gay" from its name) ensured that neither Spear nor Clark authored the bill. Julia Classen, coordinator for the coalition, suggested having Sen. Donna Peterson and Rep. Lee Greenfield, both from the Democratic-Farmer-Labor Party, as authors of the bill—a choice that proved both politically and logistically expedient as Peterson and Greenfield, though heterosexual, were sympathetic allies. Peterson was a member of the Senate Judiciary Committee and Greenfield a member of the House Judiciary Committee and the Health and Human Services Committee. Classen hoped that the legislators' heterosexuality and political clout would broaden support among various groups, including labor unions, religious organizations, feminist groups, and mental health advocates.[81] In an interview, Peterson confirmed Classen's reasoning, revealing that she had persuaded Spear and Clark, Minnesota's first openly gay and lesbian state officials, not to sponsor the bill, concerned that even supportive groups might avoid controversy and distance themselves from the bill in a post-*Bowers* climate.

Much like MCLU's strategy of highlighting the McClellans, a heterosexual married couple, in its campaign against sodomy laws, legislative efforts aimed to show how sodomy repeal would benefit heterosexual individuals as well. At the July 1986 Spear- and Clark-sponsored community forum, it was agreed that any effort to overturn the law should emphasize its positive impact on heterosexual Minnesotans. Dr. Sharon Satterfield, director of the University of Minnesota's Human Sexuality Program, cited studies showing that most heterosexuals engaged in oral and anal intercourse and encouraged forum participants to stress that the "law applies to 100 percent of the people in Minnesota, not to ten per cent [sic]," referencing the commonly assumed percentage of LGBTQ individuals.[82] Realizing that support from LGBTQ voters alone would not be enough to drive change, the Minnesota Coalition for Privacy decided to link sodomy repeal with efforts to eliminate laws against adultery and fornication. These laws, under the "Crimes Against the Family" section of the Minnesota Criminal Code, criminalized heterosexual sex outside marriage. Peterson and Greenfield criticized the state's adultery and fornication laws as "grossly sexist," with Greenfield pointing out that a married woman guilty of adultery could face a gross misdemeanor charge, a substantial fine, and up to a year in prison while a married man committing the same act might only be charged with the lesser offense of fornication.[83] Adultery prosecutions were limited to within a year of the offense and required the husband's complaint, unless he was "insane."[84] By highlighting the gender bias in these laws, the Minnesota Coalition for Privacy employed feminist rhetoric to counter claims that the public sex bill was antisex and, perhaps, even to attract support from lesbian feminists who, as seen in the antipornography movement, strongly opposed perceived power imbalances in sex.

As Spear had pledged in the July 1986 community forum, the bill, introduced by Peterson and Greenfield in the spring of 1987, lifted restrictions on consensual sexual acts between adults, including adultery and fornication, but criminalized any sexual acts in public places. The Senate and House versions of the bill—S.F. 1235 and H.F. 1379, respectively—defined "public sexual conduct" as engaging in sexual penetration in a location where nonparticipants could reasonably witness it. Classen admitted, "If you ever want to get the sodomy law repealed, you have to take an approach more palatable to all the legislators, including ones from more conservative districts."[85]

The Minnesota Coalition for Privacy followed Steve Endean's strategies from the 1970s during those initial efforts at sodomy repeal: aim for the middle of politicians and voters.[86] Under the new crime against public sex, law enforcement agencies could seek out and arrest anyone found to be engaging in sex acts in automobiles, parks, or other public spaces. Prior to the proposed bill, law enforcement agencies charged those arrested for engaging in public sex with indecent conduct—charges that included men arrested at commercial sex establishments.[87] In an interview, Peterson explained, "What's done privately between two consenting adults should not be against the law." However, "What's done publicly between two consenting adults," she added, "is something that we can say, no, you won't do that."[88] Peterson clarified that the measure did not repeal any laws relating to criminal sexual conduct, much less child abuse. In another interview, she elaborated, "The bill recognizes that intensely private decisions should be protected from government interference."[89] Regardless of their location, sex work and sex with juveniles remained "public" and, hence, open to "government interference."

Lurking behind the discussion of sodomy laws, haunting activists' forums as well as courts' decisions, was the reality of AIDS. In 1986, fear of the disease ran rampant not only in the LGBTQ community but among the broader public as well and imbued the discussions of sodomy with new urgency. Although rarely named outright, AIDS permeated official discourse in Minnesota, subtly shaping legal arguments and public health rationales that linked same-sex intimacy to disease and danger. For instance, in its ruling against Richard Gray, the Minnesota Supreme Court referenced a 1976 Iowa Supreme Court decision, *State v. Price*, which emphasized the state's interest in regulating prostitution: "Prostitution implicates more than private sexual relations between consenting adults. It affects others including the community . . . Although intimate, it is impersonal. Although involving only consenting adults at the time, it may be a factor in the spread of venereal disease."[90] Even if the Minnesota Supreme Court never explicitly mentioned AIDS, its citation of *State v. Price* hinted at concerns about HIV transmission.[91] Similarly, the prosecution indirectly alluded to AIDS in its opposition to Gray's motion to dismiss, claiming that the sodomy statute "protects the public health because it limits activities which have been shown to transmit venereal disease. One of those diseases is currently 100% fatal."[92] Despite avoiding explicit mention, both the court and the prosecution hinted at the role of AIDS in justifying regulation of sexual behaviors to protect public health.

This reluctance to speak directly of AIDS was anything but an act of discretion. No one needed to mention AIDS—it was in the news constantly—and by linking it to acts of sodomy, the court reinforced the stereotype that the epidemic arose from and was spurred on by gay men. The court was far from alone as several groups worked to cement in the public's mind the link between AIDS and gay sex, with few more active than the Berean League, a nonprofit organization of fundamental Christians founded to research, communicate, and promote Biblical principles. This organization, influential in the Minnesota Legislature, advocated enforcing the sodomy law on the grounds that gay male sex posed a public health hazard through the spread of HIV.[93] In 1985, the Berean League circulated a one-hundred-page report to policymakers titled "Are 'Gay Rights' Right?" that accused gay men of "encouraging promiscuous sex, a self-centered morality and socially irresponsible behavior that exacts huge costs from society." The heavily footnoted report added that "homosexuals must bring their mouth into contact with areas designed for the elimination of human waste, or use body apertures not constructed for sexual penetration—either of which cause serious hygenic [sic] health risks."[94]

Ironically, gay activists found common ground with conservatives and leveraged this stereotype—but in a way that would supposedly empower LGBTQ rights and finally break the stranglehold of the sodomy law in the state. While conservatives viewed all forms of gay sex as inherently diseased, gay activists believed gay sex was a vector of disease only when conducted in the wrong place. Activists wagered on mainstream society buying into this subtle difference. If gay sex was rhetorically put behind closed doors, heterosexual Americans would not have to "think" about it. In other words, gay sex would be imaginatively "quarantined" and out of the public's metaphorical face.

Proponents of the public sex bill insisted that it would protect the region's public health against the AIDS epidemic. According to Spear, some gay and bisexual men refrained from HIV testing due to fear of self-incrimination, worrying that a positive result would implicate them in sodomy-related activities and force them to disclose their sexual partners to health authorities. During Senate testimony on April 6, 1987, a physician stressed the importance of reporting AIDS contacts to combat the disease, yet, because of the sodomy law, many gay men hesitated to discuss their sexual behaviors with health-care providers. The president of the Minnesota Public Health Association (MPHA) also testified in support of the bill, emphasizing its potential to control sexually transmitted diseases, particularly AIDS.

He argued that decriminalizing high-risk sexual practices would enable public health workers to educate and assist at-risk populations in modifying their behaviors effectively.[95]

For others, sodomy repeal presented an opportunity to promote monogamous relationships among gay men. One Lutheran minister voiced his support for the bill, suggesting that by adopting the bill "we are creating a climate for gay and lesbian persons which will give rise to much more life-giving and healthier relationships." The minister did not define what he meant by "life-giving and healthier relationships," but his next words provide clues. "I firmly believe that this kind of legislation can remove some of the fear and oppression which drives those most oppressed by current laws to be unable and unwilling to be tested and *to change their behavior.*"[96] If unprotected sex with multiple partners contributed to the spread of HIV, then repealing sodomy while cracking down on supposedly indiscriminate, furtive, careless public sex would encourage gay men to date one another, have sex without the fear of arrest in private, and settle into monogamous relationships—all working together to curb the promiscuity often blamed for fueling the AIDS epidemic.

Nonetheless, the opposition drowned out supporters of the law and convinced legislators that it would not only erode public morals but also endanger public health. Mary Jane Rachner, a Republican candidate for Minnesota Secretary of State, testified against S.F. 1235, arguing that the law would allow "homosexuals [to give] AIDS to other homosexuals in the privacy of a bedroom." Rachner insinuated that judges who supported sodomy repeal based on consent "may not realize how easy it is for pedophiles to rent or own a private bedroom and get 'consent,'" perhaps alluding to Gray.[97] To Rachner, the location of the sexual activity proved irrelevant, as she viewed all same-sex intercourse to be inherently criminal and, thus, subject to public scrutiny.

While Rachner represented one extreme, law enforcement adopted a slightly more nuanced position. Previously, under Chief Bouza, the Minneapolis Police Department (MPD) had largely ignored sexual activities outside "public" spaces, but in the era of AIDS, this earlier arrangement broke down, and a locked door no longer automatically qualified as "private." In their crackdown on public sexual cultures, vice squad officers particularly concerned themselves with whether men arrested for sex knew one another—that is, if they were strangers. In the context of AIDS, the vice squad believed that anonymous sexual encounters posed a *public* health risk that warranted intervention. In an arrest report of two men from 1987, while the bill was still under consideration, two plainclothes officers described entering the basement of an adult bookstore in downtown Minneapolis that was screening X-rated gay adult films. The officers "observed 3 or 4 adult males standing by an open door and looking inside" the basement smoking lounge where the two defendants were engaged in mutual oral sex in what one of the officers described as "a position commonly referred to as '69.'" The report was graphic—clinical, even—describing how one of the defendants "continued oral sex by sucking the defendant's penis followed up by testicles and anal area." The defendants then engaged in anal intercourse with one defendant "inserting his penis into" the other's "anal cavity." The public health implications of the arrests were explicit. In one of the officer's reports, he mentioned: "It should . . . be noted that during the sexual acts, no condoms were used by either party."[98] What struck one of the police officers the most was that the men had never met one another: "It should be noted, when officers asked [defendant] how long he had known above defendant, he stated that he had never seen him before they met tonight."[99] By pointing out that the men were not using condoms, that they knew they were being watched, and that they had never met before, the vice unit officers seemed intent on emphasizing that the "deviance" of the sex could not be separated from its danger to public health. For conservatives and law enforcement alike, even in ostensibly "private" or semi-private settings, gay men would still engage in risky, casual sex. In other words, the diseased nature of gay sex was an ingrained part of gay culture that would not go away even if sex were "private." The men ultimately faced sodomy charges.

On its surface, Peterson and Greenfield's exchange of a homophobic sodomy law for one that merely targeted "public" sex—gay or straight—appeared fair. However, this compromise, like much of Minnesota's political discourse, assumed a modestly comfortable, private life in which to retreat, implicitly favoring a white, middle-class homeowner as the norm. The architects of the bill overlooked how racial and class disparities shaped the experiences of LGBTQ people in both public and private settings. Under the bill, a first offense would have been a misdemeanor, with penalties increasing for subsequent convictions. A second offense within three years would have been deemed a gross misdemeanor, and a third or subsequent offense within five years would have been classified as a felony—an even harsher penalty than sodomy itself, which was a gross misdemeanor in Minnesota.[100] The bill also allowed judges to suspend sentences and mandate treatment, based on the assumption that repeated public sex required psychiatric intervention.[101] The bill's drafters viewed public sex primarily as a recreational act—definitely not sex work—or, at worst, an "outrageous" psychological impulse driven by shame as in the case of Winton. Although neither the Senate nor the House bill mentioned prostitution, both stated that "consent to the sexual penetration [in a public place] is not a defense." Thus, whether paid or unpaid, consensual sex in public—that is, where someone could stumble upon the act—remained a crime.

By empowering law enforcement to target and arrest individuals engaged in public sex, the bill continued the criminalization of those who lacked the racial and class privileges to freely navigate public spaces or access private property for such activities. And, in the 1980s, this move spelled trouble for queer people who were precariously housed. In Minneapolis, as in other cities throughout the United States, homelessness worsened throughout the decade.[102] Starting in the 1960s and 1970s, state governments began closing mental health institutions without providing sufficient community-based services, leading to a significant increase in individuals with mental illness living on the streets. Additionally, President Reagan's budget cuts to the Department of Housing and Urban Development (HUD) drastically reduced affordable housing production.[103] In response, cities created tax incentives and repurposed single-room occupancy (SRO) hotel units for higher-income residents, further shrinking affordable housing options for low-income individuals.[104] From 1979 to 1984, Minneapolis lost 1,300 SROs, with another 500 disappearing between 1986 and 1989 due to the remodeling of the Minneapolis Convention Center.[105] Even the remaining affordable housing units were often out of reach for many Minneapolis residents. By 1990, the fair market rent for a two-bedroom apartment in Minneapolis-St. Paul was $528 per month, requiring an annual income of over $21,000—175 percent of the poverty line. Yet at the time, 22 percent of Minneapolis households lived below that figure.[106] Consequently, homelessness surged in the Twin Cities, with over 1,100 men, women, and children experiencing homelessness on any given night in 1986, a trend that continued throughout the decade.[107] A 1987 survey of twenty-six major cities revealed that applications for emergency shelter in Minneapolis and St. Paul increased by 20 and 8 percent, respectively, from the previous year. In St. Paul, families made up a third of the unhoused population, while in Minneapolis, 80 percent were single men—the highest proportion among surveyed cities. The US Conference of Mayors' Report linked the rise of the "chronic poor" in the Twin Cities to "unemployed people (who have migrated from) the urban ghettos of the South and the Midwest."[108] This term, "urban ghettos," was often code for people of color, primarily Black people. A 1990 survey of Twin Cities shelters found that the proportion of Black residents rose from 31 to 41 percent despite Black people making up only 13 and 7 percent of the populations in Minneapolis and St. Paul, respectively. Indigenous people comprised 10 percent of the unhoused population, while Latinx people made up 9 percent.[109]

The public sex bill, therefore, heightened the vulnerability of unhoused queer people of color, for whom public sex was often a necessity. Phyllis Olson, a thirty-year-old Indigenous transgender woman involved in sex work, exemplified the marginalized individuals targeted by the proposed law.[110] Described by the *GLC Voice* as a "full-time transvestite" who frequented Loring Park and downtown gay bars, Olson lacked a stable home address and resided in a cheap motel near downtown Minneapolis.[111] On September 24, 1986, while lawmakers debated the wording of the public sex bill, Olson's strangled body was discovered on a footbridge in downtown Minneapolis.[112] Olson's transient relationship to private property along with her numerous prostitution arrests dating back to 1973 enabled homicide detectives and some gay leaders to portray her death as a consequence of her "deviant" lifestyle. The MPD leaked to the *Star Tribune* Olson's positive HIV status and surmised that she, even after her diagnosis, continued to engage in sex work. Altogether, her life and the police department's indifference encouraged the public to see her as not merely an object of scorn but a viable menace. While health officials used Olson's death to call for stricter restrictions on sex workers generally, Minneapolis City Councilmember Brian J. Coyle reflected on the dangers of unregulated queer sexuality, telling the *Star Tribune*, "There's great cause for concern when anybody is discovered dead, gay or straight. And I'm also very concerned when anybody has AIDS and doesn't modify their behavior." Assuming Olson might have knowingly exposed others to HIV and did not practice safe sex, Coyle supported publicizing her HIV status "to turn up people who might have been exposed to him [sic]." Coyle's focus on Olson's behaviors, rather than addressing the systemic issues underlying her vulnerability, ignored the broader societal failures contributing to her tragic fate.[113] While Coyle expressed support for LGBTQ rights, his response overlooked the specific challenges faced by individuals like Olson, whose involvement in public sex was shaped by homelessness and economic vulnerability. Unlike Gray and Winton, who embodied a more familiar version of gay Minnesota that Coyle could comprehend, even if he condemned their actions, Olson's life was reduced to a series of pathologies by a legal system ill-equipped to address the complexities of her existence.[114]

For those in the LGBTQ community for whom sex work was not a choice but a vocation necessary for survival, the first vote on the public sex bill on

April 6, 1987, was a moment of pause. At first it appeared the bill, S.F. 1235, might sail through. The Senate Judiciary Committee, which Spear chaired, approved the bill by a vote of 11 to 4, assuring the measure would go directly to the full Minnesota Senate. However, despite the relatively liberal disposition of the Senate Judiciary Committee, composed exclusively of senators from the Twin Cities metropolitan area, the broader Senate leaned more conservatively.[115] More conservative still was the House Judiciary Committee, which heard the House version of the bill, H.F. 1379, the day after.

The morning of the House Judiciary Committee vote, the chambers overflowed with buzzing spectators, many brandishing large signs. Greenfield, the sponsor of the House bill, pleaded with committee members that Minnesotans were "entitled to the privacy of their bedroom." "The vast majority of Americans and Minnesotans," he asserted, "break these laws." Whether true or not, such arguments mattered little to those who opposed the bill on moral grounds, believing repeal would damage public morals and family values. Others cited public health as a reason *not* to decriminalize sodomy, even in private. One woman in the audience carried a sign that read: "Millions of our taxpayer's dollars spent on AIDS research. Why legalize the mode of transmission?" The Berean League, which led the charge against sodomy repeal, warned that decriminalizing sodomy would breach the barriers safeguarding middle-class white domesticity from HIV. Former state senator and then-executive director of the Berean League, Wayne Olhoft, argued that promiscuous sex constituted the primary driver of HIV infections. If anything, he demanded stricter enforcement of the existing law.[116] In a stark reversal of Greenfield's stance, Olhoft believed that criminalizing sodomy—as imperfectly enforced as the law was—acted as a dam holding back not only (as he saw it) the sin of homosexual sex but a flood of HIV infections.[117]

Swayed by Olhoft's prophesying, the Minnesota House Judiciary Committee voted 14–11 to block the measure, placing the repeal of Minnesota's sodomy law at a standstill. Spear characterized the outcome as "a major setback," attributing it not only to efforts of the Berean League but also to Phyllis Schlafly's Eagle Forum, Concerned Women for America, and antiabortion interests. Members of Minnesota Citizens Concerned for Life, an antiabortion group, fervently lobbied against the bill, arguing that decriminalizing fornication and adultery would fuel extramarital sex and, inevitably, more abortions.[118]

The House Judiciary Committee's decision sparked significant public reaction.[119] Surprisingly, the *St. Paul Pioneer Press Dispatch*, the major newspaper in St. Paul, published a scathing editorial denouncing the sodomy law as "intrusive." The editorial argued that the law criminalized sexual relations for one in ten citizens who were homosexual, restricted the only form of intimate contact available to many individuals with disabilities, and was "offensively sexist." The *Pioneer Press* also challenged conservative claims, warning that "repressive laws may make [AIDS] spread more likely, not less."[120] Yet the printed word could not counter an energized, grassroots conservative push, and last-ditch efforts to revive the proposed repeal of the state's sodomy law eventually failed.[121] On May 13, 1987, Classen conceded that the bill to replace the sodomy law with one banning public sex "looks pretty much dead."[122]

Conservative, homophobic opposition to the bill dominated the headlines, but in reality, Spear and Clark also had to fend off attacks from those who, in other instances, might have been their allies. While more moderate gay organizations like the Minnesota Committee for Gay and Lesbian Rights and Parents and Friends of Lesbians and Gays supported the bill, more radical organizations did not.[123] The Human Rights Committee of the Minnesota AIDS Project, the largest AIDS service organization in the upper Midwest, backed the repeal of sodomy but adamantly opposed the proposed public sex legislation, arguing that criminalizing public sex would only drive sex among men underground and hamper HIV prevention. Similarly, the board of the Minnesota Alliance Against AIDS (MAAA), an activist AIDS advocacy group, passed a unanimous resolution supporting sodomy repeal but opposing any new laws against public sex.[124] The *GLC Voice*, often regarded by gay moderates as a platform for its publisher, gay liberationist Tim Campbell, alleged that the executive director of the MCLU, Matthew Stark, had accused Spear and his bill of "unforgivable divisiveness."[125] Campbell, who had previously clashed with Spear over including transgender people in gay rights legislation, was so opposed to the public sex bill that he suggested, "If Minnesota legislators cannot get rid of the sodomy laws without enacting these new public sex laws . . . they would be best to leave the law alone."[126]

For gay integrationists, the loss stung, but no matter how noble their intentions, victory would have always been a Faustian bargain. Had the bill passed, some gay men and lesbians might have been accepted into the "charmed circle" of sexual value, but this inclusion would likely have been limited to those who were disproportionately white and middle- or upper-class. Gay sex that happened in quiet, modest couplings in the suburbs would be "free," but that sense of empowerment would come at the expense of the greater LGBTQ community. Those who remained closeted at home would face greater oppression, as their unchanging desires would leave them vulnerable to continued police persecution. More obviously, those with no doors they could call their own to close would still be open to public, legal scrutiny. As Dean Spade and Craig Willse point out, these partial openings into the charmed circle only "strengthen the line" between identities and practices deemed "good, healthy, and normal" and those considered "bad, unhealthy, stigmatized, and criminalized." They argue, "The line moves to accommodate a few more people, who society suddenly approves of, correcting the system and keeping it in place."[127] Including previously marginalized groups, like middle-class same-sex couples, does not challenge the systems of domination that regulate sexuality and family formation. Instead, it reinforces the authority of the state, media, and law as arbiters of normative sexuality.

While gay activists aimed to use the repeal of sodomy laws to promote HIV prevention, conservatives ultimately claimed that narrative. The sponsors of the public sex bill had a two-prong strategy. First, they argued that repealing sodomy was both fair and morally right. Obviously, religious conservatives—whether antigay or antichoice—were never going to accept this argument, but supporters hoped to appeal to heterosexual Minnesotans who wanted their own sexual practices, such as fornication and adultery, to be decriminalized. They anticipated that public support would pressure politicians to act. Yet heterosexual legislators and their constituents failed to show up. The reason lies in the second prong of the sponsors' strategy. They had claimed that decriminalizing private consensual sex while cracking down on "outrageous" public sex would reduce HIV transmission. This argument, however, gained little traction. Rather, heterosexual Minnesotans clung to the toxic stereotype that AIDS was a gay man's disease and that any gay sex posed a public health threat. One state representative, advocating for a separate bill requiring all couples applying for marriage licenses to undergo testing for HIV, circulated an article from the *Conservative Digest* claiming AIDS was linked to "loathsome homosexual practices" that "organized faggotry" was trying to conceal. When Rep. Karen Clark labeled it "hate literature," he defended his stance by saying that, as a father of seven, he had a duty to ensure the disease was not being "politically protected." The state representative had merely entered into the record a blunt statement of what many others said in private. In fact, following the *Bowers* decision, a 1986 Gallup Poll showed that 54 percent of Americans believed homosexual relations between consenting adults should be illegal, and 51 percent approved of the *Bowers* ruling.[128] For many heterosexual Minnesotans, gay sex was inherently diseased and dangerous. Despite professional criticism that mandatory HIV testing for marriage was costly and ineffective, the Minnesota House passed the bill, illustrating how deeply these prejudices shaped public policy.[129]

The Lost Bet

In a time of neoliberal ascendence, marked by an emphasis on free-market policies, privatization, and individual responsibility over collective welfare, gay leaders worked to frame gay male sexuality as "normal" by appealing to the twin pillars of privacy and property ownership. However, homophobia ultimately prevailed. Leaders had made a risky bet that by lifting a select, privileged few, the larger LGBTQ community would benefit—a bet that was always suspect on its face—and they lost. Yet, though Spear, Clark, and other proponents of the public sex bill had lost this battle, they had not necessarily lost the war to overturn the state's sodomy law, and they soon found a new ally in an entirely different branch of government. If the courts and legislature were too beholden to homophobia, Governor Rudy Perpich was not. In April 1990, Perpich appointed the Governor's Task Force on Gay and Lesbian Minnesotans to document discrimination against gay men and lesbians and recommend solutions. A year later, in 1991, the task force called for repealing the state's laws against private consensual adult sex, arguing that these laws "establish in the popular mind a connection between homosexuality and criminality" and deter gay men from seeking HIV testing for fear of incrimination—an issue the Minnesota Legislature had previously dismissed. But as a supplement to sodomy repeal, the task force advocated for legally expanding the definition of "family" to include same-sex households, stating, "Many lesbians and gay men live in committed, permanent relationships with their partners . . . It is in the best interest of society, especially in light of the AIDS crisis, to encourage stable partnerships."[130] For the task force, domestic partnerships would provide gay men with a protective barrier against the virus, but only if they were characterized by monogamy and commitment. Two years after the 1991 Governor's Task Force on Lesbian and Gay Minnesotans, University of Chicago law and economics theorists Richard Posner and Tomas Phillipson endorsed monogamy as a cost-effective solution to address the so-called gay promiscuity that fueled the AIDS epidemic.[131] If same-sex marriage were recognized, Posner and Phillipson argued, then the public costs of AIDS, such as Medicaid and other health services, would be transferred to the private household.[132]

This emphasis on privacy became a contentious issue for certain LGBTQ people, particularly unhoused queer people and especially queer people of color like Olson. For these individuals, privacy was often unattainable and not a primary concern. Queer of color critique highlights that the concept of home is not uniform for all LGBTQ people; for queer people of color, private spaces often do not ensure privacy but instead become potential arenas of heightened state surveillance and residential exclusion.[133] Excluded from the bourgeoning gay neighborhoods of the 1970s, queer people of color have nurtured kinship-like networks to navigate structural racism and economic impoverishment. The makeshift homes they forge—whether on street corners or in run-down apartments—reimagine family bonds beyond traditional legal frameworks of blood, marriage, and adoption. Instead, these homes are characterized by flexible, overlapping affective structures that transgress biological ties, age hierarchies, and conventional gender and sexual norms.[134] Such alternative homes stand in stark contrast to the homonormative homelands prompted by initiatives like the public sex bill. For queer people of color and even working-class queer people, the private bedroom has not always been a sanctuary of liberation but another reminder of their race and class marginalization in the United States.

Although its authors sought to make it as homonormative as possible, the public sex bill went down in defeat. Unlike the Minnesota Legislature, which disagreed, the Governor's Task Force parroted the Minnesota Coalition for Privacy's argument that sodomy repeal would lead to HIV prevention, and in 1993, Governor Arne Carlson, a Republican, signed legislation to amend the Minnesota Human Rights Act to include protections for LGBTQ people in housing, employment, and public accommodations.[135]

When the US Supreme Court ruled in 1986 that sodomy laws were constitutional, it incited a tempest of dissent, and LGBTQ Minnesotans were ready to harness the winds of that storm and push for repeal. What they did not expect was that they would be tacking against the wind and their journey would be painfully slow. In fact, no states repealed their sodomy laws between 1986 and 1991. On the contrary, some states even amended their sodomy laws to explicitly target same-sex conduct.[136] Minnesota can only modestly boast that it finally repealed the law—in 2001. On May 15, a Minnesota District Court declared in *Doe v. Ventura* the sodomy law unconstitutional "as applied to private, consensual, non-commercial acts of sodomy by consenting adults" because it violated "the right of privacy guaranteed by the Minnesota Constitution."[137]

Minnesota remained one of the last states to repeal its sodomy law before the US Supreme Court's 2003 decision in *Lawrence v. Texas*, which overturned *Bowers* and declared such laws unconstitutional, finally granting legal protections for private, consensual adult sexual behavior.[138] Yet the majority opinion in *Lawrence*, echoing the rhetoric of earlier gay integrationists and their allies, insisted that the ruling did not legalize all forms of sexual conduct, including sex work and much less sex with minors. LGBTQ Minnesotans, whose leaders had bent over backward not to be radical or confrontational but to conform to heteronormative ideals of sexuality—that is, middleness—had to wait fifteen years for their freedom to engage in consensual sex in private. The failed attempt to repeal sodomy in Minnesota served as a stark lesson for gay leaders, compelling them to delve even deeper into homonormativity—and, by extension, whiteness—in their pursuit of rights.

3   From Persecuted to Protected

In Search of Safe Space

On October 9, 1986, gay activists testified before the House Judiciary Subcommittee on Criminal Justice in the first-ever US Congressional hearing on antigay violence. Intended as an opportunity to discuss the extent of such violence and explore potential strategies, the hearing brought forth an array of witnesses, including law enforcement officials and social science researchers. Activists argued that antigay violence was on the rise, linking this trend to the AIDS crisis and employing the same epidemiological language that had become widespread due to the disease. The director of the National Gay and Lesbian Task Force's Violence Project testified: "The Gay community is not only battling AIDS, but is also confronting a second epidemic, one that has received far less attention from our public officials. That epidemic is anti-gay violence." Parallel sentiments were echoed by the head of the New York City Gay and Lesbian Anti-Violence Project, who described the situation as an "epidemic of violence" against gay men and lesbians. The director of San Francisco's Community United Against Violence further highlighted that the violence was fueled by a backlash against AIDS, noting, "AIDS and homosexuality have become synonymous in the American public's mind." The director added, "For the homophobic mind, AIDS is simply another justification for violence."[1]

Meanwhile, in Minneapolis, Community United Against Violence (CUAV)—an antiviolence gay activist group inspired by its San Francisco counterpart—refused to rely on an apathetic federal government to address the rising violence against gay men. Acknowledging both the ineffectiveness of the local police and the dangers posed by the "gay panic" defense, CUAV took proactive measures. Members distributed around five thousand flyers of warning literature in popular gay hangouts like bars, parks, and bathhouses. Brian J. Coyle, the openly gay city councilmember and founder of CUAV, designed these flyers "to warn everyone on Hennepin Avenue, especially the gay and bisexual community, that they must not put themselves at risk."[2] Featuring detailed accounts of eleven gay murder victims, the flyers carried a stark warning: "Play it safe! Don't go home with strangers—no matter how hot they are . . . These 11 men believed their killer was O.K.—maybe even attractive. Don't kid yourself, it could be you next!" (fig. 3.1).

While Coyle aimed to educate gay men about the physical dangers of casual, anonymous sex, the tone of the flyers, along with what some saw as a judgmental focus on the sexual behaviors of the victims, ended up alienating the very audience they were meant to reach. Some gay men dismissed the flyers, mistaking them for Christian fundamentalist propaganda.[3] If Coyle's messaging was off, his facts were not. Between 1984 and 1987, Minneapolis, a city of about 350,000 people, experienced over fifteen murders of non-heteronormative individuals, mostly gay men and some transgender women of color. Most victims were robbed and killed in their homes without signs of forced entry, leading CUAV leaders to suspect that each had invited their killer home for sex. Consequently, to warn others of the dangers of casual, anonymous sex, activists zeroed in on the sexual practices of the victims. The previously mentioned flyers cautioned gay men, in a somewhat paternalistic tone: "Despite several well publicized deaths during the last two years, some of us obviously are still putting ourselves at risk." This narrative notably excluded unhoused sex workers, particularly Black and Indigenous individuals, who lacked a home to protect. For Coyle and his allies, the safety of the home provided a spatial fix to the perils of casual, anonymous encounters. According to CUAV's logic, living in a monogamous household shielded gay men from frequenting bars, using drugs and alcohol, and engaging in risky behaviors that could result in HIV infection or a grisly death.

In demanding that the Minneapolis Police Department (MPD) address the concerns of gay victims, gay activists leveraged "tough on crime" language to flip the idea that the "gay lifestyle"—or the myth of the predatory gay man—was a threat to the public to one in which *white* gay men were instead threatened. This law-and-order rhetoric resonated with local media narratives surrounding the "Gary Syndrome," a racially charged antiwelfare discourse that blamed rising crime on "outsiders"—such as migrants, refugees, and the racialized poor. Although white gay men did not invent the Gary Syndrome, they capitalized on it to render themselves more white than gay. This process relied heavily on the symbol of the outsider—and its equivalent of the insider—a binary that served as a normalizing tool for gay activists in seeking an alliance with the police and confirms Christina B. Hanhardt's argument that US LGBTQ antiviolence practices have been

play it safe!

Don't go home with strangers — no matter how hot they are. If you do, introduce your trick to a buddy.

THESE ELEVEN MEN BELIEVED THEIR KILLER WAS "O.K." --- MAYBE EVEN ATTRACTIVE:

April 84 - D.J. JOHNSON, 60s, beaten at his Cedar Square West apartment. UNSOLVED.

June 10, 1984 - JAMES TRAETOW, 33, found shot to death. Two arrested.

Feb. 1, 1985 - JEFFREY EDMONDSON, 31, beaten to death in Tonka Bay. One convicted.

Sept. 15, 1985 - JAMES MC ARTHUR, 35 stabbed to death at 2428 Blaisdell. One arrested & found guilty.

Nov. 1985 - RICHARD GRASS, 50, killed in West St. Paul. UNSOLVED.

Dec. 17, 1985 - KYLE KASTNER, 43, strangled to death at 210 W. Grant St. UNSOLVED.

Dec. 28, 1985 - JOHN KIELEY, 58, strangled to death at 4218 Bloomington Ave. UNSOLVED.

January 1986 - RICHARD TORRANCE, 46, stabbed and burned to death at 2101 Blaisdell. One arrested and jailed.

Sept. 17, 1986 - FRED RIGA, 30, strangled to death at 1514 Chicago Ave. UNSOLVED.

Sept. 23, 1986 - FLOYD OLSON, 30, strangled on a footbridge near the Baths & 90s Bar. UNSOLVED.

Oct. 18, 1986 - ROBERT CHURCHILL, 52, stabbed and burned at 32 Spruce Place. UNSOLVED.

DESPITE SEVERAL WELL-PUBLICIZED DEATHS DURING THE LAST TWO YEARS, SOME OF US OBVIOUSLY ARE STILL PUTTING OURSELVES AT RISK.

Don't kid yourself, it could be you next!
play it safe!

JOINS US IN A GROUP EFFORT TO WARN OUR BROTHERS, MOURN OUR DEAD, PRESS FOR A THOROUGH INVESTIGATION, COOPERATE WITH THE POLICE, AND MAINTAIN A HOTLINE.

COMMUNITY UNITED AGAINST VIOLENCE

CALL COUNCIL MEMBER COYLE'S OFFICE AT 348-2206 TO VOLUNTEER AND GET OR GIVE INFORMATION REGARDING THE MURDERS.

FIGURE 3.1 Flyer from the 1986 "Play It Safe!" campaign, advising gay men against going home with strangers. From the Brian J. Coyle Papers, Box 13, Folder: Gay Violence. Courtesy of the Minnesota Historical Society.

deeply intertwined with criminalization and private development. Hanhardt's analysis of gay safe street patrols in the mid-1970s illustrates how these patrols amplified instances of antigay violence to advocate for designated gay neighborhoods, or "safe spaces." However, by attributing antigay violence to racial difference and poverty, the identity protected as "gay" became synonymous with the race, class, and gender dynamics of predominantly white, male, and middle-class neighborhoods. This alignment with safe space initiatives often coincided with gentrification patterns that displaced the racialized poor.[4] By making non-white people outsiders, gay activists in the Twin Cities implicitly positioned white gay men as "insiders," broadening the state's biopolitical category of "victim" to include them while excluding sex workers, transgender women of color, and gay men seeking intimacy in public spaces.

This chapter explores the campaign strategies and literature of gay liberal reformers and hate crime activist organizations in the upper Midwest, highlighting the links between violence awareness and HIV prevention efforts. It examines how gay activists defined both the perpetrators and victims of antigay violence during the early years of the AIDS epidemic and how they came to promote the private sphere of home as a spatial fix to both AIDS and violence.

An "Epidemic" of Violence

Violence against LGBTQ people in the Twin Cities had a long-standing history as evidenced by the high-profile deaths of Terry Knudsen, Les Benscoter, and Robert Allan Taylor in 1979. But the arrival of AIDS prompted new violence and a rhetorical response from activists. Drawing from epidemiological language, antiviolence groups documented what they termed an "epidemic of violence." In June 1984, the National Gay and Lesbian Task Force (NGLTF) released a report based on an eight-city survey of 2,074 homosexuals that found that "more than 1 in 5 gay men and nearly 1 in 10 lesbians [had] been punched, hit, kicked, or beaten because of their sexual orientation."[5] While organizations like the NGLTF acknowledged that violence against LGBTQ people had always existed, they underscored the unique severity and frequency of this surge.[6] Throughout the decade, further studies by the NGLTF continued to show a significant increase in assaults and harassment against LGBTQ people, or at least their reporting.[7] LGBTQ organizations in smaller cities also reported a rise in violence and harassment against their communities.[8]

Leaders of these antiviolence groups, mainly white gay men and lesbians, attributed the rise in violence to several factors, including the fear and hatred bred by right-wing fundamentalism, police indifference, and the widespread use of the "gay panic" defense. But the heart of the problem, as they saw it, was a backlash against AIDS. Activists argued that the epidemic forced Americans to confront homosexuality, causing those without personal connections to LGBTQ individuals to unjustly link homosexuality with the disease. According to this perspective, latent and preexisting hostility to homosexuality now had a fig leaf of justification, and many Americans unleashed their rage and fear over the disease upon the LGBTQ community. Simply put, fear of contagion led to growing violence.[9] Connecting this backlash to hate violence, the NGLTF reported that perpetrators referenced AIDS in 681, or 14 percent, of documented incidents in 1986.[10] The following year, at a press conference for the NGLTF's third annual report, the director declared, "We are a community under siege. We are battling AIDS and we're battling violence."[11] The director of San Francisco's Community United Against Violence used more blunt terms, stating to *The Advocate*, "People used to say, 'You fucking faggot'; now it's, 'You diseased faggot.'"[12] With no government mandate to document bias-related crimes, reports from activists, compiled by organizations like the NGLTF and CUAV, constituted the only sources of such data.[13] Despite potential incompleteness, the facts proved incontrovertible for LGBTQ communities across the nation, including in Minneapolis.

From April 1984 to September 1985, the rash of killings drew little attention from the MPD. Detectives solved some, while many others joined a heap of crimes that faded into mere statistics. But on December 31, 1985, the police faced a crime eerily similar to one that had occurred just a week earlier. That day, the body of John J. Kieley, a fifty-eight-year-old worker at the Veterans Administration Medical Center, was discovered in his south Minneapolis apartment after he failed to show up for work the previous evening. Homicide detectives suspected that his killer was also responsible for the murder of Lyle E. Kastner, a forty-three-year-old wealthy building contractor, whose body was discovered on December 23, 1985, by the building manager of his upscale condominium in the Loring Park neighborhood. Both men had been strangled, their homes ransacked, and they were known to frequent the same downtown gay bar, where investigators believed they had met their attacker. With no signs of forced entry at either apartment, detectives concluded that the victims had invited their killer inside. Convinced that a murderer was targeting gay men in downtown bars, the police distributed flyers seeking information. Interviews led them to a vague description of a potential suspect: a white hustler in his early twenties who had recently moved to Minneapolis—a profile similar to those linked to the cases of Knudsen, Benscoter, and Taylor.[14]

The murdered men were not, Coyle emphasized in an interview, naive dupes but, rather, older gay men who "[tended] to be more lonely and desperate for sexual contact, especially if they hadn't had much contact in a while." This longing for sexual contact, Coyle explained, often overpowered men's "fear of taking home a stranger." Still, despite this ordinary human need, Coyle thought the risks far outweighed any benefits, and he warned that any gay man "who doesn't first ask around about somebody they are interested in is making a big mistake."[15] While Coyle sympathized with the individual victims, he criticized leaders he felt were doing far too little. In an impassioned letter dated January 28, 1986, addressed to the mayor, elected officials, prosecutors, gay bar owners, and gay activists, Coyle urged everyone—both gay and straight—to "wake up to this murder wave and come together to plan . . . strategies to stop the killing." He condemned city officials for their inaction, accusing them of being "silenced by their own homophobia," and argued that if the victims had been "straight Norwegian bachelors," the response would have been far more vigorous.[16]

To a degree, Coyle's rants against the city and the community's leadership could be expected, but the remainder of his letter, in which he attacked the supposed indifference of gay men, surprised many. Coyle blasted gay bar patrons who "dismissed the growing threat and naively argued that it can't happen to them." In an unusual twist, Coyle reserved his only praise—albeit mild—for the police. Less than a year after publicly criticizing the MPD for raiding adult bookstores, he now commended them for "responding to a growing threat" and "doing an adequate job in this whole situation." Coyle noted that the police had "presented the facts in a dispassionate manner, [had] interviewed the affected community, and [had] pursued suspects where there are leads." In contrast, gay men, Coyle claimed, had failed to mobilize in response to the violence and, instead, continued to engage in casual, anonymous sex. He attributed this "complacency" to the community being "increasingly preoccupied and traumatized by the impact of AIDS." Ultimately, Coyle argued, the community had the "burden . . . to defend itself—as seriously protecting their safety as their health."[17] In 1986, the same year the local antiviolence gay movement gained momentum, Coyle learned he had contracted HIV.[18] While he did not publicly disclose his status at the time, his diagnosis fueled a growing opposition to nonmonogamous, non-coupled, and public sexual practices—essentially, advocating for homonormativity.

Coyle's shifting alliances might seem unusual, but they were grounded in a conviction he shared with the homicide detectives handling the case: that casual, anonymous sex could lead to violence against gay men. Minneapolis Police Chief Anthony Bouza supported Coyle's assertions, pointing out that the murder rate among gay men in Minneapolis had increased and was disproportionately higher than that of heterosexuals. Although Bouza conceded that gay men were "at risk" and "vulnerable," he alleged that their sexual behaviors often heightened this risk by being overly "trusting, frequently bringing strange people into their homes and seeking a good deal of casual encounters." Coyle generally agreed with Bouza but offered a more nuanced perspective. Not *all* gay men sought sexual partners at bars or public parks, Coyle countered. "A majority of gays in this town don't even go to the bars. And I am in no way claiming that a majority of people who go to bars take home strangers." There were, however, "people *out there*" willing to take those risks.[19] Coyle's gesture to "out there" ideologically and spatially distanced respectable gay men, ones who did not "take home strangers," from the reckless minority—the outsiders, those on the fringe of middleness—who did.

Two days later, on January 30, 1986, after police confirmed that a recent murder-arson victim was gay, Coyle reiterated his message during an emergency meeting at City Hall. After lashing out at the "complacent attitude" within the LGBTQ community, he led attendees, including activists, police officials, the city attorney, and six council members, to brainstorm strategies for warning gay men about the dangers of casual encounters with strangers.[20] Gay liberationist Tim Campbell stalked out the most radical position, pleading that the police permit safe escort services for middle-aged gay men. Drawing inspiration from AIDS-related buddy programs, in which volunteer caregivers assisted people with AIDS in performing ordinary domestic tasks and provided emotional companionship, Campbell also proposed a type of buddy system, Adopt-An-Auntie, in which younger gay men watched out for older gay men, ensuring that the latter did not go home with strangers. Coyle, by contrast, suggested a far less sexual approach: establishing a "Gay and Gray Center" to provide social activities, discussion groups, and outreach to closeted older gay men. Jon Tiggas, owner of the Cloud 9 gay bar, offered a sensible compromise between open sex work and platonic community centers: "I'd encourage gay men to meet a person a second time and get to know them before going home with them."[21] Despite these, at times, conflicting measures, everyone agreed on the need to alert gay men about the risks of casual sex with anonymous partners. Meeting attendees planned to post warning flyers in gay bars, revive a whistle alert campaign, organize self-defense classes, and encourage local LGBTQ newspapers to publish articles on "complacency in [the] gay/lesbian community."[22]

For many gay men, the threat of AIDS loomed larger than the fear of antigay violence. J. C. Ritter, a longtime writer for *Equal Time*, noted that "AIDS, politics, everyday survival" dominated the concerns of gay men far more than violence did. The relatively smaller risk of violence seemed insignificant compared to witnessing dozens of friends and loved ones die within weeks from the disease. Ritter clarified that gay men were not unaware of the dangers of violence, but although they might be "scared for a little while," they would soon refocus on the more immediate fear of AIDS.[23] It would take something truly horrific to shift their attention from AIDS to the threat of violence faced by LGBTQ people. In the fall of 1986, a series of brutal murders in Minneapolis did just that. The deaths of several gay men and a transgender woman captured the attention of not just the state's LGBTQ community but the entire nation. However, media coverage often focused as much attention on the "abnormal" lives of the victims—and how they differed from "respectable" gay men—as on the actual killings.

Who Is and Isn't a Victim?

On September 17, 1986, authorities found Fred Riga, a thirty-year-old gay man who was deaf and whom the police report described as "Hispanic," strangled in his south Minneapolis apartment. The fourth gay man slain in Minneapolis in the previous twelve months, Riga might have been treated like Kastner and Kieley if not for the revelation that he dressed as a woman and pursued hustlers. A few days later, a commuter on their way to work discovered the body of Phyllis Olson, the Indigenous, transgender sex worker whom Coyle had found particularly unsettling.[24] Whereas Kastner and Kieley were first and foremost victims, when officials discussed Olson, they fixated on her transient relationship to private property and her many arrests for prostitution dating back to the 1970s to suggest that her death was perhaps a predictable outcome of her "deviant" lifestyle. Unlike Kastner and Kieley, whose deaths could be ascribed to a longing for physical connection and romantic affection, the same, in all likelihood, could not be said for Olson, who came upon her assailant while looking for income.

Even more than the MPD had with previous victims, the police held an unshakeable belief that Riga and Olson bore some responsibility for their own murders. Captain Jack McCarthy of the Homicide Unit labeled them as "high-risk gays," and in an official interoffice communication, along with relevant facts, he described Riga as a "sexually active gay, known to take strangers home frequently and get into fights." Notably, with Olson, all McCarthy felt was necessary was to list her as a "transvestite prostitute"—as if that alone explained her sexual history and activities.[25] At no point did McCarthy or anyone else on the force claim either deserved to die, but as subtle shades of blame entered into official releases and then political speeches and finally media coverage, the implicit message emerged: The behaviors of the victims were as relevant to the crimes as the actions of the attackers.

In one respect, this focus was nothing new. Going back into the 1970s, police, politicians, and the media routinely suggested that gay men somehow invited the violence they faced by preying on young male hustlers. However, Riga and Olson, in addition to being "high-risk gays," differed from white, middle-class victims—men whose singular difference from most Minnesotans was that they loved and engaged in intercourse with people of the same sex. Influenced by police messaging, the media eagerly highlighted these differences. Riga, the papers announced, was a "disabled deaf-mute" who drank heavily, hustled aggressively, and took in young men struggling financially.[26] In short, in addition to fitting all the classic tropes of the gay man as a sexual predator, Riga, the media implied, was also physically and psychologically damaged. Additionally, hints of gender dysphoria were suggested. One bartender at the Gay 90s added that although Riga was not a drag queen and did not identify as transgender, he sometimes dressed as a woman. As if that were not enough to stamp him as different, the *Star Tribune* divulged that Riga not only held no job but also had no known relatives in the area—a coded but clear signifier in the language of Minnesota Nice of an outsider.[27]

Riga's and Olson's deviation from Minnesota Nice's middle-class ideals of gender and able-bodiedness marked them as inherently suspicious. For many middle-class, white gay activists and leaders, finding a group that both they and the police found apprehensive and morally dubious amounted to a common bond. Despite, or perhaps because they sought, the status of a protected minority, these activists and leaders played upon widespread and deeply held prejudices against gender nonconforming people of color. Scholars have noted that dominant actors and institutions often portray gender nonconformity as intrinsically confused and deceptive, cementing it as a "queer criminal archetype." Gender nonconforming individuals "evoke strong, often subterranean emotional associations or responses" that render them guilty even while committing no criminal act.[28] Since Riga oftentimes housed young, presumably heterosexual, men in his apartment until they found their footing and Olson was an HIV-positive prostitute who pursued heterosexual clients, their deception posed a danger to heterosexual men and their unsuspecting families. The police, therefore, only involved themselves in the murders of Riga and Olson to the extent that their lives disrupted the raced, gendered, and classed social order of America's heartland. But because their lives were not conceivable within frames of middleness, they were never fully acknowledged as lives and, thus, mourned.

In "failing" to live up to gender and sexual norms, both Riga and Olson undermined the neoliberal script that gay leaders mobilized in the pursuit of rights, rendering their deaths, as Judith Butler puts it, "ungrievable."[29] Neither murder fit the narrative leaders like Coyle wanted the public to hear. In his mind, gay men amounted to victims of a society that denied them a "normal" human experience—one that included physical connection and romantic affection. Riga could, with some stretching, be seen as an imperfect representation of this gay longing, but not Olson. Her pursuit of sex fit no acceptable pattern. An Indigenous woman, marginalized by structural racism, economic impoverishment, and centuries of settler-colonialism, her involvement in sex work likely stemmed from economic necessity. For leaders like Coyle, who sought social acceptance, gay sex was supposed to be private, far removed from the crass vulgarity of the streets and the impersonality of the markets. Only by framing gay and straight love and sex as different manifestations of the same human desire could they hope to persuade straight America to see gay men and lesbians as equals.

To convince society that gay men were "normal" and that their need for physical connection, while not always prudent, was nonetheless reasonable—and thus deserving of police protection—Coyle and other leaders had to tread carefully in their critique of deep-rooted institutional issues like racism and poverty. These were the same issues that drove people like Olson into sex work. As Roderick Ferguson has noted, this "disavowal of inequality's fundamentally structural nature" meant that emerging hate crime legislation would reinforce a homonormative racial formation and ultimately uphold white supremacy.[30] On some level, activists and leaders in the Twin Cities recognized the systemic nature of antigay violence; they argued, for instance, that the repeal of the 1978 St. Paul gay rights ordinance had given bashers free rein to attack gay men. But by 1986, their narrowly focused antihomophobia agenda failed to consider how the interconnectedness of racism, poverty, and able-bodiedness subjected certain queer individuals to heightened violence.[31] Unable to reconcile Olson's and Riga's needs with their liberal reforms, antiviolence gay activists simply erased them from the narrative.

Gay Minnesota Finds Its Common Whiteness

The growing alliance between the gay community in Minneapolis and the police in the 1980s can be partly attributed to the rise in antigay violence in the upper Midwest coinciding with an influx of poor people of color migrating from deindustrialized Rust Belt cities. The local press dubbed this migration the "Gary Syndrome," after the primarily Black and working-class town of Gary, Indiana, which had witnessed an economic exodus due to layoffs and closures associated with the restructuring of the steel industry. The Gary Syndrome threatened everything that the famous 1973 *Time* magazine cover story "The Good Life in Minnesota" had lauded. The article highlighted Minnesota's success, in part due to its low crime rate, quoting a suburban father who remarked, "There is little of the bad things up here—drugs, pollution. Being way up here, people have had a chance to see the crest of the wave coming and react to it. There's an attitude, too, that we've got a nice little thing going and let's keep it that way." At the time, Minnesota was overwhelmingly white—98 percent. However, by 1990, people who were Black, Indigenous, or Asian made up 21.6 percent of Minneapolis's population and 17.7 percent of St. Paul's.[32] This demographic shift prompted Capt. Jack McCarthy, head of the Minneapolis Homicide Unit, to tell the *St. Paul Pioneer Press*, "We've got a hell of a lot more street people. We've got a hell of a lot more minorities and gang members from Chicago and Gary. And they've brought more violence with them . . . We're becoming a big city and our population is changing."[33] Another officer, referring to the Mariel boatlift of 1980, told the *Star Tribune* that these "strangers" came from as far away as Cuba.[34]

Despite its racist implications, the Gary Syndrome avoided direct mention of race. Instead, it relied on what Ian Haney López calls "dog whistle politics," or coded appeals to white people through subliminal racial grievances.[35] Terms like "street gangs," "crack cocaine," and "welfare reform" served as veiled references to Black culture and behavior, depicting them as fundamentally deviant and depraved. During the Reagan administration in the 1980s, politicians across ideological perspectives embraced neoliberal principles like color-blindness, meritocracy, and free market individualism to downplay the impact of systemic racism in poverty. Instead, they shifted the focus to perceived cultural flaws, individual shortcomings, and the supposedly harmful effects of the welfare system.[36] Given the perception of Minnesota as a liberal state with progressive social policies, the rhetoric of Minnesota Nice rendered overt racism unacceptable. Dog whistle politics, instead, enabled local politicians and leaders to wield racial entreaties that were, on the one hand, inaudible and easily denied yet, on the other hand, still effective in provoking strong reactions from their targeted audience of disaffected white voters.

To the extent the Gary Syndrome portrayed Black people as culturally predisposed to crime, it effectively cast white people as racial victims. This phenomenon reflects what Lisa Cacho calls "white injury," a condition in which aggrieved white Americans demand "tough on crime" measures to shield themselves against shifting racial demographics. Cacho argues that this mindset reinforces broader systems of "containment, exploitation, and surveillance of communities of color."[37] That the language around crime relied on an epidemiological trope—"syndrome"—is particularly noteworthy; it depicted people of color and their supposed criminality as a foreign contagion, necessitating swift intervention to protect public health and safety. Notably, this rhetoric coincided with the era of HIV/AIDS, amplifying fears of contamination and disease. The "cure," according to advocates of the Gary Syndrome, lay in a more robust law enforcement apparatus.

LGBTQ Minnesotans already knew that the state's reputation as a bastion of liberalism, universal human rights, and inclusive multiculturalism was, at best, contingent and certainly circumspect. However, when this wave of Black urban migrants arrived, LGBTQ Minnesotans—a group that, like the state, was predominately white—faced a choice: either ally with this newly ostracized group and expose the inconsistencies and double standards that lurked within the ideal of Minnesota Nice or ally with the growing neoliberal, "law and order" culture that dominated the era's political discourse. In the end, many gay and lesbian Minnesotans, particularly integrationists, chose the latter, privileging their whiteness over their status as a sexual minority.[38]

Although Black urban migrants were not responsible for the violence against gay men—police typically arrested young, white male hustlers for these crimes—gay activists leveraged the growing public concern on crime to draw attention to the violence against gay men. On October 18, 1986, the body of Robert Churchill, a fifty-two-year-old, middle-class, white gay professional was discovered after his upscale Loring Park apartment was set on fire. His body was so severely burned that only dental records could confirm his identity. An autopsy revealed he had been stabbed in the chest before the fire. Although no evidence linked Churchill's death with that of the others, police noted that his apartment door was unlocked with no signs of forced entry, suggesting he might have known his killer. The *St. Paul Pioneer Press*, however, fixated on Churchill's sexual behaviors, depicting him as a man who "lived his private life alone and on the edge, sometimes drinking too much, hustling strangers in the so-called 'fringe bars' that neighbor the gay bars, befriending young men who were down on their luck, often providing a home and money for them until they got back on their feet." The newspaper concluded that this "private life" of hustling young men for sex "may have killed him."[39]

Two days after Churchill's brutal murder, Police Chief Bouza announced the formation of a specialized three-officer investigative team to review all fifteen unsolved homicides in Minneapolis that year. Five of these unsolved cases involved LGBTQ individuals since January 1985. Bouza tasked the team, which included a veteran homicide lieutenant and two experienced sergeants, with identifying any possible links between the murders. From January to October 1986, Minneapolis recorded forty-one homicides, involving victims ranging from "drug users and dealers" to "promiscuous homosexuals and street people," as reported by the *Star Tribune*. This tally marked the highest in a year since 1979 when the city recorded forty-nine homicides.[40] The *Star Tribune's* association of drug use—often linked in public discourse to Black criminality under the guise of the Gary Syndrome—with gay men, regardless of race, underscores how easily the public perceived gay sexuality as criminal. The unsolved murders sparked fear among residents, leading some elderly white people in Coyle's ward to barricade themselves indoors, as he told the *Star Tribune*. In an interview with the *Chicago Tribune* that spread widely, Coyle worried that Minneapolis—a city famous for being "nice" as depicted on the sitcom *The Mary Tyler Moore Show*—was descending into "a place of mean streets."[41]

Dead gay men accounted for only a small fraction of the overall rise in homicides, but gay leaders ensured that no one overlooked them as white Minnesotans became fixated on the danger new Black transplants posed to them. In acknowledging the city's record-setting fiftieth homicide, one article noted the emergence of "an underclass . . . of the type and kind found in many other major cities." Police Chief Bouza agreed, attributing the city's problems to "an influx of poor people from other cities" and cautioning, "There's a lot of mobility in this country, a great migratory pattern across the U.S. amongst all classes."[42] In July 1987, the MPD reported that two-thirds of the suspects and half the victims in the city's twenty-six homicides were "transients," newcomers who had lived in Minneapolis for less than two years.[43] In an interview, Capt. McCarthy described the victims as "people who are floating, drifting" but reassured the public that "for John Q. Normal Citizen"—someone like the patriarch quoted in the 1973 *Time* magazine cover story—"who minds his own business, has a home and a family, earns a steady paycheck, has his own circle of friends, the incidence of homicide is super rare."[44] McCarthy's observations also hinted at a sexual dimension, suggesting that what made transients suspect was not only their lack of stable housing, but also their failure to conform to the nuclear family ideal—a structure central to how Minnesotans have historically defined social belonging. Police calls for increased federal funding also painted a picture of a Minneapolis in turmoil—"a city on the edge . . . experiencing dramatic changes in its population and their extent of poverty."[45] Other media outlets documented the rise of street gangs and emphasized that gang members came from "broken" families with absent Black fathers. By focusing on the absence of two-parent households among African Americans, these news sources insinuated that restoring heteronormative structures among the Black underclass could mitigate the inequities that pushed some Black youth into the drug trade.[46]

The arrival of crack cocaine in inner-city neighborhoods across the United States, including the Twin Cities, in the mid-1980s marked a turning point in police–community relations. It also reinforced the Gary Syndrome by helping frame Black people as scourges on the welfare system, unfit parents, and criminals warranting increased policing. "Crack" accomplished something very similar to what "AIDS" had for the treatment of gay men in the public sphere, for both "crack" and "AIDS" stigmatized Black and gay people, respectively—although, of course, overlaps existed between the groups. Yet no gay leader balked when the *Star Tribune* ran images of white police officers standing protectively over a young Black boy playing with a toy assault rifle while his disheveled mother lay handcuffed on the ground. These photos, part of an exposé following the city's narcotics unit during raids on "crack houses," depicted the "hundreds of children in the Twin Cities" as being "neglected and exposed to violence by crack-using parents." The article cited police claims that Black residents occupied 90 percent of the raided "crack houses" in north Minneapolis and that of the 668 children reportedly living in these conditions, 72 percent were African American.[47] By featuring images of parents in disarray and in custody, the *Tribune* reinforced stereotypes of broken Black families while casting white police officers as heroes, but this reporting was highly selective storytelling, like the images of gay men arrested in vice raids covering their face as a testament to their sense of shame.[48] Had gay leaders drawn on their own history of facing challenges and unfair stigmatization, they might have opposed the propaganda of the Gary Syndrome and the unjust policies targeting specific communities. After all, they too had been denied fundamental rights, such as the recognition of their relationships and full access to housing. Yet no prominent voice appears in the historical record. By doing and saying nothing, gay leaders had made an important decision.

There was a clear reason why gay leaders made this decision. In his 1990 State of the City address, Mayor Don Fraser called for a stepped-up war against drugs and crime, citing crack cocaine, random violence, and gang activity as factors contributing to a growing sense of fear in Minneapolis. "Like a lightning strike," Fraser warned, "they have illuminated swiftly and starkly a destructive power within our community that threatens to unravel important strands of our social fabric."[49] Suddenly, Minneapolis, and the state more broadly, faced a group perceived as more "deviant" and "dangerous" than gay men. Gay men, once viewed by society as predatory—looking to hunt innocent boys or manipulate young straight men down on their luck—became plausible victims too. Or to be more exact, *white* gay men began to see themselves and be seen as part of a larger white victimhood, fending off a scourge of Black criminality. Even if they might have wanted to be more just, gay men had to embrace or at least ignore the racism that animated the Gary Syndrome as this discourse represented one of the few ways through which they could vouch for their entitlement to rights, benefits, and protections.

To strengthen the inclusion of gay men in the social fabric of the Midwest, Coyle and others promoted the view that sexual deviance—once a marker of homosexuality—was instead at the root of Black criminality. In an article discussing predictions for the 1990s, Coyle shared a bleak outlook, warning about "single parents having lots of children." Along with crime and drug use, Coyle concerned himself with sexual morality, arguing for the need to "define what is responsible behavior" and to hold those who practiced "immoral behavior" accountable. Coyle posed questions such as "what to do about the drug sellers, how to deal with absentee landlords, [and] what is responsible sexual behavior." Although he did not clarify what he meant by "responsible sexual behavior," it likely excluded single-parent households and certainly not gay men engaging in casual, anonymous sex despite the risks of AIDS and violence. Like supposedly lascivious heterosexual Black people who irresponsibly procreated only to neglect those children to drugs and crime or else abuse the social safety net funded by responsible taxpayers, these gay men were careless and deserved society's scorn. But Coyle made clear not *all* gay men were part of this criminal underclass; most, he suggested, were like his white, heterosexual, responsible audience: self-supporting, tax paying, coupled, sexually discreet, monogamous, and mature—that is, devotees to the politics of middleness.

Although white gay leaders embraced the rhetoric of "dangerous" Black and brown people, they were not responsible for the rise in antigay violence in the region. The Governor's Task Force on Prejudice and Violence, formed in 1987 to track bias-motivated crime and propose legislative actions, concluded that neo-Nazi "skinheads," who had an unacknowledged presence in Minnesota, committed some of the bias-related crime against LGBTQ people. Among the task force's more unsettling findings was that the Aryan Nations, a white supremacist group, focused recruitment efforts in Minnesota, especially targeting economically hard-pressed farmers.[50] The unwillingness of Minnesota Nice to directly address race, much less racism, had enabled white supremacists to gain a foothold in the state. Notably, all the assailants arrested and charged in the gay homicides were young white men, ages eighteen to twenty-one, not people of color, which supported the task force's conclusions. Yet no such vitriol was ever directed against young white men, or white people for that matter. Rather, police often portrayed the attackers sympathetically, describing them as "sexually confused." In a subtle nod to the gay panic defense, Deputy Police Chief Patrick Farrell described these assailants as "latent homosexuals" driven to violence against "older, less sought-after gay men" due to internalized "homophobia and fear of AIDS."[51] Farrell even seemed to blame the victims, suggesting that they had enticed these young, "sexually confused" men to their homes—further reinforcing the stereotype of gay men as sexual predators.

Despite the clear statistics, in September 1988, Coyle joined the rest of the City Council in voting to increase the police budget by $1.9 million, a figure intended to boost the number of officers on the streets by nearly 10 percent. City Councilmember Walter Dziedzic, a key proponent of the increase, assured, "The good people of Minneapolis don't have to look over their shoulders. The crooks who have been in Minneapolis better start looking over their shoulders, because there will be more officers in blue on the street."[52]

He did not need to, given the language of the time, specify who these "good people" saw when they glanced over their shoulders: Black men. Yet gay men were threatened first and foremost by young white men. That Coyle, who had once advocated rent control, found himself aligned with conservatives on the city council shows how compelling the culture of poverty argument could be for white Americans in the 1980s, even LGBTQ people.

Why did Coyle, who had spent much of his public career criticizing the police for targeting gay men, now support a policy that would create a new class of perennially harassed citizens? Although no simple answer exists, one possibility is that the vote came down to pure politics. Coyle came out in support for not only increasing the police department's budget and hiring more officers but also imposing harsher sentences on repeat offenders.[53] Perhaps he calculated that by giving his support to police, they would harass gay men less. Alternatively, he might have hoped that a stronger police presence would reduce crime and violence against *respectable*—that is, white—gay men (though in the past more plainclothes cops in Loring Park often resulted in more arrests of gay men). Finally, Coyle, as a product of his environment, might have been duly invested in Minnesota Nice and felt it was his duty to address the perceived threat of the Gary Syndrome. The truth is likely a combination of all three, but no matter what the reason, with his vote Coyle established an alliance with law enforcement that came at the expense of justice for people of color in the region. For the first time, respectable gay men had become more white than deviant.

The Pink Police

The alliance between gay leaders and the police marked a significant departure from the more radical actions of the late 1960s and early 1970s. During those earlier years, gay men formed the Lambda Squad, which, like the Black community's Soul Force or the Indigenous AIM Patrol, patrolled neighborhoods in Minneapolis *and* monitored police conduct.[54] Even as late as 1977, gay activists joined other over-policed groups in calling for an independent civilian review board to investigate police brutality and bias. By the late 1980s, the landscape had changed dramatically, with some segments of the LGBTQ community—particularly the affluent and property-owning—remaining mostly silent in response to over-policing and incidents like the Gary Syndrome. They were not alone in this shift. As Timothy Stewart-Winter has shown, as incidents of police entrapment of gay men and raids on gay bars sharply declined across the country starting in the late 1970s, gay activists softened their criticisms of the police and began moving toward reconciliation. Yet, in Minnesota, the quiet support from the gay community for the MPD did not result in preferential treatment.[55] As late as October 1986, Coyle was still holding press conferences at City Hall, urging the police to address the pattern of murdered gay men. Warning of further violence, Coyle called for the MPD to allocate more resources to the investigations. He commended Bouza's new task force, noting that pressure from his office had helped strengthen police efforts, but he also criticized the department for not following up on leads his office had provided. Gay men were still reluctant to contact the police directly. Coyle claimed he had received information suggesting a serial killer might be responsible for the unsolved murders, but the police, he lamented, were unwilling to pursue these leads.[56] This vacuum of urgency, effort, and concern led Coyle and other activists to form CUAV, the group that distributed the alarming flyers that had confused so many gay men.

The formation of CUAV, Coyle explained, was "necessary to shake homosexuals out of their complacency about the recent killings." Part of the reason that gay men were being targeted—at least in Coyle's mind—was due to personal irresponsibility—whether involving drugs, alcohol, or casual anonymous sex. To mitigate this risk, CUAV organized prevention seminars focused on education, stressing the dangers of casual anonymous sex and extolling the health and physical virtues of sexual discretion.[57]

Coyle firmly believed that AIDS dominated gay men's concerns, leaving them blind to the danger of physical violence. Acknowledging the success of HIV awareness campaigns, he borrowed heavily from their materials, including the "Play It Safe" tagline from the HIV-education materials of the Minnesota AIDS Project (MAP), the state's largest AIDS service organization. MAP's "Play It Safe" campaign featured posters with mostly white, masculine-presenting figures dressed in athletic gear, preparing for strenuous physical activities like biking and hockey, both popular regional pastimes. Although these ads emphasized safer sex practices, they also promoted other less scientific but morally favored measures.[58] In the November 26, 1986, issue of the local LGBTQ newspaper *Twin Cities Gaze*, a MAP "Play It Safe" ad depicted Jim St. George—Coyle's former aide and then-MAP board chairman—bent over a bike, helmet in hand (fig. 3.2). St. George, a biracial gay man with Indigenous heritage, was on a stop in Minneapolis during the first coast-to-coast AIDS bicycle fundraiser.[59] The caption beneath his photo read: "Fight AIDS by staying in control. Alcohol and drugs can mess you up. Poppers can make you go too far. Keep the caps on—and live." At the time, poppers (a slang name for the recreational inhalant substance amyl nitrite) were at the

FIGURE 3.2 1986 HIV-prevention poster from the "Play It Safe" campaign by the Minnesota AIDS Project, featuring Jim St. George. From the Leo Treadway Papers, +283, Folder 2. Courtesy of the Minnesota Historical Society.

center of a heated debate over whether they contributed to HIV transmission. Some gay activists argued that substances like poppers, alcohol, and illicit drugs impaired judgment, warranting their discouragement. Without scientific consensus, moral viewpoints heavily influenced the campaign.

While much of CUAV's language and imagery resembled those of MAP, the two organizations differed significantly in one crucial respect. Whereas MAP's "Play It Safe" campaign promoted condoms, for Coyle, this definition of "safer sex" fell far short. Condoms might have helped stop HIV transmission, but they would not stop violence. Coyle wanted nothing less than the demise of cruising and casual—even if protected—sex. Only intimate familiarity would protect gay men from physical violence, and Coyle unabashedly encouraged dating and limiting sexual partners. "Get to know someone," he advised in an interview, "before you are alone with them, and let an acquaintance know where you are."[60] By promoting dating, settling down, and embracing monogamy, CUAV could, according to its own reasoning, congratulate itself on combating violence as well as the spread of HIV.

By early 1987, compulsory homonormativity had shifted from being one of many possible strategies for gay men to follow to becoming the dominant approach in the region. Tim Campbell, the gay liberationist and counterpoint to Coyle's more integrationist aspirations, had not only joined CUAV but penned a pamphlet for the group titled "Dating." While the language and writing of the piece could only have come from Campbell—a man known for his wit and literary bite—the sentiments could have only come from Coyle. To prevent violence, Campbell outlined ten safety tips for gay men, focusing on moral conduct, sobriety, cautious choice of sex partners, and reduced sexual activity.[61] He urged gay men to "date whenever possible" and advised against having sex with "straights" and "total unknowns"—that is, outsiders. Echoing MAP's "Play It Safe" message, Campbell, who publicly acknowledged his long-term sobriety, encouraged others to "count your chemicals." Police had previously reported that several gay victims were under the influence of drugs or alcohol at the time of their deaths. Referring to some of these victims as "heavy drinkers," Campbell warned that excessive alcohol and drug use impaired their ability to make sound judgments about sexual partners: "Every drink and every additional drug consumed decreases your judgment and increases your vulnerability."[62] This merging of the radical and accommodationist wings of the gay political spectrum, though primarily focused on antigay violence activism, marked a clear victory for neoliberal approaches that emphasized personal responsibility and domestic privacy over deeper, structural issues.

The message resonated, but in the era of the Gary Syndrome and racially coded language, identifying "outsiders" meant confronting racial differences. Following Coyle's City Hall press conference, a patron of the Saloon, a local gay bar, told a reporter that he always kept "an eye out for people who [look] suspicious, who don't look like they fit in with the crowd."[63] In predominantly white Minnesota, and especially in the mostly white gay bars of Minneapolis, a person of color would have easily fit the patron's criteria. If men of color were automatically perceived as criminals due to the Gary Syndrome and if CUAV associated criminality with being an outsider, white gay men could become less inclined to "cruise" men of color for fear of assault or murder. Although patrons like this one continued to frequent bars, CUAV's fear-based campaign against outsiders led to a decline in business at the Saloon and other venues. Jim Anderson, co-owner of the Saloon, observed a shift in the social scene: "Customers dance and date and visit with friends instead of hustling strangers for the night."[64]

CUAV members had a philosophy of sexual monogamy and discretion that they wanted gay men to follow, but, in the meantime, they also wanted to save lives. With limited police action, the responsibility of ensuring safety fell on the gay community. The issue arose at CUAV's inaugural meeting on October 24, 1986, which drew forty attendees, including community leaders and several bartenders and security staff from the Gay 90s.[65] Attendees supported a "buddy system," a type of personal insurance, advising gay men to inform friends if they planned to go home with strangers. The group also discussed setting up a hotline for tips about potential suspects, allowing gay men to share information without dealing with an unsympathetic police force. CUAV would then evaluate these tips and pass relevant information to investigators.[66]

During CUAV's Violence Awareness Month in November 1986, the organization launched various initiatives to raise awareness about antigay violence. Alongside the "Play It Safe!" flyer campaign, CUAV produced public service announcements (PSAs) warning gay men about the dangers of public, anonymous sex and upping the stakes with scare tactics that, while never mentioning race, relied on similar dog whistle tropes and aesthetic practices—darkened alleys, shadowy figures, and sharpened knives—employed under the Gary Syndrome. These PSAs portrayed gay men who cruised as lonely figures prowling the streets of Minneapolis, its seedy bars, and its public bathrooms for one-night stands. One full-page PSA featured a black-and-white photograph of a hunting knife slicing through a condom lying on carpeted floor (fig. 3.3). Overlaid on that photo-

Condoms help shield against disease — but not violence.

"Safe Sex" has become a household word for stopping the spread of disease during sex.

But today, it takes more than just a condom to stop the disease of anger, hatred, and fear of Gays to protect us from the violence that has taken at least 13 Gay lives in the past two years.

VD, herpes, and AIDS aren't the only threats to gays these days. Protect yourself against harm by following some sound advice: know who you're taking home! It may be exciting to meet and pick up a total stranger, but it can be a dangerous proposition.

Know who you're taking home. Talk first. Get to know him. Ask a few questions. Don't be afraid... it's better to be safe, than sorry!

CLOUD 9

829 Hennepin Ave. • 339-4135

FIGURE 3.3 "Safe Sex Is More Than Just Wearing a Condom," a public service announcement by Community United Against Violence, published in *Twin Cities Gaze* on October 31, 1986. Tretter Collection in GLBT Studies, University of Minnesota, Twin Cities. Courtesy of the Minnesota Historical Society.

graph was the universal prohibition sign—a red circle with a line through it—implying that even sex with condoms at home was unsafe. The bolded headline read: "Safe Sex Is More Than Just Wearing A Condom."[67] Below the photograph, the PSA explained that while "condoms help shield against disease," they did not protect against "the disease of anger, hatred, and fear of Gays." It emphasized that "VD, herpes, and AIDS aren't the only threats to gays these days" and advised gay men to prevent violence by "know[ing] who you're taking home. Talk first. Get to know him. Ask a few questions. Don't be afraid . . . it's better to be safe than sorry!" Even if the message was not categorically antisex—no message demanded celibacy—it certainly encouraged caution, promoted monogamy, and strongly implied that abstinence was the safest option.

An essential aspect of the first PSA's message was the importance of knowing a partner well before inviting him into the home, a private, secure realm—anything public was inherently suspect. A second PSA reinforced this idea by focusing on the dangers of cruising. It featured a black-and-white photograph of an empty phone booth in a park, likely Loring Park, at night. The light from a streetlamp cast an eerie glow on the booth (fig. 3.4). Outside the illuminated area stood a shadowy male figure looking in the booth's direction. His body, an amorphous mass of dark matter, was undecipherable to the naked eye. Once again, a red circle with a line through it conveyed the message that even public amenities, like a phone booth, offered no safety for gay men. Bold letters above the photograph screamed out, "Be Safe!" while the caption below advised gay men to avoid dangerous places and behaviors. In this context, "dangerous" became synonymous with "public." The PSA stated, "Violence against innocent persons occurs easily in the dark shadows . . . whether in the park, on the street or in your own neighborhood . . . Avoid involvement with strangers who may have the potential for causing harm." According to the PSA, violence was possible in public ("the park . . . the street . . . your own neighborhood"), but noticeably missing from the list was the home, which was deemed safe but, as suggested by the earlier PSA, only with a monogamous partner.

Darkened, blurred—and hence dangerous—figures lurked across much of CUAV's productions, even alongside those with more homely, welcoming messages. A third PSA featured a grayscale image of a bare-chested man blurred out of focus and multiplied across the greater half of the page (fig. 3.5). Below the photo, the caption asked, "Is this your idea of Mr. Right—for tonight?" Yet just under this warning was a short message penned by a local personality from the gay nightlife scene, a character by

FIGURE 3.4 "Be Safe!" public service announcement by Community United Against Violence, published in *Twin Cities Gaze* on October 31, 1986, Tretter Collection in GLBT Studies, University of Minnesota, Twin Cities. Courtesy of the Minnesota Historical Society.

FIGURE 3.5 "Be Careful!" Community United Against Violence public service announcement, published in *Twin Cities Gaze* on October 31, 1986, Tretter Collection in GLBT Studies, University of Minnesota, Twin Cities. Courtesy of the Minnesota Historical Society.

the name of Big Mama. Appearing to be a drag queen, she embodied a matriarchal figure in kitschy midwestern fashion: florals; big, permed hair; and overly accessorized with jewelry. She offered this warning:

> Wake up and hear the birdies, kids! . . . There are persons out there killing gay guys, and there are persons running around with AIDS who just do not care who they give it to! . . . Know who you are going home with! If you don't know the person well, you are much better off going home alone. If you really want to take a stranger home, stop by and introduce him to me (or your favorite bartender), just in case something later happens to you! . . . There are some people who really care about your welfare. I happen to be one of those people . . . I care about, and love all of you! . . . Love, Big Mama.

Through Big Mama—and, by extension, CUAV—the message suggested that gay men sought fleeting connections due to low self-esteem, hinting that a maternal caretaker could uplift them and remind them of their inherent value ("their welfare"). Gay men with self-respect, the PSA implied, would not engage in dangerous practices. Only "damaged" or mentally unhealthy gay men acted in ways that put them at risk for AIDS and violence. This PSA played on the idealized image of the white American family in the Midwest inasmuch as it relayed a message of violence awareness vis-à-vis white heterosexual relations. Simultaneously, the drag element of the message implicitly acknowledged that, despite aspiring to such familial ideals, the gay men being addressed remained categorically and systematically excluded from them.

Nowhere in its "Play It Safe!" campaign or other PSAs does CUAV discuss the government's culpability in facilitating the spread of HIV.[68] No government agency or officials came under scrutiny. No questions were lobbed at the MPD for its sluggish response to gay murders. Notably, there was no suggestion of safety for transgender sex workers of color—CUAV seemed not to think they were at any particular risk. Instead, the group's literature achieved two results. First, it acclimated gay Minnesotans to the idea that it fell upon them to address or at least mitigate the violence that befell them. Second, it implicitly crafted a narrative reminiscent of the Gary Syndrome in that white gay men were the victims of violence and deserved sympathy and state protection. The old trope that homosexuals threatened public morals (a trope that had been compounded by their supposed threat to public health) had now given way to a new narrative of the victimized—*white*—gay man.

CUAV's focus on self-esteem reinforced comments from openly gay State Sen. Allan Spear that access to privacy via sodomy repeal would instill a sense of worth in gay men and, thus, discourage public anonymous encounters. Speaking at a press conference on November 6, 1986, near the scene of a gay man's murder, Spear warned gay men to avoid situations where they could be vulnerable to violence. Although he had been closeted when first elected, Spear also urged against living in the closet, stating, "We must reach out and not be forced into the closet because of the pressures of society. The only way to move forward is to make sure gays and lesbians have full rights in society."[69] According to Spear's reasoning, antigay violence would diminish with the granting of "full rights in society" to gay men and lesbians. He presumed that public, anonymous encounters stemmed from both the illegality of such interactions and a sense of shame (itself reinforced by the criminal nature of same-sex desires). Overturning sodomy laws would eliminate both issues. For Spear then, who advocated for sodomy repeal at the state level while Coyle spearheaded the antiviolence movement in Minneapolis, the right to privacy reduced the lure of casual anonymous sex and, thus, reduced the risk of violence. Only by coming out would older, closeted gay men, vulnerable to violence from young hustlers, be able to access the protections that privacy provided.

Alongside its print campaign, CUAV organized a series of events that further conflated impersonal sex with violence and that stoked the racialized specter of "outsiders" as perpetrators of crime. On November 17, 1986, about fifty gay men, along with representatives from the Minneapolis Commission on Civil Rights and the MPD, including Police Chief Bouza, gathered at a local Methodist church for a community forum focused on identifying warning signs of violence.[70] During the seminar, tensions flared between gay leaders and the police. Although CUAV had toned down its criticisms of law enforcement and made only modest requests, still the department did little. Finally, frustrated by the lack of progress in solving gay-related murders, Coyle and other CUAV members accused the police of lacking experiential knowledge of the gay nightlife scene. Campbell, on behalf of CUAV, had previously written to Mayor Fraser, Police Chief Bouza, and Police Captain McCarthy, proposing the creation of a "temporary special gay assistant to police investigators." The liaison, Campbell wrote, would work closely with police to follow leads on the murders of gay men and others who frequented Hennepin Avenue establishments, analyze data, and offer insights that might be overlooked by others.[71] Confident in the proposal's approval, Campbell prematurely announced the position to the public without authorization from Fraser, Bouza, or McCarthy. However, the police chief ultimately dismissed the idea as unnecessary.

In his reply to Campbell's letter, Bouza thanked him for the suggestion and agreed that the police department needed "a system to solicit, collect and evaluate information from a gay community that [was] clearly anxious and willing to help." Nonetheless, he considered the task force of three "top flight" investigators capable of doing the work the liaison would. Bouza, thus, concluded: "I am not sanguine about chances to fund the position you suggest, nor am I convinced it is either needed or practicable."[72] Campbell, known for his quick tongue, quickly wrote back, expressing indignation that Bouza had "given so little consideration to the idea of hiring a member of the gay community to help investigate the unsolved murders." Campbell expressed that *he* was not "sanguine" about the effectiveness of the task force. If the police department could hire civilians as decoys to entrap gay men in adult bookstores and X-rated theaters, Campbell reasoned, then it could surely hire "an assistant to investigate murders on a temporary basis."[73]

A divide between "insiders" and "outsiders" lingered in the debate over establishing a special gay liaison to the police. In an interview, Bouza remained steadfast in his opposition to such a position, stating, "We need help in assistance, but we have enough of our own investigative experts to perform the job and it's not common practice to hire *outsiders*."[74] In his refusal, Bouza did not refer to a gay liaison as part of "the public" or even the equally vague "member of the community" but as an "outsider"—the same alienating language white leaders used to frame the racialized poor from the Rust Belt and the Global South. Gay men were in Minnesota but not, according to the head of the MPD, of Minnesota. Coyle, the most accommodating and integrationist of Minnesota's gay leaders, would have none of it. When it came to these murdered Minnesotans, gay men *were* uniquely insiders. "There are just some things," he told the *Star Tribune*, "you don't know unless you're gay."[75] Without that information, he believed, these cases would remain unsolved.

Bouza's choice of words revealed the size of the cultural gap between CUAV and police leadership. During the November 17 community forum, Coyle and Campbell urged the department to actively recruit openly gay and lesbian police officers from other cities, much like it did with Black and Latinx officers. Exasperated, Bouza retorted, "We don't hire a Scandinavian when a Scandinavian is murdered, or a black when a black is murdered."

Gay men and lesbians, he countered, were already on the force, even if they were not publicly out. Far from satisfied with this defense, the crowd jeered and booed.[76]

Coyle, like the crowd that night, found Bouza's answers not only insufficient but even dismissive. He kept up pressure to establish a special gay liaison but also leveraged his official position to circumvent departmental inertia and encourage recruitment of openly gay and lesbian officers. Although Coyle lacked direct authority over police hiring, his office penned a letter to the Gay Officers Action League (GOAL) in New York City, encouraging openly gay and lesbian police officers in the New York Police Department to consider job opportunities in Minneapolis. Coyle and Campbell were particularly struck by how, despite the police leadership's disparagement of the racialized poor, the department still actively sought to recruit Black and Latinx officers and encouraged "community participation" from people of color—something it did not do with gay men and lesbians. For Coyle, Campbell, and white gay men more broadly, this shocking development underscored the extent to which their whiteness granted them insider status. They may have ended their most vocal protest against the police and become silent, assenting partners in the over-policing associated with the Gary Syndrome, but that had not bought them full membership into the regional community. To be gay—at least when it came to the MPD—was still to be outside, looking in on Minnesota Nice.

One reason Bouza believed that a special gay liaison was unnecessary in Minneapolis was because on the day of the community forum police arrested a suspect in the high-profile death of Churchill. On November 17, 1986, police in Baton Rouge, Louisiana, apprehended Willie Bias, a twenty-three-year-old white man, whom police described as a "street person." Despite his auspicious name, Bias, a young male hustler who had known Churchill and even stayed at his apartment, was not believed to have killed Churchill due to his sexual orientation.[77] "Robbery was apparently the motive for the killing," a homicide detective told the *Star Tribune*. "It had nothing to do with the victim being gay."[78] Bias's arrest cast doubt on the theory that Churchill's murder was a hate crime and weakened CUAV's suggestion of a serial killer. There was, in short, little reason to appoint a gay liaison to the police for the time being.

Notably, the fact that Bias was, like so many of the assailants attacking gay men, white still did not sway white gay leaders from an innate suspicion of Black criminality—even when evidence suggested otherwise. In the early morning hours of November 18, 1986, an anonymous tip in the killing of Phyllis Olson led to the arrest of Darryl Banks, a thirty-four-year-old Black man.[79] Capt. McCarthy explained that the tip came from someone "who knew the (suspect's) life style—that he was bisexual and prone to losing his temper."[80] Prosecutors relied heavily on a bite mark found on Olson's chest as crucial evidence against the suspect after a forensic dentist for the prosecution concluded that Banks *could* have bitten Olson. Since only weak physical evidence existed linking Banks to Olson, police focused on Banks's sexuality—"he was bisexual"—and his supposedly uncontrollable anger, which played into racialized stereotypes of Black criminality. According to this line of thinking, only someone as morally depraved as a Black man, especially a bisexual one during the AIDS epidemic (reflecting early stigmatizing portrayals of Black men "on the down low"), could have bitten his victim. Despite Banks's arrest and all the suspicion thrown upon him, he was not Olson's murderer. After spending a year in jail and less than a week before his trial was to set to begin, a Hennepin County District Court judge dismissed first-degree murder charges against Banks on October 27, 1987. DNA testing had confirmed that the blood and hair samples found at the scene did not match either Banks or Olson.[81]

Throughout Banks's ordeal, Coyle and other leaders of Minnesota's white gay community said nothing. CUAV and the Minneapolis gay community had been active—eager even—participants in helping solve other murder cases, but here, where evidence clearly refuted the suspicion against Banks, they remained strangely silent and, in so doing, gave their implicit endorsement of over-policing—especially of the racialized poor. Leaders like Coyle argued that more punitive law enforcement was necessary to stop the string of murders. Policing, in other words, could be a common good, and in this belief, Coyle was far from alone. Sodomy repeal and marriage would dominate the headlines in later decades, but if there was a moment that signaled gay Minnesota's embrace of homonormative, neoliberal ideals, its failure to confront policing or challenge the narrative of the Gary Syndrome in a serious, critical manner was it.

Lessons Not Learned

When Rep. John Conyers (D-MI) gaveled in the House Judiciary Subcommittee on Criminal Justice's historic hearings on antigay violence in October 1986, the mood of the nation's LGBTQ community was far from jubilant. Few expected immediate change, and they would be right. Despite the committee's ringing endorsement, it would take another four years before

President George H. W. Bush signed the Hate Crimes Statistics Act of 1990, mandating the attorney general to collect data on crimes committed because of the victim's race, religion, disability, sexual orientation, or ethnicity. This law marked the first time a federal statute explicitly recognized and named gay men and lesbians—though it did not include transgender people.

As the hearings commenced, Fred Riga's and Phyllis Olson's murderers were still at large (they remain so to this day), and the Minneapolis Police Department still had no special gay liaison—let alone a concerted program to hire openly gay and lesbian officers. It was easy to despair that crime and violence against gay men and lesbians would continue unchecked, but the future would be far brighter in the state, especially in a state that lagged so far behind the nation regarding sodomy repeal. Unexpectedly, Coyle and CUAV's embrace of expanded and more punitive policing—even while police leadership initially gave them the cold shoulder—was, by 1987, already beginning to pay off. By demonstrating their sympathy and willingness to ally with the department as an institution and work side by side with officers, they laid the groundwork for convincing public officials, police leaders, and ordinary officers that gay men and lesbians were "insiders" of the social fabric of the Midwest.

In February 1988, the Governor's Task Force on Prejudice and Violence released a scathing report that confirmed what gay activists had long maintained: Bias-motivated crime was on the rise. Of the 770 incidents of prejudice-driven crime, harassment, and violence documented by the task force since 1970, 22 percent was due to sexual orientation and 31 percent to race.[82] Previous attempts to pass an "anti-terrorism" law in 1981 and 1983, which would have increased penalties for crimes motivated by a person's race, color, religion, sex, sexual orientation, or national origin, had stalled because opponents cited a lack of need given no documentation.[83] But after more than thirty-six hours of testimony from 150 Minnesotans and nearly 1,300 pages of evidence, it became clear that marginalized groups, including people of color and LGBTQ individuals, were living in what the state's Human Rights Commissioner described as a "climate of hate."[84]

In April 1988, partly in response to the task force's findings, the state legislature passed H.F. No. 2340, authored by openly lesbian State Rep. Karen Clark. The law, for the first time, required police officers to track and report incidents motivated by bias.[85] The following year, Minnesota took further action by passing H.F. No 700, which classified bias-motivated crimes as gross misdemeanors, punishable by up to a year in prison, a $3,000 fine, or both.[86] State Sen. Linda Berglin, who authored the bill, argued before the Senate Judiciary Committee that increasing penalties for prejudice-driven assaults "has a substantial effect on deterring hate crimes."[87] With these legislative gains, some gay men and lesbians finally now enjoyed a degree of state protection.

These legislative gains, which represented a level of LGBTQ acceptance within the socially moderate framework of Minnesota Nice, amounted to a triumph for accommodationist politics. This success, however, came with a cost. Although white gay men might not have been the primary advocates of the Gary Syndrome, they certainly subscribed to it and leveraged it for greater police and state protection. One could reasonably argue that gay activists were compelled to form alliances with law enforcement and that the broader heterosexual mainstream imposed homonormativity as the price of acceptance. Although that may be partly true, it seems more likely that some members of CUAV, like Coyle, Spear, and even Campbell, did not accept these terms reluctantly. That is, homonormativity was not something foisted upon them; they gravitated toward it on their own. For some of these gay men, gaining acceptance from white, mainstream society was more important than affirming their gay identity. Such an investment would continue to influence their actions as gay leaders, including their responses to reports involving noncompliant HIV-positive sex workers of color.

4 The Carrier as Criminal

The Human Weapon

He looked thin but not weak, seated on a chair, facing his interviewer with the camera just off to the side capturing his profile. His face seemed tough, and the defiant—even angry—look on it masked his fatigue. The Minnesota TV crew from WCCO had been following Fabian Bridges for over a week now and had come to the crux of their interview, the moment that would capture a nation's attention. After Bridges, a thirty-year-old HIV-positive Black gay man, reportedly admitted to filmmakers to engaging in unprotected sex, the interviewer asked him on camera, "If you know how dreadful the disease is, how could you go ahead and take the chance that you might give it to somebody?" Bridges paused. He stared into the camera and softly murmured: "I don't know . . . I just guess I'm to the point where I just don't give a damn, you know? I really don't."

Lost in this interview were the ways that the period's racist neoliberal policies—cuts in public services, including housing and health care—had actively cheated Bridges and then ignored him in his hour of need. Rather, in place of facts came fictions that Bridges was a prostitute, cruelly indifferent to the suffering he spread. In late September 1985, a flurry of newspaper and television accounts throughout the country reported on Bridges as a "transient" who willingly had sex with others despite knowing he had AIDS. *Time* magazine called him a "pitiful nomad."[1] The *Los Angeles Times* described him as an "awful, awful person," a "miserable, wretched, uncaring victim-turned-victimizer who used his body as a lethal weapon."[2] Meanwhile, the *Wall Street Journal* disparaged Bridges as a "gloomy, remote, acne-scarred stranger" who came across as "pathetic rather than threatening—a scruffy little plague ship adrift in the lower depths."[3] These portrayals, often fixating on his physical appearance to underscore his alleged monstrosity, reinforced harmful historical narratives that conflated sex workers with crime and disease—though Bridges was neither a criminal nor a sex worker.[4]

While vigilante assailants held white gay men as responsible for the spread of AIDS and targeted them for individual acts of private, criminal violence, Black figures became the target for institutional, legal acts of punitive violence. Sex workers—both those who made a career of it and those who entered it episodically—spanned the spectrum of racial, gender, and sexual orientation in the upper Midwest, but despite this diversity, only Black sex workers became emblematic of the "noncompliant" and "recalcitrant" infected individual who threatened the health and stability of Minnesota by "recklessly" or, at worst, "knowingly" having sex with white married men. The Gary Syndrome, apparently, posed a problem for public health departments as much as it did for police departments. Originating from a racialized antiwelfare discourse prevalent in local media, the Gary Syndrome attributed rising crime to "outsiders," including migrants, refugees, and the racialized poor, and proposed a robust law enforcement apparatus as a solution to the perceived problem. In the same way that white criminals attacking gay men could be excused for succumbing to "gay panic" but Black crime in largely white Minnesota was an inevitable outcome of a culture of poverty and broken families, so too could white sex workers be excused for their career and any infections they might have caused—they simply needed treatment and help—but Black sex workers were inherently, irredeemably irresponsible and indifferent and had to be forced into doing what was right.

Whereas the neoliberal spatial fix for respectable, middle-class (and generally white) gay men in Minnesota who were vulnerable to violence consisted of the choice to retire to the secure, intimate, and ultimately safe private home for sex—a positive quarantining and removal of sexuality from the public sphere—when it came to sex workers whom officials defined as unruly and recalcitrant because of their race, quarantining was not voluntary but mandated. Because sex workers could not afford to—or, as officials often alleged, *chose* not to—stop their profession and act in the service of the public good, they fell outside the ambiguous but very real boundaries of Minnesota Nice. They became viral versions of the racialized criminals of the Gary Syndrome—elements subject to control rather than potential partners in cooperation—and were subjected to punitive-oriented solutions.[5] As neoliberal spatial fixes, "penality" and "privacy" were not opposites. They were neither antagonistic nor fundamentally separate. Instead, they were two points on a biopolitical spectrum that wrapped around into a coherent whole, resembling Gayle Rubin's concept of the "charmed circle."[6]

The criminalization of disease transmission—previously not considered a crime—solidified the carceral intent of the neoliberal state, a practice Trevor Hoppe describes as "punitive disease control."[7] In Minnesota, this dynamic manifested in the fusion of the Gary Syndrome and the AIDS epidemic. Through inflammatory news accounts of Black sex workers as contagious and irresponsible, the mainstream media pressured public health officials and law enforcement authorities to abandon the civil liberties of sex workers in favor of protecting the public good. Nationwide, municipalities and states implemented a range of strict measures designed to banish, constrain, and discipline individuals who knew they had HIV yet continued to engage in specific behaviors, usually sexual activity, without first disclosing their seropositive status. But, like the Gary Syndrome, HIV criminalization indexed exaggerated white fears of injury—in this case, concerns over immunological safety—as grounds for carceral cures to social ills. As the Reagan administration slashed welfare supports in the 1980s, it lavished funds on broken windows policing, diverting resources away from redistributive liberal policies toward carceral solutions.[8] HIV criminalization, therefore, revealed at once both new modes of austerity and privatization around health services and the state's enduring reliance on incarceration as its primary method for managing what Karl Marx termed "surplus populations"—the unemployed and underemployed in capitalist societies.[9]

Although mass incarceration in the United States is often attributed to the post–civil rights movement and post-Keynesian period of the 1970s, imprisonment has long defined the state's treatment of Black bodies from chattel enslavement to the convict lease system. The 1970s witnessed an intensification of that incarceration but with the added deployment of colorblind "law and order" rhetoric.[10] Ruth Wilson Gilmore, in her analysis of California's post-Keynesian state-building project, argues that the upsurge in US incarceration rates since the late 1970s reflects less an actual increase in crime than a particular neoliberal response—a "spatial fix"—to surplus populations. In California, the state metabolized the economic and social changes of the 1960s by erecting scores of prisons, manufactured out of the capital, labor, and land surplus that a newly consolidated postindustrial political economy could not assimilate. To justify the systemic warehousing of "disposable" populations, the US government at all levels launched a series of wars on crime, drugs, and poverty—wars that dovetailed with and amplified the state's punitive response to HIV transmission.[11]

Through analyses of media, state, and gay community responses to "noncompliant" Black people with AIDS, including Fabian Bridges, the Black gay protagonist of a special AIDS-themed episode of the Public Broadcasting Service's (PBS) documentary series *Frontline*, this chapter examines HIV criminalization—its strategies of quarantine and incarceration—as a neoliberal spatial fix confronted by Black sex workers. The moral panic associated with AIDS fulfilled racial and political objectives, as the state exploited fears of non-white sexual transmission to justify managing the racialized poor less through welfare and public assistance, and more through surveillance and mass incarceration. This public health construction of Blackness as injurious to the white body politic facilitated the metamorphosis of, typically, white gay men from a viral menace to a protected class. Other groups learned the same lesson. The Black press, hoping to quarantine parts of the Black community that might drag it down, also reified a dichotomy of "innocent" and "guilty" carriers of HIV in hopes of avoiding the stigma of disease applied to gay men and intravenous drug users.

Panic and Quarantine

Black rates of HIV infection outstripped their proportion of the population, but this fact hardly explains their overwhelming presence in media accounts of HIV noncompliant sex work. When even reputable news organizations investigated the risk sex workers posed to the spread of HIV, they often highlighted Black faces as much as, if not more than, white ones. Certainly, the most flagrant examples involved Black individuals. In the winter of 1987, Tyrone Matthews, a twenty-eight-year-old Black man, alarmed the residents of Jackson, Mississippi, with the news that he was a "homosexual prostitute" with AIDS who actively engaged in sex with married, heterosexual men.[12] The *New York Times* underscored that on the night of his arrest, Matthews was with a well-known, "married, white, gray-haired and overweight" businessman. The reporter noted that Matthews had been arrested over sixty times for street prostitution, with a "diverse" clientele that included "married and single men, black and white men, young and old."[13] After a grand jury declined to indict Matthews on felony sodomy charges, a Mississippi epidemiologist issued a quarantine order requiring Matthews to disclose his HIV-positive status before engaging in sex.[14] Although female sex workers with AIDS had faced similar restrictions in California, Florida, and Nevada, the Mississippi quarantine order against Matthews was one of the first imposed on a male sex worker. It would not be the last.

By the time Bridges's interview aired in 1986, America saw Black bodies as disobedient and justifiably—even necessarily—subject to penal solutions to secure behavior that benefited a white embodiment of "the public." Regulation, in that year, was, politically speaking, a dirty word, but not when it came to the behavior of profit-seeking actors outside or transgressive to legal markets.[15] These actors, who were of markets but not legally allowed into markets, became defined through the popular press as figures of angst and terror. When major news outlets covered AIDS in relation to sex work, they often invoked racist tropes of Black sex workers as sexual predators threatening "innocent" white victims. These narratives, in turn, accomplished the important ideological work needed to garner support for invasive and draconian disease control mechanisms. As with past moral panics, the popular press stood behind it all.[16] In the 1980s, the dominant news media—in concert with conservative forces—repeatedly stoked the public's racial and sexual anxieties to cultivate an AIDS moral panic.[17] These sensationalist stories affirmed the public's suspicion of not only the deviance of sexual minorities and communities of color but also their desperate need for policing.

It was not always like this, for in the early years of the epidemic, commercial news outlets construed AIDS as an affliction of white gay men.[18] The federal government's deafening silence as the epidemic leeched into all corners of society created an information vacuum that the mainstream media readily exploited. In May 1982, the *New York Times* published its first mention of GRID (gay-related immunodeficiency) to describe the epidemic, reinforcing the public impression that the disease mainly affected gay men.[19] A month later, Tom Brokaw, the anchor for *NBC Nightly News*, reported on the crisis by stating that "the lifestyles of some male homosexuals has triggered an epidemic of a rare form of cancer." However, it soon became apparent that HIV *could* pose a threat to the general population when, in January 1983, the CDC identified AIDS in the female partners of men who had the disease.[20] Thereafter, the mainstream media expanded its coverage of the crisis.[21] Major US newspapers and magazines published cover stories on the imminent danger the virus posed not to major risk groups, such as gay or bisexual men and intravenous drug users, but to white, heterosexual, middle-class, suburban Americans. In effect, news editors and journalists framed the former as the cause of AIDS and the latter as its victims. The most blameless of these lamentable victims were, according to Douglas Crimp, white, middle-class, hemophiliac children, depicted as "so innocent that they [could] even be shown comforted, hugged, and played with."[22] In contrast, in the entirety of the *Frontline* episode, not a single person ever touched Bridges, and he wore the weight of that isolation on him like a garment of shame. But these children, the newspaper editors and TV producers decided, deserved to be shown surrounded and protected because, after all, they had contracted HIV through no fault of their own.

There were many of these white children beginning in 1984 who captured the public's eye and sympathy—like Dwight Burk from Crescent, Pennsylvania, the first child born with AIDS to a person with hemophilia, and the Ray brothers, Ricky, Robert, and Randy, who contracted HIV in 1986 from blood transfusions and were later targeted by arsonists. But the most well-known was Ryan White, a teenager from Kokomo, Indiana, diagnosed with HIV in 1984 following a blood transfusion.[23] His school's demand that he not attend drew national attention like no other HIV positive person had before. Celebrities like Elton John rushed to his support, and politicians listened when he testified before the President's Commission on the HIV Epidemic. White died in April 1990, months before Congress passed the Ryan White Comprehensive AIDS Resources Emergency (CARE) Act, the largest federally funded program providing care and treatment for low-income people living with HIV/AIDS. It was no coincidence that White personified the bipartisan, national response to the AIDS epidemic because his name fittingly described the kind of person with HIV/AIDS for whom the public could feel unqualified sympathy.

The pervasive images of white children with hemophilia gravely distorted who encountered the virus. A 1987 study by the Center for Media and Public Affairs found that television depictions of people with AIDS showed heterosexuals eight times more often than gay or bisexual men, even though there were roughly eight times more gay or bisexual men with AIDS than heterosexuals.[24] Not only were heterosexuals overrepresented, but they were also consistently depicted as white and middle-class despite AIDS among heterosexuals being disproportionately concentrated among Black and Latinx individuals. Between 1981 and 1986, while Black and Latinx people accounted for 25 percent and 14 percent of the 24,576 reported AIDS cases, respectively, they represented 50 percent and 25 percent of heterosexual cases.[25] Nonetheless, through stories of helpless, white, heterosexual victims—particularly women and children—news media stoked the flames of white injury, fanning outsize fears of white heterosexual transmission. Out of this alarm arose what Susan Faludi, writing in the context of the post-9/11 era, describes as the guardian myth, a media-generated moral panic that white civilization had to be wrestled away from racial and sexual savagery.[26] In this construct, who deserved protection came down to notions of sexual fragility while who should provide protection came down to patriarchal notions of responsibility.[27] Because dominant news media cast white women and children as the privileged subjects of community outrage, white, heterosexual men became the default protectors. Even when the sexual contacts of white married men ostensibly endangered white women or children, news outlets downplayed their role as potential vectors of transmission in favor of outrage against sex workers. As Melinda Chateauvert notes, white women and children, playing on gendered racial differences, inspired political action in ways that gay men, intravenous drug users, and even Black women and children did not.[28]

Ryan White may have been the most socially and politically acceptable face of AIDS, but when it came to women and children with the disease, the reality was that they were disproportionately Black. In October 1986, the CDC reported that Black women accounted for 51 percent of the then-1,634 cases of AIDS among women at the time. Among the 304 cases of AIDS among children, 58 percent were Black. A staggering 90 percent of children with perinatally acquired AIDS were either Black or Latinx.[29] Reagan's America, of course, did not want a Black victim. Notably, the Black community and Black news sources also wanted to avoid AIDS having a Black face. At least until Earvin "Magic" Johnson's 1991 announcement of his HIV status, Black media outlets reinforced a binary between "innocent" victims and "guilty" disease carriers. As Cathy J. Cohen shows, Black publications like *Jet* and *Essence* portrayed AIDS as affecting middle-class, heterosexual Black women who courageously told their stories—about either their own struggles with the virus or those of friends or family members.[30] The Black press opted for this angle to counter a larger media narrative depicting AIDS as a stigmatized illness and, thus, protect against the further demonization of Black people, in a process Cohen calls "secondary marginalization."[31] But in so doing, the Black press centered its coverage on a particular cohort of community members that Black readers and officials deemed more sympathetic: Black women and children. That the impact of AIDS on Black women largely focused on women of child-bearing age suggests that the Black press perceived HIV as a threat to the role of Black women as custodians of future generations.[32] Even as the Black press emphasized aspects of AIDS that differed from mainstream narratives—highlighting the positive attributes of Black communities—it still propagated moralistic understandings of the disease and sidelined Black gay and bisexual men as well as Black intravenous drug users, who comprised most of the people with HIV/AIDS in Black communities.[33] If, however, the Black press cordoned off some part of its community as "innocent"—which implicitly meant that others were morally and sexually irresponsible—then perhaps that small faction could still engender sympathy and maybe even some of the few resources that might arise to help battle or at least offset the worst aspects of the disease. From a distance, the gay press employed the same narrative and applied it to a select group within its community: middle-class white gay men.

Concerns about sex workers spreading HIV arose nationwide, with some cases, particularly those reinforcing public racial biases, receiving more attention than others. The high-profile case of Tyrone Matthews was not an isolated instance of public health officials working with law enforcement to regulate the movement of sex workers; instead, it confirmed a disturbing trend toward a more punitive approach to disease control.[34] The media played its part by portraying sex workers as especially dangerous due to their perceived lack of basic knowledge about the virus. In a newspaper interview, Matthews, "wrapped in an old fur coat as he sat on his dank mattress in the Jackson City Jail," disputed the charges against him and questioned his AIDS diagnosis, pondering: "I've been told that I have the AIDS virus . . . But I don't feel like I have anything."[35] The *New York Times* concluded that Matthews did "not seem to understand the implications of the virus he carried or the need to avoid sexual contact with others."[36]

The newfound relationship between public health and law enforcement manifested in the high-profile case of Brenda Williams, a precariously housed twenty-eight-year-old Black woman in Minneapolis with a history of drug abuse and prostitution arrests.[37] Williams's arrest in the spring of 1986 made the local news only after the MPD, as it had with the slain Indigenous transgender woman Phyllis Olson, leaked to the *Star Tribune* that Williams had tested positive for HIV three months prior. Concerned about her presumed public health risk, the judge set her bail at $3,000—three times the amount prosecutors had requested. Hoping to deter future customers and notify previous ones, the judge ordered the release Williams's photograph to the local press. The *Star Tribune* went further. It published her home address. As shocking as this tactic might seem, news outlets, including respected ones like the *New York Times* and *The Advocate*, routinely published the names, mug shots, and home addresses of accused noncompliant HIV-positive people, particularly of Black people. With Williams, the practice had arrived in Minnesota.[38] In a place where modesty and not standing out—for either good or bad—were hallmarks of fitting in, her defamation in the paper marked her as an outsider fit for vilification.

As part of Williams's conditional plea, authorities issued a restraining order requiring her to provide the Minnesota Department of Health (MDH) with the names of anyone she might have put at risk.³⁹ But in a subsequent court memorandum, the MDH alleged that despite Williams's agreement to cooperate with health officials, undergo HIV transmission counseling, and avoid behaviors that could expose others to HIV, she "has done absolutely nothing to evidence a scintilla of awareness of her potential health threat."⁴⁰ The MDH diminished and degraded her intellect, dehumanizing Williams as a brute. Law and legal authorities, meanwhile, portrayed her as a savage on the prowl, a characterization that subsequently justified the application of punitive measures. When the MPD initially released Williams from prison, the head of the vice squad, Lt. Lyle Goodspeed, informed the *Star Tribune*, "I don't think she'll be on the street" but assured readers that the police would be "watching her closely."⁴¹ In the fall of 1987, after Williams was evicted from her south Minneapolis apartment and subsequently rearrested, a prosecutor told the *Tribune* that Williams differed from the average prostitution misdemeanor case: "It is akin to someone walking down the streets carrying a bomb."⁴² To law enforcement and the courts, Williams was like a downed power line, dangerous and unpredictable. She was drug-addicted and, because she was Black, sexually licentious. These characteristics were enough for the authorities to explain her behavior. In the eyes of the criminal justice system, she could not be reasoned with or rehabilitated, only confined. This stigmatizing language often accompanied language that over-sympathized with the potential victims of noncompliant HIV-carriers. When, a few months after her spring 1989 release from prison, Williams relapsed, an MPD deputy chief told the *Tribune*: "She is committing an act of violence as surely as if she took a gun and shot someone . . . She is not only knowingly infecting her customers, but wives and girlfriends and untold other *innocent* victims."⁴³ That Williams was rendered a feral beast—a monstrosity, even—without a voice of her own (she is never quoted in any news article) sanctioned her confinement and foreclosed any collective sympathy from the public.

While dominant news sources depicted Black and Latinx women as "guilty, irresponsible, and drug-addicted" pariahs, white women remained innocent victims of HIV transmission, often through blood transfusions.⁴⁴ Most famously, HIV-positive white women were represented by figures like Elizabeth Glaser, the wife of actor and director Paul Glaser and a cofounder of the Pediatric AIDS Foundation in 1988, and Mary Fischer, who spoke at the 1992 Republican National Convention. Even at the local level in Minnesota, white women with similar narratives emerged as sympathetic. In the summer of 1991, after Williams was rearrested for loitering with the intent to commit prostitution, the *Star Tribune* published a lengthy story on Nancy Simon, a twenty-seven-year-old, middle-class, white heterosexual housewife from rural Minnesota who enjoyed baking cookies when not tending to her three children.[45] Simon embodied the image of a stereotypical stay-at-home mom were it not that she was also HIV-positive. Like Glaser and Fisher, she contracted the virus through no fault of her own—her high school sweetheart husband, who had been exposed in 1983 through a blood transfusion while serving in the military, unknowingly infected her.[46] The *Tribune* emphasized the tragedy of Simon's story when it revealed that their four-year-old daughter had been born with the virus. It also underscored Simon's distinctiveness among AIDS cases: She was a woman, heterosexual, and from a small town, contrasting with the 85 percent of AIDS cases in the state being gay or bisexual men, with the disease largely concentrated in urban areas.[47] Simon's identity, in short, suggested she was *not* supposed to have acquired HIV. The *Tribune* argued as much when it stated that Simon and her husband felt "robbed"—he because his "only 'risky' behavior was having a blood transfusion. Nancy's 'risky' behavior was making love with her husband, and [her daughter's] was being born." Because white heterosexual Minnesotans could identify and sympathize with Simon and her family, high schools and churches throughout small-town Minnesota welcomed her as a speaker. The family was even invited to speak at the first National Children with AIDS Awareness Day in Washington, DC.[48]

Meanwhile, after Williams's rearrest for prostitution in the summer of 1991, the Minneapolis Deputy City Attorney assured the public that the city would keep her off the streets "as long as we can," implying the use of vagrancy-like measures that criminalized a person's "status" rather than their "conduct." Although Williams's public defender argued that she had committed no crime, was no longer involved in sex work, and was only being hounded by the police and news media, the *Tribune* once again published Williams's photo and place of residence.[49] For women of color with AIDS like Williams, they could never warrant generosity or sympathy, but rather, like their "close cousin," the mythical "welfare queen," they needed to be checked and policed lest they threaten the social fabric and economic well-being of Minnesota.[50]

Unspoken but lurking behind the spread of HIV among women of color, the "sexualized drug economy" haunted women like Williams.[51] Mood-altering substances anesthetized people from their trauma and offered an escape from people's everyday suffering, particularly as people faced the economic shift from manufacturing to low-wage service jobs and the erosion of the social safety net. For some women of color and working-class women, sex work in the informal labor market became, in part, a means to obtain drugs—reflecting the structural conditions that contributed to their disproportionate vulnerability to HIV/AIDS. While Minneapolis authorities could have easily responded with rehabilitation for Williams's narcotics addiction, they instead responded with incarceration, increasing the likelihood of Williams's recidivism, especially when her basic human needs, like shelter, went unmet. From the onset of the drug epidemic in the Twin Cities, like in most of urban America, American politicians, news media, and law enforcement consistently treated drug abuse as a criminal justice problem—not a medical one.

To the degree HIV transmission in the Black community was a medical issue, most health providers viewed it as beyond their control. Of course, Black people were more susceptible to HIV/AIDS for several reasons—not the least of which included the ongoing "structural vulnerabilities" of racism and economic impoverishment—but health officials largely ignored this dynamic and focused instead on alleged behaviors.[52] In a 1987 interview, Minnesota's chief state epidemiologist, Dr. Michael Osterholm, attributed the "relatively high rates" of sexually transmitted diseases (STDs) among Black people in the Twin Cities to having multiple sexual partners, which, he argued, increased their likelihood of acquiring HIV. The "high rate of out-of-wedlock births among blacks" reflected the early and frequent sex Black Minnesotans allegedly had—behavior that elevated their STD risk.[53] The following year, Osterholm clarified that while being Black was not a risk factor in itself, sexual promiscuity and drug abuse were "relatively common" behaviors among inner-city poor Black people.[54] Unlike the depiction of white women and children as sexually innocent and in need of protection by men and the state, Black women and children were not afforded the same narrative. Instead, they were frequently portrayed as hypersexual—engaging in sex at a younger age, having multiple partners, or smoking crack. Medicine, though presumed to be impartial and free of rank biases, often reinforced these stigmatizing images and helped justify the punishment of marginalized groups. Similar to how criminologists implicitly constructed notions of "innocent" white suburban victims of Black crime and violence under the Gary Syndrome, medical professionals too conjured images of innocent white victims but this time of Black sexuality and disease.

White sex workers came under scrutiny as a vector of disease, but compared with the dehumanization, ridicule, and confinement Black sex workers like Brenda Williams confronted, the media, health professionals, and law enforcement treated them with far more charitable generosity—even when their sexual contacts, as in the case of Scott Reynolds, were much greater.[55] In 1986, Reynolds, a twenty-nine-year-old white gay man living with HIV in Minneapolis, ignited a public health frenzy when he informed WCCO-TV, the CBS affiliate in Minneapolis, that he had engaged in unprotected sex with as many as a thousand married heterosexual clients while working for Minneapolis Men, a local escort agency, from 1979 to 1986. Many of these clients were from the Twin Cities suburbs, with some being traveling businessmen. Minneapolis Men, one of the two male escort services in the area, employed about eight to ten men, advertised locally in *City Pages* and nationally in *The Advocate*, and served approximately three hundred to five hundred regular customers.[56] Reynolds's revelations sparked as much panic as Williams's—if not more—given the affluent background of his clientele. In the two days following the broadcast, the Red Door Clinic, Hennepin County's venereal disease clinic, received eighty-five to one hundred calls, more than double its usual volume. A clinic health worker noted, "We've had just a flood of calls," including "from women who thought their previous boyfriends may have been gay."[57] The reaction from legal and health authorities to Reynolds, however, could not have been more different from Williams's. Whereas Williams suffered demonization and imprisonment, Reynolds received an offer to enter a drug treatment program and served no prison time.[58] From the onset, Hennepin County Attorney Tom Johnson announced that his office would approach the matter as "a health issue first" because authorities desperately hoped to locate customers and their families.[59]

One reason Reynolds suffered so little for his actions is that while legal and health authorities had only a perfunctory, largely rhetorical concern for Williams's clients and their families—poorer, marginalized Minnesotans—Reynolds's clients were white, suburban, and much wealthier. At Minneapolis Men, services cost $20 per hour—when the federal minimum wage was $3.35—but customers were expected to tip generously, around $75 an hour.[60] On one New Year's Eve, Reynolds earned $1,200 in fees and tips from just four clients—equivalent to about $3,500 in 2024 dollars.[61] These affluent Minnesotans mattered, and health officials wanted to find them and warn them about the danger they faced. Reynolds's life, as such, mattered but only insofar as it helped protect the lives of those the state truly prioritized: white women and children. Williams could offer no such purpose. Moreover, as a high-end escort, Reynolds conducted outcalls to private hotels and even residential homes when his clients' families were away. Williams, much like most other Black, Indigenous, and transgender sex workers in the Twin Cities, worked on the streets, often meeting clients in cars, alleys, or parks. As Tim Campbell noted in the *GLC Voice*, the MPD primarily targeted street-based sex workers, who were disproportionately Black or Indigenous women and/ or "transvestites." White sex workers, often operating out of saunas that advertised in newspapers, rarely faced arrest, a difference Campbell criticized as racist. "Believe me," he wrote in the *GLC Voice*, "certain hookers don't work the streets because they want to, nor because they have less respect for the law than sauna hookers. They do it because the saunas won't hire them."[62]

Officials refused to rely on Reynolds's memory alone, and the morning after WCCO's interview with Reynolds, Minnesota's Commissioner of Health, Sister Mary Madonna Ashton—a Catholic nun with a strong prolife stance—held an emergency press conference. She urged "all men who may have had sexual contacts with male prostitutes" since 1977, even before Reynolds claimed to have started working as a sex worker, "to receive appropriate counseling and be tested immediately." If men tested positive, Ashton implored them to inform their wives so they could also be counseled and tested. During the press conference, Ashton failed to address sex workers as members of the public most at risk in this crisis but rather treated them as a besieging army encircling the state's vulnerable suburban families. "If we have a ring of prostitutes," Ashton warned, "and there is even one and possibly more of them who have been infecting a sizable group of bisexual and gay men in our city, there's the potential of the infection spreading to wives, to mothers, to children." Ashton, who referred to women only to the extent that they were wives or mothers, stopped short of promoting safer sex practices, refusing to address questions pertaining to the effectiveness of condoms. Ashton and state public health officials had begun to see the battle against AIDS like a war of attrition, one in which they might have to write off some groups as either hopeless—as was the case with Williams—or undeserving because of their immoral actions. That perspective became evident in 1989 when Ashton told members of ACT UP/Minnesota, "It's my job to prevent the AIDS virus from entering into the general population and starting to infect *innocent* victims."[63] Only after an outcry over the Minneapolis Men scandal became public did Minnesota's health officials implement a large-scale safer-sex campaign. Upon learning male sex workers, such as Reynolds, were potentially spreading HIV to married, heterosexual men, the MDH spent about $10,000 in April 1986 alone on an HIV campaign featured in suburban newspapers that urged readers to undergo testing.[64]

Sentencing the "Guilty"

The United States has had a long tradition of regulating and restricting the sexual behavior of both its non-white citizens and colonized populations, but whereas previous quarantines had been civil matters and carriers seldom faced criminal charges, AIDS changed this practice. The marginal status of sex workers made it all that much easier to infringe on their rights and push for criminal punishment.[65] The first moves in this direction were clumsy—targeting everyone with a positive status—and, thus, relatively ineffective, but over time they became focused and forceful. In July 1983, the Rev. Jerry Falwell, in his *Moral Majority Report*, called for quarantine, contact tracing, and mandatory testing.[66] These sentiments were clearly displayed on the accompanying cover, which featured a white family—father, mother, and two children—wearing surgical masks, with the headline "Homosexual Diseases Threaten American Families."[67] By blaming gay men and intravenous drug users for the spread of HIV, pundits played on public fears of AIDS, leading most Americans to support conservative measures. Opinion polls from 1985 and 1986 showed that between 28 and 51 percent of Americans agreed that "people with AIDS should be put into quarantine to keep them away from the general public."[68] A 1987 poll found that 68 percent of Americans favored "criminal sanctions against people with acquired immune deficiency syndrome who remain sexually active."[69] Meanwhile, a poll from 1988 revealed that 63.7 percent of Americans backed a government mandate requiring anyone with HIV to wear identification tags.[70] These beliefs extended to the upper Midwest. A 1987 statewide poll of 762 randomly selected Minnesotans found that 68 percent agreed that gay men and intravenous drug users should undergo mandatory HIV testing, while 83 percent supported quarantining HIV-positive people who engaged in "high-risk" behavior.[71] Despite such widespread support, health officials, at least in the continental United States, never enacted extreme measures like mass quarantine of HIV-positive people, opting instead for the incremental criminalization of people with HIV/AIDS.[72]

The first wave of laws criminalizing HIV in the United States unfolded in the mid- to late 1980s with Florida, Tennessee, and Washington passing such legislation in 1986. In this initial effort, state lawmakers introduced quarantine and isolation orders for persons with HIV/AIDS classified as "non-adherent" to public health ordinances. Between 1985 and 1987, nine states either amended existing quarantine laws or created new ones granting health officials the authority to isolate noncompliant individuals with HIV. The laws varied widely due to the lack of a unified approach to the epidemic. For instance, Colorado's law required up to three months of isolation, while North Carolina allowed health officials to indefinitely restrict the "freedom of movement or action" of those with communicable diseases. Other states enacted laws outright criminalizing HIV transmission. Under Alabama's law, anyone acting "in a manner likely to transmit" a sexually transmitted disease could face criminal sanctions.[73]

Minnesota's 1987 non-compliant carrier law mirrored similar measures in other states but stood out for its aggressive approach to quarantine duration. The law authorized the state health commissioner to intervene on behalf of people "who pose a health threat to others or who engage in noncompliant behavior." If a carrier of an infectious disease refused to follow a health directive, the health commissioner could pursue legal action. The courts could then mandate counseling, treatment, or periodic monitoring. But, in the law's most controversial measure, the courts could also impose civil commitment at "an appropriate institutional facility" for up to six months.[74] Opposition to the law was widespread, with groups like the Minnesota Civil Liberties Union (MCLU), the Minnesota Alliance Against AIDS, and the Minnesota Gay and Lesbian Legal Assistance voicing concerns.[75] Even health authorities harbored reservations. The Hennepin County Health Director testified that the bill would cost about $50,000 per year for each person the courts deemed to show a "careless disregard" to public health. In the era of budget cuts, the director warned that this law would consume 90 percent of AIDS resources for less than 2 percent of the population served.[76] Despite opposition from AIDS activists and gay men, openly gay State Sen. Allan Spear and openly lesbian State Rep. Karen Clark voted in favor of the bill, arguing that it provided greater due process to those accused of noncompliance.[77] In fact, among politicians, the bill commanded sweeping bipartisan support. At a subcommittee hearing, State Sen. John Brandl (DFL-Minneapolis) acknowledged the challenges posed by quarantine but emphasized the need for society to protect itself from "a handful of people who refuse to be responsible."[78] Within four months of its enactment, health authorities invoked the law on four occasions.[79]

When it came to the risk of spreading HIV, lawmakers could be punitive—although supporters implied that only gay men and intravenous drug users would confront these laws and not the "general public." However, when it came to sex workers—"prostitutes" in most legislative discussions—lawmakers could be draconian. In 1985, Nevada set a significant precedent by becoming the first state to mandate HIV testing for an estimated 400 legal brothel workers. Under this policy, if sex workers tested positive yet continued working, they could be charged with attempted murder.[80] (Three years later, the Nevada Board of Health further escalated this approach by approving a policy that alerted the media whenever a sex worker in one of the state's thirty-five legal brothels tested positive for HIV.[81]) By 1988, at least thirteen states had passed laws requiring HIV testing for convicted sex workers. In Colorado, even the suspicion of sex work could trigger mandatory testing. Police there would test anyone charged with solicitation, regardless of whether a trial or conviction had taken place.[82] In 1989, California introduced a law stipulating that if a sex worker with HIV/AIDS were arrested for prostitution while on probation, they could be charged with a felony and face a harsh prison sentence.[83] The federal government also supported stricter measures, as shown in the 1988 report by President Reagan's Presidential Commission on the HIV Epidemic, which called for criminal sanctions against anyone whose behavior might transmit HIV. The Ryan White CARE Act of 1990 further tied federal funding to the prosecution of the "intentional transmission of HIV."[84]

AIDS activists were well aware of whom these laws targeted. The US PROStitutes Collective (US PROS), a multiracial network of female sex workers, argued that using prostitution laws to curb the spread of HIV falsely shifted the blame onto sex workers.[85] Nan D. Hunter, head of the American Civil Liberties Union's AIDS Projects, agreed, characterizing these laws as "a setup for selective enforcement against prostitutes and people of color."[86] The disparities in enforcement seen in Minneapolis with Brenda Williams and Scott Reynolds reflected a pattern that would be repeated across the country. These laws could only remain popular and in effect because middle- and upper-class white communities felt insulated from their impact, believing they only applied to the "guilty."

The last chance for a reasonable voice to counter this wave of harsh measures rested with the medical establishment. Had health authorities come out strongly against these laws, it would have weakened public support for them, but in 1985, the same year Nevada sought to charge sex workers with attempted murder, medical experts grappled with their own moral panic. An explosive report from Walter Reed Army Medical Center revealed that more than 1 percent of 279 soldiers tested at Fort Bragg, North Carolina, in 1984 had contracted HIV from sex workers in the United States and Europe.[87] The shocking report offered evidence of the spread of HIV from women to men through sexual contact, which had rarely been documented in the United States. In 1985, of the more than 14,000 reported HIV cases, only sixteen had been attributed to men infected through intercourse with women.[88] (What went unreported, or discreetly ignored, was the likelihood that some soldiers who tested positive may have been concealing homosexual intercourse or drug use, since these behaviors could lead to dishonorable discharge.)

Despite most health authorities assuring the public that HIV could not be transmitted through casual contact, some medical experts began promoting a hypothesis that framed sex workers as a "bridging" population. According to this view, sex workers could spread the virus from the dangerous, infected "urban" world to the otherwise safe, "innocent" world of the American heartland. Medical authorities cited studies that found high levels of HIV among female sex workers and their heterosexual clients in several central and eastern African countries as evidence that HIV could potentially become widespread in the American heterosexual population.[89] In 1985, following the release of ELISA, the first commercial HIV test, the *Star Tribune* reported that four Twin Cities sex workers voluntarily underwent HIV testing. According to the chief of the venereal disease program at the MDH, the women "were all concerned about the risk and they wanted to know what their status was." Although no HIV-positive sex workers had been identified in Minnesota at that time, the chief warned that it was "only a matter of time" before positive test results would appear among people engaged in prostitution.[90]

This fear of an influx of HIV-positive sex workers was heightened by the racial undertones embedded in the bridging hypothesis. Dr. Mathilde Krim, a renowned immunologist and cofounder of the American Foundation for AIDS Research (amfAR), voiced a prophetic concern in a 1985 interview with Randy Shilts, warning that heterosexual transmission would be the next phase of the AIDS epidemic. She expressed alarm over the national implication of AIDS among female sex workers, stating: "In my opinion, it is out already. Think of all the salesmen who come to spend a weekend [in New York City] and go back to Cincinnati to their wives and families. It's scary."[91] Without directly addressing race, Krim's words carried a racial subtext, framing AIDS as an "urban" disease spreading from city to suburb or rural town—never the reverse. This dichotomy echoed the anxieties tied to the Gary Syndrome, but with an epidemiological twist. It also placed the onus of responsibility on urban sex workers, not those (presumably white) "salesmen" from Cincinnati. Thus, for Krim, sex workers were not just killing their clients, they were also endangering the lives of innocent wives and children, in a similar fashion to how Minneapolis authorities spoke of Brenda Williams. Krim's explicit reference to "salesmen" also hinted at concerns about the economic risks posed by sex workers of color, positioning them as threats not only to the nation's physical health but also to its economic stability.

Medical professionals indulged in this panic despite the minimal risk of HIV transmission from female sex workers to heterosexual clients. In 1986, Dr. William W. Darrow of the CDC oversaw the then-largest study of AIDS among female sex workers in the country. The data, collected from 835 participants across seven cities, showed that only 98 women—roughly 12 percent—had tested positive for HIV. The study highlighted two key findings: female sex workers were more likely to contract HIV through intravenous drug use than sexual activity, and they were more at risk of acquiring HIV than transmitting it.[92] In short, unless they shared needles with clients, female sex workers rarely spread HIV. Two additional studies in New York City found only three potential cases of HIV transmission from female sex workers to male clients out of 627 cases reviewed.[93] Despite these studies, the CDC's preliminary findings, published in the March 27, 1987, edition of the *Morbidity and Mortality Weekly Report*, echoed the Reagan administration's stance on HIV criminalization, calling for not only "counseling and HIV-testing programs" but also "additional control measures by local public health and law enforcement agencies."[94]

Male sex workers, on the other hand, garnered far less attention from researchers. In 1989, a team from Georgia State University published a study on male sex workers recruited from Atlanta's taverns, parks, and streets. The survey revealed that 27 percent of the 152 participants were HIV-positive, with the primary risk factor being the number of years they had engaged in sex work.[95] A later study conducted between 1988 and 1989 on fifty-six young male sex workers in New Orleans found a similar HIV rate of 23.4 percent.[96] Although higher than the national average for female sex workers in the CDC study, these figures were still much lower than the wildly high rates of infection among male sex workers as reported in popular news outlets, which, while never offering any evidence, implied that most if not all were carriers.[97]

The fixation on sex workers as a bridging population overshadowed their proactive efforts to reduce risks. As early as 1985, Rebecca Rand, a former sex worker turned prominent Minneapolis activist, recognized how HIV had led local sex workers to reassess their work practices. "Women of my acquaintance are concerned about it," Rand said. "We read the news reports and the national press. Many have made a decision to refuse service to known or obvious users of intravenous drugs." Rand's comments indicate that female sex workers understood modes of transmission and wanted more safer-sex information. Priscilla Alexander, education coordinator for COYOTE (Call Off Your Old Tired Ethics), a national sex worker advocacy group, confirmed to the *Star Tribune* that sex workers were "requiring customers to use condoms and they are turning down customers who won't."[98] Through stories like those of Brenda Williams, Minnesota health officials and the media promoted an image of female sex workers as an attacking force needing to be held back, but in truth these women were already some of the best defenders of the public's health and should have been embraced as allies. If they served as a "bridge," it was one through which education and intervention could have been disseminated to partners, friends, and the broader community.

The criminalization of HIV represented the illogical but nearly unavoidable extension of the Gary Syndrome, adding dangerous sexuality to the latter's toxic narrative of race, crime, and drug abuse. In this expanded narrative, criminal sexuality became a "gun" or a "bomb"—in short, a biological weapon with which to terrorize law-abiding citizens. Even after science debunked these fears, Minnesotans remained gripped by them. Only a thin line separated quarantine and imprisonment, and both served as another manifestation of a neoliberal spatial fix. A twisted, obligatory version of "privacy," imprisonment sanctioned the removal and confinement from the public sphere of those bodies marked as guilty—namely, Black sex workers. The media images of Fabian Bridges—drawing on a long history of linking crime, drug abuse, and dangerous sexuality with young Black men—resonated deeply with the public, even among white gay men, reinforcing the trend toward turning HIV transmission into a crime.

The Victim as the Villain

Race, crime, and prostitution all came together in the story of Fabian Bridges—even though he was no prostitute or criminal. He was Black and HIV-positive, and in Reagan's America that alone amounted to condemnation. That reality, how disease and institutions failed Bridges, never made it into the infamous *Frontline* episode, which, instead, standardized the myth of the dangerous, uncontrolled sex worker for a national audience and conferred upon America a face to fear.

FIGURE 4.1 Fabian Bridges featured in the PBS *Frontline* episode "AIDS: A National Inquiry," which aired nationwide on March 25, 1986.

Ironically, WCCO-TV, the CBS affiliate in Minneapolis, had not set out to tell Bridges's story. In a planned story about the epidemic's impact, WCCO-TV, in partnership with PBS, searched for subjects to feature in a special episode of the documentary series *Frontline* and came across Bridges. Penniless, hungry, and dying of AIDS, Bridges was determined by producers to be worthy of his own episode (fig. 4.1). As one of the first primetime productions on the US AIDS epidemic, the 1986 *Frontline* episode, titled "AIDS: A National Inquiry," followed the last, lonely months of Bridges as he wandered from city to city in an unsuccessful attempt to secure shelter and support. A resident of Houston, Bridges had earned a respectable salary as a county employee until disease disabled him. In April 1985, doctors diagnosed Bridges with several AIDS-related opportunistic infections. They expected him to die, but he survived, and after three months of in-patient treatment, Bridges was no longer sick enough to stay. While that might seem like welcome news, Bridges's treatment had cost him his job, his savings, and his home. The only shelter he had, the hospital, now wanted him out, and in an ethically dubious—though not uncommon—move, hospital officials lured him away with a one-way plane ticket to Indianapolis, where Bridges's sisters lived. There, matters did not improve. Bridges's sisters refused to take him in as their husbands feared HIV transmission through casual contact. Bridges's brother-in-law admitted on camera that he feared for his young son: "He doesn't know what AIDS is. He doesn't know what homosexuality is. He's . . . he's innocent."[99] Mainstream media had long portrayed innocence through a white lens, but within the Black community, a similar—though less publicized—narrative emerged, one to which Bridges's brother-in-law and the Black press alluded.

Without money, Bridges drifted around Indianapolis, sometimes staying in homeless shelters. As circumstances taxed his health, his six-foot frame withered to a mere 125 pounds. In desperation, he stole a bike, and, upon his arrest, jailers placed him in isolation so that, in the words of one, "he wouldn't contaminate" the other prisoners. Upon learning of Bridges, a municipal judge rushed Bridges's case to his courtroom, where he pulled twenty dollars out of his own pocket and demanded Bridges "get out of town." In exchange for leaving Indianapolis immediately, authorities dropped the charges and gave him with a one-way bus ticket to Cleveland, where his mother lived. But she, like his sisters with their husbands, also bowed to her husband's objections and refused to let him come home.[100]

In Cleveland, without a place to stay and no suitable facilities available, the WCCO crew, which had followed him from Indianapolis, provided Bridges with money for a hotel room. The show's narrator explained that Bridges "said he had no money, so sometimes we bought him meals, and we had his laundry done. One day Fabian saw a small portable radio he liked, so we bought it for him." Anticipating criticism about journalistic ethics, the narrator defended these gifts as a way to keep Bridges away from commercial sex establishments and sex work. "Fabian hung out on the streets and said he made friends there. He spent time in adult bookstores and movie houses and he admitted, it was a way, he helped support himself." On camera, Bridges revealed, "Sometimes I do it for money, especially when I don't got any. I did it for money yesterday. I made five dollars." The interviewer never asked what "sometimes" meant, leaving viewers to imagine a long career in sex work. But it is clear that Bridges never engaged in sex work while holding down a well-paying job in Houston, and never once did the Indianapolis courts mention prostitution charges. It could be that Bridges did, in the last few desperate weeks of his life, carry out a handful of sexual transactions to sustain himself. It is equally likely that—like his announcement that he "didn't give a damn"—

in his frustration and desperation, he lied to shock and antagonize his white interviewers.

More shocking, Bridges confessed that he did not disclose his AIDS status to his sexual partners. In a voiceover, the narrator reacted to the admission: "After Fabian told us he was having unsafe sex, we faced a dilemma. Should we report him to authorities or keep his story confidential, knowing that he could be infecting others?"[101] Bridges's story had suddenly changed, the narrator remarked. "He was no longer just a victim." Instead of contacting an AIDS service organization, which might have been better equipped to address Bridges's health and housing needs, the WCCO crew contacted the president of the Cleveland City Council. In a sequence emblematic of the broader failure to address the crisis, the council president convened health, legal, and social services officials to figure out a course of action. City ordinances only allowed for a ten-day quarantine hold, leaving the group to brainstorm ways to hold Bridges for longer. Their actions skirted legality, and the ethics were questionable, but they believed the stakes could not have been higher—they saw this as a literal life-or-death situation. One panelist even remarked: "The guy's got a gun and he's out shooting people. You don't die in fifteen seconds; you die in two years."[102] The gun here was metaphorical, but the deaths, in his mind, were not, and in both cases, Bridges was a dangerous criminal—a biological terrorist—whose free movement threatened white middle America with a slow, painful death. While the city brainstormed steps to restrict Bridges's movement, local and national news outlets picked up Bridges's story and ran with the claim that he engaged in sex work despite knowing he had AIDS. Bridges had also finally begun receiving disability benefits, but his mother, in an uncharitable move, confiscated the check, saying she needed it to pay for his inevitable funeral. Upon learning his mother's plan, Bridges took the money and fled back to Houston, where a media circus awaited him.

With every breathless, dehumanizing report, doctors and police officers considered ever more draconian measures. In Houston, the county public health director sent Bridges a letter warning him to refrain from "sexual activities and particularly from prostitution" and threatening to withhold medical assistance if he continued to "misbehave." Meanwhile, the Houston Police Department refused to wait until Bridges had committed any crime; its vice squad launched a multiday manhunt to apprehend him, even, at one point, trying to entrap him into having sex.

Pessimistic about the medical establishment's ability to assist him when it was actively sending him threats, Bridges ignored the warnings and evaded the police. Filmmakers traveled down to Houston, where they encountered an unhoused Bridges intermittently living in bathhouses.[103] After Bridges allegedly informed the WCCO crew that he continued to engage in sex to meet his housing needs, the WCCO crew provided him with funds to secure a room. Unlike the previous time, this offer came with a stipulation. "Because Fabian didn't know where he was going to sleep," the narrator explained, "we gave him the money on the condition that he not practice unsafe sex and that he stay away from the bath houses." In the end, Bridges did not use the $15 a night on housing—there was none that inexpensive to be had. When *Equal Time* asked why WCCO gave him so little, the station's public affairs director admitted that it would have been "inappropriate to support him in a style [of living] to which he was not accustomed."[104]

Eventually, Bridges found housing assistance—what he had needed from the start—through the KS AIDS Foundation, one of Houston's early AIDS service organizations, which also offered him support and shielded him from the press. Though he finally had someone on his side and a place to call home, a week after moving in, Bridges returned to the hospital. On November 17, 1985, Bridges died. Since his family lacked the funds to bury him, Bridges received a pauper's funeral in the county cemetery. He was thirty years old.

In eight months, America's inadequate response to AIDS had reduced Fabian Bridges from a stable, middle-class man to a vulnerable, defensive invalid, yet nothing in the *Frontline* episode traced out this arc. Rather, in its telling, Bridges emerged as a dangerous criminal roaming the streets of middle America, a full-blown prostitute on the prowl looking to score some pitiful sum no matter what the cost to public health. Like the deviant criminal class into which the producers worked to squeeze him, Bridges could not be made to care about the enormous costs that arose from his paltry earnings. Yet, according to Ray Hill, the Houston gay activist who helped Bridges when he returned to Texas, Bridges "was not, is not, and has never been a prostitute."[105] Despite the fact that Bridges was not a sex worker and may never have actually engaged in any form of sex work, for the Minneapolitans who followed him and tried to make sense of his life, Bridges was, by his race, a danger and his sexuality his weapon.

The show's insinuation that Bridges was a sex worker encouraged the audience to imagine how many *other* AIDS-stricken sex workers of color not only remained sexually active but lurked in the shadows ready to strike. In a particularly striking scene near the end of the episode, Houston's health commissioner, with palpable fear and disdain, warns that "Fabian was only diagnosed last April. He might live another two years, and furthermore [he] is in remission now. He's not demonstrating any signs of illness!" Even though Bridges's status as a sex worker was always dubious and there was no clear number of sexual encounters he had, the commissioner projected onto him a pathological impulse to infect as many people as possible, people who would have no indication of the danger he posed. Bridges embodied the Gary Syndrome on the most intimate of levels. Since he could not be trusted and partners could not tell, the only remedy for his criminal impulses, in most officials' eyes, was surveillance and confinement.

During filming, as the national media picked up Bridges's story, a group of white gay men picketed the WCCO headquarters in downtown Minneapolis. Organized by the Gay Rights Alliance of Minneapolis (GRAM), protesters carried signs ranging from "WCCO SHAMEFUL CONDUCT" to "SOME CANNOT PROTEST." One participant told *Equal Time* he worried the media's circulation of such damning images of people with AIDS would fuel public fear and hatred, increasing violence against them.[106] Expecting further backlash from the gay community when the episode aired, producers included a disclaimer. Host Judy Woodruff began the episode by acknowledging its controversy: "It's a portrait of a man with AIDS who continued to be promiscuous." Woodruff recognized that gay men, like those in Minneapolis, were protesting out of concern that the public might incorrectly "conclude that this man's behavior is the rule rather than the exception." After the broadcast, PBS hosted a live discussion from the National Institutes of Public Health, but many AIDS experts declined to participate, fearing that the public would view Bridges as representative of most people with AIDS. Those who did participate did not challenge the moral or narrative of the episode, instead conceding that while Bridges may have engaged in "deviant" behavior, he was an "aberration."[107] This too was the unarticulated message of the Minneapolis protests: WCCO may have acted "shamefully," but not necessarily toward Bridges. The station had "shamefully" associated white, middle-class, respectable gay men with him. In the end, the fears of the gay community were both validated and dismissed. On the night it aired, KCET, the PBS-affiliate in Minneapolis, logged 168 calls, the largest telephone response to any program in a decade. Of the seventy-three callers expressing opinions, sixty-nine were negative.[108]

Gay integrationists countered with what they considered more affirmative depictions. In anticipation of WCCO's local broadcast of Bridges's story in March 1986, Brian J. Coyle, the openly gay member of the Minneapolis City Council, and Gary Rankila, an attorney and Minneapolis civil rights commissioner, appeared before a town hall–style meeting organized by WCCO-TV. Because organizers of the event did not provide Coyle and Rankila with a preview of the program, the two agreed not to discuss the ethics of the film. Instead, they accepted the invitation to provide the public with what they deemed were "positive" representations of gay men. Speaking about the meeting's organizers, Rankila told the local gay press, "We rolled with their dice and played their game rather than to be ignored. We had a very sharp discussion [on the issue of ethics] (off camera) and decided to take part so *we could present a positive side about who gays are.*"[109] Even as Rankila opted to forego lambasting WCCO for its treatment of Bridges, he used the meeting to highlight the favorable racial, class, and gender attributes of gay men like Coyle and himself. In essence, to circumvent the devaluing stigma attached to AIDS and homosexuality, Coyle and Rankila pointed to other signs and signifiers of social value—namely, middleness via morality and respectability.

Coyle and Rankila flattered themselves that they took the moral high road, presenting positive images of gay men—all white—and avoiding mentioning Bridges's sordid story, but more confrontational activists were happy to pick a fight with *Frontline*. At a press conference after the episode aired, Tom Agar, a member of the direct-action group Minnesota Alliance Against AIDS (MAAA), accused filmmakers of "contributing further to this society's irrational response to AIDS." He criticized the portrayal of Bridges, saying, "We regret that uninformed viewers will be left with the mistaken impression that Mr. Bridges's behavior is typical." Agar added, "Broadcasting images like that of Fabian Bridges is equivalent to yelling 'Fire' in a crowded theater."[110] Agar's incendiary words might be explained by the horrible, panic-induced reactions he anticipated would come from the show. He was right to worry, for on March 18, 1986, the same month that PBS affiliates aired the *Frontline* episode, the *New York Times* published an editorial by conservative author William F. Buckley in which he proposed that people with AIDS "should be tattooed in the upper forearm, to protect common-needle users, and on the buttocks, to prevent the victimization of other homosexuals."[111]

The most prominent figure in the Twin Cities gay community who questioned the accuracy and fairness of the reporting regarding Bridges was the seasoned gay liberationist Tim Campbell, who, as the most radical of the mainstream leaders, often stood alone in his positions. At the same press conference where Agar spoke, Campbell, who claimed to have known "hundreds of male prostitutes," questioned whether Bridges was truly a sex worker. He argued that filmmakers had created a "Black Typhoid Mary" narrative around Bridges, pointing out that Bridges was "not flirtatious . . . did not cruise . . . [and] was not particularly sensual." Campbell seemed to imply that if Bridges were a sex worker, he was not a particularly successful one. Rather, Campbell suggested that Bridges, with his last bit of agency, may have "manipulated" the WCCO crew into paying for a hotel room, which Bridges then squandered on admission to a bathhouse.[112]

A voice in the wilderness, Campbell questioned Bridges's particular story, but segments of the Twin Cities gay community effectively acquiesced to the notion that there was, in fact, a plague of people—sex workers and sex workers of color in particular—recklessly spreading HIV and worsening the AIDS epidemic. The only viable strategy, in their minds, was to distance themselves from these social outlaws and tap into a politics of middleness. They actively encouraged a monogamous sexual life safely ensconced within the privacy of the home because they assumed it would bestow legitimacy upon them. In nurturing that respectability, leaders like Coyle and Spear did not exert much energy and conviction defending Bridges—or any other sex worker—from unfair and baseless attacks. While they could have shown more passion in understanding the economic necessity that drove sex workers—especially sex workers of color—into their profession, they accepted at face value those the broader society labeled "deviant." There is no evidence that either man consciously or maliciously engineered it, but historically speaking, they helped shift the gaze of Minnesota's heterosexual public upon a population even more "deviant" than they, and, by comparison, white middle-class gay men came away seeming less perverse and, ultimately, less culpable for the AIDS crisis.

The Black community faced a similar dilemma, but rather than fret that America would see Bridges as first and foremost gay, it worried America would see him as Black. In response, Black leaders largely ignored the issue, and, consequently, Bridges's story, while coming close to being a national obsession, hardly appeared in the Black press. They policed the boundaries of acceptable Blackness with a silence that marginalized those living with HIV. As Cathy J. Cohen has pointed out, Black political leaders failed to treat AIDS as a "consensus issue"—or a matter pertinent to the entire Black community, deserving of attention and resources.[113] By omitting stories like Bridges's, the Black press avoided having to "own" a narrative that cast a negative light on the entire Black community. In doing so, they reinforced a politics of respectability—privileging a morally upright, heteronormative image of the Black community over the lives of its most vulnerable members.

Giving a "Damn"

Who really knows what Fabian Bridges meant when he uttered, "I just guess I'm to the point where I just don't give a damn, you know?" A man ruined in equal measure by disease and a nation that refused to do enough to confront it, the larger gay community sacrificed him to the media while the Black community disowned him. He was, in every sense, alone. He might have meant he had grown tired of people assuming what he did sexually simply based on his race and sexual orientation. He might have simply meant he was frustrated emotionally and exhausted physically and no longer willing to play the role of a villain for a mere $15. But no one in a position of power or influence stopped to ask what he really meant. The white, mainstream audience members watching *Frontline* that March night in 1986 assumed they knew: He did not give a damn about *them* or their safety. This unjustified fear, in turn, drove politicians and health officials to feverishly imagine what Bridges was doing instead of exploring why, and, consequently, when they responded, it was in a host of oppressive legal measures.

The worst-case scenarios, like tattooing people with AIDS or imprisoning them in AIDS sanatoriums, remained dreams of the far right, but since 1985, thirty-five states have passed HIV-specific criminal laws—even though antiretroviral therapy and pre-exposure prophylaxis (PrEP) have radically changed the face of AIDS.[114] In addition to sex and sharing needles, even actions that have virtually zero risk of spreading HIV, like biting, spitting, or throwing bodily fluids, can land a person in jail. And these laws do not sit dormant on the books. In 2020, the Sero Project, a network advocating against HIV criminalization, documented more than one thousand instances of charges filed under these laws since the 1980s.[115] Proponents insist that these measures encourage HIV-protective behaviors, like disclosing HIV-positive status to sexual or needle-sharing partners.[116] However, critics counter that these laws perpetuate HIV-related stigma and discourage people from getting tested, as knowing one's status can lead to criminal culpability.[117]

And who is ultimately helped? Certainly not people like Bridges. Had he received the same leniency and even sympathy that Scott Reynolds enjoyed—or even just a modest amount of support—he might have lived out his last days with a modicum of dignity and peace. He might even still be alive today. Instead, kicked from one place to another, forced into dire situations, he hustled and said what he needed in order to survive.

It is no surprise that WCCO, a station from Minneapolis, fixated on Bridges's story above all the others it could have told, for he amounted to the biological equivalent of the ubiquitous Gary Syndrome: an "outsider," criminal in his willingness to transgress community norms, deadly dangerous, and, ultimately, Black. Even before filmmakers began to interview him, the story had already been laid out and so too the moral: Bridges refused to check his impulses for the benefit of others—only carceral cures of the neoliberal state could rein him in. Even as some white gay men in the upper Midwest subscribed to the Gary Syndrome, they continued to experience hate and discrimination. But, precisely because of the Gary Syndrome, respectable, white gay men could increasingly position themselves as not "deviant" and, thus, much less dangerous than these racialized sex workers.

Even exceptions to the rule still proved it. In 1989, police arrested Carmen Gonzalez, an HIV-positive woman, and charged her with attempted murder for spitting at officers during a domestic disturbance.[118] This was not an isolated incident. Minnesota witnessed several high-profile cases where people with AIDS were convicted of assault with a deadly weapon for biting police officers. In Gonzalez's case, however, members of ACT UP/Minnesota responded in protest outside the Minneapolis Police Department headquarters, blasting the city's handling of Gonzalez's case as tainted by "AIDS hysteria, sexism, racism, and homophobia."[119] Though the courage of the protest was impressive, for those paying attention, more notable were their small number and the deafening silence of Minnesota's other powerful LGBTQ organizations and political representatives. There is no historical record of them speaking out about Carmen Gonzalez and all the other HIV positive people arrested under these laws.[120] One reason for this silence was that some white gay men (and lesbians) wanted the American public to understand that not all people with HIV/AIDS should be lumped together. In their minds, crucial distinctions of race and class existed, and these laws helped reinforce those boundaries.

Ultimately, by making the spread of HIV a crime, that is, the moral responsibility of one individual choosing to act in a way counter to the social good, these laws discouraged—and still discourage—a wide and thoughtful exploration of why HIV spread so rapidly in some communities and how state-sanctioned policies create and exacerbate inequities—inequities that, in turn, might drive people into behaviors like drug abuse or survival sex work. As with the Gary Syndrome, racist, unjust solutions help hide or obscure the fact that the very problems they are meant to fix arise from racist, unjust policies. Locking up and dehumanizing Brenda Williams was a simpler solution than confronting the poverty and drug economy that shaped her life. Threatening to incarcerate Fabian Bridges was easier than questioning why an AIDS diagnosis could strip a man of his middle-class life and leave him unhoused. Incarceration did not just imprison and remove from the public people who needed help, it locked up probing, uncomfortable questions too.

5 Minneapolis "Matures" Past Bathhouses

Closure and Quarantine

In the early morning hours of May 16, 1987, Richard "Dick" Brown, a sixty-year-old gay Minneapolis resident who worked as a book distributor and was a former bathhouse patron, marched toward the 315 Health Club, one of the largest and busiest bathhouses in operation between Chicago and the West Coast. Holding a sign that read, "AIDS Kills, Avoid Gay Bathhouses," Brown stood outside the last remaining bathhouse in Minneapolis to "call attention to the danger" of the premises (fig. 5.1). He believed bathhouses were major contributors to the spread of HIV, claiming they offered "vulnerable" men, whom he referred to as sex addicts, opportunities for casual, anonymous sex. Despite these alleged dangers, Brown accused AIDS activists and gay elected officials of running a "propaganda campaign" in defense of the 315 Health Club. Brown, along with Clint Heim, a former employee of the 315 Health Club, made it their mission to fight them. "How many," Heim said to a journalist, "must die from the virus before it sinks in that this place is an absolute disgrace?"[1] Unwilling to wait and find out, Brown and Heim began distributing pamphlets to patrons, warning them of the potential dangers.[2]

As the AIDS death toll rose in cities across the country, commercial sex establishments, like the 315 Health Club in Minneapolis, became prime targets, but there was little new in this endeavor; commercial sex establishments had already been subject to regulation long before the AIDS epidemic.[3] The bathhouse raids of 1979 and 1980 set the stage for an unofficial policy by the vice squad: Sex in private areas of the premises—that is, behind closed doors—would be tolerated, but nothing in public and certainly nothing with minors or sex workers. While most Minnesotans (even if they did not agree) allowed this arrangement, conservative forces disagreed and looked for ways to crack down on the remaining commercial sex establishments. The emergence of AIDS became a convenient pretext for advancing their agenda. In their minds, AIDS was a godsend that reshaped the terms

FIGURE 5.1 Dick Brown protesting outside the 315 Health Club, as featured in *Equal Time* on May 27, 1987. Photo by John Ritter. Courtesy of the Tretter Collection in GLBT Studies, University of Minnesota, Twin Cities.

of the debate. Meanwhile, as Minneapolis transitioned from a manufacturing economy to one centered around the creative class, city planners remained eager to attract capital, tourists, and residents. For city planners, vice districts hampered scarce but necessary investment in downtown cores. Already under pressure from those seeking to "clean up" urban spaces, businesses that sold sexually explicit material or that furnished public and semi-public sexual cultures found that the AIDS epidemic provided their enemies with even more ammunition.

AIDS, with the support of a diverse coalition—including religious groups, urban policymakers, vice squad officers, and antipornography feminists—dramatically reshaped and ultimately dismantled the status quo surrounding commercial sex establishments. Adult, consensual sex in private booths was to be criminalized. As one of the most vilified institutions in the wake of the AIDS epidemic, bathhouses stood at the center of the battle, and, more than any of the commercial sex establishments that catered to a predominantly gay male clientele—which also included adult bookstores and X-rated theaters—bathhouses closed.[4] Many reasons exist as to why, but one of the most powerful remains that the conservative forces looking to shutter these institutions found a growing, powerful, and committed voice within segments of the gay community. While an older generation of gay activists celebrated bathhouses as institutions of sexual liberation, others, like Brown and Heim, demonized them as breeding grounds for promiscuity and sexually transmitted diseases. They would be joined by politicians and business leaders, and, in the end, as bathhouses came to be viewed as threats to public health, their closure paved the way for a homonormative culture and politics in Minnesota.

This chapter examines how the urban renewal efforts of the late 1980s, combined with public health concerns, influenced gay elected officials' decision to support a 1988 ordinance that, in essence, shuttered Minneapolis's last remaining bathhouse, the 315 Health Club, which management had renamed from the "Locker Room" to make it appear more respectable and discreet. The ordinance regulated the architecture of commercial sex establishments to reduce opportunities for men to engage in sexual activity and, in theory, prevent the spread of HIV. A second front in the fight against public sex (the first one being the repeal of sodomy in exchange for a public sex law), the ordinance confined gay sex to the private, "safe" sphere of the home. The antibathhouse ordinance, thus, can be viewed through the lens of middleness, for it reflected a desire to control and discipline gay male sexuality into a moral standard that emphasized privacy in matters of intimacy. Some gay leaders supported the idea and promoted a narrative that only emotionally and morally stunted men patronized commercial sex establishments in the wake of AIDS. Their "immature" and "irresponsible" actions proved that they had been warped by the trauma of homophobia. This idea carried strong racialized overtones, casting casual, anonymous sex as a form of "primitive" sexuality while emotionally developed, "civilized" gay men nurtured committed, lasting relationships.

The closure of bathhouses, championed by some within the gay community as a public health necessity, had broader implications beyond public health concerns. It served as a pivotal element in the gentrification of Minneapolis. While some in the gay community looked to shutter bathhouses, Minneapolis looked to tear down low-income housing and demonize lurking "crack houses." Both initiatives shared a common goal to "clean up" the city's image and invite a more conservative—neoliberal—vision of modern urban living. Gentrification, therefore, was not just about changes in land use or rising property values—it was also driven by shifting sexual norms. It gave gay men (and, to a lesser extent, lesbians) opportunities for racial and class mobility within a new ideological and physical space where they could demonstrate their fitness for mainstream social acceptance, particularly through adherence to domestic norms.[5] However, this process required gay men to distance themselves not only from the spaces that once accommodated their non-normative sexual practices but also from those in the community who continued to be seen as "perverse."

The Challenge to the Status Quo

Dick Brown had, before 1985, never made a public issue of bathhouses and what transpired within them. He had even patronized them. Like Police Chief Bouza, the Minneapolis Police Department (MPD), and other critics, he found the sexual activity there "icky" but generally turned a blind eye. AIDS changed his stance dramatically. Suddenly, the city's tolerant attitude to semi-public sex enraged him, and he fumed that officials, effectively, allowed gas to be poured onto the raging fire of AIDS. Brown believed that state regulation of sexuality—not condoms—served as the most effective form of HIV prevention, rejecting the notion that commercial sex establishments could play any role in education efforts. As such, he urged the City of Minneapolis to strictly enforce regulations that prohibited any type of sexual conduct in semi-public spaces including bathhouses, adult bookstores, and public parks. Brown sent city officials literature, pamphlets, and newspaper clippings, admonishing them to regulate the 315 Health Club and accusing gay activists and AIDS advocates—whom he referred to as "gay militants"—of endangering gay men through their "sexual liberation" tactics.[6] In an interview, Brown questioned why gay elected officials defended the bathhouse, stating: "The baths are not only a lethal place for the spread of AIDS but I also fail to understand gay politicians who defend the baths. Is that how they think of ourselves, as primarily desperate and stupid queens whose true environment is a whorehouse?"[7] Brown charged openly gay Minneapolis City Councilmember Brian J. Coyle and Jim St. George, chairperson of the Minnesota AIDS Project (MAP), with "whitewashing this 24-hour sex center as a 'safe' place because condoms [were] distributed."[8] And, since "gullible" gay men were "so used to being victims, so vulnerable to manipulation," Brown argued, they willingly participated in this "con game," allowing themselves "to be marched right into the gas chamber at 315 First Avenue North" (fig. 5.2).[9]

Management at the 315 Health Club downplayed the occurrence of sex on the premises in hopes of shifting the public perception of the establishment. One manager disputed claims that patrons used the sauna, whirlpool, and steam room for sex. Describing the business as a "private health club for gay men," the manager emphasized that the bathhouse had "very specific rules and regulations regarding sexual activities in the public areas,"

FIGURE 5.2 Clint Heim protesting outside the 315 Health Club, as featured in the *Star Tribune* on June 13, 1987. Photo by Rita Reed. Copyright © Star Tribune Media Company LLC. Used with permission. All rights reserved.

referencing earlier police raids justified by allegations of public sex.[10] The manager also highlighted the club's role as one of "the major forces in our community involved in daily AIDS awareness and prevention," stating that "gay men, even in the face of AIDS, will not stop expressing their sexuality. Our club offers a needed, safer environment for that expression of what we are."[11] Even as management downplayed sex on the premises, it defended the bathhouse as "one of the gay community's most responsible elements in AIDS prevention efforts," offering men a safe space to gather, away from unsafe sex and antigay violence. It maintained that what patrons did in the privacy of their rented rooms was their own business.[12]

Despite Brown's and Heim's efforts, city and state health officials, along with gay activists, refused to close the bathhouse. In the summer of 1986, State Health Commissioner Sister Mary Madonna Ashton responded to Brown's pleas with a restrained announcement that while "the situation" continued to be monitored, legal action to shut down the bathhouse would require significant personnel and resources.[13] Instead, she praised the management for distributing free condoms, closing rooms for group sex, improving lighting, and hosting safer sex workshops. Echoing Ashton, Coyle told *Equal Time* in December 1986 that the bathhouse did not pose "a huge problem" since its management was actively "creating an environment with fewer opportunities for unsafe sex." By then, Coyle had met with the mayor and city health officials, and they all agreed that there was no need to become "sex police" as long as educational efforts continued. Although Coyle acknowledged that unsafe sex practices occurred at the 315 Health Club, he believed that these behaviors did not outweigh the benefits of the bathhouse's sex education initiatives.[14]

One of Brown's most formidable foes was the MAP, the state's largest and most recognized AIDS service organization. MAP directly challenged Brown's claims, stating that it was unsafe sexual practices, *not* commercial sex establishments, that spread HIV. In an interview, Jim St. George, MAP's chairperson, acknowledged, "No one would say unsafe sex does not happen [at the 315 Health Club]. But it is the activity, not the location that counts." As long as safer sex practices were promoted within the bathhouse, MAP argued, there was "no logical reason" to shut it down.[15] The organization emphasized the 315 Health Club's importance in reaching a population—often closeted, married, or engaged in anonymous sex—that would otherwise be hard to access.[16] Eric Engstrom, MAP's executive director, argued that closing the bathhouse would be "counterproductive" as it would not stop men from seeking "anonymous sexual encounters" but would instead push them into more clandestine and potentially dangerous locations like parks or public restrooms.[17] Support for this perspective came from the Hennepin County Health Department, which warned that closing the club could lead to an increase in "sexually compulsive behavior" in public restrooms, indirectly stoking police concerns that children could be exposed to such activities.[18]

Brown flattered himself a principled, benevolent, public-spirited man, but he dipped into crude, racist tropes to relay his message. In the April 15, 1987, issue of *Equal Time*, he ran a public service ad featuring a stock image of a nameless, dark-skinned Aboriginal man with a stern expression, shirtless and arms crossed, a piece of fabric covering his genitals. Above the image, Brown added the mocking caption: "Trust me. I do safe sex with everybody." Beneath the image, he wrote: "Safe sex is a slogan, not a guarantee" and "Multiple sexual contacts and anonymous bathhouse partners increase your risk of getting AIDS." By using this imagery, Brown implied that condoms were so simple to use that even so-called primitive races could manage them. Yet his message seemed to suggest that sex with condoms must not have been that safe precisely if "less advanced" races were

FIGURE 5.3 HIV prevention public service announcement by Dick Brown, published in *Equal Time* on April 15, 1987. Courtesy of the Tretter Collection in GLBT Studies, University of Minnesota, Twin Cities.

using them with such ease (fig. 5.3). In likening bathhouse patrons to racialized primitives, Brown depicted these gay and bisexual men as effective savages who thoughtlessly parroted back HIV prevention catchphrases.

If those in bathhouses could be rendered racialized primitives, then those outside, who could "control" their urges, became implicitly more "civilized" and therefore more white.[19] For Brown, the promiscuous homosexual struggled to reconcile his internal, primitive, and infantile demands with the need to consciously regulate one's sexual behavior amid the AIDS epidemic. The cure to this hedonism and racialized infantilism lay in what gay integrationists heralded as romantic commitment—the pursuit of a lasting, monogamous relationship.[20] Unlike the "immature" expressions of gay male sexuality, such as casual encounters at parks, bookstores, and bathhouses, romantic commitment represented a more mature and, in the context of AIDS, a more hygienic form of development.

Brown's shrill and disturbingly racist efforts hardly moved the needle. Many gay and bisexual men continued to frequent the bathhouse, a smaller minority criticized and critiqued them, and most of the gay community, whether they saw the bathhouse as harmful or not, turned a blind eye to what transpired inside. Only something shocking could shake the status quo, and that arrived when beloved farm activist Richard "Dick" Hanson discovered he had HIV. Saddened, the gay community's feelings turned to a heady mixture of fear and anger when it surfaced that Hanson might have contracted the virus at the 315 Health Club. Suddenly, his story of ascent became a warning to other white gay men of what could happen to them if they strayed too far from their Midwestern, small-town values.

From Stories of Victimhood to Stories of Martyrs

Few in the gay community opposed bathhouses and the "primitive" hedonism they embodied well into the 1980s, but AIDS began to change that—not all at once, but with a slow trickle of stories that morphed into a raging torrent. It started with the mainstream press, which, since the earliest days of the epidemic, popularized a narrative that HIV/AIDS was a disease of gay men and intravenous drug users, people who had become sick due to weakness and their own moral failings. Enraged at this simple, homophobic story, gay activists mounted a wide-scale campaign to reframe HIV-positive gay men as "victims," whose whiteness and ties to heterosexual Minnesotans made them sympathetic figures. As fundamentally good people led astray, gay men needed a villain, someone or something that preyed upon their social isolation and emotional vulnerability; bars, bookstores, and especially bathhouses would play that part. It was present as early as June 1982, in the story of Bruce Brockway, the first identified case of AIDS in Minnesota. A cofounder of the newspaper *Positively Gay* and MAP, Brockway attributed his infection to a "promiscuous phase" during which he frequented the Locker Room, a place he called a "hotbed of gay promiscuity."[21] His patronage arose out of necessity, with him saying, "Just about the only place we had to meet other gays then was at the bars or the baths." In blaming his "bathhouse liaisons" for his infection, Brockway issued a warning against visiting such places: "You don't find butterflies in sewers and you're not going to find useful friends in places where useful friends don't congregate."[22]

As the cases mounted, a narrative emerged that painted commercial sex establishments, once seen as institutions of support and camaraderie, as destructive forces, luring in good men and ruining them. The December 12, 1984, issue of *Equal Time* profiled Bill Runyon, a gay man in his thirties and the fifth known person with AIDS in the state.[23] Titled "Profile: Bill Runyon, Helping Others Fight AIDS," the article said little about condoms or other safer sex practices but instead delved into how Runyon's sexual behaviors allegedly contributed to his infection.[24] The story amounted to one long lament by Runyon over his sex life. "If I had to do it over," he confessed, "I'd have fewer sex partners than I had and I'd exchange a lot less bodily fluids." He regretted having "three-ways" with his lover and blamed the bars for enabling his "promiscuous" lifestyle: "I was caught up in the bar scene and it was always easy for me to trick. I thought it was something attractive gay men did—go to bars, socialized, pick up tricks." A sympathetic piece, the story cast Runyon and other gay men as small-town boys led astray by the intoxicating pleasures of gay urban nightlife, men lured into the Twin Cities from neighboring Midwestern states and deceived by the promise of gay liberation, copious socializing, and even more sex.[25] In a separate article on gay nightlife, Jim Anderson, co-owner of the Saloon gay bar, reminisced about these early years of gay flight to the cities. The "'70s were a tremendous time for liberation, excitement, promiscuity," Anderson recalled. On Friday and Saturday nights, the bars were "quite Fellini-like . . . because there were no holds barred." Sex at the back of the bar was common, drugs flowed freely—the Saloon even sold poppers. "There was a sense," Anderson noted, "that you were in a space where you were free to be whoever you wanted to be."[26] Though the Runyon profile never demonized him and Anderson never mentioned Runyon, both stories conveyed a clear moral: The dream of expression, liberation, and sexual freedom had tragically given way to the nightmare of AIDS. Runyon's contribution to "fighting" the disease was simply to warn other "uninformed" gay men against following the same path.

In their effort to cultivate a sense of victimhood, gay publications emphasized themes of weakness and vulnerability, often to the point of evoking pity. One such example was the story of Howard Backer, featured in the July 10, 1985, issue of *Equal Time*. A "lonely and scared" gay man dying of AIDS at the Hennepin County Medical Center, Backer had cruised bars, bathrooms, and parks since the age of twelve. Backer floated around the country, working as a "gay houseboy" and then as a sex worker. When he did not meet someone at the bars, Backer ventured off to adult bookstores and cruised until daybreak. He spent entire weekends at bathhouses, using the same "germ-filled jar of lube" for months. Interviewed as he lay in a hospital bed, a "reflective, almost remorseful" Backer confessed, "I never took care of myself like I should have. I was sexually addicted. I couldn't stop. I liked the sleazy side of being gay—bathhouses, bookstores, [and] parks. I slept around every night. I could sleep with 10 different men in a night at the baths. And it wasn't always clean."[27] Yet, the article implied, these were the only places readily available to him, and he wallowed in their squalor. As long as they existed, weak, stunted men like Backer would fall prey to them. These stories reiterated that gay men had no other venues to explore their sexuality, suggesting that mainstream society, in its homophobia, contributed to the suffering of gay men with AIDS by denying them the chance for normative sexual development.

Equal Time never intended to present Backer as representative of HIV-positive gay men—the title itself, "Not a Typical MN AIDS Case," made that clear—but he was, for those who sought to push a narrative of victimhood, an amplified, extreme version of the psychological suffering and emotional isolation that so many men experienced. Readers would see in Backer a trope with which they could, on some level, identify or, failing that, pity. "I always wanted a lover and never found one," Backer lamented. "Five times with one guy [having sex] was like a relationship. I never knew what a relationship was like." The story concluded by spotlighting the ongoing risks men took at bathhouses, with Backer condemning their actions as rooted in loneliness and addiction. "You go to the baths and there are still 100 men there on a Saturday night having sleazy, sloppy sex. No matter how many guys die of AIDS there will always be those addicts who can't stop."[28]

Brockway, Runyon, and especially Backer fit a narrative that, by 1987, had become well established: Young, white gay men, damaged at an early age by shame and homophobia, arrive in the city, embrace its racialized decay, immorality, and hedonism, and ultimately fall victim to its blight. But what about men like Dick Hanson, a prominent activist in the radical farm movement, a lobbyist for the National Farmers Organization, a Democratic-Farmer-Labor (DFL) leader elected to the Democratic National Committee in 1980 (serving two terms), a 1984 US Congressional candidate, and a member of the ACLU, the National Organization for Women, and the Rainbow Coalition? A devout churchgoer in a stable, loving relationship, Hanson labored on his century-old family farm in rural Glenwood, Minnesota, and if not for his sexuality could have been a poster child for rural Minnesota.[29] He also had AIDS, and in June 1987 the *St. Paul Pioneer Press Dispatch* featured him in its Pulitzer Prize–winning investigative series AIDS in the Heartland (fig. 5.4).[30] Jacqui Banaszynski, a reporter for the *Pioneer Press*, had been covering gay rights issues for several years when the 1985 death of Rock Hudson forced Americans to confront the AIDS epidemic. In a complete reversal of both tone and intent of *Frontline* and WCCO's coverage of Fabian Bridges, Banaszynski and her editors wanted "to humanize people afflicted with this terrifying new illness" by following the story of a person with AIDS from diagnosis to death. After nearly a year of searching for the right subject, Banaszynski found the perfect story in Hanson.[31] In the piece, Banaszynski helped craft the genre of AIDS homecoming narratives—in which white gay men, often returning from large cities under financial and medical duress, live out their final months among caring families in rural and suburban towns across the United States.

In the 1980s, as Reagan dismantled the social safety net, thousands of gay men without a private home they owned or a partner—or a close group of friends—to care for them found the only option available was to return to their small Midwestern hometowns. There, they relied on their families of origin for emotional support, housing, and medical care. Typically, these AIDS homecoming narratives folded the Midwest into the story of AIDS, but only as a symbolic counterpoint to the urban, coastal metropolises where HIV supposedly originated. A 1987 *New York Times* article told the story of a small-town, All-American boy who, like many gay men, had gone to the "glamorous metropolis" in order to come out. Once there, he lived among a dense urban population of gay men where HIV spread quickly. The article reported that, with their dreams dashed, "they returned to their small towns, not in triumph over successes in the city but instead to die," oftentimes returning "to Mom, because her arms are usually open, even as so many doors are slamming."[32] While challenging the stereotype of small-town homophobia, the article reinforced the idea of cities as dangerous and diseased. The portrayal of HIV as traveling exclusively from racially diverse urban areas to predominantly white suburbs and rural towns perpetuated a narrative of urban decay versus small-town virtue, with whiteness as the standard of tolerance and compassion. In this framing, gay men were reintegrated into the nuclear family though a nexus of whiteness coded as small-town traditional values.

FIGURE 5.4 Dick Hanson (*right*) and Bert Henningson (*left*) pose outside their farm in Glenwood, Minnesota, in a scene reminiscent of Grant Wood's iconic painting American Gothic. This photograph appeared in the *St. Paul Pioneer Press Dispatch* on June 21, 1987. Photo by Jean Pieri. Copyright © MediaNews Group. Used with permission. All rights reserved.

These homecoming stories both shared key elements of victim narratives and transcended them. Whereas most stories of victimhood circulated among the gay press and helped explain the prevalence of AIDS in the gay community, homecoming narratives were first and foremost for a heterosexual audience. They transformed gay men from sexual deviants into human beings who shared more with the reader—as sons and brothers—than they differed. As Heather Murray shows, AIDS homecoming narratives offered parents, relatives, and allies the chance to discursively redeem these men from the moral lassitude often attributed to intravenous drug users—imagined as Black, brown, and poor.[33] The *Pioneer Press*'s managing editor, Mark Nadler, made this dynamic clear in his preface explaining the decision to publish Hanson's story. Nadler described Hanson as "one of us—a native Minnesotan, a farmer, a political activist, someone's son and brother and uncle." He contrasted Hanson with the widespread narratives of AIDS involving "drug users and homosexuals with promiscuous lifestyles who prefer to die in the anonymity of large cities." Hanson and his partner, Bert Henningson, were different, Nadler noted, because they "live[d] together as a committed couple with a deep relationship." In an effort to humanize Hanson, Nadler reflected, "Whatever you may think of his politics or sexual orientation, it is impossible to read his story and think of him as anything other than a decent, sensitive man determined to make some sense of the tragedy that has *befallen* him and thousands of others. His is the great tragedy of our times, and his is a story worth telling."[34] Nadler framed Hanson within a social value system tied to a universal, white, heteropatriarchal order. Apart from his homosexuality, Hanson embodied the racial, class, and gender markers necessary to evoke sympathy from white heterosexual Minnesotans. Nadler's preface urged readers to set aside their biases and focus on the universality of Hanson's experience, particularly his Midwestern whiteness. This approach worked, as a diverse group—gay and lesbian activists, feminists, fellow farmers, and prominent DFL politicians including Gov. Rudy Perpich, St. Paul Mayor George Latimer, and Minneapolis Mayor Don Fraser—rallied around Hanson at a fundraiser.[35] Gov. Perpich even mailed Hanson a personal check to help cover rent.[36] Mark Dayton, then Minnesota's commissioner of economic development and later a US senator and the governor of Minnesota, maintained a close friendship with Hanson, visiting him in the hospital and holding his hand.[37] Hanson's social value, amplified through Nadler's framing, translated into tangible support. He became one of the first people with HIV/AIDS in Minnesota to receive the experimental drug AZT, marking him as an early recipient of the state's medical advances.[38]

Due to his deep roots in the Minnesotan heartland, Hanson became one of the state's most prominent figures living with HIV/AIDS. Alongside Henningson, he regularly gave interviews to local news outlets and frequently spoke at AIDS education seminars held in churches and schools across Minnesota. On May 5, 1987, Hanson addressed a special state Senate meeting on AIDS, where more than 250 people listened to him declare, "My name is Dick Hanson and I have AIDS. But I am more than a statistic; I am a human being. I love and need to be loved, I live with hope and don't take it away from me."[39]

The *Pioneer Press* forsook any mention of the economic, political, and social factors that allowed HIV to proliferate, instead focusing on Hanson's committed and loving relationship with Henningson, a professor of international trade at the University of Minnesota, Morris. To celebrate five years together, Hanson and Henningson hosted a ceremony with close friends, exchanging rings in a nod to traditional heteronormative customs. Banaszynski underscored how relatable their relationship was, writing: "They are farmers who have milked cows, slopped hogs and baled hay like everyone else. Their politics and sexual orientation may disturb some. But their voices and values are most familiar, and perhaps better understood, than those of their *urban* counterparts."[40] In contrast, someone like Backer, dying alone and repentant in a county hospital, would never have received such a fair and sympathetic portrayal. His death symbolized urban decay and disease, part of a world deemed beyond saving. AIDS was, in that telling, a collaborator with crack and racialized crime working to undermine the public well-being and prosperity of the region. To be rural, on the other hand, meant belonging to a white, healthy world in which disease only "befell" otherwise good people.

Significantly, AIDS in the Heartland asserted that Hanson and Henningson contracted HIV at the 315 Health Club, and the series emphasized the role of commercial sex establishments in supposedly facilitating high-risk sex. Since neither man had come out until their thirties, they spent the early 1980s exploring their same-sex desires, "making up for 15 years of self-denial." They were avatars of Brown's Aboriginal man. Before the epidemic, Hanson frequented San Francisco and New York City for what he described as "political and sexual junkets." After coming to terms with his homosexuality, he often traveled to the Twin Cities for weekend getaways, engaging in "anonymous encounters" at the 315 Health Club.[41] There, Hanson met men from neighboring states and all walks of life. "There were a lot of people from Wisconsin, Iowa, the Dakotas doing the same thing,"

Hanson recalled. "They were farmers, businessmen, teachers, [and] priests. We just had an awful lot in common, living in an environment that wasn't acceptable to us being ourselves." Banaszynski's detailed account of Hanson's infection reflected a broader media pattern, especially in the Midwest, of externalizing the source of the virus to urban and coastal areas. Such narratives reassured white, heterosexual audiences that AIDS, like crime, came from outside middle America. Yet Banaszynski's retelling complicated this view, suggesting that society's homophobia pushed decent men like Hanson—men who, when presented with the choice, would have opted for homonormative relationships—into bathhouses, where they contracted an "outside" disease. Only the return and acceptance by their white, rural origins could alleviate the suffering into which their urban sojourns had led them. In this seminal homecoming narrative, Banaszynski did nothing less than put "Minnesota Nice" on trial and show how, in its own small way, rural America helped fuel the AIDS epidemic.

As with most stories on people with HIV/AIDS in the 1980s, on July 25, 1987, with Henningson by his side, Hanson died, becoming the 125th Minnesotan to die of AIDS. His funeral took place at his lifelong church, a gesture the gay press noted as a sign of re-acceptance by a community that had once been uneasy with his homosexuality. His ashes were scattered on the Glenwood farm, a poignant final resting place.[42] After Hanson's death, a representative from MAP told the press that Hanson had helped put "the humanity of AIDS . . . to the forefront," shifting the public perception from "high-risk nameless people" to real, recognizable lives.[43] At the request of his family, Henningson returned to Ortonville, Minnesota, to spend his final months with them. In an epilogue to the AIDS in the Heartland series, Henningson's mother explained, "I couldn't see him going to the Twin Cities and living in some tiny apartment alone. At least [Hanson] had [Henningson] to look after him—but he would have had no one. And we were taught you take care of your own . . . It will show the communities, too, that these men can come home and live out their days. They don't have to be herded into the cities and die alone."[44] Before his own death on May 9, 1988, Henningson wrote the epitaph for the AIDS memorial quilt that honored his and Hanson's lives: "Openly gay and at home on their family farm in rural Minnesota, their love ran deep as the prairie soil."[45]

By presenting Minnesotan readers with a story of someone with whom they could relate, Banaszynski and her editors succeeded in humanizing *certain* people with AIDS. While the first installment of AIDS in the Heartland initially received about 70 percent negative feedback, public perception shifted significantly by the end of the series. The final piece, which focused on Hanson's death and its impact on his loved ones, garnered overwhelmingly positive responses from readers. This praise extended to the Pulitzer board, which unanimously acclaimed the series. As the board secretary noted, "There was pretty general agreement from the start that it was the winner in the feature category."[46]

Homecoming stories became a particularly heart-wrenching tool for the white gay community in the upper Midwest to garner public sympathy. Parents reassured the public of their sons' "innocence" by downplaying the sexual aspect of the disease and instead emphasizing the emotional bonds between sons and white, heterosexual families of origin. It was an effort tied to the politics of middleness that gay elected officials had been cultivating since the 1970s. In the context of the AIDS epidemic, the home and family became crucial arenas for countering the stigma surrounding homosexuality—particularly by staging a middle-class Midwestern fantasy in which white gay men could be morally redeemed through domestic respectability and imagined racial harmony. Yet from a more critical perspective, these narratives did more than reconcile estranged sons with their families: they enabled a form of racial reconsolidation, in which certain forms of same-sex identity were selectively reabsorbed into the normative project of whiteness—through kinship, grief, and legible forms of suffering. This quiet accommodationism, which grew in the wake of the AIDS epidemic, marked a significant victory for the politics of middleness. The political potential of middleness, not at all obvious in the 1970s when gay integrationists actively encouraged it, became apparent only in the crucible of the AIDS epidemic.

Before Hanson's diagnosis, Minneapolis's hands-off policy toward bathhouses and commercial sex establishments promoted only scattered—but occasionally vocal—dissidents, such as Dick Brown. Gay men were dying, but unknown and alone or else "guilty" of their own sexual failings, they served in the gay press as a warning to others. With Hanson's death, gay Minnesotan men had a martyr—one that even straight Minnesotans could recognize—sacrificed on the altar of "unhealthy" and, as we will see, fundamentally "immature" sexual excess. His death began to shake the existing agreement that officials would turn a blind eye to what happened in sex establishments as long as it stayed out of public view. This consensus would come crashing down with the unexpected arrival of Randy Shilts to the Twin Cities to promote his book *And the Band Played On*.

The Status Quo Breaks: Closure as Quarantine

After the Hennepin Baths closed in 1979 and Big Daddy's followed in 1983, only the 315 Health Club, formerly the Locker Room, remained. That made it the sole target of Dick Brown's ire, but as late as August 1987, he could claim few victories. That summer, inspired by regulatory measures in New York City, Brown escalated his efforts by sending a report titled "How AIDS Was Spread in Minnesota" to members of the Minneapolis City Council, including President Alice Rainville, and Sandra Hilary, chair of the Public Health and Safety Committee.[47] In the report, Brown urged the city to impose several spatial and structural changes on the bathhouse, such as shutting down the third floor, which housed over fifty private sex rooms, installing brighter lighting in the showers, steam room, and whirlpool, and closing at midnight to "discourage patronage by late night customers of nearby gay bars who come to the bathhouse high on liquor and/or drugs after the bars close." Brown argued that the city council had a "moral obligation" to pass a regulatory ordinance, warning that failure to do so would lead to infection rates similar to those of San Francisco and New York City.[48]

In response to Brown's efforts, the city offered him a reply so noncommittal it amounted to a polite dismissal. Hilary thanked Brown for his "concern" and assured him that both the city and state health departments were working on a solution "beyond the educational and preventive efforts to date." She concluded by saying that his suggestions "would be considered as part of this review."[49] Behind the scenes, however, Minneapolis Commissioner of Health David Lurie concurred with Brown and wrote to Hilary, noting that Brown's proposals were in line with public health guidelines and the city had the authority to implement them.[50] The issue gained momentum when Rainville criticized Lurie and the Minneapolis Health Department for their inaction, calling for a review of how other cities handled similar issues with bathhouses.[51] After examining laws nationwide, Lurie recommended that Minneapolis adopt an ordinance similar to Marion County, Indiana's, which had been upheld in federal court.[52] Like Marion County, Minneapolis could regulate high-risk behaviors associated with HIV transmission by prohibiting establishments, including bathhouses, adult bookstores, X-rated theaters, and saunas, from allowing such activities. Designed to police the boundaries between public and private, the ordinance aimed to suppress anonymous sex by altering the interiors of sex-related businesses. It banned partitions with "glory holes"; required adequate lighting in all viewing booths, stalls, or rooms; mandated that at least one side of these areas be open and visible to adjacent spaces; and prohibited private rooms unless the establishment was a "validly operating" hotel, motel, apartment complex, condominium, or rooming house. Finally, the ordinance granted the health commissioner "full power and authority" to inspect and enforce the law.[53] The city attorney estimated that the ordinance would affect twelve to fourteen businesses.[54] By extending surveillance into private cubicles where men engaged in sex, the ordinance reversed previous agreements between the police chief and gay activists that sexual activity inside private cubicles would not be policed.

While Lurie considered whether the Marion County law would garner enough political support, a pivotal event took place that shifted countless perspectives. In 1987, Randy Shilts, a feisty, fast-talking thirty-six-year-old journalist who had been covering gay health issues for the *San Francisco Chronicle* since 1981, published *And the Band Played On*, a five-hundred-page tome of the early years of the US AIDS epidemic. The book landed with the force of an asteroid, exposing the Reagan administration's criminal indifference and the full scope and devastation of the AIDS crisis. Shilts also highlighted the factors that allowed the disease to proliferate, chief among them being the bathhouses, which he blasted as incubators of the virus.[55] "Bathhouses guaranteed the rapid spread of AIDS among gay men," Shilts wrote. Although he acknowledged that HIV would have spread across the United States even without bathhouses, Shilts insisted that "these foci of sexual activity fueled the brushfire propagation of the infection more than any other single element of American society."[56] By focusing on bathhouses and similar public sex venues, Shilts implied that these locations were the primary sites of infection. Like Brown, Heim, and others who attacked bathhouses as disease vectors, Shilts's fixation on the geography of sex overlooked the role of sexual practices—what one did or did not do—in spreading the virus.

Central to Shilts's contention that bathhouses were a major site for the spread of HIV among gay men was Gaëtan Dugas, a charismatic and unabashedly promiscuous French Canadian flight attendant. Historically remembered as "Patient Zero," or the very first case of AIDS in the United States, Dugas became in Shilts's account a "Typhoid Mary" who boasted more than 2,000 lifetime sex partners including 40 of the first 248 people with HIV/AIDS in the United States. Despite little solid evidence, Shilts implied that Dugas bore responsibility for introducing the virus to the country and spreading it nationwide. Dugas allegedly continued to patronize bathhouses despite being diagnosed with an infectious disease, a fact Shilts used to condemn the establishments.[57]

While Dugas's story was sensational, later research proved it to be incorrect. However, in November 1987, when Shilts arrived in the Twin Cities on the eleventh stop of his seventeen-city national book tour, no one knew that, and the story, as well as Shilts's moralizing, had taken deep root among important people.[58] Shilts had already influenced Brown, who heavily cited him in calls for the city to regulate commercial sex establishments, but he also began to reach a broader audience, including heterosexual legislators in Minneapolis.

In fact, Chairperson Hilary pointed to *And the Band Played On* as a key factor in the city council's Public Safety and Health Committee unanimously voting in March 1988 to advance the bathhouse ordinance, which followed Lurie's recommendation. She explained that prior to the book's release, the ordinance would not have passed due to an unfavorable political climate in Minneapolis. "Politically we were in hot water just talking about it," she said.[59] Previously, any discussion about closing bathhouses risked being labeled homophobic, but Shilts's work gave health and government officials the backing to address the issue. The ordinance gained additional credibility when Sister Mary Madonna Ashton, the state's commissioner of health, endorsed the Minneapolis plan, arguing that it would reduce HIV infections by limiting opportunities for at-risk people to engage in high-risk sex with multiple partners. The Minneapolis Police Department, known for its history of arresting gay men on the flimsiest of pretensions, also supported the measure. Vice Officer Dean Severson filed an affidavit stating that he had made hundreds of arrests between 1982 and 1988 in adult bookstores and saunas for indecent conduct and prostitution, witnessing acts such as masturbation, fellatio, and unprotected anal sex with strangers.[60] With two high-profile public officials backing the ordinance and none opposing it, its momentum only increased.

During his visit to the Twin Cities, Shilts described Minnesota as "an oasis of sanity in dealing with AIDS." A Midwesterner himself, Shilts praised the gay men of the heartland, saying, "I've been in Minneapolis several times, and have found sexuality is much more conservative on the whole. [Minnesota gays] would go out to bars during the weeknights and they'd clear out at 10 because everybody got up the next morning to go to work . . . Where they were roaring in San Francisco and New York every night, it was just much more of a conservative lifestyle here."[61] Shilts suggested that this culture of compulsory homonormativity and related emphasis on work and responsibility—key components of middleness—had helped protect Minnesota's gay men from HIV and even bolstered the region's economic vitality.

Nonetheless, Shilts railed against the continued operation of the 315 Health Club. "In 1983, supporting the bathhouses was a measure of denial against AIDS," Shilts claimed. "In 1987, it's insanity and political cowardice."[62] As Shilts left his mark on Minneapolis, pushing for stricter regulations on bathhouses, the gay community began to grapple with a crucial question: Was closing the 315 Health Club and similar establishments the right step in the fight against AIDS?

A Very Public Fight over "Private" Spaces

Of all the minds Shilts changed, none had a greater impact on Minneapolis than Brian J. Coyle, the city's only openly gay city councilmember. Initially, Coyle opposed any regulation of the bathhouse, arguing that it provided essential safer sex education. On November 20, 1985, after being successfully reelected, Coyle sent a letter to his constituents outlining "our strategy for dealing with the politics of AIDS as we enter 1986." Alongside legal protections for people with HIV/AIDS, Coyle talked about feeling "afraid that some City officials are going to move to try to close the baths within the next couple months. This is a deceptive and dangerous issue."[63] But, by February 1988, after Hanson's death and his own undisclosed HIV diagnosis, Coyle's perspective began to shift. In an interview, he acknowledged that "these last few months have affected me. I've had personal conversations with the people who are going [to the 315 Health Club] and they admit to me that safer sex is not being practiced. And then I read 'And the Band Played On.'"[64]

During his stop in the Twin Cities, Shilts emphasized that just as important as making the *New York Times* bestseller list was how his book had prompted Coyle to support an investigation of the 315 Health Club. He proudly noted that Coyle's shift on bathhouses represented the kind of direct, life-saving change he had hoped to inspire. "I had a real mission to tell this story," Shilts explained. "I wanted to say, 'Don't make the same mistakes we did or you'll be going to funerals every day.'" His sense of triumph was well founded—Coyle later admitted, "The Shilts book has helped me reconsider whether I've been too soft and liberal about the bathhouse. If they can close it legally, they won't get any fight from me."[65]

Although no representatives from the 315 Health Club or the adult entertainment industry spoke at the Public Health Advisory Committee hearings in February 1988 regarding the controversial ordinance, much of the gay male audience viewed the measure as a political maneuver rather than a health issue.[66] They argued that the ordinance was antigay, part of a moral campaign to shut down commercial sex establishments, not address AIDS. In response, the Gay and Lesbian Community Action Council (GLCAC), along with the Minnesota Alliance Against AIDS (MAAA) and the Gay and Lesbian Freedom Pac, organized a community forum titled Bathhouses, Sexual Freedom, and the Law at the Hennepin County Government Center on February 9, 1988. GLCAC aimed to provide "balanced and responsible information" about the "complex and controversial" relationship between AIDS and commercial sex establishments.[67] As expected, Dick Brown used the forum to reaffirm his support for the ordinance, excoriating radical queer activists who defended the bathhouse: "What scares me more is the gay establishment, not the straight community."[68] However, the biggest surprise for the fifty "fretful" gay men in attendance, as the *GLC Voice* described them, came when Coyle voiced his support for closing the bathhouse.[69]

In his opening remarks, Coyle made a startling admission: "I now favor closing the bathhouse." Addressing the shocked crowd, he explained his change of heart, noting that he had previously supported the 315 Health Club because MAP distributed condoms there, the management had shut down the "orgy room," and glory holes were removed. He also pointed out that, at the time, "there was only one bathhouse in town, a few bookstores, and . . . these were not central to Minneapolis gay life."[70] But Shilts's book had changed his mind, and he encouraged the crowd to read it as well. Throughout the night, he referenced Shilts's account of the AIDS crisis in San Francisco, using it as a cautionary tale for what could happen in Minneapolis if the bathhouse ordinance failed. Coyle aligned himself with the "brave individuals" in San Francisco who were labeled "sexual Nazis" by gay liberationists simply for asking, "What are we doing to ourselves?" and condemning the "publicly licensed murder" happening in the bathhouses. Quoting Shilts, Coyle remarked that "everybody agreed the baths should have been closed sooner, [and] they agreed health education should have been more direct and more timely." Nevertheless, as Coyle warned the audience of Minneapolis gay men, "By the time everyone agreed . . . it was too late. Instead, people died. Tens of thousands of them."[71]

Brown and Coyle stood alone in supporting the ordinance at the community forum, as every other panelist opposed it, arguing that it targeted gay men unfairly. Eric Shambach from MAAA denounced the ordinance as "blatant bigotry," while Robert Halfhill, also representing MAAA, warned that closing the bathhouse would push gay men to seek sexual encounters in public spaces like "shrubs and trees." Halfhill even suggested replacing Coyle on the Minneapolis City Council, accusing him of ignoring the concerns of his gay constituents. Carrie Orth, director of the MCLU, criticized the ordinance for being driven by moral assumptions about sexuality, calling it "morally motivated private purpose" legislation and citing violations of the First, Fourth, and Fourteenth Amendments.[72] In short, the panelists raised concerns about both the ordinance's questionable motives and its potentially harmful outcomes.

Amid the barrage of countervailing responses, Coyle clarified that he changed his mind after receiving reports from local gay men and medical professionals about unsafe sex practices continuing at the 315 Health Club. As he told the *Pioneer Press*, "I've been listening to my community" and realized that "the majority of gays" shared his evolving views.[73] If Coyle sincerely believed this sentiment, he had not been speaking with a particularly large or diverse group of gay men. Many still supported the previous approach: The bathhouse not only promoted safer sex but also served as a vital hub for education and testing, especially for men who had sex with men yet did not identify as gay. Defenders of the 315 Health Club argued that without the bathhouse's free condoms and constant messaging about safer sex, men—regardless of their openness about their sexuality—would continue to have sex, but in riskier places and ways, worsening the epidemic. A local gay male resident wrote a letter to Coyle defending the bathhouse as a safe space where men were likelier to practice safer sex, thanks to the health messages posted throughout. The letter warned that if the bathhouse closed, "many patrons may choose to take partners home, where the chances of transmission (anal intercourse in bed!) are greater!"[74] One of the bathhouse managers agreed, noting that its clientele tended to practice safer sex more diligently than those who brought partners home from bars occasionally, mistakenly assuming lower risk due to fewer sexual contacts. Another manager reiterated that closing the bathhouse would push "sex out on the streets," where men would be more vulnerable to antigay violence and harder to reach with outreach efforts. The executive committee of MAP echoed the management's concerns in a detailed statement opposing the bathhouse's closure.[75]

Coyle's dramatic reversal ignited a fierce backlash from within the gay community, fracturing key alliances and prompting accusations of betrayal from collaborators like Tim Campbell. Long opposed to any restrictions on public sex, Campbell saw the ordinance as clearly unrelated to public health. At a committee hearing, he declared, "It's an ordinance against gay sex. It's an ordinance about morality, not about health or high-risk sex. It's an ordinance to close down bookstores and *our* bathhouse under the guise of getting at high-risk sex."[76] Campbell also pointed out that the city ignored places like singles bars where heterosexuals met and arranged sexual liaisons.[77] Despite their past disagreements, Coyle maintained a cordial relationship with Campbell, who held influence in the gay community as the editor of one of the most widely read LGBTQ newspapers in the upper Midwest. Coyle, however, remained firm on the bathhouse issue, and Campbell retaliated. In a *GLC Voice* op-ed following the Bathhouses, Sexual Freedom, and the Law forum, Campbell accused Coyle of pulling "the most clearly offensive stunt of his career." He claimed that Coyle "deliberately and publicly stomped" on "strong, convincing, objective data from non-gay health officials" showing that gay men had changed their sexual behaviors. Campbell referenced Minneapolis Health Department records, which showed that tests at the 315 Health Club between January 1985 and February 1988 revealed no syphilis cases and only one case of gonorrhea in February 1986.[78] Campbell argued that these numbers indicated that gay men, particularly bathhouse patrons, had adopted safer sex practices.[79] Furious that Coyle had dismissed these statistics, Campbell accused him of being "a gay bearing false witness against gays to enhance his own imagined credibility with straights. It is lying. It is abuse of gay credentials. It is treason."[80] Campbell believed men like Coyle had been misled by the frenzied fears of those aiming to dismantle a cornerstone of the gay community, and he urged the council to reject the ordinance.

Campbell was not alone in viewing the ordinance as a thinly veiled moral crusade; other activists and organizations also condemned the measure as a dangerous rollback of hard-won sexual freedoms and gay public space. At a separate committee hearing, Robert Halfhill of the Minnesota Alliance Against AIDS (MAAA) voiced opposition to the plan, asking the Public Health Advisory Committee, "What are you going to close down next?"[81] Drawing attention to the history of police raids on Minneapolis's commercial sex establishments, MAAA argued that closing the 315 Health Club under the pretext of HIV prevention would be "the culmination of these unprovoked attacks on us, attacks which involved many instances of police brutality, and would be the final kick in the face to the Gay Community."[82] For supporters, keeping the 315 Health Club open had become a symbol of the legacy of that gay activism. Likewise, the LGBTQ newspaper *Twin Cities Gaze* warned of a potential domino effect, where other gay community spaces—like adult bookstores, massage parlors, and even the YMCA—might also face closure.[83] Bathhouses, more than adult bookstores, X-rated theaters, or saunas, represented an undeniably and distinctly "gay space." Whereas Brown and Coyle lamented that homophobia had forced gay men into bars, bookstores, and bathhouses, Campbell and Halfhill saw them as valuable spaces offering alternatives to the domestic privacy embedded in Minnesota Nice.

Criticism from gay liberationists toward Coyle was not new, but its intensity was. Although he had been elected to the city council on a progressive platform, some of his gay constituents accused him of becoming too centrist. According to Jim St. George, Coyle's former aide, Coyle grew frustrated with leftist critiques of his perceived lack of radicalism. He told St. George, "I can't go off and say or do crazy things and still have any credibility with my colleagues" on the council. St. George explained that Coyle believed he had to be "more responsible, more reasonable, to have credibility" and "couldn't just shoot off at the mouth."[84] In navigating the political landscape, Coyle also prioritized a polished appearance, often donning stylish suits. His friend and former roommate, Jerry Fladmark, recalled Coyle's penchant for "really nice suits," joking that Coyle believed that "the better I dress, the more I can get away with saying more lefty things." Coyle told Fladmark that if you wear sharp suits, people "will not critique you the same way," whereas if you are "wandering around in jeans with holes in the knees" and say, "something lefty, they just kind of roll their eyes."[85] Both St. George and Fladmark assert that Coyle's commitment to progressive politics never faltered. However, as Minneapolis's first openly gay councilmember, Coyle understood the need to present a respectable image to influence heterosexual perceptions of gay men. This sense of responsibility also led him to speak out against spaces he believed contributed to the spread of HIV.

Coyle defended his reversal on the ordinance by citing medical professionals who substantiated reports that bathhouse patrons were "using the privacy of the booths and stalls to have high-risk sex."[86] At the Bathhouses, Sexual Freedom, and the Law forum, Coyle shared a letter from Dr. Scott Strickland, a well-known local gay physician. Strickland, who had previously opposed regulation, explained that his work with patients who continued to visit these venues had led him now to support regulation.[87] Mental health professionals further escalated the debate by writing to Coyle, arguing that commercial sex establishments fueled "sexual addiction" among gay men.[88] One therapist recounted experiences with clients exhibiting "compulsive sexual behavior," including two who contracted HIV after visiting the bathhouse and adult bookstores. The therapist described a cycle of loneliness, deprivation, and substance abuse that drove risky sexual behavior and criticized the depiction of the 315 Health Club as "a responsible community organization" when "nothing could be further from the truth."[89]

In a more direct critique, a substance abuse counselor questioned the integrity of supporting venues that contributed to the spread of HIV while advocating for more funding for AIDS education and research, arguing, "We don't retain any credibility when we support the promiscuous places where AIDS is spread and yet cry 'foul' when the straight community won't give more money for AIDS education, research, etc."[90]

Some gay men who supported the ordinance believed it was both unfair and insufficient to limit gay sex by merely closing commercial sex establishments. Embracing a culture and politics of homonormativity, they advocated that sex, along with the love and attachment from which it should spring, needed to be channeled into the private sphere of the home where "mature," lasting relationships could thrive. In December 1987, a month after Shilts's visit, a gay couple wrote to *Equal Time*, agreeing that bathhouses needed to close but criticizing Dick Brown's language for scapegoating gay men as "responsible for the development of the disease." This, they said, reduced "gay men to little more than homosexual animals in the minds of many," when in reality, they desired what everyone else had. The couple noted a pattern of "trash[ing] gays yet deny[ing] [them] legal recognition and societal support for maintaining healthy same-sex relationships" but remained hopeful that public health officials were "beginning to realize that encouraging stable or monogamous gay relationships is a significant aspect of AIDS prevention."[91] Bathhouses, they argued, needed to be shut down not only because they spread disease but because they also hindered efforts to secure what gay men truly wanted and deserved—and what would most effectively curb the spread of AIDS: domestic partnerships. Another letter writer condemned bathhouse patronage as a sign of immaturity, contrasting it with the maturity of monogamous relationships. He expressed frustration, saying he was "sick of so-called 'leaders' of the gay community defending our 'right' to go to baths," when these leaders should instead be fighting a "society that denies our right to form lasting, mature relationships" and "forced most gay men to be so deeply closeted . . . that the only way to express their sexuality was in the most anonymous and degrading manner."[92]

Advocates of domestic partnerships sought to reinforce the sexually "conservative lifestyle" that Shilts had praised for protecting Midwestern gay men, believing that the health and dignity of the gay community were at stake. They viewed bathhouses and the gay "liberation" they symbolized as merely a hedonistic, "youthful" phase that the gay rights movement had outgrown on its path to mature, stable relationships. Those who clung to bathhouses as a cultural legacy might have been pitied for their nostalgia—if it had not carried such dangerous consequences. AIDS thrived on the folly of youth, and these gay men wanted the community to grow up—fast. There were other advantages as well. Dick Hanson had shown that exchanging rings, settling down, and adopting heteronormative customs earned goodwill and seemed to reduce homophobia. In this sense, Campbell and others opposing the ordinance were right—a bathhouse was distinctly, even exclusively, gay, and, as such, it would have to go. Growing up meant going straight.

From "Dirty" Bathhouses to Swanky Spas

Before the AIDS epidemic, neoliberal restructuring of urban space had already made bathhouses vulnerable to redevelopment. Even before the proposed 1988 ordinance, the 315 Health Club was facing an uncertain future. As early as 1979, the city targeted all bathhouses with a proposed zoning amendment requiring any establishment offering a central steam bath and private rooms to the public to provide two parking spaces for each individual cubicle. For a bathhouse with fifty cubicles, this would mean a hundred off-street parking spots. This proposal was clearly designed to make opening a new establishment along Hennepin Avenue nearly impossible. The real target was Club Baths, a chain planning to open at 113 N. 1st St., where the Minneapolis City Council had previously failed to mount a $500 million redevelopment effort. The city council president even admitted, "I don't think that a gay bathhouse is a good start for the area."[93] While the proposal never went anywhere, it sent a clear message along Hennepin Avenue: The city had its sights set on the vice district and would seize any chance to replace anything with the whiff of sex with family-friendly and, more to the point, investor-friendly, "clean" businesses.

Gay liberationists had linked the increase in police harassment against gay men during the "reign of terror" from 1979 to 1985 to gentrification, calling the police and city planners "willing partners." In 1982, Claude Peck, producer of the *Fresh Fruit* radio show, and Robert Halfhill, then-director of Target City Coalition, coauthored an op-ed criticizing the Minnesota Committee on Gay and Lesbian Rights' (MCGLR) proposed reforms for the MPD. "Developers who want to make downtown and near-downtown neighborhoods attractive to suburbanites are anxious to clear 'undesirables,'" the men claimed, "such as pimps, winos, and, of course, gays out of these areas."[94] Peck and Halfhill implicated the MPD in these efforts, noting that most vice-related arrests were made on land primed for redevelopment, such as Loring Park and the downtown adult bookstores. Tim Campbell, writing for the *GLC Voice*, went further, reporting that Mayor Don Fraser admitted that "he has 'used the vice squad by direct and implicit order' to further the plans of city development."[95] But, when it came to bathhouses, the MPD's vice squad did not have to try too hard as business was already winding down.

Between 1979 and the summer of 1987, bathhouses in Minneapolis—like those in most major US cities—as a rule, closed rather than opened.[96] Amid growing concerns about AIDS, the party had all but died despite disco music continuously playing throughout largely empty spaces. By the time the Minneapolis ordinance reached committee hearings in early 1988, it could be argued that it was no longer necessary; some nights, the 315 Health Club hosted as few as ten men.[97] That year, Brad Theissen, the publisher of *Twin Cities Gaze*, acknowledged the shrinking customer base, writing, "I used to go to the [315 Health Club]. I stopped going around the time most others stopped going—about three or more years ago." AIDS had cut into the bathhouse's customer base, Theissen observed, and "its revenues have dwindled ever since the health crisis became identified."[98]

In 1985, management introduced several changes aimed at attracting more customers and shedding the business's "sleazy" reputation. Its goal was to rebrand it as a "clean" and welcoming space for relaxation, exercise, and socializing among gay men. According to one manager, the 315 Health Club was "not just a place for sex" but "for socializing and meeting people . . . a place for gay men to gather, a place to relax."[99] One of the main attractions was the "country's biggest steam room," a five-hundred-square-foot space with a fountain, plenty of seating, and a maze of passageways.[100] Reflecting the fitness craze of the 1980s, the manager even considered hiring a weight trainer. The television viewing area was also remodeled for "more comfortable seating and greater capacity." On weekends, campy films like *Gone With the Wind* replaced X-rated movies. To further open up the club and integrate it into the neighborhood, management added a daylight-moonlight lounge overlooking 1st Avenue. This lounge, featuring natural lighting for the first time at the bathhouse, allowed patrons to observe the passage of time and feel less "underground" (fig. 5.5).[101]

Although it is difficult to confirm if these efforts boosted patronage, management eventually shifted focus, moving from downplaying sex to promoting the bathhouse's role in HIV prevention. In 1986, it launched its own "Play It Safe!" public service announcements in LGBTQ newspapers, encouraging

FIGURE 5.5 The 315 Health Club, 1984. Photo by Norene Roberts. Courtesy of the Hennepin County Library.

gay men to visit for condoms and safer-sex literature. The ads emphasized that "'safe sex' doesn't have to mean becoming 'asexual.'"[102] Management, with partial funding from MAP, distributed free condoms with every towel, ultimately handing out more condoms at the 315 Health Club than any other location in Minneapolis. During a five-month stretch in late 1987 and early 1988, employees distributed over sixteen thousand condoms—about two or three per customer.[103] Even before the prospect of the ordinance, management in 1986 shut down the "orgy rooms" to prevent group sex and boarded up the "glory holes" to curb anonymous encounters. They plastered "safer sex" posters all over the walls and made brochures readily accessible. Posters featuring muscular men in various stages of undress reinforced the benefits of safer sex, with one patron commenting that it was impossible to turn a corner without "seeing a poster that tells you to use a condom."[104] Along with the extensive condom distribution, management expanded free venereal disease testing at its in-house Body Shop Clinic from two nights a week to four.[105] But, in the end, the bathhouse was still a business, and management had to balance prevention efforts with profit. As early as 1986, it lowered prices on lockers and rooms while assuring patrons in ads that "the party's just beginning."[106] However, by 1988, as business sharply declined, so did maintenance. The once-thriving establishment became known as a "dirty" and dank place, a far cry from its glory days in the 1970s.

Despite the heated debate the ordinance sparked within the gay community, the 315 Health Club quietly shut its doors on March 28, 1988, just four days before the city council's vote.[107] The potential legal battles over building regulations likely factored in the decision to close, but if business had been booming like it was in 1979—when commercial sex establishments took the city to court—there might have been more resistance. For all that bathhouses symbolized to gay men—a carefree, optimistic era of potential liberation, a space uniquely theirs, representing a distinct culture—by 1988, men from the upper Midwest simply stopped going. Whether this reflected the "maturing" of the region's gay identity, as pro-ordinance advocates claimed or, more realistically, the overwhelming impact of AIDS, which had touched every aspect of public life, some gay men turned away from the spaces that had once openly celebrated their sexuality. While it is unclear whether gay sex became a strictly private affair at home, it was no longer proudly public.

The closure of the 315 Health Club represented a watershed moment, providing city officials a foothold to advance their redevelopment plans in the heart of the sex district.[108] The same week it closed, the bathhouse's owner sold the building to BSR Properties, a private real estate firm eager to capitalize on its location in the "trendy redevelopment area" of the warehouse district. BSR announced plans to convert the first floor into an upscale restaurant and the upper floors into studio lofts.[109] A developer with BSR told the *Star Tribune*, "I can assure you that whatever is done, the building will be gutted. There's nothing to save in that place . . . All the interior will be sandblasted to remove the years of *dust and dirt*. The only thing remaining will be the brick."[110] Concurrently, city councilmembers were also pushing forward on broader redevelopment efforts, such as proposals to demolish parts of Hennepin Avenue and replace affordable housing with a $115 million luxury development in Loring Park known as Laurel Village.[111] These efforts aligned with the city's broader strategy to attract young urban professionals, a vision consistent with Richard Florida's concept of the "creative class."[112]

At the same time that the 315 Health Club closed, the city seized all of Ferris Alexander's sex-related businesses following his conviction for racketeering. Block E, a section of downtown Minneapolis once home to several commercial sex establishments, fell to the wrecking ball. City Council President Alice Rainville had urged her colleagues to support a plan to tear down the businesses on Block E and temporarily turn the land into a parking lot, pending the development of a mixed-use facility. Rainville argued that despite Minneapolis's reputation as "the dominant business, commercial and retail center of the Midwest," Block E, with its "problem population" that included gay men frequenting sex-related businesses, remained "downtown's problem child."[113] Hardly an isolated incident, Rainville's attitude and language toward Block E reflected a broader trend in urban renewal that Neil Smith describes as "revanchist urbanism," or the removal of potential threats to property values and consumer-driven gentrification.[114] In the neoliberal imagination, businesses linked to vice are seen as incompatible with family-friendly entertainment and residential zones, thus deterring economic investment. City officials use exclusionary metaphors to suggest reclaiming inner cities from the supposed moral threats of alcohol, pornography, and casual sex with anonymous partners. Practically acting like a fountain of revanchist urbanism, Rainville proclaimed, "We must send a message that Hennepin is still downtown's turf, and we will reclaim it."[115]

As urban renewal surged, the future looked bleak for commercial sex establishments and only grew more so when the City of Minneapolis, on

April 1, 1988, finally voted in favor of the High Risk Sexual Conduct ordinance, amending the city's Code of Ordinances relating to contagious diseases. The ordinance essentially criminalized both homosexual and heterosexual sex outside private bedrooms.[116] Unsurprisingly, Coyle voted for the ordinance, to the disappointment of many of his gay constituents. On the eve of the vote, Coyle acknowledged the emotional strain the looming vote had caused him, saying: "For me, this is not easy. I have some people who won't speak to me. This is one of the tougher issues because it's so emotionally laden and passionate."[117] As the first openly gay Minneapolis City Councilmember, Coyle may have felt pressure to align with the preferences of most gay men, but no clear consensus existed. Except for Dick Brown, the most vocal gay voices opposed the ordinance. On April 7, 1988, Mayor Don Fraser, who had previously vetoed two antipornography ordinances authored by Catherine MacKinnon and Andrea Dworkin, signed the anti-bathhouse ordinance into law.[118]

In Coyle's mind, the bathhouse was less a symbol of gay pride than of gay pathology. It was a place that existed only because of the homophobia and self-loathing of the past, where scared and scarred men went wild with youthful abandon in a catharsis of sexual release. But as more men like him came out, staked their place in society, and embraced their same-sex desires without shame, a more stable, loving, and coupled—that is, homonormative—future could be theirs. Coyle told the *Star Tribune*, "I have a lot of confidence that the gay community is out. It's here to stay out," adding, "We're maturing as a community." To Coyle, those who opposed the ordinance perversely clung to their own trauma—men emotionally unable or selfishly unwilling to give up casual, anonymous sex. By failing to mature beyond the sexual excesses of steamy bathhouses and sweaty dance floors, they literally endangered the livelihood of the "community." Coyle's perspective, however, overlooked the possibility that some simply enjoyed casual sex and failed to consider the ordinance's impact on those without the race and class privilege to retreat to the private sphere.[119] These two groups would not disappear simply because the ordinance passed.

Coyle used the passage of the ordinance to assert a gay identity that he and Shilts claimed was distinct to the upper Midwest—an identity they positioned in contrast to the more well-known gay "meccas" of San Francisco and New York City. Drawing on Shilts's ideas, Coyle urged his critics to "Wake up. The '70s are over. Unlimited anonymous sex was never all that big in Minneapolis, but its days are over . . . Unlike San Francisco, Minneapolis has never been terribly dependent on these practices." Coyle flipped previously negative stereotypes of the upper Midwest—its provincialism, rural values, and overwhelmingly white population (seen as less cosmopolitan compared to coastal cities)—to his advantage. What might have once caused embarrassment, he reframed as markers of moral superiority and sexual responsibility among gay men in Minneapolis—signs of the region's middleness. In San Francisco or New York City, gay men remained—like popular images of "crack addicts"—"dependent" on irresponsible, "immature," and even self-destructive practices. But not in Minneapolis. In fact, when Coyle sat with Shilts during his visit to Minneapolis, Jim St. George, Coyle's former aide, recalled that as the men discussed the AIDS epidemic in San Francisco and New York City, Coyle used "his hands to sort of outline the East Coast and the West Coast" and said, "'You know, [the] guys on the coasts think [they're] the story . . . Actually, [they're] the parentheses. The story is here in the middle of the country.'"[120] While Coyle's remarks reflected a sense of pride in what he saw as a way of life resilient to the devastation of AIDS, time would prove him right in ways he could not foresee. With his brand of homonormativity on the rise, the so-called heartland would come to have as much—if not more—impact on gay identity in the years ahead than the celebrated "meccas."

Not everyone welcomed Coyle's praise; many of his gay constituents felt betrayed by his vote. In a letter published in *Equal Time*, a local gay man likened Coyle's support for the bathhouse ordinance on Good Friday to Judas's betrayal of Jesus: "We of the gay community know how Jesus felt when his 'friend' let him down, as you have done with us. He sold out for thirty pieces of silver. How many straight votes have you sold us out for?" The letter highlighted the widespread discontent among Coyle's gay constituents and vowed to rally "time, effort, and money" against his reelection.[121] Sensing the brewing controversy, Coyle seems to have kept a low profile. One of his supporters wrote, expressing concern over his absence from gay social spaces: "I've missed you at the 'Cloud 9' [gay bar] lately and now I think I know why—it's not so pleasant probably for you to be socializing in the gay community."[122] Coyle's retreat from public life may also have been shaped by his health; by this point, he was likely grappling with the effects of AIDS-related illness, which may have deepened his sense of vulnerability and isolation amid the political fallout.

While some gay men protested Coyle's vote by distancing themselves from him socially, others chose to take more direct action. On June 3, 1988, Tim Campbell, along with Ferris Alexander and an unnamed "John Doe," filed a lawsuit against the City of Minneapolis. They alleged that the bathhouse ordinance violated their First and Fourteenth Amendment rights. Campbell and Doe, as patrons of adult bookstores, claimed the ordinance would deter them from using the coin-operated booths for viewing films or live performances. Alexander, who owned six of the eight adult bookstores in Minneapolis, stated that his business was harmed because the ordinance prohibited doors, curtains, or other barriers in these booths. He reported a decline in profits as a result. A US District Court acknowledged Alexander's financial losses but considered them insignificant in light of the public health issues the ordinance aimed to address. The court also rejected Campbell's and Doe's argument that their right to privacy extended to watching sexually explicit films or live dancing in these establishments. It clarified that while privacy rights cover "the personal intimacies of the home, the family, marriage, parenthood, procreation, and child rearing," they do not extend to viewing explicit material in public venues.[123] In short, commercial sex establishments were not protected "zones of privacy." The case eventually reached the Eighth US Circuit Court of Appeals, which, on March 2, 1990, ruled in favor of the City of Minneapolis. The court upheld the city's authority to require the removal of booth doors as part of its AIDS prevention measures.[124] The court firmly established that commercial sex establishments were public spaces, where patrons had no fundamental right to view explicit material or engage in sexual activity, especially during a public health crisis. With this ruling, the previous agreement forged during the "reign of terror" was effectively undone.

The public nature of commercial sex establishments made them vulnerable to continuous state surveillance. At the Bathhouse, Sexual Freedom, and the Law forum, Coyle—who had successfully removed the vice squad from bathhouses a few years earlier—acknowledged that although he had changed his stance on their risks, he remained concerned about how the new ordinance would be enforced. While he assured the audience that "enforcement power would come from the Director of Public Health," Coyle expressed fears that "the police or health department [would use] entrapment to build evidence for action."[125] On the eve of the vote, his doubts persisted.[126] "I support the ordinance as a public health measure as long as it is enforced by public health authorities."[127] In response, City Councilmember Hilary issued a memorandum clarifying that the Minneapolis Health Department would be solely responsible for inspecting affected businesses and ensuring compliance with the ordinance.[128] She emphasized that police involvement would be limited to charging individuals who removed warning signs from noncompliant establishments—deemed "hazardous sites"—with misdemeanors.[129]

Coyle's fears about the ordinance leading to vice squad raids would be proven correct. From May to October 1993, the vice squad, citing the bathhouse ordinance, raided several adult bookstores, including Buns and Roses and the Broadway Bookstore, after receiving reports of "high-risk" behaviors. Undercover officers witnessed men "groping genital areas" and "propositioning others for sex" while also finding discarded condom wrappers on the floor. Multiple patrons were arrested for "indecent conduct," and the store owners were fined. A memo from an aide to then-Mayor Sharon Sayles Belton accused the MPD of overstepping its authority with these so-called health-related raids. "In reality . . . what the police should be doing," the aide pointed out, "is contacting the Commissioner of Health, who then based on the information the police provide declare the place a Health Risk."[130] The vice squad had returned in full force to its old stomping grounds—but now, cloaked in the language of public health rather than morality, it wielded the ordinance as a tool to surveil and criminalize sex between men.

The Political Potential of Sex

Despite no real evidence that "public" or "commercial" sex automatically meant "unsafe," the antibathhouse ordinance fostered this perception among the public. Ironically, the ordinance hindered efforts by gay community leaders to challenge the stereotype that gay male sexuality was compulsive, immoral, and deadly. Instead, it reinforced the idea that AIDS stemmed from gay immorality and that the bathhouse was ground zero. The panic and contempt sparked by the bathhouse debate outlasted even the public's fear of AIDS itself. By 2017, nearly thirty years after the ordinance's passage, medical advancements had transformed AIDS from a death sentence to a chronic but manageable condition for those with access to treatment. Yet in January of that year, police officers, working on behalf of fire and housing inspectors, raided The Warehouse—an unlicensed sex club in north Minneapolis, near the former site of the 315 Health Club. For three nights a week, gay men of all ages paid $15 to enter and have casual, often anonymous, sex. Like Dick Brown a generation earlier, a local gay man, John Mehring, opposed the club's activities and took it upon himself to shut it down. When critics accused him of bitterness due to his HIV-positive status, Mehring insisted his concerns were strictly about safety and licensing.

The basement lacked a fire escape, he argued, and people could be trapped in an emergency.[131] Mehring tried every angle, contacting news outlets, politicians, and even the police, until city inspectors finally shut down the club for being unsuitable for commercial use. The party moved to a smaller, private residence, but without the free HIV testing and safer-sex messaging provided by the Red Door Clinic. By 2025, the entire operation had closed, leaving Minneapolis as one of the few American cities without a designated gay sex venue.[132] Despite the passage of time, little has been done to amend—let alone repeal—the ordinance, as gay men, having won so much in the intervening years, do not want to breathe new life into the damning images of irresponsible and "immature" sexual hedonism.[133]

What did gay men lose—and continue to lose—after the ordinance passed? Beyond the physical space of sexual expression, one perspective argues that the ordinance curtailed a broader horizon of gay political possibility—foreclosing solidarities and counterpublics fostered through erotic freedom in favor of a politics of middleness grounded in respectability. As Samuel Delany notes, bathhouses and sex clubs facilitated and even encouraged contact among men of different races, classes, and sexualities. Through both anonymous and non-anonymous encounters, these men formed what Delany calls "contact relations," creating powerful cross-race and interclass bonds. "Given the mode of capitalism under which we live," Delany observes, "life is at its most rewarding, productive, and pleasant when the greatest number of people understand, appreciate, and seek out interclass contact and communication conducted in a mode of good will."[134] Building on Delany's ideas, José Esteban Muñoz sees commercial sex establishments and the public and semi-public sexual cultures they nurture as enabling a queer counterpublic. In this space, "the transformative potential of queer sex and public manifestations of such sexuality" serve "both [as] a respite from the abjection of homosexuality and a reformatting of that every abjection."[135] For both Delany and Muñoz, the presence of massed bodies engaged in queer public sex signals political power, challenging the idea of sex business patrons as "isolated perverts." Instead, these bodies, united in collective libidinal pleasure, gesture toward a queer sexual architecture built outside the spatial blueprints of heteronormative—and now homonormative—confinement.

This corporeal mass, however, becomes increasingly elusive as the crackdown on sexual dissidence intensifies. The Minneapolis antibathhouse ordinance sought to ban physical contact between patrons—precisely because it was this shared touch, and the communal intimacies it generated, that threatened the state's rigid separation of public and private spheres, a division central to neoliberal ideals of property and respectability. The erotic and emotional connections fostered through public sex and acts of communal care disrupt the public-private divide that underlies Western regulation of sexuality. Nonetheless, such intimacies expand our understanding of who deserves care and reveal the deeper investments that emerge from this recognition. While figures like Coyle, Brown, Hanson, and other advocates of homonormativity in Minneapolis may have been seen primarily as white, educated, affluent men—whose same-sex desire was treated as incidental—Delany and Muñoz argue that queer public and semi-public sex is essential to imagining a world beyond neoliberal containment. Only by rejecting the solitary "pervert" model associated with public sex and affirming a collective identity of sexual dissidence can true transformative power be realized.

During the 1980s and early 1990s, as integrationist politics gained momentum, those who witnessed the defeat of liberationist ideals often point to the 1988 antibathhouse ordinance as a turning point. As bathhouses faded into memory, so did the idealism of an earlier era—when being gay was synonymous with being subversive, and men like Dick Brown, who championed "decency" and "respectability" stood on the outside, frustrated by the reluctance of others to adopt these values. With the ordinance's passage, the tide turned in Brown's favor, as more gay men in Minnesota reconciled with a world that had marginalized them and then largely blamed them for a disease under which they suffered disproportionally. Now, men like Campbell would be on the outside, wondering why their community could be bought off with the hope of fitting into an unfair world. As bathhouses, bookstores, and X-rated theaters withered in Minneapolis, liberationists scrambled to preserve a culture of cruising. But this practice would, in turn, draw unwanted attention of its own.

6 Cruising All the Way Home

The Draw of the Park

On the night of August 3, 1989, State Representative Glen H. Anderson (DFL), a powerful figure in Minnesota politics, drove from his small farming town of Bellingham to Loring Park in Minneapolis. At fifty, Anderson was a seventeen-year veteran of the legislature, chair of the House Appropriations Committee, and a married father of three. That Thursday, he offered an undercover police officer $20 for sex and was arrested in a Minneapolis Police Department (MPD) sting targeting prostitution in the park. The fallout was swift. Anderson issued a public apology, denied any homosexual tendencies, and blamed his behavior on pornography. He vowed to seek psychiatric help and called on the Minnesota Legislature to "find a way to close the porn shops."[1] With the closure of the 315 Health Club, Anderson would not be the last high-profile figure caught engaging in public sex at the parks. Just a month later, in September 1989, vice officers arrested twenty-eight men for soliciting sex in Loring Park, including a priest, a psychologist, and two social workers.[2] The MPD referred to these operations as "fag detail," a crude counterpart to their "john detail" stings. Undercover officers would lure men into isolated areas of the park before making arrests. If the men suspected entrapment and attempted to flee, officers could still use force and arrest them for disorderly or indecent conduct.[3] Despite the heavy police presence, men kept coming. One officer, astonished by the persistence, compared it to "wagons circling out there."[4]

By 1989, the Minneapolis City Council, under the pretense of HIV prevention, had cracked down on the city's last bathhouse and nearly driven its adult bookstores and X-rated theaters out of business. Councilmember Brian J. Coyle believed that shutting down these commercial sex establishments would encourage gay men to pursue long-term, monogamous relationships, which he saw as key to combating AIDS and reducing violence. This spatial fix, however, had pushed some gay men further into the streets, sparking complaints from residents concerned about their quality of life and property values. As the centerpiece of public sexual cultures in Minneapolis, Loring Park inevitably became the next target for regulation. After all the previous battles to clamp down on the physical institutions and cultural practices that accommodated public and semi-public sex, cruising became the next front in the fight against queer social practices.

Cruising, as Phil Hubbard describes it, encompasses a "subtle subversion" of the typical choreography of city life.[5] Often occurring at night to maintain the anonymity of participants—some of whom may not identify as gay—cruising involves a "sexual vernacular," a nonverbal language of "looks, glances, and gestures that may culminate in exposure, touching, masturbation," and oral or anal sex, sometimes in the presence of others.[6] Taking place in public spaces like parks or semi-public ones like restrooms—both environments where sexual activity is typically deemed inappropriate—cruising blurs the line between public and private, creating what Michel Foucault calls "heterotopias"—counterpublic sites that invert everyday space and their associated norms.[7] For this very reason, cruising can also come with great risk as it exposes men to police and others seeking to enforce social order.

Why did Loring Park become a hub for certain social activities? While Minneapolis boasted several parks, Loring Park stood out due to its proximity to what a gay liberationist collective in the 1970s dubbed a gay "ghetto."[8] In 1980, a gay periodical tried to measure the growth of the city's LGBTQ population from 1970 to 1978 by looking at the concentration of young, single, childless households. Though an imperfect measure, childless unmarried people were often used as a proxy for identifying concentrations of gay men and lesbians. Minneapolis's single population rose from 22 percent in 1970 to about 30 percent by 1978, with nearly half of all renter households consisting of single individuals. The renter population was also very young, with 40 percent under thirty years old.[9] If the number of young, single people served as a rough indicator for LGBTQ residents, then Loring Park, according to census data, had the largest LGBTQ population in the city. In 1980, Loring Park's population was 5,908. By 1990, it had grown to 6,586, with the percentage of residents ages twenty to forty-four rising slightly from 50.8 percent in 1980 to 54.5 percent.[10] Despite the fact that more residents had reached what the city's Department of Community Planning and Economic Development referred to as "family formation age" by 1990, the neighborhood remained largely childless throughout the 1980s. In fact, Loring Park had only 871 family households in 1990, the fewest among Minneapolis neighborhoods.[11]

Loring Park's cultural and physical layout shaped a distinctive sexual geography, one that stood in contrast to the traditional link between sexual intimacy and domestic spaces.[12] In addition to its proximity to the city's gay bars in downtown Minneapolis and its cheap rooming houses, the thirty-four-acre park offered dark pathways and lush foliage that contributed to its anonymous, forbidden male sexuality. However, the same features that attracted gay men also made the park dangerous.[13] While Loring Park had a reputation for late-night cruising, it became a target for bashers and robbers preying on gay men. The 1985 murder of James McArthur, stabbed to death by a young man he encountered while cruising the park, prompted Coyle to warn others "to be wary of the park."[14]

Loring Park's location—just steps from downtown Minneapolis and the Hennepin Avenue commercial corridor—also made the neighborhood prime real estate for city planners. Following the city's clearance and redevelopment of 40 percent of downtown under the Gateway Urban Renewal Plan of the 1950s, attention turned to Loring Park.[15] In 1973, the city established the Loring Park Development District, aiming to "rebuild" a nine-block area by replacing aging brownstone apartments and single-room occupancy hotels with upscale condos and townhomes. This so-called revitalization displaced about a thousand residents—roughly one-sixth of the neighborhood's population—most of them working-class and many who relied on public spaces for intimacy, kinship, and care.[16] Urban renewal in Loring Park did more than alter the built environment; it reconfigured the neighborhood's social and spatial dynamics. With the emergence of AIDS, city planners increasingly framed spatial clearance as a form of public health management. Such narratives allowed redevelopment to be recast as both protective and progressive, even as these interventions disproportionately impacted populations already rendered vulnerable by race, class, and sexuality. The transformation of Loring Park thus reflected not simply a drive for economic growth but a remapping of queer urban life—one that privileged privacy, domesticity, and consumerism over older patterns of communal intimacy.

This chapter examines a proposed anticruising ordinance aimed at curbing public sexual cultures in and around Loring Park. Similar to other spatial fixes, the ordinance sought to privatize expressions of intimacy in ways that aligned with the neighborhood's ongoing gentrification. Some gay residents, particularly white gay men, supported the ordinance, seeing it as a path to sexual normativity that would ostensibly protect property values. However, in the flush of AIDS moral panic, this push also targeted the elimination of public sexual cultures and the spaces that incubated them. In contrast, queer activists—gay liberationists—opposed the ordinance, linking the crackdown on public sexual cultures to historical concerns of over-policing and oppressive moralism. This chapter concludes by discussing Coyle's fix that finally resolved the debates: legally recognized domestic partnerships. These partnerships represented a solution to both AIDS and urban blight by encouraging monogamy—that is, privatized over communal forms of intimacy—and enhancing property values without the heavy-handed policing and surveillance that had long shaped the LGBTQ community's relationship with law enforcement.

A Crown Jewel of Urban Renewal

Once a wealthy enclave at the turn of the twentieth century, Loring Park underwent a transformation into a more modest neighborhood by the 1940s. After the demolition of the Gateway District—the city's original downtown and "Skid Row"—in the 1950s, some of its displaced residents moved into Loring Park, drawn by its subdivided houses and affordable apartments.[17] Robert Halfhill, a gay liberationist and longtime resident of the area, recalled that the Gateway had been home not only to "pimps, winos, and prostitutes" but also to queer people, and when urban renewal came for their homes, they, like others, looked to Loring Park. "George," an elderly gay man interviewed by *Equal Time*, confirmed that while Loring Park "had always been gay . . . it increased after the Gateway was torn down." Although some bars in the Gateway turned a blind eye to the homosexuality of patrons, when the 19 Bar opened in Loring Park in 1957, it openly catered to gay men and lesbians. A younger generation of LGBTQ people, inspired by civil rights and the social movements of the 1960s, helped establish an identifiable community within the neighborhood. According to Halfhill, "Loring Park was becoming the new area where those that society did not want were relegated."[18] In 1973, the *Minneapolis Tribune Picture Magazine* noted that Loring Park "has to be the most incredibly diverse community in Minneapolis, with its many elderly, retired people and young singles who like walking to their jobs downtown . . . It is also home for what is probably the city's largest concentration of gay people . . . and it also includes a large number of Indians, blacks in stylish clothes, bearded white males in ragged denim, young married couples, [college] students . . . wine-drinking panhandlers and even an occasional prostitute."[19] While city planners viewed this population as "undesirable," they saw the neighborhood itself as a source of untapped profit.

In the 1960s, with a hemorrhaging tax base, the City of Minneapolis launched a campaign to attract corporations, boost the job market, and increase housing options near downtown. A key part of this initiative was Metro Center '85, a plan created by the Department of Community Planning and Economic Development, which proposed building modern housing in the Loring Park neighborhood, conveniently located within walking distance of the central business district.[20] As part of that effort, the Office of the City Coordinator in 1971 finalized a redevelopment plan for the area between Loring Park and Nicollet Mall. The proposal included extending Nicollet Mall to Grant Street, creating a greenway linking the mall to the park, constructing more housing for downtown office workers, and expanding the Minneapolis Community and Technical College (MCTC). At the time, the nine-block area generated less than $900,000 in annual real estate taxes, but the city projected that full redevelopment could bring in nearly $5 million a year.[21] The potential to attract high-income residents and revitalize downtown led the city council to officially designate the nine-block area as the Loring Park Development District (LPDD) in 1972.

Surveys from the 1970s revealed that the LPDD was home to a largely poor, transient, and single population, which influenced the decision to pursue demolition. The area marked for redevelopment included 1,043 housing units, mainly apartments, efficiencies, and hotel rooms, with rents ranging from $60 and $100 per month. Residents were mostly young adults, many of whom were LGBTQ, or elderly, with 46 percent age sixty or older and 75 percent living alone. A substantial portion, 38 percent, were retired, unemployed, or dependent on welfare, and 69 percent had annual household incomes below $6,000.[22] In addition to the residential demographics, the commercial scene along Nicollet Avenue, the neighborhood's main business corridor, further reflected economic hardship. Liquor stores and entertainment venues made up 32 percent of the occupied businesses, while 14 percent of storefronts stood vacant.[23] These statistics underscored the disconnect between the existing residents and businesses and the wealthier population and commercial enterprises envisioned in the city's Metro Center '85 redevelopment plan.

Though neighborhood groups won some victories against the wrecking ball, chunks of Loring Park still succumbed to new developments. One such project was the Greenway Gables, a $4.5 million endeavor consisting of

FIGURE 6.1 Booth Manor Condos and Greenway Gables Townhomes in Loring Park, with Loring Green West under construction in the lower right corner, 1980. Courtesy of the Hennepin County Library.

forty-three gated townhomes. Each unit boasted vaulted ceilings, gabled exteriors, private patios, and scenic views of Loring Park and the downtown skyline. The development, marketed with images of young heterosexual couples in formal attire sipping cocktails in a private courtyard, exuded an air of sophistication and privilege. While the city sold the land to developers for a mere $85,000, the townhomes were listed between $90,000 and $150,000.[24] Similarly, condos in the nearby Loring Green complex, promoted as "the essence of refinement . . . and elegance," ranged from $115,000 to an impressive $436,000. Advertisements for Loring Green positioned it as "a prestigious address for discerning families who place a premium on luxury, privacy, state-of-the-art security and the peace of mind that comes with financial stability."[25] Indeed, residents of these developments were financially well off, with a median income of $75,000 at Greenway Gables in 1985—equivalent to roughly $227,000 in 2025. A quarter of residents earned between $50,000 and $100,000, or approximately $152,000 to $303,000 in 2025 (fig. 6.1).[26] As redevelopment transformed the area, *The Minneapolis*

Tribune noted, "Many of the living quarters of bums and prostitutes are no longer there."[27]

Upon completion of all projects associated with the LPDD in 1986, the real estate journal *Downtown Profile* praised the initiative as an "overwhelming success," highlighting its role in "transforming the district from a typical decaying urban albatross into a renewed residential neighborhood with many attractive amenities."[28] However, concerns about safety remained a challenge throughout the LPDD's development. Before redevelopment, the Loring Park neighborhood had a notably high crime rate, with assaults occurring 5.5 times more often than the city average. Acknowledging the need to address these safety issues, the LPDD adopted principles from defensible space theory, which suggests that crime can be reduced through strategic environmental design, such as encouraging natural surveillance to allow residents to monitor public areas from their homes. The goal was to extend residents' influence beyond their own dwellings, fostering a sense of community vigilance that could help deter crime.[29] The Department of Housing and Urban Development (HUD), drawing on defensible space concepts, noted that new buildings in the LPDD would feature "structures . . . around the perimeter of the parcels"—that is, gates—and "controlled access." These elements were meant to enhance visual surveillance of semi-public spaces, with apartment windows and balconies serving as the "eyes" of the community. Residents were expected to keep an eye on the streets and report any criminal activity or violations to the MPD.[30]

The building designs functioned as intended, and by 1979, as tower cranes dotted the Loring Park skyline, new property owners began reaching out to the MPD for help in addressing a growing issue in the neighborhood: cruising. Among these new owners, Loring Hill Properties wrote to Minneapolis Deputy Police Chief Leonard Brucciani on March 19, 1979, stating, "A certain element of the male population of this community finds the sidewalks, stairs, and entry of the Building to be a convenient meeting and pick-up location during the evening hours seven days a week . . . As owners of the building, we would appreciate any efforts on the part of the Minneapolis Police Department which might eliminate the costs, complaints and notoriety which result from these gatherings." In response, Brucciani forwarded the letter to officers of the downtown police precinct responsible for patrolling Loring Park, urging them to "Please respond to their needs." A scribbled note at the bottom of Brucciani's memo—"Please don't blame us for having to harass the gays"—hinted at potential backlash, implying that officers were simply carrying out the demands of Loring Park's new, affluent residents.[31]

As developers constructed new condos and wealthier residents moved in, complaints only grew louder, highlighting the looming threat of gentrification to the neighborhood's bohemian character. At the center of this debate was Citizens for a Loring Park Community (CLPC), a group formed in 1972 when residents banded together to prevent the demolition of the historic 1906 Loring Park Shelter Building. CLPC had long championed historic preservation and, in the mid-1970s, even opposed the demolition of low-income housing, condemning the displacement of low-income residents. By the 1980s, however, CLPC began to shift—from an emphasis on broad-based resident inclusion in city decision-making to a stance more closely aligned with the priorities of city officials and real estate developers. As more condo owners joined, the group increasingly focused on issues related to property values, building maintenance, and neighborhood investment. Signs of this transformation surfaced during an August 1980 CLPC meeting, where a resident of the newly constructed Loring Way Condominiums complained about noise and slow police response times.[32] At a follow-up meeting the next month, representatives from the MPD and Minneapolis Park Police listened as one resident expressed frustration, saying, "You can sit and have coffee at 3:00 or 4:00 a.m. and see them sitting on the steps," referring to gay men who cruised the area. An MPD officer encouraged residents to report disturbances and assured them that gay men would be arrested. He also emphasized that the vice squad was actively patrolling the neighborhood and, despite LGBTQ concerns over recent raids on bathhouses and bookstores, defended the squad, insisting its officers were "very good people."[33]

Concerned property owners targeted the sources they could identify, including gay bars. Developers of new properties, such as the LaSalle Court and the Parkway, lobbied flamboyant pro-business city councilmember Barbara Carlson to act against the 19 Bar. In response, gay liberationist and Loring Park resident Robert Halfhill circulated a flyer warning gay renters: "With gentrification of the Loring Park neighborhood, the pressure to expel Gays from the area is continually increasing." Halfhill's concerns were echoed at a neighborhood meeting, where one property owner suggested that rising rents might be enough to drive these "undesirables" out. Fears about tenants witnessing "embarrassing" incidents from their windows led to discussions of increased police surveillance, though the meeting's focus on elaborate sting operations left some property owners feeling unsatisfied, reflecting ongoing tensions within the community over policing.[34]

Worried about gay expulsion, Halfhill urged gay renters to attend CLPC meetings "so that gay interests will be adequately represented in the organization." However, he missed an essential new dynamic: Some gay men were among those advocating for stricter measures against cruising.[35] In 1980, Halfhill could be forgiven for not seeing this, as these voices were still few. But as more gay renters became property owners, they migrated increasingly into the position of the integrationists. Poorer gay renters, as a general rule, had fewer problems with cruising in the neighborhood, but the arrival and fear of AIDS would give added ammunition to the arguments of the property owners.

Cozying Up to the Cops

The arrest of Anderson in Loring Park in August 1989 occurred at an auspicious political moment. Throughout the 1980s, complaints about cruising persisted, but little action was taken. Then, in the middle of a tough reelection campaign in 1989, city councilmember Barbara Carlson proposed an amendment to the city's traffic code aimed at reducing late-night traffic and noise associated with perceived prostitution in Loring Park. In cold northern climates like Minnesota, men often cruised by car for much of the year, but Carlson's measure prohibited "the operation of a motor vehicle past a traffic control point three or more times" between 9:00 p.m. and 6:00 a.m. If an officer saw a driver pass through a designated "no cruising zone" more than twice, that motorist would receive a warning, including written notice that a third pass would result in a crime.[36] On the third pass, the driver could be fined up to $200 and/or arrested (fig. 6.2). While the ordinance was meant to address public concerns, it failed to distinguish between cruising and prostitution, casting suspicion on all public expressions of gay male sexuality. As a result, it faced criticism for its overly broad scope and potential for police abuse.

Representing Minneapolis's wealthiest ward, Carlson claimed she was responding to her constituents' complaints that cruising had worsened over the past year. Residents reported that late-night cruising by men seeking male sex workers disturbed the neighborhood, generated criminal activity, and tarnished the area's reputation.[37] The community responded with organized efforts, such as block clubs and pressure on law enforcement, aiming to eliminate what the *Star Tribune* described as "the tawdry elements that have turned the name of their once elegant neighborhood into a code word for gay cruising."[38] Real estate agents and other stakeholders

FIGURE 6.2 Two men depicted "cruising" in Loring Park, as featured in the *Star Tribune* on September 24, 1989. Photo by Brian Peterson. Copyright © Star Tribune Media Company LLC. Used with permission. All rights reserved.

concerned with property values shrieked that "the park's notoriety as a center for gay vice may depress condominium sales, disappointing those who hoped the area would enjoy an economic resurgence with an influx of young professionals."[39]

Critics accused Carlson of doing the developers' bidding, as she had received more donations from them than any other councilmember. Carlson, however, dismissed the accusations, stating that developers valued her "business background" and her understanding of the "needs of business."[40] The two sides finally faced off at a neighborhood meeting on September 14, 1989. More than a hundred people packed into the assembly room of the Oak Grove Apartment building, and tensions quickly flared. On one side were both gay and straight residents who argued that the ordinance was not an attack on LGBTQ people but rather a measure to protect "quality of life."[41] A gay male resident of Loring Park emphasized that his sexual orientation had nothing to do with his support for the ordinance. He was more concerned about the freedom from "dangerous" people loitering and the constant noise, including "Madonna blasting from car radios."[42] Another gay male resident of Loring Park echoed these concerns in an interview with

Equal Time, saying, "We got tired of calling 911 when trouble came up . . . I have lived in the neighborhood for five years and prostitutes' attitudes have really become more aggressive and violent."[43] At the meeting, the most vocal supporters put aside their differences and united as property owners, worried that the ongoing public sex and drug exchanges would cause their relatively new condominiums—most built within the past fifteen years—to deteriorate and drag the neighborhood back into decline.

On the other side, opponents scoffed at the notion that the ordinance was a mere "quality of life" issue. For them, it amounted to nothing more than a homophobic overreaction and a restriction on free movement. They peppered the night with shouts of "Move to the suburbs!" and jabs at Carlson. At one point, an angry attendee asked her, "When did you discover the gay community?" To this accusation, Carlson raged back that she had long been a supporter of the gay community, adding, "I understand the pain of the johns who are closeted, but this is a problem of violence and drug abuse in an era of AIDS."[44] The meeting turned chaotic at times, but in between the shouting and heckling, opponents raised substantive issues. They questioned how anyone could trust the MPD, known for harassing LGBTQ people, to determine who was and was not a resident of Loring Park. Officer Tom Sawina, assigned to the park, tried to reassure the crowd, stating, "The police are not out to get the residents. Prostitutes and people cruising do not live in the area."[45] In short, they were outsiders. Some attendees grew uneasy about the possibility of having to prove they lived in the neighborhood, but Sawina convinced them that officers generally knew who lived there and that the ordinance would not be enforced nightly—occasional enforcement would be enough to send a message. Ten days later, a journalist who accompanied the vice squad on a routine prostitution sting in the park reported that none of the "johns" arrested lived in Loring Park: "One was from Bloomington, one from Minnetonka," both suburbs of Minneapolis, "and the other from Cuba."[46]

Critics of the ordinance argued that its rationale made little sense, raising suspicions of a more insidious motive. Tim Campbell, staunch liberationist and publisher of *GLC Voice*, along with others, questioned why "closeted gay johns looking for hustlers, drug peddlers looking for clients and gay bashers looking for victims" would draw attention with a "parade of cars" if they were truly causing such disturbances.[47] Instead, many queer activists—including the surviving gay liberationists from the 1970s and a growing group of younger sex radicals—viewed the city's anticruising ordinance as an attack on civil liberties. ACT UP/Minnesota voiced opposition, warning that the ordinance would disperse sex workers and hinder safer-sex outreach programs. Eric Shambach, a member of ACT UP/Minnesota, likened the restrictions on movement to apartheid policies in South Africa.[48] While some found this comparison extreme, many still expressed concern about the police deciding who had the right to be in the neighborhood. One former Loring Park resident, writing to a newspaper, argued that construction, not prostitution, was responsible for the noise and parking issues and feared the ordinance would target queer sociality, "especially with the historically documented antigay/lesbian sentiment of the Minneapolis Police Department."[49] Another resident shared that while cruising did not scare him, he feared gay bashers and the "police, after being harassed a few times. They will stop you if you 'look' gay; I've personally experienced this."[50]

Frustrated, liberationists, including Campbell, fumed that if a community of racial minorities had been "redlined" like Loring Park, "there would have been an uprising."[51] Robert Halfhill, a fellow ACT UP/Minnesota member, agreed and called for militant action. He saw the ordinance as part of a broader effort to push gay men underground, telling *Equal Time*, "First it was closing the bathhouses, and they're still going after bookstore arrests, now it's Loring Park."[52] But, as Halfhill maintained, Loring Park served as a vital social hub for gay men, explaining, "Straights have to realize that they have the entire society to meet each other in, we don't."[53] Another gay male resident echoed this sentiment, asking: "Where do gays meet, where do we find friends? In some people's lives, it's the park." These statements reflected the growing frustration among gay men, who felt city regulations were restricting their public spaces to meet. Not all gay men supported the state's suppression of distinctly gay spaces under the guise of public health or safety, and some decided merely complaining about it was not enough.

With bathhouses long gone, X-rated theaters giving way to home videos, and adult bookstores just barely holding on in the face of political pressure and increased policing, some gay men responded with bold, public action to protect another distinctly queer space and practice. On September 17, 1989, just days after the contentious meeting at the Oak Grove Apartment building, a group splintered off from ACT UP/Minnesota. Frustrated that some members did not believe cruising fell under the group's mission, they formed F.A.G.S. (Friends Against Gay Suppression).[54] Richard Simon, who oversaw F.A.G.S., modeled it after Queer Nation, coming up with the name to reclaim the slur "fag." Simon explained, "I thought it would be good to kind of give the word a positive [spin]. When you heard the word, you would think of our group and [the] positive things that we worked on."⁵⁵ Promoting the concept of "outrageous activism" or "a blend of direct political action, gay-guerilla street theater, protest marches, and civil disobedience," F.A.G.S. challenged the idea that public sex was inherently unsafe and defended commercial sex establishments as essential for HIV education and prevention. It sponsored rallies and even organized voter registrations all in the name of defeating Carlson. Rejecting the culture of middle-class respectability embraced by gay property owners, F.A.G.S. represented one of the first groups, since the liberationist days, to pursue a broader political agenda.

F.A.G.S. wasted no time organizing a protest aimed at both the figure it held responsible for the proposed law and the ideals behind it. Two weeks after its founding, in the early hours of Sunday, October 1, 1989—right after the bars closed—F.A.G.S. members staged a "cruise-in" outside Carlson's upscale Kenwood Isles home. Protesters had distributed handbills at gay bars two days earlier, urging patrons to "Cruise around Barbie's house," a mocking reference to Carlson (fig. 6.3).⁵⁶ Dean Asmundson, a member of both ACT UP/Minnesota and F.A.G.S., recalled, "We took the cruising out of Loring Park and into Kenwood [Isles], which is a posh area of town." The media was also invited, and the event turned into quite a spectacle. "We had a real circus going on. People were driving around, honking their horns . . . It was an obnoxious thing to do, but it was a total zap type action"—a term for surprise, direct confrontations with political or corporate entities.⁵⁷

Around eighty people showed up, some dressed in black and pearls to mimic Carlson's signature look, while others in the crowd held up defaced Carlson campaign posters. As they reached Carlson's street, protesters found it blocked by rubber traffic pylons. Under the lights of television cameras, an irate Tim Campbell, a frequent critic of Carlson, grabbed a cone and slammed it repeatedly against her front door.⁵⁸ When Carlson and her husband appeared at the front door, they were dressed, as Asmundson recalls, like "Ozzie and Harriet"—she in a fancy nightgown and pearls, he in pajamas and slippers.⁵⁹ As Carlson gave a television interview, behind her, in full view of the television cameras, Campbell scuffled with Carlson's husband before being wrestled to the ground by a neighbor. The entire scene on Carlson's front porch was both slightly ridiculous and entirely shocking, but at least one man there that night, Wolfgang Wolf, a F.A.G.S. member, declared the cruise-in a rousing success. In one respect, he was right.⁶⁰ The next day, all four of the city's TV news broadcasts led with coverage of the anticruising ordinance.⁶¹

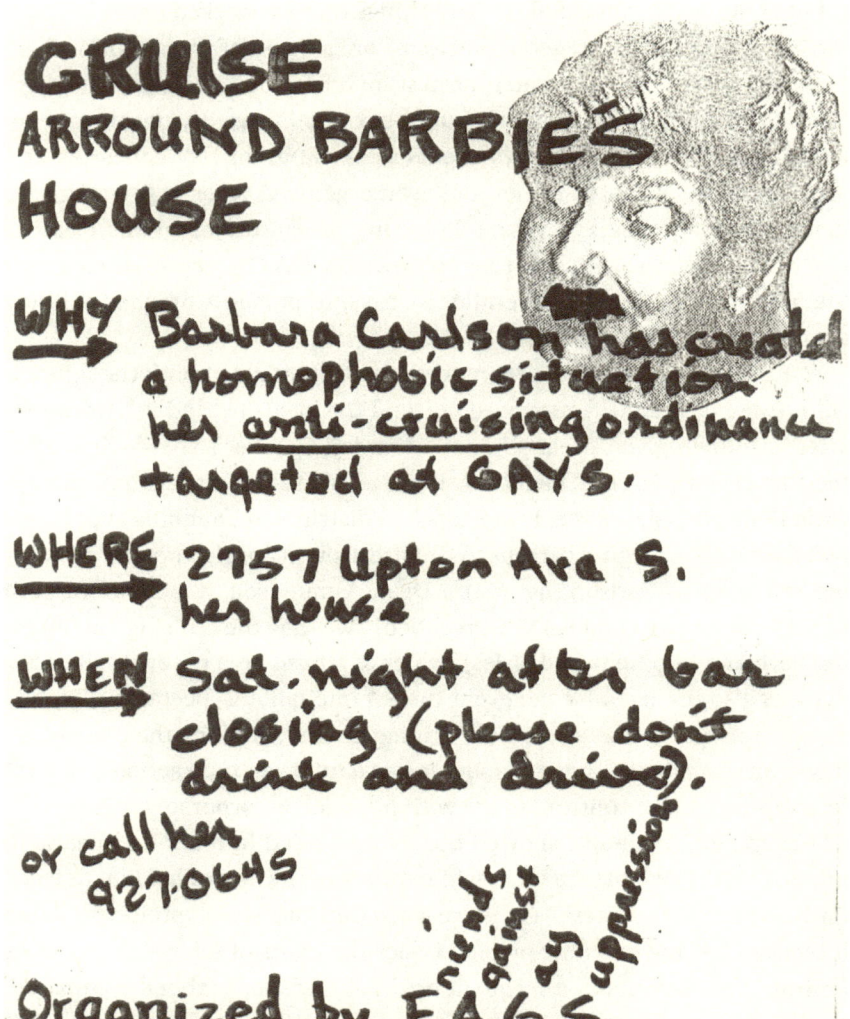

FIGURE 6.3 Flyer created by F.A.G.S. (Friends Against Gay Suppression) promoting a "cruise-in" at Barbara Carlson's home, 1989. From the Tretter Collection Information Files, Box 2, Folder: Cruising Ordinance, Minneapolis, 1980s. Courtesy of the Tretter Collection in GLBT Studies, University of Minnesota, Twin Cities.

In response to Campbell's altercation with Carlson's husband, the emergent integrationist faction of gay Minneapolis voiced its criticism.[62] One letter to the editor of *Twin Cities Gaze* featured a man apologizing to Carlson on behalf of the local gay community for Campbell's behavior: "As a member of the Twin Cities Gay Community, I would like to apologize for the unconscionable behavior of Mr. Tim Campbell regarding your proposed 'anti-cruising' ordinance in Loring Park." He added that, despite Campbell appointing himself as the community's spokesperson and the media accepting this narrative, "nothing could be farther from the truth. What Mr. Campbell is doing is grand-standing and making a general nuisance of himself, and giving all of us a bad name."[63] Another gay man, writing to the *Star Tribune*, urged heterosexual readers to "not judge the gay community" based on Campbell's "irresponsible behavior," adding that such conduct "cannot be condoned by a community which seeks to have its own privacy rights respected."[64] For these men, Campbell's indecorous behavior was on par with his pernicious politics. A letter to *Equal Time* argued that the only attack on the gay community came from Campbell, and his "outrageous behavior and claim of being the 'Great Gay Spokesman'" had "once again cast embarrassment on the entire gay/lesbian community." The letter further suggested that Campbell perpetuated the homophobic stereotype of the gay community as a group who "only knows anonymous sex in dark and public places."[65] As gentrification solidified bourgeois ideals of public and private comportment, the promiscuous homosexual seeking intimacy in public spaces stood as the antithesis of homonormativity's focus on the private home. A rising gay bourgeoisie was all too willing to side with politicians and developers in labeling public sex as hazardous, morally corrupt, and, in the era of AIDS, unsanitary.

Indeed, the anti-Campbell crowd defended the ordinance as a crucial measure for HIV prevention. They claimed that the gentrification of Loring Park would help mitigate HIV transmission by reducing spaces where gay men engaged in rushed, furtive, and careless sex. A commentator in the *Twin Cities Gaze* criticized married men for cruising the park and then returning home to their families, asserting that the ordinance was not just about improving quality of life but protecting public health. "From a public health point of view," he wrote, "it is time that the city took action to discourage the hustlers and their customers (mostly married men), who meet the hustlers and take home God-knows-what diseases to their unsuspecting wives." A gay male resident of Loring Park and former board member of CLPC wrote to the *Twin Cities Gaze*, urging people to support the ordinance not just for residents' right to "peace and quiet" over "some 'straight' from the 'burbs' in a quest for anonymous sex" but also because "this type of sexual activity relates to the spread of AIDS."[66] Supporters of the cruising ordinance grew frustrated with individuals like Campbell and groups like F.A.G.S., who, as one writer to *Equal Time* sarcastically remarked, defend cruising as if it were "a part of the gay lifestyle which needs to be protected like some ancient ritual."[67] Another gay male resident of Loring Park told *Equal Time* he welcomed a stronger police presence, saying it would help some gay men finally feel safe, comfortable, and welcome in their city—a turn of events that would have undoubtedly shocked gay liberationists of the early 1970s.[68]

By his own admission, Campbell could have cared less what his critics thought, as he had little desire to cultivate mainstream acceptance. Instead of confronting a homophobic society, Campbell noted that many of his detractors were simply "trying to get by on being polite," a "survival technique" to which many gay men clung. "Faggots," he found, "aren't supposed to get angry."[69] He also remarked that some people wanted to frame the gay rights movement as a civil rights issue rather than part of the broader sexual revolution. However, Campbell argued that most people needed to experience their own sexual revolution before they could fully engage with civil rights. To him, gay civil rights would only arise from a strong and proud gay identity, which meant embracing all aspects of gay sexuality—including cruising. "Admitting that we have sex," he clarified, "is not admitting that we are obsessed by it."[70] Without sex, gay men lost a crucial aspect of themselves, a vantage point from where they could critique heteronormative structures. For Campbell, moderate gays like Brian Coyle wanted "to render gay men eunuchs and asexual beings" in the eyes of straight society—a dangerous compromise that, in his view, stripped gay men of their personal pleasure and the collective political power that arose from it.

For Campbell, gentrification posed one of the greatest threats to the political power he believed gay men derived from their shared sexuality—especially as neoliberal policies sought to privatize the public spaces where that sexuality had historically been expressed. He viewed the anticruising ordinance as a thinly veiled attempt by city officials, working in concert with gay politicians and private developers, to remake Loring Park in line with redevelopment priorities. In an op-ed for the *GLC Voice*, Campbell lamented the displacement of gay residents by a wave of "yuppie" newcomers: "Before the return of the gentry to the inner city, gays were considered the most desirable of the folks of modest income who were interested in living in the Loring area. Now, the landlords hope they can rent to the yuppie gentry and overt signs of gay lifestyles have to go."[71] Campbell was both right and wrong. On the one hand, he was right in noting that gay men viewed themselves as modern white "pioneers" of a once "run-down" neighborhood, and the anticruising ordinance would have undoubtedly served the interests of landlords and homeowners aiming to boost property values. On the other hand, Campbell was wrong in drawing a firm distinction between gays and "yuppies." Some gay residents—those with racial and economic privilege—had no fear of gentrification. As homeowners, they desired the "peace and quiet" needed to appease investors and attract buyers who would drive up their own home values. Like their heterosexual counterparts, they saw public gay sex as essentially prostitution and, therefore, a hindrance to the neighborhood. A Minneapolis gay couple, "Joe" and "Pete," eagerly awaited the anticruising ordinance. In letters to two newspapers, they wrote, "As homosexuals, we do not condone nor support prostitution any more than does the heterosexual population." In one quick rhetorical turn, the couple had turned all gay men cruising Loring Park into mere prostitutes. These so-called prostitutes, the couple continued, "are no more or no less a part of our community than are prostitutes in heterosexual society a part of that society."[72] The couple insisted that same-sex couples, like heterosexual couples, felt and viewed the world in the same way. "One of our greatest tasks in today's society," they declared, "is to show the majority that our lifestyle is no different than that of heterosexuals." Like a gay Silent Majority, the couple thought that even though "many people perceive gay people as being sexually out of control" and having no "values and morals around sexuality," they represented the "majority" of the gay community who "seek the same compassion, caring, tenderness and commitment that heterosexual people seek."[73] Even if "Joe" and "Pete" did not say so explicitly—they had no need to, they all but announced it in their equivalence to broader society—they no doubt also believed that gay property owners were just like their straight peers and interested in appreciation above all else.

Two days after the traffic pylon incident at Carlson's home, on October 2, 1989, the Minneapolis City Council's Public Health and Safety Committee held its first public forum on the anticruising ordinance. F.A.G.S. members made a striking appearance, donning masks of Carlson—some with added snake tongues and one even drawing "a little Hitler mustache" (fig. 6.4).[74] Halfhill wore a woman's nightgown and pearls, parodying Carlson's appearance during the cruise-in. Also in attendance were gay residents and

FIGURE 6.4 Members of F.A.G.S. (Friends Against Gay Suppression) protest the anticruising ordinance at a city council hearing on October 2, 1989, by wearing Barbara Carlson masks and her signature pearls. The demonstration was featured in the *Star Tribune*. Photo by Donald Black. Copyright © Star Tribune Media Company LLC. Used with permission. All rights reserved.

property owners from Loring Park, and with them stood Dick Brown, famous for his bathhouse protests, who worried that the public might mistake Campbell's position as representative of the gay community. "Some of the gay fanatics," he claimed, "are so concerned about gay rights they don't have any respect for anyone else's rights."[75] Others joined his critique, with one resident describing Loring Park as a great neighborhood with "mostly gay professional residents" but lamenting that it was "invaded" by outsiders after the bars closed. Another attendee spoke of the need for residents to "gain back their community."[76] Despite the palpable tension, the *Star Tribune* reported moments of "thoughtful debate on domestic tranquility vs. civil liberties," though the meeting eventually unraveled into chaos. Gay activists shouted at city council members, one of whom walked out and asked the police to file charges. A gay protester sarcastically shouted, "The rich are taking over the city, and the poor can go to hell!" Attacks became personal, even misogynistic, when Wolfgang Wolf, a member of F.A.G.S., dismissed the idea that Minneapolis had a "prostitution problem," boldly claiming that the only real prostitute was the "political whore" on the city council exploiting gay men's civil liberties for personal gain.[77] Faced with the escalating tension, the committee postponed further discussion on the ordinance until after the November election, citing the need for refinement and a desire to avoid politicization.[78]

The committee's action reflected their concern that this issue would be even more explosive than the bathhouse ordinance from just a few years earlier.[79] While the bathhouse fight, though contentious, focused on establishments that had become largely symbolic and were already in decline by 1986, cruising remained a vibrant and thriving part of gay culture. It brought together a volatile mix of class, sexuality, and privacy issues. More than any previous challenge faced by Minnesota's gay community, cruising drew a sharp divide between those who embraced homonormativity and those who resisted it. But it also put something tangible—not merely symbolic—on the line. For gay men opposed to the ordinance, the risk was losing one of the few public spaces they could truly claim as their own. Campbell underscored this point when he spoke at the Public Health and Safety Committee, stating, "Actions have been taken against bathhouses and beaches and now they're trying to hit Loring Park."[80] He argued that the ordinance was "a frontal attack on an age-old social custom distinctively associated with the gay community."[81] While he may have been right about the "custom" of cruising, he was wrong about a singular gay community. Already, divisions had emerged over the notion of a "maturing" gay identity, divisions that homeownership only deepened. A person's stance on the ordinance was often determined by their socioeconomic status—particularly whether they rented or owned property. Jerry Fladmark, a Loring Park resident and future president of the CLPC, recalled, "There was a faction in the gay community who were doing well and were well off" who loathed the idea that being gay meant, in the public's mind, sleazy or having "promiscuous sex or anonymous recreational sex. Those kinds of things were just anathema to them. And they felt that that was going to hinder their ability to get better gay rights." As Fladmark saw it, the ordinance was not designed to make Loring Park less gay but, rather, "to make being gay more respectful."[82]

With "hustlers" and their "johns" being used like weapons for either side, Richard Osborne, a gay attorney who had served on the Minneapolis Commission on Civil Rights and was himself arrested in 1983 for "indecent conduct," entered the debate to puncture the pretense of middle-class respectability among those who defended the ordinance.[83] In a letter published in *Equal Time* titled "A word to the 'holier-than-thou,'" Osborne addressed the gay community, calling out the "self-righteous" gay property owners who supported the ordinance and reminding them of a critical point: Sodomy, whether in a public place like Loring Park or in a private, monogamous bedroom, was still illegal in Minnesota:

> I have news for these holier-than-thou people: you are just as much a criminal as your brother who picks up a hustler or has sex under the bridge at Loring Pond. You might think that because you limit your sex life to 'doing it' in your bedroom with your monogamous lover you are going to be seen as OK in the eyes of nongay society; you are wrong. Even if the ass that you fuck or the pussy that you lick is that of a faithful, lifelong lover and even if you confine it to the privacy of your home, you are guilty of the crime of Sodomy, and that's a gross misdemeanor, while Prostitution and so-called Indecent Conduct are only misdemeanors. You are worse crooks than those at whom you so smugly cast stones!

If the law reflected morality, then, strictly speaking, these supposedly law-abiding homeowners corrupted the neighborhood and damaged their property values more than the men cruising the park. Of course, it was all rhetorical, but it raised the question of why these men would betray their fellow gay men for a society that rendered them, if they acted in any sexual fashion, criminal?[84]

By 1989, sodomy remained illegal in Minnesota, but cruising in Loring Park—walking about a public space in search of sex—did not. Due in part to F.A.G.S., Carlson's bid for city council went down in defeat as did her anti-cruising ordinance. The city council's Public Health and Safety Committee declined to advance the ordinance, and after Carlson's electoral loss, no other councilmember wanted to take up the controversial measure. While the proposal quietly disappeared, the anxieties that fueled it did not. The debate would take a darker turn just two years later, when a series of murders in and around Loring Park forced the LGBTQ community to reevaluate its relationship with public spaces and law enforcement.

Old Foes Become Fast Friends

The 1989 ordinance debate breathed new life into Citizens for a Loring Park Community (CLPC) after a period of inactivity, and as the group revived, it came to reflect broader shifts in urban politics and LGBTQ priorities. Ken Darling, a police reporter for the *Milwaukee Sentinel*, and Jerry Fladmark, a former aide to State Sen. Allan Spear, emerged as key figures in reshaping the group's mission around the concept of "livability." Both openly gay, their perspectives, shaped by professional and personal experiences, highlighted the increasingly complex relationship between neighborhood politics and gay rights. Yet visions within the group were not always aligned, and internal tensions emerged as the CLPC sought to balance competing concerns.[85] Rather than emphasizing rights or even acceptance, many members prioritized safety—particularly the sense of safety felt by young, urban professionals whose presence was seen as vital to the neighborhood's economic and symbolic revitalization. Visitors to the park who did not conform to this constituency's "sense of community" quickly became a "safety issue."[86] As the AIDS epidemic unfolded, the LGBTQ community's engagement with public spaces also evolved. As Stathis Yeros observes, the struggle expanded from the right to inhabit neighborhoods to a broader demand for equal participation in shaping urban futures.[87] This shift opened new channels for cooperation between LGBTQ residents, law enforcement, and real estate interests—partnerships that reflected both hard-won legitimacy and the limits of inclusion.

Under Darling's leadership, the CLPC reframed concerns about noise and safety in Loring Park as opportunities for civic engagement, emphasizing collaboration between residents and police. As vice president and chair of the Committee to Reduce Noise and Improve Safety, Darling expressed concerns to the *Twin Cities Gaze* in the summer of 1991, noting that Loring Park felt "unlivable" on some late weekend nights: "The noise can make it hard to sleep and all the street and pedestrian traffic can be intimidating to some residents, Gay and straight." According to Darling, Loring Park had changed, "becoming more stable and professional—and people are just not wanting to put up with the noise level on weekends anymore."[88] While CLPC members feared the neighborhood risked turning seedy, they acknowledged that addressing the issues would require police involvement—a fact that still raised apprehensions. Darling emphasized that the police needed to understand that "not everybody on the street at night [was] a prostitute."[89] To sensitize officers, Darling advocated for community engagement in neighborhood policing, explaining, "Our goal all along was to involve community members, particularly Gay men, in any increased police activity, to ensure that the police were responding to our needs, not that we were reacting to their actions."[90] This strategy marked a departure from the confrontational tactics of F.A.G.S., reflecting the CLPC's growing willingness to work with law enforcement to resolve neighborhood issues.

The CLPC's efforts paid off when it secured the support of officers who were attuned to the concerns and experiences of LGBTQ people. Led by Darling, the CLPC worked with Inspector William Jones, MPD commander for the 4th precinct, to launch a trial late-night police patrol initiative.[91] This program added extra squad patrols and involved the community in foot patrols, aiming to reduce street noise and prostitution on late Friday and Saturday nights.[92] The CLPC began its foot patrols on June 13, 1991, and a week later, two MPD officers joined it.[93] The patrol initiative coincided with a city pilot program that used a van to pick up "chronic inebriates" in the neighborhood.[94]

After a month of patrols, Darling presented a positive report at a CLPC meeting, highlighting noticeable improvements in the neighborhood's atmosphere. Before the program began, an informal traffic count conducted on a Saturday night in June recorded 234 cars passing through a particular intersection within fifteen minutes. In contrast, a similar count on the night of July 6, 1991, a month into the patrols, showed only 173 cars passing through during the same time frame.[95] While not all CLPC members were convinced that the patrols were necessary, many noticed a real improvement in the neighborhood's ambiance—until the night of July 31, 1991. Around 11:45 p.m., twenty-one-year-old Joel Larson, after a long day of work, "decided to go for a walk" through Loring Park, according to his roommate.[96] Nine days earlier, news of Jeffrey Dahmer's grisly murders in Milwaukee, Wisconsin, had rattled gay men in the Twin Cities. Larson, a legally blind, white gay man who had moved to Minneapolis from Des Moines, Iowa, seven months earlier and worked in sales, met another man at the park that night.[97] According to witnesses, after talking briefly, the man tried to lead Larson to a more secluded area, but they began arguing. Larson managed to escape, but the man pursued him. Near the park's Dandelion Fountain, just a block from his home, the man shot Larson. Screaming for help, Larson ran a few hundred feet to an intersection where bystanders gathered but were helpless as Larson succumbed to a gunshot wound to the back. The following night, Loring Park residents held a candlelight vigil with more than two hundred attendees, including Larson's mother.[98] A neighbor described Larson as "just a nice kid living here, up on the city for the first time . . . He should have lived."[99]

Initially, the MPD believed Larson's death was the result of a botched robbery, but that theory quickly fell apart when, ten days later, another attack occurred at a different popular cruising spot in the Twin Cities. On August 10, 1991, about 5:30 a.m., one man was killed and another seriously wounded along the Mississippi River Flats, a secluded area along the river near the University of Minnesota campus. During the day, the East River Parkway neighborhood attracted joggers and cyclists, drawn by its lush lawns and river vistas. But at night, it transformed into "Bare Ass Beach," a well-known location for casual encounters among men dating back to the 1930s. The reputation of the Flats for anonymous sex was so established by the 1980s that the Minnesota AIDS Project had installed condom dispensers on trees (fig. 6.5).[100] On that August day in 1991, all of Minnesota would become familiar with the spot, for the man killed was well-connected, forty-eight-year-old former DFL State Senator John Chenoweth. He was shot twice in the upper left chest and once in the left arm. His companion, nineteen-year-old Cord Draszt, was shot twice in the back but survived.[101]

The attack sent shockwaves through Minnesota's political circles and prompted a swift and forceful response (fig. 6.6). Suddenly, police no longer viewed Larson as a lone victim. At a press conference following Chenoweth's death, Police Chief Laux announced that investigators had "strong reason" to believe the shootings of Chenoweth, Draszt, and Larson were connected.[102] In a revealing turn, ACT UP/Minnesota—typically aligned with liberationist politics and firmly opposed to the closing of bathhouses precisely because of the dangers faced in public sex—adopted a tactic more commonly associated with integrationist strategies. In an effort to build trust between the LGBTQ community and law enforcement, the group called for the hiring of openly gay and lesbian officers.[103] At an August 12 meeting with Deputy Police Chief David Dobrotka, queer activist Dean Asmundson, speaking in front of rolling cameras, told a visibly uncomfortable Dobrotka that "having openly gay officers would help to ease the gay community's distrust of the police and the police department would be more knowledgeable about fighting bias crime."[104] The move was not without internal friction. Some within ACT UP/Minnesota were uneasy with this shift in approach—Asmundson later admitted that "that wasn't necessarily what we do"—but legal activists convinced the group that it was essential to get "a gay foot in the door."[105] The decision paid off almost immediately. The editorial board of the *Star Tribune* publicly endorsed the activists' demands, advocating for "a much closer relationship"

FIGURE 6.5 A Minnesota AIDS Project condom bucket placed above an antiviolence message at "Bare Ass Beach." Featured in the *Star Tribune* on August 13, 1991. Photo by Marlin Levison. Copyright © Star Tribune Media Company LLC. Used with permission. All rights reserved.

REWARD, ANONYMITY,

FOR INFORMATION LEADING TO FORMAL CHARGES AGAINST A SUSPECT OR SUSPECTS IN THE MURDERS OF JOEL LARSON AND JOHN CHENOWETH.

CRIME STOPPERS INC.

CALL:

45-CRIME

Calls are neither recorded nor traced. You will be known by a code number.

Joel Larson

John Chenoweth

UP TO $2,000 EACH CASE.

21-year-old Joel Larson was shot to death about 5 minutes before midnight on Wednesday July 31st at Grant and Willow Streets in Loring Park.

48-year-old John Chenoweth was shot to death about 5 a.m. Saturday August 10th on a popular gay beach on the East bank of the Mississippi River below Shriner's Hospital. Cord Draszt, 19, was seriously wounded in the same attack.

FIGURE 6.6 A reward flyer from 1991 seeking information on the homicides of Joel Larson and John Chenoweth. Source: Leo Treadway Papers, Box 38, Folder: Hate Crimes, undated (1990–1993). Courtesy of the Minnesota Historical Society.

FIGURE 6.7 Protesters, including Richard Simon (center), hold a rally and press conference at City Hall following the shootings of Joel Larson, John Chenoweth, and Cord Draszt. The event was covered in the *Star Tribune* on August 20, 1991. Photo by Joey McLeister. Copyright © Star Tribune Media Company LLC. Used with permission. All rights reserved.

between the MPD and the LGBTQ community. They even urged the department to establish a "gay citizen committee" or appoint a "gay liaison," echoing earlier calls made by the Minnesota Committee for Gay and Lesbian Rights in the 1970s and Community United Against Violence in the 1980s. The editorial board concluded, "Police may not understand what beckons men out at night in public parks to commit murder or attract anonymous sex. But it is a law enforcement officer's responsibility to apprehend the fellow and safeguard the rest."[106]

The murder of Larson and Chenoweth marked a breaking point, galvanizing the LGBTQ community into one of its most visible and emotionally charged protests in the city's history. While Minnesota Governor Arne Carlson had earlier proclaimed March 6 Gay and Lesbian Hate Crimes Awareness Day—a symbolic gesture of growing LGBTQ acceptance—promises and proclamations would not be enough.[107] On August 19, 1991, about five hundred people stormed the main entrance of Minneapolis City Hall, demanding justice for the slain men (fig. 6.7). Even with lingering tensions over the CLPC and MPD's anticruising patrols, the violence briefly united the

LGBTQ community. Blowing whistles and chanting, "No more violence—stop the bashing now!" protesters marched in a long column behind a banner that read: "We've Survived Queer Bashing." Evoking the direct action and street theater of AIDS activism, they carried mock tombstones bearing the names of antigay violence victims and draped the podium at City Hall with a yellow crime-scene-style tape that read: "Queer Safe Space." At City Hall, Asmundson stood behind the podium, wearing a bulletproof vest, and asked, "Is this what I have to wear now to be queer?! Do I have to wear this like a condom to keep myself alive because our government doesn't care?!" The crowd erupted into a thunderous "No!" as Asmundson hurled the vest to the ground. State Sen. Allan Spear, a friend of Chenoweth, also spoke, linking antigay violence to the ongoing AIDS crisis. "This past Saturday, I spent my morning at a funeral. And I don't know about the rest of you but I've been attending too many funerals lately." The crowd clapped in agreement. "I've been attending funerals for friends who have died of AIDS and last Saturday I attended a funeral for my friend John Chenoweth who was murdered solely because he was a gay man. And a week earlier Joel Larson died solely because he was a gay man . . . This cannot continue."[108]

Moved by the violence and the public outcry, Mayor Don Fraser and Police Chief Laux promised demonstrators they would work to improve police–LGBTQ community relations. In an unprecedented move, they committed to sensitivity training for officers and actively involving the LGBTQ community in addressing hate crimes.[109] Despite intense pressure, it took the MPD nearly three months to identify a suspect. On November 26, 1991, police named a thirty-two-year-old Black man, awaiting trial for robbery at the Saloon gay bar, as the prime suspect in the murders of Larson and Chenoweth. In the era of the Gary Syndrome, Marcus James seemed to fit the profile.[110] He had recently migrated from Indiana, where he had served six years in prison for robbery. The case against him relied on the testimony of a white gay employee of the Saloon, who believed that James resembled the police's composite sketch of the shooter. In an interview with Gaze-TV, a local LGBTQ-themed cable show, the employee, describing the "natural high" he felt after reporting his suspicions to the police, urged other gay men with information to trust the police and come forward. In the segment, Gaze-TV reported that the suspect was "frequently working [Loring Park], including holding people up for ten to twenty dollars to supposedly buy coke or crack." The host added, "Apparently, there was a crack house down a few doors down the street from the fountain area where Larson was shot."[111] The suspect's history of incarceration and possible substance use seemed to support the MPD's theory that the murders were robberies, not hate crimes.[112] Detectives even traveled to Indiana to interview his family.[113] In the end, the MPD had the wrong man.

In February 1992, a six-page letter surfaced at local news outlets and LGBTQ rights organizations, revealing information only the killer could have known. Raging against gay men who engaged in public sex, the author justified the murders as part of a crusade to stop the spread of HIV by targeting the locations where gay men gathered for sex and to "drive faggots back into the closet where they belong." While expressing regret that people had to be harmed to "send a message to the promiscuous, filthy gay community," the author saw the violence as necessary to force gay men into hiding. Signed as the "AIDS Commission," the letter warned gay men "not to flaunt your sickness before those of us who will not accept it."[114]

Some initially dismissed the letter as a hoax, but on February 17, crime victim advocate Patti Abbott of the Gay and Lesbian Community Action Council (GLCAC) received a phone call from someone claiming to be the author. The caller was upset that people were not taking him seriously. While Abbott kept him on the line, a colleague contacted the police. The caller shared enough accurate details that Abbott and the police believed he was the killer. When he called Abbott again on February 20, the police traced the call to Jay Johnson, a twenty-three-year-old closeted Black gay man living in a Roseville, Minnesota, boardinghouse.[115] (Police records identified Johnson as Black, though his landlord noted he appeared "mulatto" and speculated he might have been adopted, as his parents were white.)[116] In their report, officers described Johnson as effeminate and noted his "acned/pockmarked" face.[117] A search of his possessions revealed the .38 caliber revolver used in the murders, along with a journal where Johnson expressed his desire "of committing homicide on a large scale and entering the ranks of the nation's most notorious serial killers; [an] ambition which had grown as dormant as the AIDS virus now in my cells . . . reawakened." At the time of the murders, Johnson worked as a restaurant host and had previously been a student at Bethel University, a private evangelical Christian school where his father served as vice president for enrollment and program development. Johnson was also active in the Republican Party.[118] Later, Johnson would attribute his actions to internalized homophobia and the antigay rhetoric preached by conservative Christians, turning to murder to exorcise desires the church deemed wicked. He would confess, "I was disgusted with what I was doing. And quite frankly, I just thought to myself, 'If I shut these places [cruising spots] down, my temptation to do that would be less.' I would think to myself, 'This is a constructive, moral thing to be doing.' And I certainly didn't just come up with that idea. I watched *The 700 Club* sometimes with Pat Robertson—they're constantly talking about gays."[119] Johnson moved from idealization to action with his positive HIV diagnosis. His shame over his desire became a raging anger at the sex acts and spaces that had made him "diseased." Despite identifying as Christian, Johnson viewed his violent actions as righteous retribution. He was sentenced to two concurrent life terms for the murders of Larson and Chenoweth, along with an additional fifteen years for wounding Draszt.

The partnership between the GLCAC and the MPD proved pivotal in solving the murders, a fact publicly recognized by Police Chief Laux, who awarded Patti Abbott a medal for her contributions. "I can't emphasize enough," Laux stated, "how important the relationship [between] the police department and the Gay and Lesbian Community Action Council has been in this case."[120] Since the November shootings, the GLCAC and MPD had worked to improve police–community relations, a strategy that not only helped crack the case but also led to Sgt. Sharon Lubinski coming out as the first openly LGBTQ police officer in the MPD two months later.[121] Lubinski explained her decision, citing the need for better law enforcement for LGBTQ individuals. "A police department needs to deal with gay and lesbian crime victims," she told the *Star Tribune*. "If they can't deal with a fellow gay employee, how can they deal with a crime victim?"[122] Surprisingly, the president of the Minneapolis Police Federation shared this view, acknowledging the importance of Lubinksi coming out for other LGBTQ officers.[123] Ken Darling, vice president of the CLPC, supported Lubinski's announcement, recalling her as the ideal candidate—"college educated and clearly articulate and was one of these new officers who believed in community policing."[124] Her decision also prompted Chief Laux to call for greater understanding and support for LGBTQ officers within the department.[125] In response, Laux established the Gay and Lesbian Police Community Task Force to assess the MPD's internal climate and enhance services for the LGBTQ community.[126]

The task force represented the most momentous step yet in bridging the divide between the MPD and the LGBTQ community. In March 1994, it released a report acknowledging the long-standing tensions, citing past raids and crackdowns on cruising as major sources of distrust. At the same time, the report highlighted recent progress, pointing to the arrest of Johnson for the murders of Larson and Chenoweth as evidence of "the benefit of increased trust between police and the gay community." To build on this momentum, the task force recommended creating a special police liaison team, requiring diversity training on gender and sexual orientation, and adopting policies to prohibit discrimination on those grounds. Still, the report recognized that serious challenges remained, starting with rank-and-file officers.[127] Surveys revealed a range of candid, often inflammatory, attitudes. When asked if they knew someone who was gay or lesbian, responses varied from "I have many homosexual friends" to "They make me sick" and "I find the life-style disgusting and the effort to give it respectability abhorrent." AIDS fears surfaced repeatedly. One officer reported feeling safe "unless [a gay or lesbian officer were] bleeding or in need of CPR—I would not be comfortable with first aid in this scenario." Another officer added, "Knowing their life-style has high incidence of AIDS, I would not perform CPR or stop bleeding of an injured gay officer." A third stated that they would work with a gay or lesbian officer but insisted, "No physical contact. It could be tough if he were injured." When asked about their interactions with the LGBTQ community, one officer described the experience as negative: "AIDS, drunk, overly defensive flaming fags. These do not represent the normal gays or co-workers." It is no surprise, then, that when officers were asked what reforms might make the department more welcoming to openly gay and lesbian colleagues, many either favored maintaining the status quo—which encouraged closeting—or supported even stricter measures. One officer asked, "Why should [openly gay or lesbian officers] or the department make a person's sexual preference an issue?" Others called for the MPD to fire or ban openly gay and lesbian officers "like the military" because "this is not a job for a homosexual." These comments emerged amid allegations that officers responding to Larson's attack failed to administer emergency care due to fear of HIV transmission, though the MPD denied these claims.[128] Yet the survey responses lent credibility to those suspicions. One investigator's report on Chenoweth's death "advised property room personnel" handling clothing and jewelry removed from the body "that the victim who wore these clothes was HIV positive" despite no public evidence "and that they should take the appropriate precautions since the clothes may have blood on them."[129] Acknowledging how deeply AIDS-related fears had intensified hostility toward openly gay and lesbian colleagues, the task force recommended mandatory HIV/AIDS training for all MPD personnel.[130]

Police harassment had long shaped the experiences of openly gay men, distinguishing them from the broader white, middle-class mainstream. Yet the coordinated responses to Johnson's arrest, along with the public statements from the mayor, police chief, and task force, suggested that a shift in the relationship between the LGBTQ community and law enforcement might be underway. Still, survey responses from officers tempered this optimism, revealing deep-seated resistance to the kind of community-police cooperation that Chief Laux envisioned, even in places like Loring Park. Bridging that divide would require more than policy—it would demand cultural change within the department. In the wake of Larson's and Chenoweth's deaths, however, a shared opposition to cruising created unexpected common ground between law enforcement and an emerging homonormative faction of the LGBTQ community, opening the door to a new, if uneasy, alliance.

By 1994, while residents of Loring Park still complained about cruising—and the accompanying noise and drugs some associated with it—people from outside the neighborhood had noticed a change. That fall, the *Star Tribune* praised Loring Park for its transformation from a place "riddled with drunks, crime and decay" into a "trendy neighborhood" that preserved its historic mansions and brick-and-brownstone walk-ups while embracing a bohemian mix of new condos, cultural centers, and restaurants. The *Tribune* credited this revitalization to gay men, likening Loring Park to other "gayborhoods" like Greenwich Village in New York City, Dupont Circle in DC, and Capitol Hill in Seattle. Police officer Tom Sawina echoed this view, noting that crimes like gay bashings and muggings had been curbed. "It's a good neighborhood—a friendly neighborhood. If I was going to pick a neighborhood in the inner city [to live in], that's the one I would pick."[131]

The *Tribune*, however, overlooked a crucial element: It was not just gay men alone who brought about this miraculous transformation, but gay men in conjunction with an active police presence. After the murders of Larson and Chenoweth, the relationship between the police and the gay leadership of the CLPC grew gradually. For proponents of gay integration, epitomized by their support for Carlson's ordinance, these murders underscored the perils of gay promiscuity, not only tarnishing the neighborhood's reputation but also fueling concerns about AIDS and violence. This climate of fear may have prompted some gay men to prioritize monogamy as a form of protection—a message promoted by gay integrationists since the 1970s. Monogamy, with its associations to privacy, stability, and homeownership, emerged as a moral and material counterweight to promiscuity, safeguarding both individuals and Loring Park's appeal to potential residents and investors. In this context, the campaign against public sex served as a pivotal rebranding effort, reshaping Loring Park from a locale known for gay public sex to one where gay men could aspire to property ownership.

In the spring of 1992, shortly after the MPD apprehended Johnson, police ramped up enforcement efforts in Loring Park. Although the recent murders had made some gay men more cautious, cruising continued. One April night, the CLPC counted more than three hundred cars passing through a Loring Park intersection in just fifteen minutes. What was different this time was the growing rapport between the police and gay property owners in the neighborhood. And the police used this rapport to justify its increasingly aggressive tactics in the park. First, the vice squad shifted its decoy operations from adult bookstores to public parks, arresting men and seizing their cars under an ordinance that permitted the confiscation of vehicles used in the solicitation of sex. Officer Tom Sawina told the *Star Tribune*, "We want to get the word out that if you are cruising Loring Park, the guy on the corner you pick up may be a cop. Hopefully, that will make some people think twice about coming down here."[132] Second, the MPD brought in younger, more conventionally attractive men as decoys—men who otherwise might not pay the older gay or closeted men arrested any attention.[133] A *Star Tribune* reporter followed "Scott," a police decoy, as he cruised Loring Park. Dressed in "stone-washed jeans with a hole in one knee and red baseball cap," the undercover officer, as the reporter described, "seemed to bring people in like a beacon," receiving several offers for paid sex in under three minutes.[134] During one weekend in April 1992, a four-hour decoy operation led to the arrest of three men and the confiscation of a car.[135]

While some members of the CLPC supported the MPD's sweep of Loring Park—Vice President Ken Darling rode along as an observer to ensure no one was beaten or harassed—not everyone in the group backed the prostitution sting.[136] The CLPC had long prioritized crime reduction and openly opposed cruising, but the police tactics prompted a moment of reckoning. At the April 13, 1992, meeting, CLPC President Jerry Fladmark resigned in protest. As president, Fladmark had worked to make Loring Park safer and more welcoming for LGBTQ people. However, he later remarked that he did not become president "to do stings" or "have undercover officers pick up johns." Although the CLPC board formally opposed the operation, some property owners bypassed the leadership altogether, contacting the police directly to press for a crackdown on cruising. Fladmark recounts:

> I remember specifically because I became friends with some of these landlords, and I was outraged . . . I think one of the guys that got arrested was like 21 . . . and he had a grand total of . . . $18 in his pocket. And they ended up arresting him for soliciting gay sex in the

park. And I remember telling one of the landlords, I said, "Do you really, really honestly believe that he drove down here with the idea of paying for sex with $18 in his pocket?" I mean, that's just ridiculous. "You've ruined a person's life. He was in school" . . . I think he was from one of the suburbs. But I said, "This is what you're doing. You're ruining people's lives with this stuff."

The young man had been arrested on prostitution charges, illustrating how easily police conflated any public sex between men with criminality. At the same April 13 meeting, Fladmark called the operation a waste of resources and criticized officials for refusing to delay the operation to address community concerns. As other speakers compared the MPD's tactics to entrapment, it became clear that the CLPC was conflicted. While it aimed to discourage cruising, many members recoiled at the police department's methods.[137]

No amount of decoy units or perfectly planned strategies were ever going to fully stop cruising among gay men at well-known spots. Try as neighborhoods might, men seeking sex still made pilgrimages there. After the controversy over the decoy operation, the CLPC maintained its partnership with the MPD. In June 1993—during Pride month, no less—the CLPC, the MPD, and the Loring-LaSalle Owners and Managers Association distributed hundreds of flyers titled "Loring Community Standards" to drivers passing through Loring Park. The flyers emphasized the neighborhood's expectations for quiet, respectful behavior and warned against illegal activity on the streets or in the park.[138] A member of the CLPC's Noise and Safety Committee, who helped organize the flyer distribution, stressed that it was not a "cruising crackdown," stating, "I'm personally gay and I know how sensitive that is in the neighborhood."[139] To further reassure the community, Sgt. Sharon Lubinski, who had recently come out as a lesbian, also participated in the campaign.[140]

The partnership between the CLPC and MPD played a pivotal role in reshaping Loring Park—not only as a safer neighborhood but as a newly branded gayborhood aligned with city-led redevelopment goals. In the early 1990s, Minneapolis launched the Neighborhood Revitalization Program (NRP), a $400 million, twenty-year initiative designed to reverse neighborhood decline. Eager to secure a share of these funds, the CLPC submitted the Loring Park Neighborhood Action Plan, a $3.6 million proposal focused on improving infrastructure, safety, housing, and economic development. The plan identified parking, crime, noise and safety issues as key concerns, while also expressing unease about the neighborhood's central location attracting "homeless and indigent people."[141] Echoing the goals of the 1970s Loring Park Development District, the new plan emphasized design considerations to address safety—such as enhanced pedestrian lighting and tree placement. To combat "a negative media image of Loring Park . . . as unsafe for shopping and visiting," the CLPC proposed rebranding the neighborhood as an arts district. A key component of the plan was an expanded collaboration with the MPD. The CLPC allocated $45,000 to hire off-duty officers for neighborhood patrols and to support the Loring Community Oriented Policing Program (L-COPP) Center, a local substation operated by the CLPC and staffed by volunteers and work-study students from Minneapolis Community and Technical College. A luxury apartment building owner donated office space for the L-COPP, allowing students to patrol the area during the day, serve as "goodwill ambassadors," and report any "illegal behavior" to the police.[142] The plan stressed that increasing police visibility would help "reduce incidents of public drunkenness, panhandling and prostitution," while also building trust between law enforcement and neighborhood residents.[143]

As part of the broader push to revitalize Loring Park, efforts to crack down on public sex grew increasingly aggressive. In May 1995, the CLPC's Noise and Safety Committee ramped up its campaign to reduce traffic and noise by expanding citizen patrols. Unlike earlier efforts, which focused on late-night surveillance, these new patrols systematically recorded the license plate numbers of cars that circled specific blocks "an unusual number of times." The initiative became more coordinated with the installation of mechanical car counters. On a single weekend night in June 1995, one counter registered more than three hundred cars passing between 3:00 a.m. and 4:00 a.m., despite ample street parking. Community volunteers shared these license plate numbers with the MPD, which then mailed letters to the motorists, notifying them that the "neighborhood is concerned about cruising, and the neighborhood will be watching." The letters also "requested" that motorists voluntarily contact the MPD to explain their presence in Loring Park.[144] With the CLPC and MPD working in lockstep to curb cruising, the Neighborhood Revitalization Program Policy Board approved funding later that year for the CLPC's Loring Park Neighborhood Action Plan. Surprisingly, the plan secured the support not only from property owners and realtors but also from the Twin Cities Gay and Lesbian Pride Festival, which had long hosted Pride at Loring Park, and the Gay and Lesbian Community Action Council.[145]

The gentrification of Loring Park, driven by rising rents, displaced many long-term residents, including gay liberationists who had long relied on affordable rental housing. Among them was Richard Simon, a working-class member of ACT UP/Minnesota who worked in the food service industry. Like Simon, many of the group's core activists, though primarily young white gay men, shared similar financial hardships. Dallas Drake, a firefighter, recalled spending nearly half his monthly paycheck on ACT UP activities, while Dean Asmundson, a hairstylist, often covered travel, meals, and printing expenses out of pocket, rarely expecting to be reimbursed.[146] For Simon, the cost of activism was more than symbolic. He hesitated to participate in some direct actions—such as the 1990 Aquatennial Torch Parade protest in downtown Minneapolis—because he feared he could not afford bail if arrested.[147] This financial pressure, combined with Minnesota's broader cultural aversion to public disruption, contributed to the more measured tone of ACT UP/Minnesota's activism, setting it apart from the confrontational tactics seen in larger cities like San Francisco and New York City.

As gay liberationists were pushed out of Loring Park, gay integrationists within the CLPC grew so closely aligned with the MPD that, to some observers, they were indistinguishable. Eric Shambach, a member of ACT UP/Minnesota, wrote to the LGBTQ-focused *Gaze Magazine*, urging the community to patrol the patrols by closely monitoring the CLPC's citizen patrols and reporting any abuses to ACT UP. His letter ended with an uncompromising call to action: "We call upon our community to join us and demand that these homophobes STOP THESE ASSAULTS."[148] The "homophobes" in Shambach's calculation were not the police—or, at least, not the police alone—but also members of the CLPC. Lt. Scott Gerlicher, who oversaw the Loring Park sweeps, defended the MPD's approach, claiming they were merely "trying to target behavior, not particular groups of people." Yet he also acknowledged that the aim was deterrence. "If somebody knows they risk being arrested or having a letter sent to their house, and they are married, they might think twice about going to that area." Although cruising was technically legal, Gerlicher revealed that police would stop and flag men suspected of cruising for any minor traffic violation, such as broken lights or failing to signal turns. While Shambach might have seen this as targeted harassment, Richard Anderson, then vice president of the CLPC, remained unconcerned and defended the sweeps, insisting that residents, including gay men, supported them. These residents, he argued, were tired of being solicited for sex when they came home at night. "To us it is a noise and traffic issue, not a gay issue . . . We don't care what people in the cars are up to, but their driving around affects the livability of *our* neighborhood."[149] Important distinctions had, by 1997, arisen within the LGBTQ community. If Shambach was willing to excommunicate some men from the larger community and lump them in with traditional adversaries like the police, those men simply shook it off. For them, the idea of an LGBTQ community no longer held sway; their identities extended beyond it. In addition to being "gay," they also saw themselves as part of an emerging "creative class." As the spaces available to cruise dwindled and the practice faded, a larger question lingered: What would replace the forms of intimacy, collectivity, and resistance that cruising once embodied?

The "Mature" Solution

In the late 1980s and early 1990s, as debates about cruising heated up in Minneapolis, one prominent gay voice remained unusually quiet. Brian J. Coyle did not fit well into either side of the issue. On the one hand, he was weary of Carlson's 1989 anticruising ordinance, fearing it could be used to target the LGBTQ community. "How," he asked, "can you discern if someone is cruising or looking for a parking space?" Yet, at the same time, Coyle strongly opposed cruising, stating, "This doesn't mean that I support gay cruising and/or prostitution. I'd rather people have relationships."[150] In short, Coyle stood equally against over-policing and what he saw as morally harmful public sexual practices. The first was patently unconstitutional and the second morally stunting. Both, he thought, undermined gay rights and broader social acceptance. Unlike Tim Campbell, Coyle refused to defend cruising in Loring Park as a "gay institution" worth preserving. In an interview with *City Pages*, he declared that the era of anonymous public sex in parks was over: "To romanticize [cruising] as [Campbell] did, as some kind of legacy of the gay culture—I don't buy that."[151]

Instead, beginning with his first term on the city council in 1983, Coyle advocated for a domestic partnership ordinance that would legally recognize long-term, monogamous relationships.[152] In his view, domestic partnerships addressed multiple concerns at once: they would encourage gay men to come out of the closet, reduce the demand for cruising and gay prostitution (along with their associated noise and disturbances), and lessen the need for excessive, unjust policing. He also saw such partnerships as consistent with the city's 1970s emphasis on neighborhood stabilization through homeownership, believing that legal recognition would help anchor and strengthen communities.[153] For Coyle, the policy offered clear public benefits with little downside.

Coyle found early inspiration in a 1983 effort by the Minneapolis Commission on Civil Rights to draft a domestic partnership ordinance. But the proposal emerged at a politically inopportune moment—just as the city became embroiled in the controversy surrounding the antipornography ordinance authored by Andrea Dworkin and Catherine MacKinnon. The resulting backlash siphoned political capital away from the domestic partnership effort, and the initiative stalled.[154] Undeterred, Coyle revived the ordinance the following year, making it a centerpiece of his city council campaign. Once elected, he became its leading advocate, working closely with gay constituents to refine its provisions and secure its passage. He envisioned the measure as "precedent setting legislation" that would greatly benefit the community by expanding access to credit, extending dependent health benefits, granting hospital visitation rights, and providing legal recognition for same-sex relationships.[155] Yet support for the ordinance proved elusive. Religious conservatives opposed anything resembling gay marriage, and the city worried about the cost of providing benefits to the domestic partners of city employees. Additionally, the "business community" was wary of the possibility of Minneapolis-based companies being required to offer similar benefits.[156] Meanwhile, some gay liberationists criticized the ordinance for limiting partnership rights to city employees, leaving out the broader LGBTQ population.[157]

The domestic partnership debate remained dormant—until AIDS reframed it as a public health issue. Advocates began to argue that legalizing domestic partnerships could curb sexual promiscuity, limit cruising, and ultimately protect gay men from HIV. Local LGBTQ publications echoed this message, often casting monogamy as both a moral and medical imperative. In its ten-part series on the impact of AIDS on gay men, *Twin Cities Gaze* dedicated an entire issue to the topic of dating. The newspaper posed a provocative question: "Are we willing to be monogamous and faithful to one imperfect human being to preserve our health and start regaining some sanity to our sexual lives, instead of acting like spoiled children who feel they deserve anything they want any time they want it?"[158] The comparison of gay men to spoiled children underscored a growing discourse of personal responsibility and restraint, portraying promiscuity as a reckless indulgence. In a *Star Tribune* op-ed, *Twin Cities Gaze* publisher Brad Theissen went further, comparing public sex to sexual addiction. He claimed that men were drawn to the "danger, risk, darkness and intrigue" of cruising in parks because it offered a "physical high not available elsewhere." Theissen argued that such behavior should be discouraged not through punishment but through reform: by decriminalizing sodomy and lifting legal barriers to same-sex partnerships. His message was clear—only by granting gay men access to the private, respectable space of the home, anchored in monogamous coupledom, could the epidemic's spread be meaningfully curbed.[159]

As HIV spread across the upper Midwest, *Twin Cities Gaze* introduced a real estate column aimed at "empower[ing] Gay men and Lesbians in the real-estate marketplace." Written by a Twin Cities real estate agent who identified as a gay man, the column not only explained industry jargon and market conditions to potential buyers but also boldly declared, "The Gay ghetto is more or less a thing of the past." According to the real estate agent, gay men were now "seeking shelter of their own in all areas of the Twin Cities and suburbs." Though the column did not directly mention AIDS, it likely hinted at the epidemic when it claimed that the gay ghetto—and the sexual practices associated with it—were a thing of the past. Once seen as spaces where men with same-sex desires could freely come together and engage in casual sex, gay ghettos had also been associated with racialized stereotypes of "dirty" slums, renting, and criminality. Now, however, these once-liberating sexual networks were increasingly blamed for the spread of HIV. The solution, the column suggested, was to leave them behind. To protect themselves, gay men were encouraged to "seek shelter" in residential spaces once off-limits: suburban single-family homes, far removed from the perceived danger and decay of the racialized ghetto. While the virus threatened the physical health of gay men, the real estate agent noted that the housing market was the "healthiest" it had been in years.[160] In other words, escaping the gay ghetto was not just a lifestyle upgrade — it was recast as a survival strategy.

Like their heterosexual counterparts, gay men found that buying a home increasingly required a two-income household. For Coyle and others, this reinforced the belief that stable, long-term relationships were not just emotionally fulfilling but economically necessary. In 1990, seven years after first proposing a domestic partnership ordinance, Coyle introduced a new bill to the city council. When it became clear that that the council could not muster the necessary votes to pass the original measure, Coyle compromised.[161] In January 1991, amid growing concern over the AIDS epidemic, Minneapolis adopted a more limited ordinance. It allowed city employees to use sick or bereavement leave to care for or mourn a live-in partner. Additionally, any unmarried couple, regardless of city employment, could register their relationship with the city clerk for a $6 filing fee. Though largely symbolic, the gesture offered official recognition for relationships that had long been ignored by the state. Coyle explained to the *Star Tribune* that the ordinance served as "a form of acknowledgement of [gay and lesbian] relationship[s] and says the city of Minneapolis believes these forms of family have value."[162] Even with the concessions, the city council, at Coyle's urging, had expanded the definition of "immediate family" to include unmarried couples, both heterosexual and homosexual, who shared a household.[163]

Coyle likely introduced the ordinance to the city council due to his deteriorating health. In the 1980s, he had been on a steady rise, becoming vice president of the city council, the highest position held by an openly gay person in Minneapolis at the time. He had once aspired to run for mayor and seek higher office, but his HIV diagnosis altered that trajectory. "By 1986, he knew he had AIDS," recalled his former aide, Jim St. George, "and I think [he] recognized that that was no longer in the cards."[164] Like many others diagnosed with AIDS in the 1980s, Coyle felt compelled to act while he still had time. As his friend Jerry Fladmark put it, "If he was going to make progress, now was the time to do it."[165]

A few months after the ordinance passed, on April 23, 1991, Coyle publicly revealed that he had been diagnosed with AIDS in 1986, shortly after being elected to his second term. Until then, he had only told a few close friends. Publicly, he stated that he likely contracted the virus through unprotected sex with a former lover, but in his private journals, Coyle attributed it to "addictive patterns of behavior."[166] After more than eight years on the Minneapolis City Council, Coyle passed away on August 23, 1991, at the age of forty-seven, due to heart failure and complications from AIDS.[167] His obituary in the *Star Tribune* remembered him for being "the architect of a plan to provide sick and bereavement to the unmarried domestic partners of gay, lesbian, and heterosexual city workers."[168]

Coyle's domestic partnership ordinance, though scaled back, marked the culmination of his efforts to reduce the risk of HIV transmission. Even after his death, his name continued to be invoked in debates about strengthening and expanding the ordinance.[169] While his declining health likely added urgency to his push, Coyle's motivations extended beyond legacy-building. He genuinely believed that committed, monogamous relationships offered gay men not just legal recognition but emotional stability, dignity, and protection amid a devasting epidemic.[170] His promotion of domestic partnerships—and his opposition to bathhouses and cruising—reflected a vision shaped by both pragmatism and care. These were not simply political calculations but part of a deeply held conviction: that gay men's lives could be saved through integration, personal responsibility, and the pursuit of stable, intimate bonds. It was a vision of gay rights that fit squarely with the Midwestern consensus of middleness. To be gay in the Midwest, as the 1980s gave way to the 1990s, increasingly meant shedding the sexual transgression celebrated by 1970s liberationists like Campbell. In short, being gay had shifted from vice to nice.

Who Gets Locked Out of the Home?

In her analysis of the rise of gay marriage following the AIDS epidemic, Sarah Schulman reminds us that the very idea of same-sex marriage was once considered "preposterous."[171] This view was shared not only by conservative opponents but also by the gay liberation movement. For activists who embraced a vision of radical solidarity and collective care, marriage symbolized a retreat into privatized, heteronormative respectability. Adopting the nuclear family model, they feared, would not only undercut queer cultural innovation but also sap the communal energy that had fueled the movement's most transformative demands. In this context, marriage was not liberation—it was capitulation.

AIDS changed all this. By 1991, the link between public sex and disease had firmly taken root, and the idea that fewer sexual partners—in private—was one of the few effective ways to curb the spread of HIV enjoyed wide circulation. Yet as Schulman argues, we must look beyond these practical, homonormative responses to confront the deeper emotional and psychological wounds the epidemic caused. "The trauma of AIDS—a trauma that has yet to be defined or understood, for which no one has been made accountable," she writes, "has produced a gentrification of the mind for gay people. We have been streamlining into a highly gendered, privatized family/marriage structure en masse."[172] AIDS, in this view, prompted a retreat from expansive, collective visions of queer life toward a more contained and assimilationist politics—what Schulman calls a metaphorical "gentrification of the mind," mirroring the physical gentrification of once-liberatory queer spaces. The effects of this psychic shift were profound, reflected in the growing willingness of influential figures within the CLPC to collaborate with law enforcement—a partnership that would have been unthinkable in earlier eras of gay activism circles (fig. 6.8).

FIGURE 6.8 The downtown Minneapolis skyline overlooking Loring Park, 1995. Courtesy of the Hennepin County Library.

This new alliance was, first and foremost, a marriage of convenience for gay homeowners seeking to protect their property. But in their efforts to crack down on cruising and eliminate so-called vice districts, they also disrupted the social fabric of spaces where people, united by little more than shared sexual desire, found rare opportunities to connect across lines of race and class. By targeting these encounters, they reinforced social hierarchies and helped ossify class distinctions. As Schulman observes, this shift ushered in "racial and class stratification, homogeneity of consumption, mass-produced aesthetics, and familial privatization."[173] The move from community-based politics—exemplified by the direct-action and solidarity of gay liberation—to a homonormative agenda centered on assimilation and private gain marked a profound loss of collective resistance. What emerged in its place was a politics that upheld the status quo and benefited those already positioned to thrive within it.

For gay men with access to privacy and financial stability, the loss of cruising spaces often came with new opportunities—to integrate more fully into mainstream, middle-class life. One outcome of the physical

Cruising All the Way Home   229

and psychological gentrification of AIDS is the rise of what Amin Ghaziani calls "cultural archipelagos," or "new residential and leisure queer spaces [that form] across the city, and beyond its borders as well."[174] One example is Golden Valley, a first-ring suburb of Minneapolis, where, according to a gay male resident, "gay couples go to settle down."[175] Beginning in the early 1980s and continuing through the height of the AIDS epidemic later that decade, growing numbers of gay couples began moving to Golden Valley, which soon earned the nickname of Lavender Hills.[176] A local gay real estate agent noted that he guided "a lot" of gay couples to the neighborhood during that time: "Usually, if someone gay was selling, somebody gay bought." Neighbors, described as "well-educated, liberal, accepting people," had no issue with the new residents' sexuality, so long as they maintained their homes and yards—in other words, so long as they maintained property values.[177] By 2019, Golden Valley had become one of the Twin Cities' more affluent suburbs, with a median household income of $98,058 and a median home value of $304,700. The suburb remained overwhelmingly white—about 85 percent in 2021.[178] Because gay men often referred friends to available homes in the area, they ensured that new buyers aligned with the neighborhood's class and demographic profile. As one longtime gay resident explained in a 2017 *City Pages* article: "Just recently, we had a house go up for sale in the neighborhood. We immediately made a phone call to a [gay] couple that had brunch with us in Golden Valley. They looked at it and they bought it."[179]

Here in Golden Valley reside both the highest number of same-sex households in Minnesota—even, proportionally, more than Minneapolis—and the state's first "family-friendly Pride," which explicitly celebrates "the diversity of our suburban residents" in contrast to the "more urban-focused" and "raucous" Twin Cities Pride festival.[180] It stands as a bastion of the "new" gay—a site far removed both physically from urban life and ideologically from the toxic stereotypes mainstream America circulated about gay men: removed from the so-called predators hunting children; from the stigmatized vectors of disease laying siege to "innocent" suburban purity; from flamboyant "queens" demanding to wear dresses to work; from shadowy figures lurking in the park, looking to do something "dirty" in a darkened corner. Rather, Golden Valley embodies a spatial expression of the politics of middleness, where gay identity is comfortably folded into the status quo. Like other Midwesterners, gay couples here want their home prices to go up. They want their schools—they have children, too—"safe" and their children to be above average. And they are comfortable calling the police when threatened.

For figures like Brian J. Coyle and many gay integrationists, these men entered a "mature" home, where what they do in the privacy of their bedrooms is incidental to their civic rights and overall identity. They are proud Minnesotans, practitioners of "Minnesota Nice," and only parenthetically attracted to men and, ideally, in love with only one. But for figures like Tim Campbell and many gay liberationists, this was not progress but retreat. These men, they believed, were politically anesthetized, apostates who have forsaken a unique, valuable position in society, who gave up far too much and got far too little in return. Leading by example, they might have lifted others up—those the status quo did not, people like Fabian Bridges—but, instead, they helped close the door behind them. Their racial and class privilege stayed strong, and the status quo freed them. It is an open question whether they, or anyone else, is the better for it.

Epilogue
What Space Can Be

Flyover to Epicenter

Return to *The Daily Show* segment that opened this book. Hardly a sociological study—its first obligation was humor—the show nonetheless struck several important chords, proving the axiom that there is more than a grain of truth in every joke. Scenes of the "old" gay include sex shops, parades, a choir of no fewer than a hundred gay men singing and dancing together, and the Castro, a well-defined LGBTQ neighborhood. The "new" gay of Minneapolis, by contrast, is defined by private, coupled scenes in the home: preparing dinner or sipping coffee with homemade bread. The only scene outside the home is a trip to a big box store to buy household goods. Essentially, the show presents the "old" gay as deeply rooted in community, while portraying the "new" gay through a noticeable lack of it. Community gives way to interiority. This transformation is no accident. Neoliberal spatial fixes—engineered responses to the social crises and economic pressures of recent decades—have subtly but powerfully shifted LGBTQ life in Minneapolis from the street to the living room, from the collective to the privatized, at least for those with the cultural and financial capital to do so.

But what about everyone else? What about the poorer, Black, brown, and Indigenous queer people? What about the broader LGBTQ community—those who, because of their gender, are denied the privileges gay men enjoy in a patriarchal society? There is a moment, toward the end of the segment, in which a leader of the "old" gay in San Francisco warns that a private life of home, car, and store does little to serve the "movement," to which *The Daily Show* correspondent replies—with unnerving seriousness—"Maybe the movement has already moved." It is easy to assume this is the case, for the "new" gay dominates the headlines with every gay marriage bill passed, every gay celebrity adoption, or every rising gay politician—like Pete Buttigieg, the Midwesterner who won Iowa's Democratic presidential caucuses in 2020. Meanwhile, the older, more radical traditions of gay liberation seem to have fallen by the wayside.

So has gay liberation gone dormant—or, worse, died—without the efforts of wealthier, whiter, and more politically connected gay men to guide it? Is there a community still attuned to the revolutionary potential of what José Esteban Muñoz calls the "brown commons," "a sphere of being with, between, across, and alongside each other in various positions of striving, flourishing, and becoming"?[1] If this book offers any conclusion, it is that, yes, there is and there needs to be one. If all are to be healthy and secure and *stay* healthy and secure, there must be one.

While *From Vice to Nice* charts the rise of integrationist politics and its neoliberal, private spatial "fixes," the spirit of gay liberation—though less visible after the early 1990s—never truly disappeared. To find its lasting presence, one must look beyond the white mainstream and into the vibrant legacies of Black, Latinx, queer, and Indigenous antiracist and feminist health activism. Within these communities, the ethos of "radical care"—a transformative, inclusive approach to wellness that challenges the social, political, and economic forces behind health disparities—remained active and thriving.[2] Advocates of radical care emphasized that true wellness cannot be achieved in isolation. Instead, they foregrounded how systems of power—racism, sexism, colonialism, classism, and homophobia—take root in the body. They argued that the solution to these injustices lay not in accumulating individual wealth and personal security, but in understanding how these systems impact the human body—and working collectively to address them in order to promote healing.[3]

Ironically, white, middle-class gay communities in Minnesota once understood this as well. A key example is Gay House, founded in 1971 by John Preston and Michael McConnell, two young white gay men. One of the nation's first LGBTQ community centers, Gay House offered counseling, medical referrals, and a safe space for youth grappling with their sexual orientation or gender identity. McConnell later described it as "a place to find help not easily or comfortably addressed in general social service environments."[4] Through pamphlets and newsletters, Gay House volunteers affirmed same-sex desire and gender variance as natural expressions of human experience. They rejected stereotypes that cast LGBTQ people as lonely, depressed, or incapable of long-term relationships—insisting that it was homophobia and social isolation, not any inherent pathology, that caused suffering. At Gay House, emotional and physical healing lay in community. Long before AIDS, its volunteers were already raising awareness about venereal diseases and the importance of testing.[5] Gay House fostered a politics of intimate, communal belonging—family, really—that challenged heterosexual norms of domesticity and made room for everyone. Like many radical organizations of its era, Gay House closed by the end of the 1970s. But its legacy endured, carried forward in memory, practice, and the radical conviction that health begins with solidarity.

The Rise (and Fall) of a Revolution

By the late 1980s, in response to the AIDS crisis, the Twin Cities had developed a robust AIDS social service infrastructure. Yet many of these organizations struggled to confront the deeper forces driving the epidemic, such as racism, poverty, and homophobia. Unlike the early gay and lesbian health and VD clinics of the 1970s, which blended community organizing and political activism with their services, these AIDS service organizations focused primarily on delivering medical and social services, gradually evolving into health-care bureaucracies.[6] As detailed in the preceding chapters, wealthier and predominantly white gay men could make their peace with this dynamic. For queer people of color, it was never that simple.

In 1987, a group of queer Indigenous people, including Sharon Day (Bois Forte Band of Ojibwe) and Lee Staples (Milles Lacs Band of Ojibwe), founded the Minnesota American Indian AIDS Task Force (MAIATF). Beyond its use of Indigenous culture and iconography in its program and outreach materials, MAIATF centered its work on "Ganawenima," an Ojibwe term meaning "to take care of"—a collective ethic of care that prioritized the well-being of all Indigenous people, including those whom society discarded as underserving.[7] As MAIATF's executive director, Day drew from her upbringing: "The way I was raised . . . the first thing you do is take care of your family, your band, your clan, your tribe . . . That's part of your clan responsibility . . . That's what we try to figure out with the Task Force. Take as many people with us as we can and move forward."[8] The organization understood health not just as physical wellness but as shaped by social determinants, like homelessness and substance abuse, that increased vulnerability to HIV.

MAIATF's programs included monthly Talking Circles, where Indigenous elders led participants through prayer, reflection, and open discussion. Other volunteers used Indigenous craft traditions to foster social connection and mutual support.[9] Groups like American Indian Gays and Lesbians, cofounded by Richard LaFortune (Yup'ik), followed MAIATF's example, working to reconnect alienated queer Indigenous people with their tribes and cultural teachings, especially those who had relocated from reservations to urban areas. Far from seeing health as an individual problem, all these activists argued that isolation exposed Indigenous people to heightened risk for HIV—an isolation that "white organizations," as Staples put it, failed to address.[10] Their focus on racism, poverty, settler-colonialism, *and* Indigenous ways of knowing ultimately led to the first international gathering of "two-spirit" people in 1988.[11]

By 1990, this collective approach to community health and queer HIV/AIDS activism remained largely ensconced in Minnesota's Indigenous community. Just as mainstream white society had long marginalized Indigenous life, so too did mainstream HIV/AIDS activism overlook Indigenous-led efforts. But in 1994, that began to change.[12] That year, Nick Metcalf, a Lakota student from South Dakota's Rosebud Reservation, arrived in Minneapolis. Troubled by the persistently high rates of HIV among Black and Latinx communities, Metcalf decided to address how the mainstream LGBTQ community excluded queer people, people who used drugs, and people who engaged in sex work.[13] Together with Edd Lee, a gay Korean American man, they formed Minnesota Men of Color (MMC). Initially, the group was informal, with members gathering for meals to talk, vent, and share ideas. By 1997, however, they had become the nucleus of a politicized network of young men of color. "Everyone was hungry," Lee recalls, and with the help of a modest grant, MMC transitioned from kitchen-table conversation into public, collective action.[14]

By 1999, MMC achieved tax-exempt status and caught the attention of the county health department. Soon, with a six-figure budget, MMC launched HIV outreach programs like Somos Familias (We Are Families) and Ikĉé Wiĉáŝa (Common Man), named in Spanish and Lakota, respectively.[15] Behind it all, MMC carried forward MAIATF's belief that individual health flourishes only within the well-being of the community. Drawing inspiration from the region's two-spirit renaissance, it promoted the idea that to truly thrive—rather than merely survive—one must embrace both body and soul. MMC's outreach materials enthusiastically celebrated sex and sexual practices, emphasizing that people needed to live for something beyond mere survival.

MMC rejected racist and heteronormative hierarchies of moral value, reframing culture not as a risk factor but as a vital pathway for prevention and healing.[16] This embrace of culture was no superficial gesture that masked an otherwise traditional or orthodox AIDS service organization. Antiretroviral drugs, doctor visits, and condoms constituted only part of MMC's response to the AIDS crisis. True to two-spirit politics, MMC wanted its clients not just to survive but to use their diagnosis as an opportunity to heal both body and soul. Roxanne "Rox" Anderson, a Black, mixed-race, gender non-conforming, masculine-presenting transgender community outreach worker at MMC, summed it up: "We engaged with our community through the lens of culture."[17] In an era of rising conservatism, in which the neoliberal model of care not only severed individuals from their communities but anointed only those who could afford care as worthy of it, MMC's work was nothing short of revolutionary.

The region hungered for what MMC offered, and by 2001, it had expanded to serve 5,320 people. Of these, 60 percent were African American, 15 percent Latinx, 10 percent Native American, and 1 percent Asian/Pacific Islander.[18] Defying its own moniker, MMC became one of the first organizations in the region to provide targeted support to transgender women through a program called Gender Girls.[19] That same year, a full 25 percent of MMC's clients were either transgender or cisgender women. Its unapologetic embrace of the full LGBTQ spectrum—and its defense of the rights, needs, and health of everyone—earned it both admiration and backlash.[20] At Twin Cities Pride in 2000, the region's largest LGBTQ celebration, a young trans woman of color was ejected from, ironically enough, the "Stonewall Stage" for performing a song with vulgar lyrics. Distraught, she made her way to MMC's modest booth—the one place she knew she had allies. As one staffer recounted, she tearfully explained that every year, organizers targeted "queens of color," regularly kicking them off stage. "What the fuck are y'all gonna do about this shit?" she implored.[21]

For the MMC staff working the booth, the scene was neither new nor particularly shocking. Yet, true to their belief that health—and, really, vitality—only came with a sense of belonging, MMC stepped in to defend the performer and take on the well-funded, well-organized institution of Twin Cities Pride (TCP). It started with a constructive but direct letter, offering observations and suggestions. When it received no response, it decided it needed more than just a small booth at Pride.[22] It wanted a tent—the "biggest tent," one staffer demanded—featuring music that resonated with queer people of color. MMC began attending TCP board meetings regularly but found them "super uncomfortable" and "not fun," full of microaggressions like dismissive tones and exaggerated eye rolls.[23] More blatant acts of exclusion followed: MMC staff were not invited to sit at the board's table and were passed over when the meeting agenda was distributed. To the TCP board—composed of white gay men—the young queer people of color from

MMC did not seem to have a right to participate in decision-making. But through persistence, the power dynamics at the meetings gradually shifted. In 2001, MMC successfully hosted the "Power to the People" stage, named after the rallying cry of slain Black Panther Party leader Fred Hampton and Public Enemy's 1990 rap anthem.

Located, as one MMC staffer put it, "in a no man's land" with little appeal aside from nearby bathrooms, the tent nonetheless drew crowds with a powerful lineup: local Aztec dancers, Native drummers, jazz musicians, and a roster of rising of hip-hop artists.[24] Two-spirit organizing had always privileged culture, and now MMC was harnessing that cultural power to create one of the most vibrant spaces at Pride. The stage became a site of visibility and joy, where queer people of color could see and celebrate themselves—not as guests at someone else's event, but as people who fundamentally belonged. When an Indigenous dancer took the stage or a Latinx drag queen belted out Selena, they even became, arguably, the life of the party. This was, after all, MMC's vision all along: people living their most authentic selves, not only in political solidarity but also with care and concern for those around them.

The Power to the People tent only grew, and MMC invited others—community-based organizations that although not queer-serving did serve people of color.[25] The group embraced a broader definition of queerness, one that included heterosexual people who, while not identifying as LGBTQ, were "queered" because they stood outside gender, sexual, and domestic space norms.[26] Within a few short years, Power to the People became the festival's second-largest stage, drawing devoted crowds and attracting vendors eager for nearby space. Yet, despite this success, tensions with TCP organizers persisted. As Metcalf put it, "Pride did not want us there."[27] One year, security swarmed the tent over allegations of marijuana use—though Indigenous elders had simply been burning sage. Another year brought accusations of fire code violations for barbecuing on-site. And almost every year, organizers lodged the same complaint: the R&B and hip-hop performances were too loud.

MMC weathered years of resistance at Pride and continued putting on a good show. But in 2003, it faced a challenge it could not overcome. That February, the state Office of the Legislative Auditor received an anonymous complaint about MMC's financial management. Based solely on this tip, the auditor's office launched an investigation into the $337,349 in funds awarded to the MMC by the Minnesota Department of Health between 1999 through

2003, uncovering $27,227 in questionable expenses.[28] The auditor's report not only deemed MMC "noncompliant" with the terms of the grant but also cast doubt on the very effectiveness of its programs. Despite having no expertise in public health outreach, the auditors dismissed MMC's HIV prevention work, claiming that "many of the materials the Minnesota Men of Color submitted for review and approval appeared to promote the organization's social events, rather than the HIV/STD disease prevention program."[29] The auditor's office failed to recognize that cultural events and activities *were* part of MMC's HIV outreach efforts. Nevertheless, the press eagerly pumped the story out, and soon board members—especially those from corporate, high-paying backgrounds—disappeared while politicians looking to find a radical boogeyman to blame for overspending on social services popped up.[30] By winter, MMC shuttered many of its programs and scaled back the rest. Metcalf and others carried on—with varying degrees of success—but in 2009, MMC officially disbanded.

One could easily read the demise of MMC in the 2000s—alongside the dissolution of ACT UP/Minnesota in the 1990s, F.A.G.S. in the 1980s, and Target City Coalition in the 1970s—as evidence of gay liberation's failure and the final triumph of homonormative ideals. Indeed, over the same period that MMC rose and fell, integrationists seemed to roll from victory to victory. In 1993, State Sen. Allan Spear and State Rep. Karen Clark amended the Minnesota Human Rights Act to include protections for sexual orientation and gender identity, making Minnesota the eighth state to pass such legislation. In 2001, a Minnesota District Court struck down the state's longstanding sodomy law. In 2012, voters rejected a ban on same-sex marriage, and that year, Janeé Harteau became the first openly LGBTQ police chief of the Minneapolis Police Department. The following year, same-sex marriage passed easily through the state legislature. Even a committed liberationist like Tim Campbell, who died in 2015, might have celebrated these milestones—though likely with some ambivalence. Yet these gains came largely apart from—or even at the cost of—what *The Daily Show* segment dubbed the broader "movement." As the dominant gay culture of Minnesota—the more educated, typically wealthier, and largely white gay men—embraced neoliberal spatial fixes, they shifted from acting as a queer vanguard to functioning as property-owning taxpayers in same-sex marriages: gay ambassadors of Minnesota Nice. With the help of highly active antiretroviral therapy (HAART), they became "safe" behind the gates and walls of their private homes, but these "fixes" only spared *their* space from HIV infection, not others.

The radical care that MMC operationalized at the turn of the twenty-first century remains urgently needed. As recently as 2021, 36,136 people were diagnosed with HIV in the United States and its territories. The racial disparities that defined the virus's early years have persisted more than four decades into the pandemic. That year, Black/African American people made up 40 percent of new HIV diagnoses despite comprising just 13 percent of the population. Similarly, Latinx people, 18 percent of the population, accounted for 29 percent of new diagnoses.[31] These patterns are echoed in Minnesota. Of the state's 298 new HIV cases in 2021, African American and African-born Black Minnesotans accounted for nearly 42 percent while representing only about 8 percent of the population. Latinx Minnesotans made up 14 percent of new cases despite being just 6 percent of the population, and while American Indians represented 1.4 percent of Minnesotans, they accounted for 3 percent of new diagnoses.[32] In a climate of structured impoverishment and compromised health, viral infections like HIV—and now COVID-19—continue to strike hardest in racially segregated and economically divested neighborhoods.

Despite occasional claims to the contrary, these disparities cannot be reduced to individual choices or personal failings.[33] By 1997, HAART had become widely available—but only to those with the resources to access it. As more white gay men began to live longer, ironically some of the most radical and ambitious AIDS groups began a slow death. With them went the attention, concern, and funding they once commanded, leaving HIV/AIDS as a problem for those on the margins. For queer people of color in particular, the fight goes on. While some gay men and lesbians managed to escape the "gay ghetto," both in a literal and figurative sense, they did so at the cost of leaving others, more marginalized than them, behind. Yet even this "emancipation" will always remain suspect and vulnerable—one hateful political zealot or bigoted law away from crumbling.

On that note, while it might be tempting to read *From Vice to Nice* as a criticism of the mainstream gay movement in Minnesota since its inception in the 1970s—and a lament for its effects on the racialized poor—that is not its true intent. Instead, this book prompts readers to ask, "What if?" What if the wealthy, powerful, and privileged in the gay community had not embraced a politics of middleness? What if, even in the face of the AIDS crisis, the movement had held fast to its liberationist ideals? What if sex had remained a public act of political solidarity and not a "private" one to be discreetly passed over in silence? What if MMC had the clout and political muscle of the Minnesota AIDS Project to push back against one unfair report? And what if, even at the risk of losing a corporate sponsor or two, TCP had infused the entire festival with the same spirit that enlivened the Power to the People tent?

Another way to convey the same idea is to read this work as a call—a call to see being gay as not incidental but profound. To see being gay as not a minor issue to be politely overlooked but a positionality, a vantage point, that needs to be emphasized. It is a valuable perspective from which to critique power and a unique bridge that unites some of society's most privileged and most despised. It should not be diluted to be palatable for mainstream America. Rather, it may well be just the *fix* this nation needs.

Notes

Introduction

1. Kim Palmer, "Gayest City? Magazine Says It's Minneapolis," *Star Tribune*, January 15, 2011.

2. *The Daily Show with Jon Stewart*, "Minneapolis Is the New Gay," aired May 9, 2011, on Comedy Central, https://www.cc.com/video/ys5uqo/the-daily-show-with-jon-stewart-minneapolis-is-the-new-gay.

3. Kohnen, *Screening the Closet*, 1–2; Halberstam, *In a Queer Time and Place*, 23. I use "LGBTQ" as an umbrella term encompassing diverse sexual orientations and gender identities, while "gay" refers specifically to cisgender gay men—those attracted to men and identifying with their gender assigned at birth. This distinction ensures precision in discussing specific groups. "Homosexual" is used in historical contexts, particularly in legal and public health discourse. I use "queer" in the expansive sense articulated by Cathy J. Cohen—not simply as shorthand for LGBTQ identity, but as a term denoting non-normativity, particularly forms of cross-gender identification and same-sex expression grounded in practices of radicalism, subversion, and opposition to dominant structures. In this usage, "queer" resists conflation with homonormativity or the politics of middleness and instead signals a disruptive potential that challenges the status quo. See: Cohen, "Punks, Bulldaggers, and Welfare Queens," 438.

4. Duggan, *The Twilight of Equality?*, 50.

5. Manalansan, "Race, Violence, and the Neoliberal Spatial Politics in the Global City," 142.

6. See also Eng, *The Feeling of Kinship*; Vaid, *Virtual Equality*.

7. See D'Emilio, *Sexual Politics, Sexual Communities*; Armstrong, *Forging Gay Identities*.

8. Gentrification involves not only the privatization of public urban spaces but also the regulation of nonnormative sexualities, reinforcing what Cheryl I. Harris calls "whiteness as property"—the social and economic privileges associated with being white in the United States. Harris, "Whiteness as Property," 1714.

9. British sociologist Ruth Glass coined "gentrification" in 1964 to describe the transformation of working-class neighborhoods into affluent communities, where wealthier residents move in, raising property values and rents, and displacing lower-income residents. Glass, "Introduction: Aspects of Change," xviii–xix.

10. "Minneapolis Has Fourth Highest Rate of Same-Sex Couples among Big Cities," *The Washington Independent*, August 30, 2011.

11. Baird Helgeson, "Movement to Legalize Gay Marriage Gains Steam," *Star Tribune*, November 8, 2012; Sasha Aslanian and Eric Ringham, "Eighteen Months to

History: How the Minnesota Marriage Amendment Was Defeated—Money, Passion, Allies," *MPR News*, November 9, 2012, https://www.mprnews.org/story/2012/11/09/marriage-how.

12. Kathy Bergen, "Gay Marriage Proposal: Wed in Minneapolis," *Chicago Tribune*, September 5, 2013. For how cities market themselves as "gay friendly" as a means of profit, see Rushbrook, "Cities, Queer Space, and the Cosmopolitan Tourist."

13. Human Rights Campaign, "Municipal Equality Index," 2019, https://hrc-prod-requests.s3-us-west-2.amazonaws.com/HRC-MEI-2019-report.pdf.

14. Weston, "Get Thee to a Big City," 255.

15. Halberstam, *In a Queer Time and Place*, 36–37.

16. Enke, *Finding the Movement*, 274.

17. LGBTQ scholarship has challenged metronormative and bicoastal narratives by examining the histories and experiences of LGBTQ people in overlooked regions. Notable works include Biro Walters's *Wide-Open Desert*, Forstie's *Queering the Midwest*, Cartwright's *Peculiar Places*, Janovy's *No Place Like Home, Queering the Countryside* (Gray et al.), Johnson's *Just Queer Folks*, Johnson's *Sweet Tea*, Herring's *Another Country*, Gray's *Out in the Country*, Howard's *Men Like That*, and Sears's *Lonely Hunters*.

18. Bonilla-Silva, *Racism without Racists*, 152.

19. Howard, *Men Like That*.

20. Lassiter and Crespino, "Introduction," 7.

21. Manalansan et al., "Queering the Middle," 1.

22. Emphasis in original. Lassiter and Crespino, "Introduction," 11.

23. Hoganson, *The Heartland*, xiv. For further discussion on the cultural mythology of the heartland Midwest, refer to Cayton and Gray's *The American Midwest* and Cayton and Onuf's *The Midwest and the Nation*.

24. Atkins, *Creating Minnesota*, 242.

25. Minnesota's predominantly white population stems from exclusionary state policies and community practices. Yet people of color have long lived and thrived in the Midwest. Recent scholarship, such as Sdunzik's *The Geography of Hate*, Montrie's *Whiteness in Plain View*, and Reid's "The Whitest of Occupations?, " challenges the notion of the Midwest as overwhelmingly white.

26. Leslie Feinberg, "Early Gay Liberation: Anti-Racist Solidarity," *Workers World*, May 27, 2022, https://www.workers.org/2022/05/64387/; Artyukhina, Morgan. "'Our Armies Are Rising': Sylvia Rivera and Marsha P. Johnson," *Liberation School*, October 13, 2020, https://www.liberationschool.org/our-armies-are-rising-sylvia-rivera-and-marsha-p-johnson/; Diwas, "Of Consciousness and Criticism"; Leighton, "'All of Us Are Unapprehended Felons,'" 866–71.

27. Stein, *City of Sisterly and Brotherly Loves*, 13.

28. Stewart-Winter, *Queer Clout*, 1–2, 8.

29. Armstrong, *Forging Gay Identities*.

30. Howard, *The Closet and the Cul-de-Sac*.

31. Meredith May, "Gay Men's Chorus Carries On," *San Francisco Chronicle*, June 4, 2006.

32. Dallas Drake in conversation with the author, February 2023.

33. For foundational work on LGBTQ rights and urban politics, see Valentine and Bell, *Mapping Desire; Castells, The City and the Grassroots*; and Knopp, "Some Theoretical Implications of Gay Involvement in an Urban Land Market." For studies that explicitly consider the impact of AIDS on urban politics, see Yeros, *Queering Urbanism*; Sides, *Erotic City*; Colgrove, *Epidemic City*; Stewart-Winter, *Queer Clout*; and *Policing Public Sex*, ed. Dangerous Bedfellows.

34. Key early works in AIDS historiography include Shilts's *And the Band Played On*, Patton's *Inventing AIDS*, Epstein's *Impure Science*, Treichler's *How to Have Theory in an Epidemic*, and Crimp's *Melancholia and Moralism*. Studies that foreground race and sexuality in the context of the US AIDS epidemic include Cohen's *The Boundaries of Blackness*, Román's "Not-About-AIDS," Muñoz's *Disidentifications*, Roque-Ramírez's "Claiming Queer Cultural Citizenship" and "Gay Latino Histories/Dying to Be Remembered," and Manalansan's *Global Divas*.

35. Brier, *Infectious Ideas*.

36. Refer to the following works: Hobson's *Lavender and Red*, Carroll's *Mobilizing New York*, and Royles's *To Make the Wounded Whole*. These studies are further enriched by several edited collections, including "The AIDS Crisis Is Not Over," edited by Hobson and Royles in *Radical History Review*; *The Black AIDS Epidemic*, edited by Bailey and Bost in *Souls*; and *AIDS and the Distribution of Crises*, edited by Cheng et al.

37. Batza, "Opening DOORWAYS and Closing Others," 229.

38. Wall text, *AIDS at Home: Art and Everyday Activism*, The Museum of the City of New York, New York City. See Vider, "Public Disclosures of Private Realities."

39. See Batza, *Before AIDS*, 130.

40. Harvey, *A Brief History of Neoliberalism*, 2; Gerstle, *The Rise and Fall of the Neoliberal Order*, 2.

41. Pattillo, "Race, Poverty, and Neighborhood Planning in Chicago from the New Deal to Neoliberalism," 13, 20.

42. See Sears, *Arresting Dress*; Goluboff, *Vagrant Nation*.

43. See Esparza, "'We Lived as Do Spouses.'"

44. Hoganson, *The Heartland*, xxi.

45. Harvey, *The Condition of Postmodernity*, 180; Harvey, *The Limits to Capital*, 431–38, 442–45.

46. See Warner, *The Trouble with Normal*, 149–93.

47. Halverson and Reno, *Imagining the Heartland*, 12.

48. Hoganson, *The Heartland*, 301.

49. Halverson and Reno, *Imagining the Heartland*, 52; Puar, *Terrorist Assemblages*, 3; Chow, *The Protestant Ethnic and the Spirit of Capitalism*, 3.

50. Myers and Ha, *Race Neutrality*, 17, 24, 55–58; Randy Furst and MaryJo Webster, "How Did Minn. Become One of the Most Racially Inequitable States?," *Star Tribune*, September 6, 2019.

51. Greg Wierzynski, "The Good Life in Minnesota," *Time* magazine, August 13, 1973; Dave Kenney, "'State That Works' Cover Offered a Minnesota Image That Doesn't Fit as Comfortably Today," *MinnPost*, August 13, 2013, https://www.minnpost.com/community-voices/2013/08/state-works-cover-offered-minnesota-image-doesnt-fit-comfortably-today/.

52. Sugrue, *The Origins of the Urban Crisis*, xviii.

53. In 1990, Minnesota's white population was 94 percent. By 2020, this figure had decreased to 84 percent. Ricardo Lopez, "Minnesota's Decades-Long Failure to Confront Police Abuse," *The New Yorker*, June 10, 2020.

54. Domestic citizenship, as Vider describes it, involves "the rights, responsibilities, and recognition that stem from the performance of normative domestic scripts." It gains legitimacy by contrasting itself with racialized and queered "Others," who are portrayed as unwilling to protect the private home and, therefore, unworthy of its protections. Vider, *The Queerness of Home*, 14.

55. Beginning in the 1990s, a wave of immigrants from East Africa, South Asia, and Latin America transformed the Twin Cities metro area. In Minneapolis, the white population had declined to 288,967 by 1990, down from 513,250 in 1950. Meanwhile, the city's census-designated "minority population" grew 68.5 percent over the 1980s, reaching 79,416 by 1990. By then, people of color made up 21.6 percent of Minneapolis's population, compared with less than 2 percent in 1950. "Minneapolis Population and Racial Change, 1950–1990," 1991, box 27, folder Minneapolis Population Racial Change, 1950–1991, Department of Community Planning and Economic Development (CPED) Records, Hennepin County Library, Minneapolis, MN.

56. "Quick Facts: Minneapolis City, Minnesota," United States Census Bureau, July 1, 2021, https://www.census.gov/quickfacts/minneapoliscityminnesota.

57. "Quick Facts: Minneapolis City, Minnesota," United States Census Bureau, July 1, 2021, https://www.census.gov/quickfacts/stpaulcityminnesota.

58. Evan Comen, "The Worst Cities for Black Americans," *24/7 Wall St.*, last updated January 15, 2020, https://247wallst.com/special-report/2019/11/05/the-worst-cities-for-black-americans-5/4/; Kim-Eng Ky, Ryan Nunn, and Libby Starling, "People of Color Face Systemic Disparities in Minnesota's Labor Market," *Federal Reserve Bank of Minneapolis*, November 13, 2020, https://www.minneapolisfed.org/article/2020/people-of-color-face-systemic-disparities-in-minnesotas-labor-market.

59. Montrie, *Whiteness in Plain View*, 202.

60. The Homestead Act of 1862 allowed white settlers to claim 160 acres of public land for free by living on it for five years and making improvements like farming or building a house. Within three years, over 75,000 settlers had moved to Minnesota, rapidly populating the prairie. "What Is a Homestead?," Minnesota Historical Society, https://www.mnhs.org/sites/default/files/forestsfieldsfalls/farming/farming-slide08.html, accessed January 13, 2022; Wolfe, "Settler Colonialism and the Elimination of the Native," 397; Hugill, *Settler Colonial City*, 12.

61. Child and White, "'I've Done My Share,'" 198; Snipp, "American Indians and Alaska Natives in Urban Environments," 176.

62. Snipp, "American Indians and Alaska Natives in Urban Environments," 177.

63. Shoemaker, "Indians and Ethnic Choices," 434; "The Plight of the Urban Indian," *Minneapolis Tribune*, April 11, 1968.

64. On the racialized dispossession of Black communities under urban renewal, see Taylor, *Race for Profit*; Satter, *Family Properties*; and Rothstein, *The Color of Law*.

65. Sarah Holder, "Why This Started in Minneapolis," *City Lab*, June 5, 2020, https://www.citylab.com/equity/2020/06/george-floyd-protest-minneapolis-history-racism-minnesota/612481/. On the racialized dispossession of Black communities under urban renewal, see Taylor, *Race for Profit*; Satter, *Family Properties*; and Rothstein, *The Color of Law*.

66. "Twin Cities Tear Down the Old to Make Room for the New," *Engineering News Record*, August 16, 1962, box 17, folder Engineering News Record: The Twin Cities Tear Down to Rebuild August 16, 1962, CPED Records, Hennepin County Library.

67. Tom Beer, "Neighborhood Resistance to I-94, 1953–1965," *MNopedia*, Minnesota Historical Society, last updated July 16, 2021.

68. "Loring Park Development District," undated, box 1, folder Irvin Projects: Loring Park Progress and Development, undated, 1972, 1973, 1975, 1980, Lawrence Irvin Papers, Hennepin County Library.

69. Ben Horowitz, Kim Eng Ky, Libby Starling, and Alene Tchourumoff, "Systemic Racism Haunts Homeownership Rates in Minnesota," *Federal Reserve Bank of Minneapolis*, February 25, 2021, https://www.minneapolisfed.org/article/2021/systemic-racism-haunts-homeownership-rates-in-minnesota#_ftn1; David Leonhardt, "The Minnesota Paradox," *New York Times*, June 1, 2020.

70. "Gateway Center Progress Report Number Three," January 1965, box 17, folder Downtown Development History, 1950s–1980s, CPED Records, Hennepin County Library; "Minneapolis Housing and Redevelopment Authority milestones," undated, box 1, folder SCMC M/A 2014.04.01 MHRA: Overviews, Accomplishments, Summary 1962–1978, CPED Records, Hennepin County Library.

71. Terrion L. Williamson argues that Black experiences in the Midwest are distinct from those in other regions, partly because they receive little sustained attention to their lives. National focus on Black Midwestern lives, Williamson notes, tends to surface only in moments of crisis in cities like Chicago, Flint, Detroit, and Ferguson. Williamson, *Black in the Middle*, 15.

72. Adams, "'New Life, New Vigor, and New Values'"; Phillips-Fein, "The Politics of Austerity." Also see Connolly, *A World More Concrete*; Diamond, *Chicago on the Make*; Cohen, *Saving America's Cities*; Holtzman, *The Long Crisis*.

73. Kwamé Holmes argues that urban sexual regulation has profoundly shaped queer experiences and identities in the United States. Through laws, policing, and zoning, cities have historically controlled sexual behavior, influencing the development of queerness. Damon Scott similarly argues that urban renewal has been used to eradicate "queer land uses," which he defines as "patterns of commercial activity that accommodated non-normative sexual desires, provoked anxieties about urban decline, undermined land values, and fueled postwar urban revitalization projects." For further reading, see Holmes, "The End of Queer Urban History?," 161; Scott, *The City Aroused*, 19; Gray Fischer, *The Streets Belong to Us*; Lvosky, *Vice Patrol*; Plaster, *Kids on the Street*; Stewart-Winter, *Queer Clout*; Hanhardt, *Safe Space*.

74. "Underwriting Manual: Underwriting and Valuation Procedure Under Title II of the National Housing Act," Federal Housing Administration (Washington, DC: US Government Printing Office, 1938), https://www.huduser.gov/portal/sites/default/files/pdf/Federal-Housing-Administration-Underwriting-Manual.pdf.

75. Howard, *The Closet and the Cul-de-Sac*, 71–72.

76. Canaday, *The Straight State*, 3–4, 8.

77. Geary, *Antiblack Racism and the AIDS Epidemic*, 66–67. Also see Hanhardt, *Safe Space*, 35–80; Stewart-Winter, *Queer Clout*, 71–93.

78. While scholars have made important contributions to understanding AIDS in relation to spatial politics, much of this work has focused on the physical and intellectual losses experienced in urban life in major cities such as Los Angeles, San Francisco, and New York City. See Colgrove, *Epidemic City*; Sides, *Erotic City*.

79. Wallace et al., "The Hierarchical Diffusion of AIDS and Violent Crime," 935. For a detailed analysis of how race and space shaped the varying HIV risks faced by Black people, see Shabazz's *Spatializing Blackness*, 97–113. For additional key works on the medical geography of the AIDS epidemic, refer to Gould's *The Slow Plague*; Drucker's *A Plague of Prisons*, 19–36; and Wallace and Wallace's *A Plague On Your Houses*, 123–36. While scholars have made important contributions to understanding AIDS in relation to spatial politics, much of this work has focused on the physical and intellectual losses experienced in urban life in major cities such as Los Angeles, San Francisco, and New York City. See Colgrove, *Epidemic City; Sides, Erotic City*.

80. Schulman, *The Gentrification of the Mind*, 23–26.

81. Geary, *Antiblack Racism and the AIDS Epidemic*, 24.

82. "Minnesota Department of Health Disease Control Newsletter," January/February 1988, box 11, folder Bathhouse Ordinance, 1988, Brian J. Coyle Papers, Minnesota Historical Society, St. Paul, Minnesota; Lewis Cope, "302 Cases in State at the End of '87," *Star Tribune*, January 17, 1988.

83. Yeros, *Queering Urbanism*, 18; for an analysis of bathhouse closures, see Bérubé, "The History of Gay Bathhouses," and Woods and Binson, *Gay Bathhouses and Public Health Policy*. For a queer ethnographic account of men having sex with other men in Times Square's pornographic movie theaters, see Delany, *Times Square Red, Times Square Blue*.

84. Castells, *The City and the Grassroots*, 138.

85. Brier, "AIDS and Action (1980–1990s)," 100–102; Brier, *Infectious Ideas*, 156–89. See also Carroll, *Mobilizing New York*, 131–61; Gould, *Moving Politics*, 181–212.

86. Brown, *In the Ruins of Neoliberalism*, 108.

87. See Moreton, *To Serve God and Wal-Mart*, 5; Murphy, *Deregulating Desire*, 15–16.

88. A growing body of scholarship examines "institutions of intimacy," a concept introduced by Lauren Berlant and Michael Warner to explore the intersections between domesticity, LGBTQ culture, community, and politics. In addition to Berlant and Warner's "Sex in Public," 553, see Vider's *The Queerness of Home*, Gutterman's *Her Neighbor's Wife*, Howard's *The Closet and the Cul-de-Sac*, Winunwe Rivers's *Radical Relations*, Pleck's *Not Just Roommates*, and Macías-González, "Transnationalism and the Development of Domesticity in Mexico City's Homophile Community, 1920–1960."

89. Bob Collins, "No Pride for Area Police," *MPR News*, June 22, 2017, https://blogs.mprnews.org/newscut/2017/06/no-pride-for-area-police/; "Pride Fest Leaders Apologize, Invite Cops to March in Parade," *MPR News*, June 23, 2017, https://www.mprnews.org/story/2017/06/23/pride-fest-leaders-change-course-allow-cops-parade.

90. Black and Latinx people, already facing poorer health outcomes, often live in segregated neighborhoods with limited health-care access and in crowded, multigenerational households where social distancing is difficult—creating environments where viruses thrive. Many also work low-wage "essential" jobs without paid sick leave, rely on public transportation, and cannot work remotely. While there is no biological predisposition to COVID-19, higher rates of comorbidities such as diabetes and heart disease increase Black and Latinx people's risk for severe illness. These racial disparities stem from long-standing inequities in housing, employment, and health care—not individual "risk behaviors"—paralleling the structural factors that shaped the racial profile of AIDS. Richard A. Oppel Jr., Robert Gebeloff, K.K. Rebecca Lai, Will Wright, and Mitch Smith, "The Fullest Look Yet at the Racial Inequity of Coronavirus," *New York Times*, July 5, 2020.

91. Christopher Dreher, "Be Creative—or Die," *Salon*, June 7, 2002, https://www.salon.com/2002/06/06/florida_22/.

92. Rodríguez, *Queer Latinidad*, 39.

Chapter 1

1. White, *States of Desire Revisited*, 192.
2. White, *States of Desire Revisited*, 192–93.
3. Koreen Phelps, "What Happened to Minnesota Gay Activists?," *Minnesota Daily*, November 13, 1974; "Oral History Interview of Koreen Phelps," November 5, 1993, AV1994.173, Twin Cities Gay and Lesbian Community Oral History Project, Minnesota Historical Society, St. Paul, MN; "Panthers Get FREE Nod," *The Advocate*, November 25–December 8, 1970, 5; Bronson, *A Quest for Full Equality*, 11–12.
4. Clendinen and Nagourney, *Out for Good*; Strano, "Minnesota," 1021.
5. Bronson, *A Quest for Full Equality*, 22.
6. Jack Star, "The Homosexual Couple," *Look* magazine, January 26, 1971, box 42, folder Photos 01—College Courtship and Commitment, 1965–1972, Michael McConnell Files, Tretter Collection.
7. McConnell et al., *The Wedding Heard 'round the World*.
8. Endean, *Bringing Lesbian and Gay Rights into the Mainstream*, 11.
9. Endean, *Bringing Lesbian and Gay Rights into the Mainstream*, 12.
10. Endean, *Bringing Lesbian and Gay Rights into the Mainstream*, 1.
11. Endean, *Bringing Lesbian and Gay Rights into the Mainstream*, 18.
12. Endean, *Bringing Lesbian and Gay Rights into the Mainstream*, 14.
13. "What Can We Do About Anita Bryant and Florian Chmielewski?," undated, box 11, folder MCGR 1976, Leo Treadway Papers, Minnesota Historical Society.
14. Deborah Howell, "State Sen. Allan Spear Declares He's Homosexual," *The Minneapolis Star*, December 9, 1974.
15. Spear, *Crossing the Boundaries*, 274.
16. Spear, *Crossing the Boundaries*, 274, 281.
17. "Letter from Spear to Howard," February 4, 1974, box 7, folder Minnesota Committee for Gay Rights (MCGR), 1972–1979, Allan Spear Papers, Tretter Collection.

18. Eric Pianin, "Council Protects 'Gay' Rights, Picks Lake-Nicollet Developer," *The Minneapolis Star*, March 29, 1974; Nick Coleman, "Council Enacts 'Gay Rights Ordinance,'" *Star Tribune*, March 30, 1974.

19. Lars Bjornson, "Broad Protection Offered in Minneapolis," *The Advocate*, April 10, 1974, 16.

20. Lars Bjornson, "Rights Bill Passed in Minneapolis," *The Advocate*, April 24, 1974, 6–7; Jim Chalgren, "Steve Endean: No Stranger to the System," *The Advocate*, September 8, 1976, 13–14; Gerri Williams, "St. Paul Council Passes Gay-Rights Amendments," *Star Tribune*, July 17, 1974.

21. Kim Ode, "Tim Campbell: Gay Activist Ignites Controversy on Journey to 'Promised Land,'" *Star Tribune*, July 14, 1986; "Vote Tim Campbell for Mayor," 1979, box 2, folder Timothy Campbell, Tretter Collection Information Files.

22. Endean, *Bringing Lesbian and Gay Rights into the Mainstream*, 236.

23. Endean, *Bringing Lesbian and Gay Rights into the Mainstream*, 120.

24. "Ghetto," undated, box 1, folder MCLU—Gay Task Force—Gay Rights, 1975–1993, MCLU records, Tretter Collection.

25. "Letter from Campbell to Endean," August 1, 1974, box 7, folder MCGR, 1972–1979, Allan Spear Papers, Tretter Collection.

26. Kay Miller, "Gays Fight First for Acceptance, then for Life," *Minneapolis Star Tribune,* February 22, 1987.

27. Endean, *Bringing Lesbian and Gay Rights into the Mainstream*, 121.

28. Clendinen and Nagourney, *Out for Good*, 237.

29. Endean, *Bringing Lesbian and Gay Rights into the Mainstream*, 277.

30. Clendinen and Nagourney, *Out for Good*, 236–38.

31. In some flyers, the group identifies itself as "FAB," while in others, it calls itself "FACT." "FACT flyer," undated, box 10, folder Gay Rights Legislation 2 (1970–1975), Michael McConnell Files, Tretter Collection; "Picket Baker's House," June 1975, box 11, folder MCGR 1975, Leo Treadway Papers, Minnesota Historical Society.

32. Carl Griffin, Jr., "'No Compromise' Gay Coalition May Sink Rights Bill," *The Advocate*, May 7, 1975, 4; Neil Miller, "Minnesota: Ideological Infighting," *Gay Community News*, June 7, 1975.

33. "Editorial," *The Advocate*, May 7, 1975, 30.

34. "Dump Spear!" Location +240, folder Oversize, Thom Higgins Papers, 1950–1994, Minnesota Historical Society.

35. "Gay Rep. Faces Vote Challenge," *Gay Community News*, October 11, 1975; "Dump Spear Flyer," undated, box 10, folder Gay Rights Legislation (1970–1978), Michael McConnell Files, Tretter Collection.

36. See Frank, "'The Civil Rights of Parents.'"

37. "MCGR Newsletter," April 21, 1978, box 11, folder MCGR 1978, Leo Treadway Papers, Minnesota Historical Society.

38. "Citizens Alert for Morality Pamphlet," 1978, box 10, folder Gay Rights Legislation (1970–1978), Michael McConnell Files, Tretter Collection.

39. Bronson, *A Quest for Full Equality*, 39.

40. L. J. Hessburg, "The Gay Rights War: A House Divided vs. Hard and Pious Politics," *Twin Cities Reader*, September 23, 1977, 10–13, 34.

41. "Tactics Split Minneapolis Activists," *The Advocate*, October 5, 1977, 41.
42. Both Wichita, Kansas, and Eugene, Oregon, repealed similar regulations.
43. "Minnesota Poll Split," *The Advocate*, November 30, 1977.
44. Bronson, *A Quest for Full Equality*, 38.
45. In 1995, the Human Rights Campaign Fund removed "Fund" from its name.
46. White, *States of Desire Revisited*, 319.
47. Chalgren, "Steve Endean: No Stranger to the System."
48. White, *States of Desire Revisited*, 320.
49. White, *States of Desire Revisited*, 320.
50. Bill Josephs, "Minneapolis and St. Paul: The Twin Cities," *Ciao!* 3, no. 4 (August 1975): 6–9.
51. Bérubé, "The History of Gay Bathhouses," 188.
52. Chauncey, *Gay New York*, 208, 219.
53. "'Bath Houses' Memo by Dick Brown," 1987, box 18, folder Bathhouse "high risk sex" ordinance, Minneapolis 1988, Tretter Collection Information Files, Tretter Collection.
54. Tim Campbell, "New Bathhouse Stirs Friction," *GLC Voice*, January 1980, 1.
55. Hanson, *History of the Minnesota Gay and Lesbian Legal Assistance (MnGALLA)*, 7.
56. Goluboff, *Vagrant Nation*, 47.
57. Lvosky, *Vice Patrol*, 3, 10, 21, 98–103.
58. "The Cop as Candidate," *Newsweek*, May 12, 1969, 63; Finlay Lewis, "Detective's 61.8% of Vote Beats Cohen," *Minneapolis Tribune*, June 11, 1969.
59. Hessburg, "The Gay Rights War"; "Minneapolis Police Harassment Escalates," *The Advocate*, October 6, 1976; "Minnesota Muddle," *Gay Community News*, November 29, 1975.
60. Manuel and Urban, "'You Can't Legislate the Heart,'" 202–4.
61. Hanson, *History of the Minnesota Gay and Lesbian Legal Assistance (MnGALLA)*, 7.
62. Tom Webb, "Grand Jury Decides to Take No Action in Bathhouse Raid," *Minneapolis Tribune*, October 30, 1979.
63. Frank Allen and Debra Stone, "Police 'Visit' to Bathhouse Called Harassment of Gays," *The Minneapolis Star*, June 29, 1979.
64. Allen and Stone, "Police 'Visit' to Bathhouse Called Harassment of Gays"; Frank Allen, "Aide's Role in Raid Irks Gays," *The Minneapolis Star*, August 2, 1979.
65. "Gay-Rights Activists Arrested after Sit-In," *Minneapolis Tribune*, July 3, 1979.
66. Thom Higgins and Bruce Brockway, "'A Preposterous Coverup of Unlawful Conduct,'" *Positively Gay* 1, no. 5 (September 1979).
67. H. G. Bissinger, "8 Protesters in Hofstede Office Jailed," *St. Paul Pioneer Press*, July 3, 1979.
68. "Editor," *Positively Gay* 1, no. 3 (August 1979).
69. Bruce Brockway, "'Tell Them to Elect Their Own Mayor,'" *Positively Gay*, August 1979.
70. "Jury Plans No Action in Bathhouse Raid Case," *The Minneapolis Star*, October 30, 1979; Bruce Brockway and Thom Higgins, "Deputy Mayor Raids Gay Bath,"

Positively Gay, August 1, 1979; Tom Webb, "Policeman Suspended for Conduct during Raid," *Star Tribune*, January 30, 1980.

71. "The Schroeder Taunt," *Positively Gay*, September 1979.

72. Tim Campbell, "Bathhouse Raiders Collect City Favors," *Positively Gay*, October 1979.

73. Tom Webb, "DeMars: Bathhouse Plan Meant to Block Chain," *Star Tribune*, December 8, 1979; Tom Webb, "Some Gays Criticize DeMars's Bathhouse Plan," *Star Tribune*, December 7, 1979; Tim Campbell, "New Bathhouse Stirs Friction: Pesis Quells Mutiny," *GLC Voice*, January 1980.

74. Tim Campbell, "An Open Letter to the New Police Chief: Mayor's Social Justice Record Is Good," *The Minneapolis Star*, February 27, 1980.

75. Tim Campbell, "Gays Don't All Come Out Alive: A Look at Police Activities," *GLC Voice*, August 1980.

76. See Gray Fischer, *The Streets Belong to Us*, 11–12.

77. "Statement of Don Fraser about the Minneapolis Police Department," August 10, 1979, folder Issues: Police Department, Donald M. Fraser Papers, Minnesota Historical Society.

78. Van Cleve, *Land of 10,000 Loves*, 145; Blade, "'Sodom on the Mississippi.'"

79. Eric Pianin and Patrick Marx, "Pornography Helped Build an Alexander Fortune," *The Minneapolis Star*, November 17, 1975; Randy Shilts, "Big Business: Gay Bars and Baths Come Out of the Bush Leagues," *The Advocate*, June 2, 1976; David E. Early and Katherine Skiba, "Another Vice-Law Battle Brewing," *The Minneapolis Star*, November 21, 1980. See Billund-Phibbs, "Steam Rooms."

80. "Statement of Sgt. G. Weimar to MPD," December 1, 1979, box 6, folder MCGR/Target City Coalition Literature/Vice Squad Raid Accounts, MCLU Records, 1965–1979, Tretter Collection.

81. "Statement of Sgt. Nelson to MPD," December 1, 1979, box 6, folder MCGR/Target City Coalition Literature/Vice Squad Raid Accounts, MCLU Records, 1965–1979, Tretter Collection.

82. "Statement of Sgt. G. Weimar to MPD," December 1, 1979, box 6, folder MCGR/Target City Coalition Literature/Vice Squad Raid Accounts, MCLU Records, 1965–1979, Tretter Collection; Robert Halfhill, "Herbert Convicted on Disorderly House Charge," *The Gaily Planet*, November 12, 1980, 1, 8.

83. Tom Webb and Doug Stone, "9 Arrested, 116 Tagged inside Gay Bathhouse," *Star Tribune*, December 2, 1979.

84. "Statement of Sgt. Nelson to MPD," December 1, 1979, box 6, folder MCGR/Target City Coalition Literature/Vice Squad Raid Accounts, MCLU Records, 1965–1979, Tretter Collection.

85. "Statement of Officer T. Billings to MPD," December 1, 1979, box 6, folder MCGR/Target City Coalition Literature/Vice Squad Raid Accounts, MCLU Records, 1965–1979, Tretter Collection; Tim Campbell, "Great Raid Backfires," *The GLC Voice*, January 1980, 4.

86. Tom Davies, "Fraser Hints Misgivings about Gay Bathhouse Raid," *Star Tribune*, December 14, 1979.

87. "Men Arrested in Raid Facing Lesser Charge," *The Minneapolis Star*, December 6, 1979.

88. "Transcript of Police Chief Donald Dwyer's Press Conference," December 1, 1979, box 18, folder Bathhouses, Tretter Collection Information Files, Tretter Collection.

89. "City Plans to Charge 9 Arrested in Bathhouse with Misdemeanors," *Minneapolis Tribune*, December 7, 1979.

90. Brian Lambert, "Inside the Baths: Doug Victor's Lonely Ordeal," *Twin Cities Reader*, January 16, 1980.

91. Campbell, "Gays Don't All Come Out Alive."

92. "6 of 9 Men Arrested in Bathhouse Raid Fined," *Minneapolis Tribune*, December 19, 1979; Tom Webb, "Man Arrested in Bathhouse Raid Pleads Not Guilty to 4 Charges," *Minneapolis Tribune*, December 12, 1979.

93. "News Notes," *Gay Community News*, April 11, 1981; "Doug Victor Found Not Guilty on Three Counts, Guilty on One Count," *GLC Voice*, January 1981.

94. "The Courage of Our Convictions," *GLC Voice*, January 1980.

95. "Transcript of Police Chief Donald Dwyer's Press Conference," December 1, 1979, box 18, folder Bathhouses, Tretter Collection Information Files, Tretter Collection.

96. Lambert, "Inside the Baths."

97. "Local Judges Uphold Vice Law Constitutionality," *The Gaily Planet*, September 10, 1980.

98. *State of Minnesota, City of Minneapolis v. Douglas Edward Victor* (1980), Municipal Court First Division, Minneapolis.

99. Margaret Zack, "City Police Again Raid Bathhouse," *Star Tribune*, February 11, 1980; Dan Daniel, "Second Bathhouse Raid in 3 Months Nets over 100," *Gay Community News*, March 1, 1980.

100. "'Last-Chance' Raid on Minneapolis Bathhouse," *The Advocate*, April 3, 1980.

101. Larry E. Johnson, "Raid Victim Picks Up the Standard for Gay Rights," *The Minneapolis Star*, April 24, 1980.

102. Tom Webb, "Vice Squad Tickets Assistant County Attorney," *Minneapolis Tribune*, February 2, 1980.

103. Katherine Skiba, "Bouza Takes Over as Chief—amid Cheers, Jeers, and Sneers," *The Minneapolis Star*, February 12, 1980.

104. R. T. Rybak, "Judge 'Believed Juveniles Were in Locker Room,'" *Star Tribune*, February 12, 1980.

105. Lee Mitgang, "City Faces: Minneapolis's Fiery New Police Chief," *Associated Press*, May 21, 1980; Christine Hudgins, "Justice System Copes with Cuban Crime," *The Minneapolis Star*, August 20, 1981.

106. Mitgang, "City Faces."

107. Philip B. Taft Jr., "Tony Bouza of Minneapolis: Is He a Reform Chief or a 'Flake'?" *Police Magazine*, January 21, 1982.

108. Christine Hudgins, "Policy on Gays Has Fraser, Police Battling on Beaches," *The Minneapolis Star*, October 14, 1981.

109. Daniel, "Second Bathhouse Raid in 3 Months Nets over 100."

110. Tom Davies, "Police Chief's Honeymoon Over before It Begins," *Star Tribune*, February 12, 1980.

111. Daniel, "Second Bathhouse Raid in 3 Months Nets over 100."

112. "Bathhouse Employees Acquitted in Minnesota," *The Advocate*, May 1981, 2; "MGDF Update Letter," December 7, 1981, box 1, folder MN Gay Defense Fund—Mailings, 1980–1982, MCLU Records, Tretter Collection.

113. Davies, "Police Chief's Honeymoon Over before It Begins."

114. Katherine Skiba, "Police Chief Transfers Vice, Narcotics Heads," *The Minneapolis Star*, February 13, 1980.

115. Daniel, "Second Bathhouse Raid in 3 Months Nets over 100"; Tom Webb, "Vice Unit's Leaders to Retain Old Goals," *Minneapolis Tribune*, February 14, 1980.

116. Tom Webb, "Bathhouse Raids Moved Sex behind Doors," *Minneapolis Tribune*, May 26, 1980.

117. Delegard, "Contested Geography," 166, 175.

118. Dick Dahl, "The High Price of Vice," *City Pages*, April 27, 1983.

119. David Brookbank, "DFL Opposes Vice Laws," *The Gaily Planet*, August 13, 1980.

120. "Increase in Vice Activity Reported," *The Gaily Planet*, October 15, 1980.

121. "MCGLR Newsletter," October 1982, box 8, folder MCGR, Tretter Collection Information Files, 1938–2008, Tretter Collection.

122. Paul McEnroe and Dennis J. McGrath, "150 Involved in Vice Sweep That Included Officer's Arrest," *Star Tribune*, August 1, 1984.

123. The reported number of gay men arrested by the vice squad under Bouza varies depending on the source. According to the *GLC Voice*, more than five thousand men were arrested in adult bookstores during the first five years of the Fraser administration. *Equal Time* reported that the MPD arrested 595 men for "indecent conduct" in 1982, 540 in 1983, and 373 by October 1984. J. C. Ritter, "Coyle Alerts Fraser on Police Harassment of Gays," *Equal Time*, October 3, 1984; Tim Campbell, "Bookstores Sex: Therapy Is the Answer. Who Should Get It?" *GLC Voice*, January 7, 1985.

124. Only 5 percent of men charged with indecent conduct chose to take their cases to court. "Letters: Coyle and Bouza Face-Off," Equal Time, June 13, 1984.

125. David E. Early and Katherine Skiba, "Another Vice-Law Quarrel Brews," *The Minneapolis Star*, November 21, 1980; Doug Stone and R. T. Rybak, "Sauna, Bookstore Operators Battling with Police Once Again," *Star Tribune*, November 21, 1980; Stoney Bowden, "Judge Orders Halt to Vice Squad Harassment," *The Gaily Planet*, November 26, 1980.

126. Robert Halfhill, "Conflict over Vice Squad Ruling," *The Gaily Planet*, December 3, 1980.

127. "Conference Suggested on Police Sauna Tactics," *The Minneapolis Star*, December 11, 1980.

128. Delegard, "Contested Geography," 166.

129. The case was "closed," and no significant changes resulted from it. Mark Kasel, "Political Leaders Protest Vice Squad," *Equal Time*, March 6, 1985; Margaret Zack and Paul McEnroe, "Alexander Accuses City of Harassing His Customers," *Minneapolis Star and Tribune*, February 20, 1985.

130. Jim Parsons, "Accustomed to Controversy," *Star Tribune*, July 30, 1990.

131. J. C. Ritter, "The Month of August Is Hot for Gay Arrests," *Equal Time*, September 5, 1984.

132. Paul McEnroe, "Bouza Curtails Bookstore Patrols," *Star Tribune*, February 22, 1985.

133. Jim St. George in conversation with the author, March 2023.

134. Jerry Fladmark in conversation with the author, March 2023.

135. Kasel, "Political Leaders Protest Vice Squad"; Jim Schroeder, "Vice Squad Steps Up Activity," *Equal Time*, May 13, 1987.

136. Harriet Guthertz, "Karen Clark Settles into Legislative Role," *Gay Community News*, April 18, 1981; "Who Is Karen Clark," *GLC Voice*, November 1980.

137. Robert Halfhill, "Feminists Split on Vice Issues," *The Gaily Planet*, November 5, 1980.

138. Kasel, "Political Leaders Protest Vice Squad."

139. McEnroe, "Bouza Curtails Bookstore Patrols."

140. Paul McEnroe, "Bouza Denies Gay Pressure on Bookstores," *Star Tribune*, February 23, 1985.

141. Paul McEnroe, "Vice Squad Crackdown Sets Record in August for Arrests in One Month," *Star Tribune*, September 12, 1983; Paul McEnroe, "Vice Squad Officers Arresting Fewer Gays for Indecent Conduct," *Star Tribune*, April 26, 1985.

142. Katherine Skiba, "Competitor of Raided Gay Bath Offering Tours," *The Minneapolis Star*, February 14, 1980; Dan Cohen, "Look Out, Chief, It May Get Icky!" *The Minneapolis Star*, February 19, 1980.

143. Terry Wolkerstorfer, "Gay Group Alleges Police Laxity, Plans Vigilante Assault Defense," *The Minneapolis Star*, September 11, 1974; Lars Bjornson, "Minneapolis Gays Cite 'Queer-Baiting,' Ask Park Protection," *The Advocate*, October 23, 1974.

144. Another brief gay patrol was the "Loring Gay Defense Squad," founded by Thom Higgins. Bjornson, "Minneapolis Gays Cite 'Queer-Baiting.'"

145. "Gay House Newsletter," September 1975, box 1, folder Gay House—Associated Documents, 1971–1975, Gay House Records, 1971–1975, Tretter Collection.

146. These early documentation efforts, however, failed to differentiate between types of violence, such as random street violence, domestic abuse, or interpersonal sexual assault. Kay Miller and Christopher Evans, "Gays Say Violence Has Not Let Up," *The Minneapolis Star*, June 26, 1981.

147. Brenda Ingersoll, "St. Paul's Repeal of 'Gay Rights' Increases Membership of Groups," *The Minneapolis Star*, December 4, 1978.

148. "Memo from Woodward on No More Assault Project," August 18, 1978, box 11, folder MCGR—"No More Assault Project"—1978, Leo Treadway Papers, Minnesota Historical Society.

149. "Men Beating Men Flyer," undated, box 11, folder MCGR 1978, Leo Treadway Papers, Minnesota Historical Society; "MCGR Newsletter," January 12, 1979, box 11, folder MCGR—"No More Assault Project," 1979–1980, Leo Treadway Papers, Minnesota Historical Society.

150. Debra Stone and John Oslund, "Gay Victim an Unlikely 'Martyr,'" *The Minneapolis Star*, June 13, 1979; Tom Webb, "Man Severely Beaten in Park; Friends, Police Are Baffled," *Star Tribune*, June 8, 1979.

151. John Oslund, "Cruising Loring Park," *The Minneapolis Star*, June 21, 1979.

152. "Man Critical Following Attack," *Gay Community News*, June 23, 1979; "Inflation Calculator," Federal Reserve of Minneapolis, accessed October 26, 2024, https://www.minneapolisfed.org/about-us/monetary-policy/inflation-calculator.

153. "MCGR Newsletter," July 6, 1979, box 11, folder No More Assault Conference Program Planning, July 27–28, Leo Treadway Papers, Minnesota Historical Society; "Man Critical Following Attack."

154. Tom Webb, "Loring Park's Double Life Doesn't Always Mix," *Star Tribune*, June 13, 1979.

155. "Letter from MCGR to Hofstede," July 23, 1979, folder MCGR—"No More Assault Project," 1979–1980, Leo Treadway Papers, Minnesota Historical Society.

156. Jerry Fladmark in discussion with the author, March 2023.

157. "You Can Help Prevent Assaults Flyer," undated, folder No More Assault Conference Program Planning, July 27–28, Leo Treadway Papers, Minnesota Historical Society.

158. Dallas Drake in discussion with the author, February 2023.

159. Bruce Brockway and Alan Stombaugh, "Benscoter Murder Case Detailed," *Positively Gay*, July 1979.

160. Tom Webb, "St. Paul Gay Man's Death Questioned," *Star Tribune*, June 20, 1979.

161. Debra Stone, "St. Paul Gays Plan March," *The Minneapolis Star*, June 27, 1979.

162. Tom Webb, "Gay Man's Death Still Raises Questions," *Star Tribune*, June 29, 1979.

163. Tom Webb, "St. Paul Police Now Say That Gay Man Was Murdered," *Star Tribune*, July 11, 1979.

164. Tom Webb, "Family Bears Pain of Dead Son Being Named in Slaying," *Star Tribune*, July 13, 1979.

165. "Suspect in Gay's Slaying Died in Crash," *The Minneapolis Star*, July 11, 1979; Webb, "St. Paul Police Now Say That Gay Man Was Murdered"; Karl Karlson, "Gay's Killer May Not Be Named," *St. Paul Dispatch*, July 11, 1979.

166. Webb, "St. Paul Police Now Say That Gay Man Was Murdered."

167. Dallas Drake in discussion with the author, February 2023.

168. Oslund, "Cruising Loring Park."

169. "19-Bar Forms Loring Patrols," *Positively Gay*, July 1979.

170. Thom Higgins, "Another Month, Another Murder," *Positively Gay*, October 1979.

171. "City Man, 18, Not Guilty in Loring Park Fatal Stabbing," *Star Tribune*, March 1, 1980.

172. Emphasis added. "Loring-Area Murder Suspect, 18, Arrested," *The Minneapolis Star*, September 7, 1979.

173. Peter Ackerberg, "Plea Bargain Rejected; Jury Acquits Killer," *The Minneapolis Star*, March 7, 1980; "Statement of Officer T. Hussman," Minneapolis Police Department, Supplementary Report, CN: 79-147, 703, September 17, 1979.

174. Robert Halfhill, "Houle Described as 'Mad Dog,'" *GLC Voice*, box 1, folder *GLC Voice*, MCLU Records, Tretter Collection; Tim Campbell, "Jury Excuses Queerkiller," *GLC Voice*, March 1980.

175. Emphasis added. Ackerberg, "Plea Bargain Rejected; Jury Acquits Killer." Remarkably, in 2023, thirty-three states and five territories across the United States still permitted defendants to use the gay panic defense. "Criminal Justice: Gay/Trans Panic Defense Laws," *Movement Advancement Project*, October 3, 2023, https://www.lgbtmap.org/img/maps/citations-panic-defense-bans.pdf.

176. Margaret Zack, "2 Witnesses Identify Greg Smith as Terry Knudsen's Assailant," *Star Tribune*, June 19, 1981; Robert Halfhill, "Knudsen Murder Trials Continue," *GLC Voice*, February 1981; Margaret Zack, "Trial Begins for Man Accused of Murder," *Star Tribune*, June 18, 1981; "Terry Knudsen slaying suspect, 18, is indicted," *Minneapolis Tribune*, April 29, 1981.

177. Smith, who was sixteen at the time of the attack, was tried as an adult, convicted of third-degree murder, and sentenced to twenty-five years in prison. "Four Jurors Picked in Knudsen Murder Trial," *Star Tribune*, January 6, 1981; Margaret Zack, "Smith Sentences to up to 25 Years in Knudsen Death," *Star Tribune*, July 9, 1981; "Witness in Loring Park Killing Gets Jail Term," *Star Tribune*, April 14, 1982.

178. David Phelps and Paul Klauda, "Cruising for Male Teen Prostitutes Is Weekend Ritual near Loring Park," *Star Tribune*, November 22, 1981.

179. Phelps and Klauda, "Cruising for Male Teen Prostitutes."

180. Miller and Evans, "Gays Say Violence Has Not Let Up"; Robert Halfhill, "Bouza says Cops Rejected Training; Bookstore Arrests to Continue," *The Gaily Planet*, October 15, 1980.

181. Miller and Evans, "Gays Say Violence Has Not Let Up."

182. Miller and Evans, "Gays Say Violence Has Not Let Up."

183. White, *States of Desire Revisited*, 332.

184. Minkoff, *Organizing for Equality*, 74.

185. Vaid, *Virtual Equality*, 72–75.

186. White, *States of Desire Revisited*, xiii.

187. Thomas Trisko in discussion with the author, March 2023.

Chapter 2

1. *Bowers v. Hardwick*, 478 U.S. 186, 106 S. Ct. 2841 (1986).

2. *Griswold v. Connecticut*, 381 U.S. 479, 85 S. Ct. 1678 (1965); *Eisenstadt v. Baird*, 405 U.S. 438 (1972); *Roe v. Wade*, 410 U.S. 113, 93 S. Ct. 705 (1973); *Stanley v. Georgia*, 394 U.S. 557, 89 S. Ct. 1243 (1969).

3. Kevin Diaz, "Sodomy Law Still on Books, and No Challenge Is in Sight," *Star Tribune*, August 31, 1991.

4. "Coyle Meeting Tuesday on S.C. Decision and Justice Dept. Ruling," *Twin Cities Gaze*, July 6, 1986.

5. Kate Parry, "ACLU Offers Help in Challenge to Sodomy Law," *Minneapolis Star and Tribune*, July 25, 1986.

6. Jim Schroeder, "Rally Protests Supreme Court, Justice Dept.," *Equal Time*, July 23, 1986; Sue Hyde, "Hardwick, Sodomy Laws and Our Fight for Sexual Freedom," *Gay Community News*, March 15–21, 1987.

7. *Opinion of the Justices*, 129 N.H. 290, 530 A.2d 21 (N.H. 1987).

8. *Bowers v. Hardwick*, 478 U.S. 186 (1986).

9. Schroeder, "Rally Protests Supreme Court, Justice Dept."

10. "Demonstration against S.C. Decision Wednesday at Fed. Bldg.," *Twin Cities Gaze*, July 6, 1986.

11. For more on the historical relationship between privacy and the LGBTQ community, see Vider's *The Queerness of Home* and Howard's *The Closet and the Cul-de-Sac*.

12. *Griswold v. Connecticut*, 381 U.S. 479, 85 S. Ct. 1678 (1965).

13. Goluboff, *Vagrant Nation*, 173–76.

14. De Orio, "The Invention of Bad Gay Sex," 55.

15. De Orio, "The Invention of Bad Gay Sex," 69.

16. Jim Schroeder, "Forum Discusses Repeal of Minnesota's Sodomy Law," *Equal Time*, August 6, 1986.

17. Parry, "ACLU Offers Help in Challenge to Sodomy Law."

18. Goluboff, *Vagrant Nation*, 49–50.

19. Eskridge, *Dishonorable Passions*; Painter, "History of Sodomy Laws."

20. Painter, "Minnesota"; David Peterson, "Cautious High Court Unlikely to Throw Out State's Sodomy Law," *Minneapolis Star and Tribune*, December 4, 1986; Office of the Revisor of Statutes, "Section 609.293—Sodomy," Minnesota Statutes 1986, accessed March 28, 2022, https://www.revisor.mn.gov/statutes/1986/cite/609/pdf.

21. Jim Schroeder, "ACLU's Nan Hunter on the 'Long Fight,'" *Equal Time*, August 6, 1986; Jim Schroeder, "Repeal of Sodomy Laws Depends on Coalitions," *Equal Time*, September 3, 1986; Jim Schroeder, "Stoddard on Rights for Gays/Lesbians," *Equal Time*, October 29, 1986.

22. Diaz, "Sodomy Law Still on Books, and No Challenge Is in Sight."

23. Tim Campbell, "Summer of Police Hostility Sparks New Activism," *GLC Voice*, October 1984.

24. Ehrman-Solberg, "The Battle of the Bookstores and Gay Sexual Liberation in Minneapolis"; Murphy and Urquhart, "Sexuality in the Headlines."

25. See *State v. Nelson*, 199 Minn. 86, 271 N.W. 114 (Minn. 1937); *State v. Panetti*, 203 Minn. 150, 280 N.W. 181 (Minn. 1938); *State v. Hopfe*, 249 Minn. 464, 82 N.W.2d 681 (Minn. 1957); *State v. Anderson*, 270 Minn. 411, 134 N.W.2d 12 (Minn. 1965); *State v. Pooley*, 278 Minn. 67, 153 N.W.2d 143 (Minn. 1967); *State v. Bryant*, 287 Minn. 205, 177 N.W.2d 800 (Minn. 1970).

26. "Letter from James T. Nagle to Janlori Goldman," August 12, 1985, box 5, folder Sodomy research, data, & MPD/SPPD arrest records 1985–1986, MCLU Records, 1965–2006, Tretter Collection.

27. "Letter from Sue Aasen to Janlori Goldman," August 27, 1986, box 5, folder Sodomy research, data, & MPD/SPPD arrest records 1985–1986, MCLU Records, 1965–2006, Tretter Collection.

28. "Letter from Susan J. Bousquet to Jan Goldman," September 13, 1985, box 5, folder Sodomy research, data, & MPD/SPPD arrest records 1985–1986, MCLU Records, 1965–2006, Tretter Collection.

29. David Peterson and Christine Hudgins, "Judge Winton Subject of Sex Investigation," *The Minneapolis Star*, February 11, 1982.

30. David Phelps, "Three Youths Say on TV Winton Paid Them for Sex," *Star Tribune*, February 12, 1982; Paul McEnroe and David Peterson, "Youth Told Conflicting Stories about Winton, Sex," *The Minneapolis Star*, February 12, 1982; "Knutson Case Stays in Juvenile Court," *The Gaily Planet*, August 27, 1980.

31. "Text of Court Statement by Judge Crane Winton," 1982, box 1, folder Crane Winton Case, Allan H. Spear Papers, Tretter Collection.

32. Dennis Cassano, "New Charges against Winton Being Studied," *Star Tribune*, April 19, 1984.

33. *Complaint Concerning Winton*, 350 N.W.2d 337 (Minn. 1984); *Minnesota v. Winton*, Nos. 80369-1, 80370-1 CO. (Minn. Dist. Ct. June 21, 1983).

34. "Letter from Spear to Winton," July 2, 1982, box 1, folder Crane Winton Case, Allan Spear Papers, Tretter Collection; "Letter from Spear to Constituents," undated, box 1, folder Crane Winton Case, Allan H. Spear Papers, Tretter Collection.

35. "Opinion on Complaint Concerning Winton by Minnesota Supreme Court," May 25, 1984, box 1, folder Crane Winton Case, Allan H. Spear Papers, Tretter Collection.

36. "News Notes," *Gay Community News*, July 10, 1982; Loie Hayes, "Gay Judge Refuses to Bow to State Pressure," *Gay Community News*, June 4, 1983.

37. *Complaint Concerning Winton*, 350 N.W.2d 337 (Minn. 1984).

38. Renfro, *Stranger Danger*, 18.

39. Randy Furst and Paul McEnroe, "Donahue Was Topic of Rumors for Many Years," *Star Tribune*, April 29, 1984; Dennis Cassano, "Police Investigating Possible Adult Links in Child Abuse Case," *Star Tribune*, April 21, 1984.

40. Cassano, "Police Investigating Possible Adult Links in Child Abuse Case."

41. Kevin Diaz and Margaret Zack, "Donahue Enters Guilty Plea," *Star Tribune*, October 2, 1984.

42. Tim Campbell, "Letters from Readers: Creating 'Vampires,'" *Star Tribune*, May 15, 1984.

43. Kim Ode, "Tim Campbell: Gay Activist Ignites Controversy on Journey to the 'Promised Land,'" *Star Tribune*, July 14, 1986.

44. Sam Newlund and Dennis Cassano, "Supporter of Man-Boy Sex Attracts Protesters," *Star Tribune*, June 22, 1984; Levine, "Sympathy for the Devil."

45. Claude Peck, "Minneapolis Forum Raises Hackles, Issues," *Gay Community News*, July 7, 1984.

46. Newlund and Cassano, "Supporter of Man-Boy Sex Attracts Protesters."

47. Gene Sullivan, "Letters from Readers: Self-Serving Gays," *Star Tribune*, June 27, 1984.

48. Vider, *The Queerness of Home*, 16.

49. David B. Goodstein, "Opening Space," *The Advocate*, April 20, 1977.

50. City-Data. "Shoreview, Minnesota," accessed July 31, 2015, http://www.city-data.com/city/Shoreview-Minnesota.html.

51. *State v. Gray*, 413 N.W.2d 107 (Minn. 1987); Leonard, *Sexuality and the Law*, 170.

52. Jim Schroeder, "Shorewood Man Charged under State Sodomy Law," *Equal Time*, August 20, 1986.

53. Emphasis added. Bill McAuliffe, "Hennepin County Judge Rules State Sodomy Law Is Unconstitutional," *Minneapolis Star and Tribune*, December 2, 1986; David Peterson, "Cautious High Court Unlikely to Throw Out State's Sodomy Law," *Minneapolis Star and Tribune*, December 4, 1986; Jim Schroeder, "Sodomy Law Unconstitutional," *Equal Time*, December 17, 1986.

54. McAuliffe, "Hennepin County Judge Rules State Law Is Unconstitutional."

55. Peter Freiberg, "Minn. Gov. Signs Progay Executive Order; Court Strikes Down Sodomy Law," *The Advocate*, January 6, 1987, 15–16.

56. After the US Supreme Court upheld the constitutionality of Georgia's sodomy statute in the *Bowers* case, McClellan withdrew his lawsuit from federal court. In June 1987, the MCLU refiled McClellan's case in Hennepin County District Court. However, in March 1989, the Minnesota District Court dismissed the lawsuit.

57. "Letter from Dorsey and Whitney to Stark," 1987, box 5, folder *Gray v. Minnesota*—Legal & Notes, MCLU Records, 1965–2006, Tretter Collection.

58. Jim Schroeder, "Sodomy Vote Almost Went Other Way," *Equal Time*, July 23, 1986; Jim Schroeder, "Sodomy Statute Upheld, Mn. Court Challenge Reviewed," *Equal Time*, July 9, 1986; "MCLU Sues to Overturn Sodomy Law," *Minneapolis Star and Tribune*, February 4, 1987; Jim Schroeder, "Sodomy Law," *Equal Time*, February 18, 1987.

59. David Shaffer, "Lawsuit Challenges Minnesota Sodomy Law," 1987, box 5, folder *Gray v. Minnesota*—Press, 1987, MCLU Records, 1965–2006, Tretter Collection.

60. In 1986, although the legal age of consent in Minnesota was sixteen, certain circumstances—such as the age difference or relationship between the parties—raised the age of consent to eighteen. The law was clear that no one under the age of thirteen could legally consent to sex. For reference, see Minnesota Session Laws—1985, Regular Session, "Chapter 286-H.F. No. 848," Office of the Revisor of Statutes, May 31, 1985, https://www.revisor.mn.gov/laws/1985/0/286/.

61. Halfhill insisted that he never had sex with anyone under the age of consent and had "no sexual interest in prepubescent boys." However, he explained that he was a member of NAMBLA because he supported "the human rights of the people having this sexual orientation." "Letters: Bob Halfhill Chides MCLU Madness," *GLC Voice*, February 20, 1984.

62. Jim Schroeder, "Sodomy Repeal Still a Possibility," *Equal Time*, April 15, 1987; McAuliffe, "Hennepin County Judge Rules State Sodomy Law Is Unconstitutional."

63. "Defendant's Reply Memorandum," 1987, box 5, folder *Gray v. Minnesota*—Legal Files & Notes, MCLU Records, 1965–2006, Tretter Collection.

64. Dennis Cassano, "State Supreme Court Asked to End Enforcement of the Sodomy Statute," *Minneapolis Star and Tribune*, May 8, 1987.

65. Art Harris, "Gay Rights Legal Fight Inspired by Outrage," *Minneapolis Star and Tribune*, September 8, 1986.

66. Underlined in original. "Memorandum in Opposition to Defendant's Motion to Dismiss," 1987, box 5, folder *Gray v. Minnesota*—Legal Files & Notes, MCLU Records, 1965–2006, Tretter Collection.

67. *State v. Gray*, 413 N.W.2d 107 (Minn. 1987).

68. Hewetson, "History of the Gay Movement in Minnesota"; Dan Oberdorfer, "Court Partially Upholds Sodomy Law, Will Decide on Relevancy of Setting," *Star Tribune*, October 2, 1987; Jim Schroeder, "State's Sodomy Law Upheld in Prostitution Cases," *Equal Time*, October 14, 1987; Diaz, "Sodomy Law Still on Books, and No Challenge Is in Sight."

69. Oberdorfer, "Court Partially Upholds Sodomy Law, Will Decide on Relevancy of Setting"; Schroeder, "State's Sodomy Law Upheld in Prostitution Cases"; Diaz, "Sodomy Law Still on Books, and No Challenge Is in Sight."

70. Margaret Zack, "Charges Dropped in Sodomy Case after Key Witness Refuses to Testify," *Star Tribune*, February 26, 1988; Lou Gelfand, "To Spare Shame to a Witness, a Trial Is Scrapped," *Star Tribune*, March 6, 1988.

71. Jim Schroeder, "Clark/Spear Discuss 1987 Session," *Equal Time*, December 17, 1986.

72. Schroeder, "Clark/Spear Discuss 1987 Session."

73. Robert Whereatt, "Coalition Brings New Strategy to Sex Law Fight," *Star Tribune*, March 26, 1987.

74. For more on the "war on sex," see Halperin, "Introduction: The War on Sex"; Lancaster, "The New Pariahs."

75. Blomley, "The Borrowed View," 619–22.

76. Hubbard, *Cities and Sexualities*, 34.

77. Rubin, "Thinking Sex," 151, 153.

78. Rubin, "Thinking Sex," 151–52.

79. Schroeder, "Clark/Spear Discuss 1987 Session."

80. Whereatt, "Coalition Brings New Strategy to Sex Law Fight"; Jim Schroeder, "Civil Rights Commission Endorses Repeal of Sodomy Law," *Equal Time*, February 4, 1987.

81. Jim Schroeder, "New Bill Drafted," *Equal Time*, March 4, 1987.

82. Jim Schroeder, "Forum Discusses Repeal of Minnesota's Sodomy Law," *Equal Time*, August 6, 1986.

83. "FYI," *Twin Cities Gaze*, February 2, 1987; Schroeder, "New Bill Drafted"; Whereatt, "Coalition Brings New Strategy to Sex Law Fight."

84. "Letter from Senate Counsel to Sen. Donna Peterson," March 25, 1987, box 163, folder Judiciary Committee Vol. 2, 1987, Legislative Committee Hearings, Minnesota Historical Society; "609.36 Adultery," Crimes Against the Family, Minnesota Criminal Code of 1963, box 163, folder Judiciary Committee Vol. 2, 1987, Legislative Committee Hearings, Minnesota Historical Society.

85. Jim Schroeder, "Hearings Set to Replace Sodomy Law," *Equal Time*, April 1, 1987.

86. Endean, born and raised in the upper Midwest, was the founder of the Human Rights Campaign.

87. Schroeder, "Civil Rights Commission Endorses Repeal of Sodomy Law"; Schroeder, "New Bill Drafted"; Joe Kimball, "Panel Approves Repeal of Sex Laws," *Star Tribune*, April 7, 1987.

88. Whereatt, "Coalition Brings New Strategy to Sex Law Fight."

89. "Sodomy Law Repeal Gains," *Senate Briefly*, April 10, 1987, Legislative Reference Library, State Capitol, St. Paul, Minnesota.

90. *State v. Gray*, 413 N.W.2d 107 (Minn. 1987).

91. *State v. Price*, 237 N.W.2d 813 (Iowa 1976).

92. "Memorandum in Opposition to Defendant's Motion to Dismiss," 1987, box 5, folder *Gray v. Minnesota*—Legal Files & Notes, MCLU Records, 1965–2006, Tretter Collection.

93. "The Berean League of Minnesota Flyer," undated, box 3, folder Berean League, 1987, James Eric Chalgren Papers, 1972–2002, Tretter Collection; Parry, "ACLU Offers Help in Challenge to Sodomy Law," *Minneapolis Star and Tribune*, July 25, 1986; "Berean League: Its People, Its Purpose," *Equal Time*, March 20, 1985.

94. J. C. Ritter, "Religious Group to Launch New Attack on Gays," *Equal Time*, March 20, 1985.

95. "Testimony from Dr. Edward Ehlinger," April 6, 1987, box 163, folder Judiciary Committee Vol. 2, 1987, Legislative Committee Hearings, Minnesota Historical Society; Kimball, "Panel Approves Repeal of Sex Laws"; Whereatt, "Coalition Brings New Strategy to Sex Law Fight."

96. Emphasis added. "Testimony from Rev. Paul A. Tidemann," April 6, 1987, box 163, folder Judiciary Committee Vol. 2, 1987, Legislative Committee Hearings, Minnesota Historical Society.

97. "Testimony from Mary Jane Rachner," April 6, 1987, box 163, folder Judiciary Committee Vol. 2, 1987, Legislative Committee Hearings, Minnesota Historical Society.

98. "Minneapolis Police Department Report by Sgt. Jacobson," December 20, 1987, box 5, folder Sodomy research, data, & MPD/SPPD arrest records, 1985—1986, MCLU Records, 1965–2006, Tretter Collection.

99. "Minneapolis Police Department Record by Officer Severson," December 20, 1987, box 5, folder Sodomy research, data, & MPD/SPPD arrest records, 1985—1986, MCLU Records, 1965–2006, Tretter Collection.

100. "S.F. 1235" and "H.F. 1379," April 12, 1987, Minnesota Legislative Reference Library, accessed December 11, 2021.

101. Schroeder, "Civil Rights Commission Endorses Repeal of Sodomy Law"; Schroeder, "New Bill Drafted"; Kimball, "Panel Approves Repeal of Sex Laws."

102. Between 1981 and 1989, homelessness in the 142 largest US cities increased from 5 to 15 percent. Burt, "Causes of the Growth of Homelessness during the 1980s," 3.

103. Between 1982 and 1987, the Reagan administration slashed the federal public housing budget by 87 percent, causing a steep decline in HUD-subsidized housing starts, which dropped from 144,348 in 1981 to 17,080 in 1986. Venkatesh, *American Project*, 116; Perrow and Guillén, *The AIDS Disaster*, 166–67.

104. Cohen, *Saving America's Cities*, 375.

105. Pat Prince, "Activists Rally for Cause of Homeless," *Star Tribune*, July 15, 1988; Rob Hotakainen, "Minneapolis, Hennepin County Pool Efforts on Homelessness," *Star Tribune*, May 19, 1990.

106. Joe Selvaggio, "Commentary: Solution Needed for Growing Homelessness in Minneapolis," *Star Tribune*, May 15, 1990.

107. Steve Berg, "U.S. Mayors Report Increase in Hungry, Homeless," *Star Tribune*, December 17, 1987.

108. Berg, "U.S. Mayors Report Increase in Hungry, Homeless."

109. According to 1990 reports, white people made up 37 percent of the unhoused population, while Asian people accounted for just 1 percent. Mitchel Levitas, "Homeless in America," *New York Times Magazine*, June 10, 1990; James Walsh, "Blacks Outnumber Whites in Emergency Shelters," *Star Tribune*, August 10, 1990; US Census Bureau, "General Population Characteristics: Minnesota," 1990, https://www2.census.gov/library/publications/decennial/1990/cp-1/cp-1-25.pdf.

110. Both the mainstream and LGBTQ press, along with law enforcement and some gay leaders, referred to Olson as a "transsexual" or "transvestite." While it is unclear whether Olson identified as "transgender," I use this term to describe her because she expressed a feminine gender identity. "Transgender" serves as an umbrella term for gender identities and expressions that differ from the sex assigned at birth, whether or not an individual undergoes medical transitions. In contrast, "transsexual" specifically refers to those who medically transition and carries medical and pathological connotations, making it less inclusive. "Transvestite," now considered outdated and pejorative, refers to people who wear clothing associated with a different gender, typically unrelated to their gender identity.

111. Tim Campbell, "Seven Gay Murders in One Year," *GLC Voice*, November 3, 1986.

112. Margaret Zack, "Murder Indictment; Man Freed/Was Charged in Death of Gay Prostitute," *Star Tribune*, October 28, 1987.

113. Julie Gravelle and Kevin Diaz, "Transient Found Slain Had Tested Positive for AIDS," *Minneapolis Star and Tribune*, September 24, 1986.

114. In addition to overlooking Olson's challenges as a transgender woman, Coyle did not account for how her Indigenous identity further shaped her experiences of marginalization. This omission reflects a broader pattern in some LGBTQ legal reform efforts, in which race was often sidelined in favor of a more universalized approach to gay rights, particularly during campaigns to repeal sodomy laws. See Eng, *The Feeling of Kinship*; Somerville, "Queer *Loving*"; Shah, "Policing Privacy, Migrants, and the Limits of Freedom."

115. Kimball, "Panel Approves Repeal of Sex Laws."

116. Schroeder, "Clark/Spear Discuss 1987 Session"; Kimball, "Panel Approves Repeal of Sex Laws"; Schroeder, "Sodomy Repeal Still a Possibility."

117. Lewis Cope, "1,500 Hear Debate on Sex Education and Homosexuality at AIDS Conference," *Star Tribune*, November 8, 1987; Ritter, "Religious Group to Launch New Attack on Gays."

118. Jim Schroeder, "Sodomy Law Repeal Fails," *Equal Time*, May 13, 1987; Schroeder, "Sodomy Repeal Still a Possibility."

119. Schroeder, "Sodomy Repeal Still a Possibility"; Schroeder, "Sodomy Law Repeal Fails."

120. "Laws Are Intrusive, Should Be Repealed," *St. Paul Pioneer Press Dispatch*, April 10, 1987.

121. Schroeder, "Sodomy Repeal Still a Possibility"; Schroeder, "Sodomy Law Repeal Fails."

122. Schroeder, "Sodomy Law Repeal Fails."

123. Jim Schroeder, "Hearings Set to Replace Sodomy Law," *Equal Time*, April 1, 1987.

124. Tim Campbell, "Gay Groups Opposing Spear's New Sex Law," *GLC Voice*, March 16, 1987.

125. "Public Sex Law/Sodomy Repealer Stopped in Committee," *GLC Voice*, April 20, 1987.

126. Tim Campbell, "New 'Public Sex' Laws Pushed by Spear and Friends as 'Sodomy Repeal,'" *GLC Voice*, February 16, 1987.

127. Spade and Willse, "Marriage Will Never Set Us Free."

128. Gallup, *The 1986 Gallup Poll*, 213–14.

129. The Minnesota Senate rejected the mandatory AIDS testing bill, preventing it from becoming law. Gregor Pinney, "Senate Oks $2.2 Billion for Human Services," *Star Tribune*, May 5, 1987; Gregor Pinney, "House Bill Would Require Marriage License AIDS Test," *Star Tribune*, May 3, 1987.

130. "The Task Force on Lesbian and Gay Minnesotans Final Report," March 22, 1991, M.S. 105.H.19.6F, Governor's Task Force on Lesbian and Gay Minnesotans Records, 1990–1993, Minnesota Historical Society.

131. Philipson and Posner, *Private Choices and Public Health*, 54–56, 179.

132. See Cooper, *Family Values*, 167–214. Both Andrew Sullivan and William Eskridge advocated for gay marriage as a strategy to combat HIV. They argued that encouraging monogamous relationships among gay men could help reduce the sexual promiscuity believed to be contributing to the HIV/AIDS crisis. Andrew Sullivan, "Here Comes the Groom: A (Conservative) Case for Gay Marriage," *The New Republic*, August 28, 1989; Eskridge, *The Case for Same-Sex Marriage*, 9, 120.

133. See Reddy, "Home, Houses, Nonidentity"; Bailey, *Butch Queens Up in Pumps*; Nero, "Why Are the Gay Ghettos White?"; Manalansan, *Global Divas*.

134. Bailey, *Butch Queens Up in Pumps*, 25.

135. Donna Halvorsen, "Carlson Signs Gay-Rights Bill into Law," *Star Tribune*, April 3, 1993.

136. Parry, "ACLU Offers Help in Challenge to Sodomy Law."

137. *Doe v. Ventura*, No. MC 01–489, 2001 WL 543734 (Minn. Dist. Ct 2001).

138. *Lawrence v. Texas*, 539 U.S. 558, 123 S. Ct. 2472 (2003).

Chapter 3

1. "NGLTF Urges Gov't Action at Congressional Hearings on Violence," *Twin Cities Gaze*, October 31, 1986; Dave Walter, "Gays Testify on Homophobic Violence," *The Advocate*, November 11, 1986; William R. Greer, "Violence against Homosexu-

als Rising, Groups Seeking Wider Protection Say," *New York Times*, November 23, 1986; Rick Harding, "With Violence Escalating, NGLTF Calls on Congress," 1986, box 13, folder Gay Violence, Brian J. Coyle Papers, Minnesota Historical Society.

2. "CUAV Press Conference Speech," October 22, 1986, box 13, folder Gay Violence, Brian J. Coyle Papers, Minnesota Historical Society.

3. Kari Enger, "AIDS Campaign Not without Controversy," *Twin Cities Reader*, October 15, 1986.

4. Hanhardt, *Safe Space*, 87, 94, 105–6. For a discussion of the "queer unwanted" in gay safe spaces, see Bell and Binnie, "Authenticating Queer Space."

5. "Anti-Gay/Lesbian Victimization: A Study by the National Gay Task Force," June 1984, box 13, folder Gay Violence, Brian J. Coyle Papers, Minnesota Historical Society.

6. James Coates, "AIDS Backlash Gets Violent, Gays Say," *Chicago Tribune*, October 26, 1986.

7. "Quarterly Report and Analysis of Anti-Gay Violence, October–December 1985, CUAV," February 10, 1986, box 13, folder Gay Violence, Brian J. Coyle Papers, Minnesota Historical Society.

8. William E. Schmidt, "Atlanta Homosexuals Fear Surge in Random Violence," *New York Times*, December 2, 1986; Coates, "AIDS Backlash Gets Violent, Gays Say."

9. "Anti-Gay/Lesbian Victimization: A Study by the National Gay Task Force," 1984, box 13, folder Gay Violence, Brian J. Coyle Papers, Minnesota Historical Society; Coates, "AIDS Backlash Gets Violent, Gays Say."

10. Jean Latz Griffin, "Reports of Gay Harassment Soaring," *Chicago Tribune*, May 11, 1987; "NGLTF Press Release," April 27, 1987, box 13, folder Gay Violence, Brian J. Coyle Papers, Minnesota Historical Society.

11. "AIDS Blamed as Study Reports 42% Increase in Violence against Gays," *Star Tribune*, June 8, 1988.

12. Peter Freiberg, "Antigay Violence: Is It on the Rise?" *The Advocate*, December 22, 1983.

13. Hanhardt, *Safe Space*, 160–61, 171–73.

14. "Police Seeking Murder Suspect," *Equal Time*, January 8, 1986.

15. "Police Seeking Murder Suspect."

16. "Emergency Meeting Announcement from Council Member Brian Coyle," January 28, 1986, box 13, folder Gay Violence, Brian J. Coyle Papers, Minnesota Historical Society.

17. "Emergency Meeting Announcement from Council Member Brian Coyle."

18. Jon Jeter, "A Will to Live, to Speak Out: City Council's Coyle Reveals 5-Year Fight with AIDS Virus," *Star Tribune*, April 24, 1991.

19. Emphasis added. Dennis J. McGrath, "Slayings of Gays Prompt Meeting: Council Member Cites 'Murderous Rampage,'" *Star Tribune*, January 30, 1986.

20. Van A. Hayden, "Gay Killings Prompt 'Summit,'" *Minnesota Daily*, January 31, 1986.

21. J. C. Ritter, "Bar Owners Offer Reward to Solve String of Gay Murders," *Equal Time*, February 5, 1986; Hayden, "Gay Killings Prompt 'Summit'"; Mike Kaszuba, "Gay Leaders Ask Support from Community," *Star Tribune*, January 31, 1986.

22. "Proposal for Task Force on 'Violence Against Gays,' and Gay/Lesbian Community Response," 1986, box 6, folder Homicides—Gay Related, 1985–86, Leo Treadway Papers, Minnesota Historical Society.

23. Jacqui Banaszynski, "Murders, Fear Haunt Gays," *St. Paul Pioneer Press*, September 28, 1986.

24. Kevin Diaz, "City Man Found Strangled to Death Is Fourth Gay to Be Slain in 12 Months," *Star Tribune*, September 18, 1986.

25. "Interoffice Communication from McCarthy Pertaining to Gay-Related Homicides," November 7, 1986, box 13, folder Gay Violence, Brian J. Coyle Papers, Minnesota Historical Society.

26. Diaz, "City Man Found Strangled to Death"; Banaszynski, "Murders, Fear Haunt Gays;" Coates, "AIDS Backlash Gets Violent, Gays Say."

27. Diaz, "City Man Found Strangled to Death."

28. Mogul et al., *Queer (In)Justice*, 23.

29. Butler, *Frames of War*, 22–24. For more on the process of ascribing or denying value to racialized others, see Cacho's *Social Death*.

30. Ferguson, "Race-ing Homonormativity," 62.

31. For a critique of hate crime legislation, see Spade, *Normal Life*, 84–88.

32. Paula Klauda, "Racial Patchwork Slowly Emerging," *Star Tribune*, August 18, 1991.

33. Banaszynski, "Murders, Fear Haunt Gays."

34. Larry Oakes, "Detectives Grapple with Rise in Slayings," *Star Tribune*, November 5, 1986.

35. Haney López, *Dog Whistle Politics*, 3–5.

36. Diamond, *Chicago on the Make*, 243.

37. Cacho, "'The People of California Are Suffering,'" 415.

38. Not all LGBTQ Minnesotans supported the police, and some actively collaborated with Black and Indigenous communities to challenge unchecked police power and advocate for limits on discretionary law enforcement. In 1979, LGBTQ individuals joined Black and Indigenous residents in testifying before the Minnesota Advisory Committee on Civil Rights, calling for the creation of an external civilian review board for the MPD. Although Police Chief Bouza implemented reforms in 1980, the internal review board proved ineffective. In 1989, after a botched "crack raid" resulted in the deaths of an elderly Black couple and the assault and arrest of five Black college students, the Minneapolis City Council convened the Civilian Review Working Group, which included LGBTQ members, to explore alternatives. Their recommendations led to the establishment of a civilian review board the following year. While Coyle supported the effort, he also praised the department's competence, stating, "There's tremendous talent out there," emphasizing he was not antipolice. For Coyle and other LGBTQ Minnesotans, the issue was not policing itself, but how it was conducted. Many believed that hiring openly LGBTQ officers could help reform the system from within. "Police Federation Charged with Collusion," *GLC Voice*, 1979, box 39, folder *GLC Voice*, vol. 1, no. 7, 9, vol. 4, issue 15, November 1979, December 1980, June 1983, Michael McConnell Files, Tretter Collection; Ann Viitala and Mark Wallem, "Civilian Review of the Police," *Equal*

Time, October 25, 1989; Glen Warchol, "Watching the Cops," *Twin Cities Reader*, January 3–9, 1990; David Anger, "Victory: Minneapolis Moves toward Police Accountability," *Equal Time*, January 31, 1990.

39. Dennis J. McGrath and Kevin Diaz, "Lingering Fear Spurs Search for Links in 15 Unsolved Murders," *Minneapolis Star and Tribune*, October 22, 1986; Jacqui Banaszynski, "Gay's Private Life May Have Killed Him," *St. Paul Pioneer Press and Dispatch*, October 22, 1986; Pat Doyle, "Link to Gay Slayings Sought in Latest Case," *Star Tribune*, October 21, 1986; Coates, "AIDS Backlash Gets Violent, Gays Say."

40. Norman Draper and Carol Byrne, "Homicides in City Are Near Record," *Star Tribune*, November 23, 1986; "Minneapolis Police Forming Panel to Study 12 Unsolved Murders," *Star Tribune*, October 21, 1986.

41. Mark Brunswick, "Officials Try to Allay Fears about Slayings," *Star Tribune*, November 5, 1986; Coates, "AIDS Backlash Gets Violent, Gays Say."

42. Bruce Rubenstein, "Farewell to Arms," *City Pages*, November 16, 1988.

43. "The Homelessness among Us: A Growing Population," *Equal Time*, August 5, 1987.

44. Draper and Byrne, "Homicides in City Are Near Record."

45. "Application from City of Minneapolis to U.S. Department of Justice Bureau of Justice Assistance for Police Hiring Supplement Program Grant," 1993, 111.A.4.2F, folder Police Department, 1992–1993, Sharon Sayles Belton Papers, Minnesota Historical Society.

46. Britt Robson, "Mean Streets," *MPLS-ST. PAUL*, May 1990.

47. Paul McEnroe, "Violence, Despair Tarnish Hope for New Generation," *Star Tribune*, February 11, 1990.

48. For more on media and crack cocaine, see Humphries, *Crack Mothers*; Reeves and Campbell, *Cracked Coverage*.

49. Rob Hotakainen, "Fraser's Speech Urges City to Step Up Battle against Drugs, Crime," *Star Tribune*, January 31, 1990.

50. Jim Schroeder, "Hate Crimes Legislation Passes Senate Committee," *Equal Time*, March 30, 1988; Jim Schroeder, "Status of 'Hate Crimes' Legislation Locally, Nationally," *Equal Time*, March 16, 1988.

51. Tim Campbell, "Wave of Murders May Total Nine: Brian Coyle Calls Emergency Meeting," *GLC Voice*, February 3, 1986.

52. Rob Hotakainen, "Council Approves 72 New Police Officers," *Star Tribune*, September 3, 1988.

53. Mark Brunswick, "Officials Try to Allay Fears about Slayings," *Star Tribune*, November 5, 1986.

54. William Preston Robertson, "Strange Fruit," *City Pages*, August 16, 1989; Lars Bjornson, "Minneapolis Gays Cite 'Queer-Baiting,' Ask Park Protection," *The Advocate*, October 23, 1974.

55. Stewart-Winter, "Queer Law and Order," 62.

56. David Scheie, "Gays Push for Self-Defense, Police Protection," *The Surveyor*, December 1986; "Coyle's Anti-Violence Press Conference Speech," October 22, 1986, box 13, folder Gay Violence, Brian J. Coyle Papers, Minnesota Historical Society.

57. Scheie, "Gays Push for Self-Defense, Police Protection."

58. Enger, "AIDS Campaign Not without Controversy."
59. Jim St. George in discussion with the author, March 2023.
60. Banaszynski, "Murders, Fear Haunt Gays."
61. "CUAV Pamphlet: Dating: It's Safer," February 1987, box 13, folder Gay Violence, Brian J. Coyle Papers, Minnesota Historical Society.
62. Jacqui Banaszynski, "Gays Seeking Safety after Slaying Series," *St. Paul Pioneer Press and Dispatch*, October 23, 1986.
63. Kate Parry and Kevin Diaz, "Police Investigation into Killings of Gays Welcomed," *Star Tribune*, October 23, 1986.
64. Banaszynski, "Murders, Fear Haunt Gays."
65. Tim Campbell, "Seven Gay Murders in One Year," *GLC Voice*, November 3, 1986.
66. McGrath and Diaz, "Lingering Fear Spurs Search for Links."
67. "Safe Sex Is More Than Just Wearing A Condom," *Twin Cities Gaze*, October 31, 1986.
68. In the early years of the epidemic, the government's response was hindered by a lack of understanding about the virus, its transmission, and pervasive homophobia, leading to delays in funding and research. See Brier, *Infectious Ideas*, 78–82.
69. Banaszynski, "Gays Seeking Safety after Slaying Series"; Tina Burnside, "Gay Murders Focus of Violence Awareness Month," *Minnesota Daily*, November 7, 1986; "Press Announcement: Press Conference in Loring Park," October 31, 1986, box 13, folder Gay Violence, Brian J. Coyle Papers, Minnesota Historical Society; "Priest Urges Action to End Gay Prejudice," *St. Paul Pioneer Press*, November 7, 1986; "Leaders Hold News Conference to Call Attention to Violence against Gays," *Star Tribune*, November 7, 1986.
70. Mark Kasel, "Community United Against Violence Hosts Bouza at Forum," *Twin Cities Gaze*, November 26, 1986.
71. "Letter from Tim Campbell to Brian Coyle about Police Job Investigator," October 28, 1986, box 13, folder Gay Violence, Brian J. Coyle Papers, Minnesota Historical Society.
72. "Letter from Police Chief Anthony V. Bouza to Tim Campbell," October 30, 1986, box 13, folder Gay Violence, Brian J. Coyle Papers, Minnesota Historical Society.
73. "Respond Letter from Tim Campbell to Police Chief Anthony V. Bouza," November 5, 1986, box 13, folder Gay Violence, Brian J. Coyle Papers, Minnesota Historical Society; Scheie, "Gays Push for Self-Defense, Police Protection."
74. Emphasis added. Burnside, "Gay Murders Focus of Violence Awareness Month."
75. Parry and Diaz, "Police Investigation into Killings of Gays Welcomed."
76. Bill McAuliffe, "Bouza Cites Diligence in Probes of Crimes against Gays," *Star Tribune*, November 18, 1986.
77. "Statement of Sgt. C.W. Miles," Nov. 21, 1986, Minneapolis Police Department, CN: 86-247, 428.
78. Jim Parsons, "Man Arrested in Churchill Killing; Robbery Seen as Motive," *Star Tribune*, November 18, 1986; Jim Schroeder, "Suspect Booked in Churchill Murder," *Equal Time*, November 26, 1986.

79. Darryl Banks is a pseudonym used to protect the privacy of the individual involved. He was not a public figure, and there is no public record confirming a conviction in this case.

80. "Minneapolis Man Held in Death of Gay Prostitute," *Star Tribune*, November 19, 1986.

81. Jim Schroeder, "Hair Samples Clear Accused Man," *Equal Time*, November 11, 1987.

82. Cynthia Scott, "Hate Crimes, Anti-Gay Violence: What You Can Do," *Equal Time*, August 17, 1988.

83. John Ritter, "Statewide Public Hearings on Anti-Gay Violence," *Equal Time*, December 16, 1987.

84. Wendy S. Tai, "Hate Crimes Increasing, Panel Told," *Star Tribune*, January 30, 1988.

85. "Chapter 643-H.F. No. 2340," Minnesota Session Laws—1988, Regular Session, April 26, 1988, https://www.revisor.mn.gov/laws/1988/0/643/, accessed January 31, 2022.

86. "Chapter 261—H.F. No. 700," Minnesota Session Laws—1988, Regular Session, May 25, 1989, https://www.revisor.mn.gov/laws/1989/0/261/, accessed January 31, 2022.

87. Schroeder, "Hate Crimes Legislation Passes Senate Committee."

Chapter 4

1. Evan Thomas, Cathy Booth, and Michael G., "The Untouchables: Anxiety over AIDS Is Verging on Hysteria in Some Parts of the Country," *Time*, September 23, 1985.

2. Howard Rosenberg, "'*Frontline*' AIDS Controversy: Documentary Makers' Relentless Focus on the Lethal Life Style of a Dying Fabian Bridges Puts Minneapolis Station and PBS in the Spotlight," *Los Angeles Times*, March 27, 1986.

3. Martha Bayles, "Television: Documentary: A Case of AIDS," *Wall Street Journal*, March 24, 1986.

4. See Walkowitz, *Prostitution and Victorian Society*.

5. For further insight into how the "sexual policing" of Black women influenced the growth of police discretion and shaped modern urban landscapes—especially during the shift from midcentury practices to the "broken windows" policies of the 1980s—refer to Gray Fischer, *The Streets Belong to Us*, 5–6, 148.

6. Rubin, "Thinking Sex," 153.

7. Hoppe, *Punishing Disease*, 5.

8. Murch, "The Color of War," 141; Gray Fischer, *The Streets Belong to Us*, 184–85.

9. Marx, *Capital*.

10. See Hinton, *From the War on Poverty to the War on Crime*.

11. Wilson Gilmore, *Golden Gulag*, 54–86.

12. "Tyrone Matthews" is a pseudonym. In this chapter, I assign pseudonyms to individuals accused of being noncompliant HIV carriers to protect their confidentiality, particularly when it is unclear whether they are still alive. An exception is

made for Fabian Bridges, who is deceased and already featured prominently in a nationally televised documentary.

13. Dudley Clendinen, "Dilemma for Southern Prosecutors: Streets or Prison for Aids Carrier?," *New York Times*, January 2, 1987.

14. Dudley Clendinen, "World's Oldest Profession Meets Man's Latest Terror," *Chicago Tribune*, January 12, 1987.

15. For more on how the state has withdrawn from the market while increasing regulation of certain actors and behaviors, see Harcourt, "Neoliberal Penality," 4.

16. For more on the media's role in creating moral panics, refer to Hall et al., *Policing the Crisis*, and Cohen, *Folk Devils and Moral Panics*.

17. While much has been written about the causes and effects of the global AIDS pandemic, less attention has been paid to how the moral panic surrounding AIDS became entangled with neoliberal punishment and racial antagonism. Building on the concept of moral panic, I define AIDS moral panic as a mass movement fueled by punditry and sensational journalism, rooted in white American society's exaggerated fears about HIV transmission.

18. See Linda Villarosa, "America's Hidden HIV Epidemic," *New York Times Magazine*, June 6, 2017.

19. Lawrence K. Altman, "New Homosexual Disorder Worries Health Officials," *New York Times*, May 11, 1982.

20. Centers for Disease Control and Prevention, "Epidemiologic Notes and Reports Immunodeficiency among Female Sexual Partners of Males with Acquired Immune Deficiency Syndrome (AIDS)—New York," *MMWR Weekly* 31, no. 52 (1983): 697–98.

21. Kinsella, *Covering the Plague,* 210.

22. Crimp, *Melancholia and Moralism,* 90.

23. Kinsella, *Covering the Plague,* 219; "Youthful AIDS Victim Whose Case Prompted Warning to Hemophiliacs Dies," *Associated Press*, December 13, 1985; "Family in AIDS Case Quits Florida Town after House Burns Down," *New York Times*, August 30, 1987.

24. Center for Media and Public Affairs, "The AIDS Story: Science, Politics, Sex, and Death," *Media Monitor* (1987), cited in Kinsella, *Covering the Plague,* 220.

25. Centers for Disease Control and Prevention, "Epidemiologic Notes and Reports Acquired Immunodeficiency Syndrome (AIDS) among Blacks and Hispanics—United States," *Morbidity and Mortality Weekly Report* 35, no. 42 (1986): 655–58, 663–66, https://www.cdc.gov/mmwr/preview/mmwrhtml/00000810.htm.

26. Faludi, *The Terror Dream,* 148.

27. Jansson, "An Economy of Protection."

28. Chateauvert, *Sex Workers Unite,* 100.

29. In 1986, Hispanic women made up 21 percent of all AIDS cases among women, while 22 percent of AIDS cases among children were reported in Hispanic children. See Centers for Disease Control and Prevention, "Epidemiologic Notes and Reports Acquired Immunodeficiency Syndrome (AIDS) among Blacks and Hispanics—United States."

30. Cohen, *The Boundaries of Blackness,* 226.

31. Cohen, *The Boundaries of Blackness,* 8.

32. Cohen, *The Boundaries of Blackness,* 217.

33. Selik et al., "Racial/Ethnic Differences in the Risk of AIDS in the United States," 1539.

34. For another case study on the media's role in the criminalization of HIV, see Shevory, *Notorious H.I.V.*

35. Dudley Clendinen, "Southern Prosecutors Face Dilemma on AIDS," *St. Petersburg Times,* January 4, 1987.

36. Clendinen, "Southern Prosecutors Face Dilemma on AIDS."

37. "Brenda Williams" is a pseudonym. While some newspaper articles did not explicitly mention race, they nonetheless relied on racialized frameworks to construct sex workers as threats. For example, some reports linked AIDS to "crack cocaine," underscoring how the war on drugs helped drive the criminalization of HIV. Other articles associated the virus with the supposed danger posed by female sex workers in regions like West Africa and Southeast Asia. See John Tierney, "Urban Epidemic: Addicts and AIDS," *New York Times,* December 16, 1990; Philip J. Hilts, "Out of Africa; Dispelling Myths about AIDS: Origins, Sexual Practices, Social Values, Politics," *Washington Post,* May 24, 1988.

38. Tamar Lewin, "Rights of Citizens and Society Raise Legal Muddle on AIDS," *New York Times,* October 14, 1987; Dave Walter, "Transvestite Quarantined in Jackson," *The Advocate,* March 31, 1987.

39. Bill McAuliffe, "Woman Considered to Be AIDS Risk Is Released after Prostitution Arrest," *Minneapolis Star and Tribune,* April 2, 1986.

40. Margaret Zack, "Prostitute Who Allegedly Has AIDS Virus Ordered Not to Put Others at Risk," *Star Tribune,* August 9, 1986.

41. McAuliffe, "Woman Considered to Be AIDS Risk."

42. "Minneapolis/Judge to Hear Prostitution Case of Prostitute Who May Carry AIDS Virus," *Star Tribune,* September 25, 1987.

43. Emphasis added. Mark Brunswick, "Prostitute Carrying AIDS Virus Arrested and Released Twice," *Star Tribune,* June 7, 1989.

44. Watkins-Hayes, *Remaking a Life,* 110.

45. Randy Furst, "Prostitute with AIDS Virus Arrested; City Wants Her off Streets," *Star Tribune,* May 24, 1991.

46. The US blood supply was not screened for HIV until 1985. Centers for Disease Control and Prevention, "U.S. Public Health Service Guidelines for Testing and Counseling Blood and Plasma Donors for Human Immunodeficiency Virus Type 1 Antigen," *Morbidity and Mortality Weekly Report* 45 (1996): 1–9, https://www.cdc.gov/mmwr/preview/mmwrhtml/00040546.htm.

47. By 1991, only 12 percent of Minnesota's 921 AIDS cases were reported outside the Twin Cities metropolitan area. Kurt Chandler, "A Family Lives with AIDS," *Star Tribune,* June 30, 1991.

48. Chandler, "A Family Lives with AIDS."

49. Furst, "Prostitute with AIDS Virus Arrested."

50. Watkins-Hayes, *Remaking a Life,* 110. Also see Hancock, *The Politics of Disgust,* 23–30, 57–61.

51. Watkins-Hayes, *Remaking a Life,* 46.

52. Sonja Mackenzie defines "structural vulnerabilities" as the "power, politics, and economic forces [that] produce health and illness" and contribute to disparities in mortality rates, such as those seen with HIV/AIDS in the United States. Mackenzie, *Structural Intimacies*, 8.

53. Lewis Cope, "Twin Cities AIDS Cases Are Higher among Blacks," *Minneapolis Star and Tribune*, August 7, 1987.

54. Lewis Cope, "302 Cases in State at the End of '87," *Star Tribune*, January 17, 1988.

55. "Scott Reynolds" is a pseudonym.

56. "Keene Launches Gay Real Estate Firm," *GLC Voice*, undated, box 1, folder *GLC Voice* 1980–1987, MCLU Records, Tretter Collection; J.C. Ritter, "Escort Service Closed; Safe Sex Debated," *Equal Time*, April 2, 1986.

57. Kevin Diaz and Bruce Benidt, "Police and Others Question Role of Prostitution in AIDS," *Star Tribune*, March 28, 1986.

58. J. C. Ritter, "Stan Borman on: Prostitution, AIDS and the Health Department," *Equal Time*, May 28, 1986; Tim Campbell, "AFRAIDS in Minnesota," *New York Native*, May 26, 1986; "AIDS Takes Scary Suburban Twist," *Minnesota Law Journal* 1, no. 3, (1986), 7; J.C. Ritter, "Escort Service Closed; Safe Sex Debated," *Equal Time*, April 2, 1986; Diaz and Benidt, "Police and Others Question Role of Prostitution in AIDS"; Lewis Cope, "Male Prostitute with AIDS Virus Had 1,000 Sex Partners in Cities, He Says," *Star Tribune*, March 27, 1986.

59. Diaz and Bruce Benidt, "Police and Others Question Role of Prostitution in AIDS."

60. Earl F. Mellor, "Workers at the Minimum Wage or Less: Who They Are and the Jobs They Hold," US Bureau of Labor Statistics, *Monthly Labor Review*, July 1987, 34–38, https://www.bls.gov/opub/mlr/1987/07/rpt1full.pdf.

61. Dan Oberdorfer, "Suspect in AIDS Furor Turns Himself In," *Star Tribune*, March 29, 1986.

62. Tim Campbell, "Gays Don't All Come Out Alive: A Look at Police Activities," *GLC Voice*, August 1980.

63. Emphasis added. Wolfgang Wolf, "ACT UP Meets with Ashton, Health Department," *GLC Voice*, September 18, 1989; Paul Levy, "Who on Earth Is That Nun?," *Star Tribune*, June 24, 1990.

64. Campbell, "AFRAIDS in Minnesota," *Campbell v. Minneapolis* preliminary draft of memorandum of law, July 22, 1980, box 1, folder Draft—*Campbell v. Minneapolis*, 1980, MCLU records, Tretter Collection.

65. Refer to Craddock, *City of Plagues*, 90; Briggs, *Reproducing Empire*, 23; Shah, *Contagious Divides*, 82. For further discussion on the intersection of race and public health, see Molina, *Fit to Be Citizens?*

66. Gostin, "The Isolation of HIV—Positive Patients Reply."

67. "Moral Majority Report," *HIV and AIDS 30 Years Ago*, accessed February 11, 2022, https://hivaids.omeka.net/items/show/9.

68. Eleanor Singer, Theresa F. Rogers, and Mary Corcoran, "The Polls—A Report: AIDS," *Public Opinion Quarterly* 51, no. 4 (Winter 1987): 580.

69. "The Times Poll: 42% Would Limit Civil Rights in AIDS Battle," *Los Angeles Times*, July 31, 1987.

70. "Require AIDS Victim Wear ID Tags," General Social Survey, National Opinion Research Center at the University of Chicago, 1988. GSS Data Explorer, https://gssdataexplorer.norc.org/variables/5047/vshow.

71. Jim Schroeder, "High Number of Residents Support Mandatory HIV Testing, Quarantine," *Equal Time*, May 27, 1987.

72. In the early 1990s, the US government denied entry to hundreds of Haitian refugees who tested positive for HIV, imprisoning them indefinitely at Guantánamo Bay. See Paik, "Carceral Quarantine at Guantánamo."

73. Lewin, "Rights of Citizens and Society."

74. Minnesota Statutes 1987 Supplement, "Chapter 144: Department of Health," https://www.revisor.mn.gov/statutes/1987/cite/144/pdf#search=%22health%22, accessed February 8, 2022.

75. Robert Halfhill, "Minn. Opts for Quarantine," *Gay Community News*, June 14–20, 1987.

76. Halfhill, "Minn. Opts for Quarantine."

77. John Ritter, "'Non-Compliant' Proposal: MCLU Objects," *Equal Time*, April 15, 1987; "Letters: Criticism of Spear, Clark," *Equal Time*, June 10, 1987.

78. Ritter, "'Non-Compliant' Proposal: MCLU Objects."

79. Jim Schroeder, "Non-Compliant Law Used," *Equal Time*, February 3, 1988.

80. Lewin, "Rights of Citizens and Society.

81. "Nevada Will Notify Media of Prostitutes Carrying AIDS," *Toronto Star*, December 10, 1988; "Prostitutes to Get AIDS Testing," *United Press International*, March 19, 1986.

82. Bruce Lambert, "AIDS among Prostitutes Not as Prevalent as Believed, Studies Show," *New York Times*, September 20, 1988.

83. Laura Myers, "Oakland Prostitute Released after Prosecution Refuses to Pursue Case," *Associated Press*, July 18, 1990.

84. Presidential Commission on the Human Immunodeficiency Virus Epidemic, "The Presidential Commission on the Human Immunodeficiency Virus Epidemic Report," June 24, 1988, https://eric.ed.gov/?id=ED299531; Ryan White Comprehensive AIDS Resources Emergency Act of 1990, P.L. 101-381, https://history.nih.gov/research/downloads/PL101-381.pdf.

85. "Prostitute Women Oppose Mandatory Testing," *Gay Community News*, August 21–September 3, 1988.

86. Lewin, "Rights of Citizens and Society."

87. Margaret Engel, "Prostitutes Transmitting AIDS to U.S. Soldiers; High Incidence Found in West Germany," *The Washington Post*, September 27, 1985; also see Redfield et al., "Heterosexually Acquired HTLV-III/LAV Disease," 2095–96.

88. Erik Eckholm, "Prostitutes' Impact on Spread of AIDS Is Developed," *New York Times*, November 5, 1985.

89. See Clumeck et al., "Seroepidemiological Studies of HTLV-III Antibody Prevalence among Selected Groups of Heterosexual Africans," 2601.

90. Randy Furst and Lewis Cope, "Officials Fear Prostitution May Spread AIDS Virus," *Star Tribune*, September 29, 1985.

91. Randy Shilts, "AIDS: The Prostitute Connection and the Need for Early Education," *New York Native*, April 8–21, 1985.

92. Centers for Disease Control and Prevention, "Antibody to Human Immunodeficiency Virus in Female Prostitutes," *Morbidity and Mortality Weekly Report* 36 (1987): 157–61, https://www.cdc.gov/mmwr/preview/mmwrhtml/00000891.htm.

93. Lambert, "AIDS among Prostitutes."

94. Centers for Disease Control and Prevention, "Epidemiologic Notes and Reports Antibody to Human Immunodeficiency Virus in Female Prostitutes," *Morbidity and Mortality Weekly Report* 36, no. 11 (1987): 157–61, https://www.cdc.gov/mmwr/preview/mmwrhtml/00000891.htm.

95. Elifson et al., "Seroprevalence of Immunodeficiency Virus among Male Prostitutes," 832.

96. Simon et al., "HIV and Young Male Street Prostitutes: A Brief Report," 196.

97. Follow-up studies found that a male sex worker's sexual activities were more strongly correlated with HIV status than intravenous drug use. See Elifson et al., "Risk Factors Associated with HIV Infection among Male Prostitutes," 82.

98. Furst and Cope, "Officials Fear Prostitution May Spread AIDS Virus."

99. *Frontline*, season 1986, episode 8, "AIDS: A National Inquiry," aired March 25, 1986.

100. *Frontline*, "AIDS: A National Inquiry."

101. *Frontline*, "AIDS: A National Inquiry."

102. *Frontline*, "AIDS: A National Inquiry."

103. Bridges had reportedly used his social security funds to try to settle an old debt and "squandered the rest." *Frontline*, "AIDS: A National Inquiry."

104. James Davies, "Protestors Question WCCO's Methods, Intent in AIDS Story," *Equal Time*, November 13, 1985.

105. "Fabian Bridges Leaves Hospital, Finds Refuge with Friends," *Montrose Voice*, October 11, 1985.

106. Davies, "Protestors Question WCCO's Methods."

107. One exception was panelist Diego Lopez, director of clinical services at the Gay Men's Health Crisis in New York City. Lopez, who was HIV-positive, stated that Bridges had been victimized by "all the institutions that failed him" and called the medical field's treatment of Bridges "extremely racist." *Frontline*, "AIDS: A National Inquiry."

108. Howard Rosenberg, "'Frontline' AIDS Controversy: Documentary Makers' Relentless Focus on the Lethal Life Style of a Dying Fabian Bridges Puts Minneapolis Station and PBS in the Spotlight," *Los Angeles Times*, March 27, 1986.

109. Emphasis added. "Mixed Reviews for WCCO Documentary," *Equal Time*, April 2, 1986.

110. "Mixed Reviews for WCCO Documentary."

111. William F. Buckley, "Op-Ed: Crucial Steps in Combating the AIDS Epidemic; Identify All the Carriers," *New York Times*, March 18, 1986.

112. Campbell, "AFRAIDS in Minnesota"; Mark Kasel, "MAAA Tackles WCCO-TV 'Documentary'; Safe Sex Literature," *Twin Cities Gaze*, April 1986.

113. Cohen, *The Boundaries of Blackness*, 8. Building on the work of Melvin Dixon, Darius Bost theorizes "double cremation" as the process by which antiblackness and antiqueerness together mark the Black gay body for both social and corporeal death. See Bost, *Evidence of Being*, 3.

114. Centers for Disease Control and Prevention, "HIV and STD Criminalization Laws," last updated October 22, 2022, https://www.cdc.gov/hiv/policies/law/states/exposure.html.

115. Sero Project, "Justice Institute Toolkit," accessed March 30, 2022, https://www.dropbox.com/s/4xh4f7almkfewbv/SPJI%20Toolkit.pdf?dl=0.

116. Wolf and Vezina, "Crime and Punishment," 825.

117. Mykhalovskiy, "The Public Health Implications of HIV Criminalization," 375; Ahmed et al., "Protecting HIV-Positive Women's Human Rights," 128; Burris and Cameron, "The Case against Criminalization of HIV Transmission"; Galletly and Pinkerton, "Conflicting Messages," 453.

118. "Carmen Gonzalez" is a pseudonym.

119. "ACT UP/Minnesota Newsletter, January 1990," box 1, folder ACT UP HIV/AIDS Protest Flyers, 1990, Dallas Drake Papers, 1950–2003, Tretter Collection; Robert Halfhill, "Letters: HIV Hysteria," *Star Tribune*, January 6, 1990.

120. In 1987, Darryl Thompson (pseudonym), an HIV-positive inmate at the Federal Medical Center in Rochester, Minnesota, was sentenced to an additional five years in prison for biting two guards, neither of whom contracted the virus. The following year, a federal appeals court upheld the conviction, declaring that Thompson's mouth and teeth constituted a "deadly and dangerous" weapon. Similarly, in 1990, Tonya Brooks (pseudonym), an HIV-positive woman, was charged with second-degree assault for biting and scratching a St. Paul police officer during a domestic disturbance. Rob Hotakainen, "State Inmate Charged in Bite Linked to AIDS," *Minneapolis Star and Tribune*, April 11, 1987; Robert Halfhill, "Prisoner with HIV Convicted for Biting," *Gay Community News*, July 19–25, 1987; Conrad deFiebre, "Woman with AIDS Virus Charged with Assault," *Star Tribune,* August 9, 1990; *US v. Moore*, 846 F.2d 1163 (8th Cir. 1988).

Chapter 5

1. Walter Parker, "Group Wants Bathhouse Shut Down," *St. Paul Pioneer Press Dispatch*, June 13, 1987.

2. Bill McAuliffe, "Pickets Take Their AIDS Message to Bathhouse," *Minneapolis Star and Tribune*, June 13, 1987; John Ritter, "Dick Brown Continues Solo Campaign to Close Bathhouse," *Equal Time*, May 27, 1987.

3. Delegard, "Contested Geography," 166–69; Butler, "Sex and the Cities," 205–14; Hickey, "The Geography of Pornography," 129–33; Brest and Vandenberg, "Politics, Feminism and the Constitution," 613–29.

4. Serlin, "Bathhouses," 125.

5. For a discussion of "domestic citizenship," see Vider, *The Queerness of Home*, 12.

6. "A Moral Obligation: DLM Memorial Fund Memo," box 11, folder Bathhouse Ordinance, Brian J. Coyle Papers, Minnesota Historical Society.

7. Dick Brown, "Reader Questions Keeping Bathhouse Open," *Equal Time*, February 4, 1987; John Ritter, "The Bathhouse and AIDS Question," *Equal Time*, December 17, 1986; "Brown's Response to Engstrom," December 28, 1987, box 11, folder Bathhouse Ordinance, Brian J. Coyle Papers, Minnesota Historical Society.

8. "Letters from Readers," *Minneapolis Star and Tribune*, December 6, 1986.

9. Brown, "Reader Questions Keeping Bathhouse Open"; "Letters: Dick Brown Responds," *Equal Time*, June 10, 1987.

10. "Urgent! News Release," box 11, folder Bathhouse Ordinance, Brian J. Coyle Papers, Minnesota Historical Society.

11. Martin Kostrzab, "Letters: Gay Health Club," *Star Tribune*, November 26, 1986.

12. Mark Brunswick, "Manager Says Bathhouse Is Misunderstood," *Minneapolis Star and Tribune*, June 17, 1987; Ritter, "The Bathhouse and AIDS Question."

13. Ritter, "The Bathhouse and AIDS Question."

14. McAuliffe, "Pickets Take Their AIDS Message to Bathhouse."

15. McAuliffe, "Pickets Take Their AIDS Message to Bathhouse."

16. Jim St. George in discussion with the author, March 2023.

17. "Community Warning: Coyle Comes Out for Closing the Bathhouses," box 11, folder Bathhouse Ordinance, Brian J. Coyle Papers, Minnesota Historical Society; John Ritter, "New Ordinance May Close Bathhouse," *Equal Time*, January 20, 1988; John Ritter, "315 Health Club Closes Prior to Ordinance," *Equal Time*, April 13, 1988.

18. Parker, "Group Wants Bathhouse Shut Down."

19. In the West, long-standing taboos about where sex takes place are tied to what Norbert Elias refers to as the "civilizing process." This process, which developed alongside Western imperial expansion, reinforced distinctions between "civilized" and "primitive" societies by enforcing a strict separation between public and private spaces. Scott Lauria Morgensen expands on this idea, arguing that gay social movements in the United States engage in "settler homonationalism." By aligning themselves with the nation-state and its settler logics, these movements construct a modern sexual identity while distancing themselves from historical narratives that associate queerness with primitivism—narratives that have also been used to sexualize and marginalize Indigenous peoples. See Elias, *The Civilizing Process*, 43, 160; Morgensen, "Settler Homonationalism," 107.

20. Vider, *The Queerness of Home*, 30.

21. Jacqui Banaszynski, "Epidemic Is Topic No. 1 for Gays," *Star Tribune*, July 3, 1983.

22. Lewis Cope, "AIDS Facts Allay Some Fears about Illness," *Star Tribune*, July 3, 1983.

23. By December 1984, twenty-five cases of AIDS had been diagnosed in Minnesota, with fourteen resulting in death. J. C. Ritter, "Profile: Bill Runyon, Helping Others Fight AIDS," *Equal Times*, December 12, 1984.

24. Ritter, "Profile: Bill Runyon, Helping Others Fight AIDS."

25. Cope, "AIDS Facts Allay Some Fears about Illness."

26. Kay Miller, "Gays Fight First for Acceptance, Then for Life," *Minneapolis Star and Tribune,* February 22, 1987.

27. J. C. Ritter, "Not a Typical MN AIDS Case," *Equal Time,* July 10, 1985.

28. Ritter, "Not a Typical MN AIDS Case."

29. "Farm Activist, Democratic Leader Dick Hanson Dies of AIDS at 37," *Twin Cities Gaze,* July 30, 1987; Jacqui Banaszynski, "AIDS in the Heartland: Chapter One," *St. Paul Pioneer Press Dispatch,* June 21, 1987.

30. "Pioneer Press Dispatch Wins Journalism Award; Miami Herald Gets Three," *Star Tribune,* March 29, 1988.

31. Nick Woltman, "Pulitzer Prize-Winning Series Humanized AIDS Crisis, Divided Pioneer Press Readers," *Twin Cities Pioneer Press,* July 25, 2016.

32. Dirk Johnson, "Coming Home, with AIDS, to a Small Town," *New York Times,* November 2, 1987.

33. Murray, *Not in This Family,* 138.

34. Emphasis added. Mark Nadler, "The Human Story behind AIDS Statistics," *St. Paul Pioneer Press Dispatch,* June 21, 1987.

35. Jacqui Banaszynski, "Dick Hanson, AIDS Victims' Ambassador, Dies," *St. Paul Pioneer Press Dispatch,* July 26, 1987.

36. Brad Theissen, "Dick Hanson Memorial Sunday, Aug. 16," *Twin Cities Gaze,* August 13, 1987.

37. Jerry Fladmark in discussion with the author, March 2023.

38. "AIDS Update," *Equal Time,* May 13, 1987.

39. "Dick Hanson Obituary," March–August 1987, box 14, folder AIDS, Brian J. Coyle Papers, Minnesota Historical Society. Newspaper clippings documenting Hanson's life and death, including excerpts from "AIDS in the Heartland," appeared in the folder on bathhouses that Coyle kept alongside meeting minutes, speeches, and policy papers. Their inclusion suggests that Coyle saw Hanson's story not only as emblematic of the epidemic's human toll, but also as a tool to justify his support for the antibathhouse ordinance to future researchers.

40. Emphasis added. Banaszynski, "AIDS in the Heartland: Chapter One."

41. Jacqui Banaszynski, "AIDS in the Heartland: The Final Chapter," *St. Paul Pioneer Press Dispatch,* August 9, 1987.

42. Theissen, "Dick Hanson Memorial Sunday, Aug. 16."

43. Banaszynski, "Dick Hanson, AIDS Victims' Ambassador, Dies."

44. Jacqui Banaszynski, "AIDS in the Heartland: The Epilogue," *St. Paul Pioneer Press Dispatch,* April 3, 1988.

45. John Ritter, "Bert Henningson—Farmer, Activist—Dies at Age 41," *Equal Time,* May 25, 1988.

46. Woltman, "Pulitzer Prize-Winning Series Humanized AIDS Crisis."

47. Mark Kasel, "Are Controversies at 315 and River Flats Headed for Negative Outcomes?" *Twin Cities Gaze,* October 8, 1987.

48. "A Moral Obligation: Memo by the DLM Memorial Fund," 1987, box 11, folder Bathhouse Ordinance, Brian J. Coyle Papers, Minnesota Historical Society.

49. "Letter from Sandra Hilary to Dick Brown," August 18, 1987, box 18, folder Bathhouse "high risk" sex ordinance, Minneapolis, 1988, Tretter Collection Information Files, Tretter Collection.

50. "Letter from Lurie to Hilary," August 18, 1987, box 18, folder Bathhouse "high risk" sex ordinance, Minneapolis, 1988, Tretter Collection Information Files, Tretter Collection.

51. Rob Hotakainen, "Ordinance Would Battle 'High-Risk' Sex," *Star Tribune*, January 20, 1988.

52. "Clean Up Project Letter to Fraser," January 4, 1988, box 11, folder Bathhouse Ordinance, Brian J. Coyle Papers, Minnesota Historical Society; "David Lurie Letter to Sandra Hilary," January 5, 1988, box 11, folder Bathhouse Ordinance, Brian J. Coyle Papers, Minnesota Historical Society. See *Berg v. Health Hosp., Marion*, 667 F. Supp. 639 (S.D. Ind. 1987).

53. Ritter, "315 Health Club Closes Prior to Ordinance"; John Ritter, "Should the Bathhouse Be Regulated," *Equal Time*, February 17, 1988.

54. Hotakainen, "Ordinance Would Battle 'High-Risk' Sex"; Ritter, "315 Health Club Closes Prior to Ordinance."

55. Before the AIDS epidemic, Shilts often visited bathhouses and struggled with heavy drinking. During college, he even worked at a bathhouse in Eugene, Oregon. After the death of his friend Gary Walsh, an AIDS activist, in February 1984 due to AIDS-related complications, Shilts stopped drinking and sought help for substance abuse. In 1986, he joined the board of directors for Pride Institute, an LGBTQ-affirming substance abuse treatment facility located in Edina, a wealthy suburb of Minneapolis. Kinsella, *Covering the Plague*, 157–84; David Anger, "Shilts to Speak on Recovery, AIDS," *Equal Time*, September 27, 1989.

56. Shilts, *And the Band Played On*, 306.

57. Shilts, *And the Band Played On*, 147, 157.

58. It is inaccurate to attribute the introduction of HIV into the United States to a single individual, as the virus likely entered the country through multiple pathways. One of the earliest known cases is that of Robert Rayford, a sixteen-year-old African American youth from St. Louis, Missouri, who died in 1969. Decades later, in the 1980s, preserved tissue samples from his body tested positive for HIV, suggesting that the virus was present in the US well before it was formally identified. See Donald G. McNeil Jr., "HIV Arrived in the U.S. Long before 'Patient Zero,'" *New York Times*, October 26, 2016. Also refer to McKay, *Patient Zero and the Making of the AIDS Epidemic*, 133, 190–97; Tiemeyer, *Plane Queer*, 171–80; Kerr, "AIDS 1969: HIV, History, and Race."

59. Walter Parker, "Minneapolis Panel Oks Plan to Limit High-Risk Sex in Saunas," *St. Paul Pioneer Press Dispatch*, March 22, 1988.

60. See Christine Hudgins, "Policy on Gays Has Fraser, Police Battling on Beaches," *The Minneapolis Star*, October 14, 1981; Rob Hotakainen, "State Officials Endorse Minneapolis Plan to Fight AIDS," *Star Tribune*, January 2, 1988.

61. Lewis Cope, "Author of Book on AIDS Tells of Stigma Slowing Early Research," *Star Tribune,* November 19, 1987.

62. Jacqui Banaszynski, "Reporter Calls Account of AIDS a 'Mission,'" *St. Paul Pioneer Press Dispatch*, November 10, 1987.

63. "Letter from Coyle to Constituents," November 20, 1985, folder Minnesota Alliance Against AIDS, Leo Treadway Papers, Minnesota Historical Society.
64. Leo Skir, "The Party's Over," *City Pages*, February 10, 1988.
65. Banaszynski, "Reporter Calls Account of AIDS a 'Mission.'"
66. "Public Health Advisory Committee March Meeting Minutes," February 6, 1988, box 11, folder Bathhouse Ordinance, Brian J. Coyle Papers, Minnesota Historical Society.
67. "Gay and Lesbian Community Action Council's Invitation to AIDS Forum," February 2, 1988, box 11, folder Bathhouse Ordinance, Brian J. Coyle Papers, Minnesota Historical Society.
68. Ritter, "Should the Bathhouse Be Regulated."
69. Judy Martin, "Coyle Says 'Bathhouse Must Go!,'" *GLC Voice*, February 15, 1988.
70. "'Bathhouses, Sexual Freedom, and the Law' Speech by Coyle," February 9, 1988, box 11, folder Bathhouse Ordinance, Brian J. Coyle Papers, Minnesota Historical Society.
71. "'Bathhouses, Sexual Freedom, and the Law' Speech by Coyle."
72. Ritter, "Should the Bathhouse Be Regulated"; Martin, "Coyle Says 'Bathhouse Must Go!'"; Louis Porter II, "Bathhouses Proposal Puts Coyle on Spot," *St. Paul Pioneer Press Dispatch,* 1988.
73. Ritter, "New Ordinance May Close Bathhouse."
74. "Letters to Coyle Opposing Bathhouse Ordinance," January 21, 1988, box 11, folder Bathhouse Ordinance, Brian J. Coyle Papers, Minnesota Historical Society.
75. J.C. Ritter, "Goal at 315 Health Club Is Building New Social Image," *Equal Time*, October 30, 1985.
76. Emphasis added. Hotakainen, "State Officials Endorse Minneapolis Plan to Fight AIDS."
77. Tim Campbell, "Politicos Eye 'Progressive Measures' against Commercial Sites where AIDS Could Be Spread," *GLC Voice*, September 8, 1987.
78. Ritter, "New Ordinance May Close Bathhouse."
79. For a literature review on 1980s research regarding the connection between AIDS and bathhouses, see Woods's and Binson's *Gay Bathhouses and Public Health Policy*. The general consensus among public health experts is that bathhouses were unlikely to have been a major factor in the spread of HIV.
80. Tim Campbell, "Coyle Should Retract False Witness," *GLC Voice*, February 15, 1988; Porter II, "Bathhouses Proposal Puts Coyle on Spot"; Tim Campbell, "Minneapolis Discusses New Laws Supposedly for AIDS," *GLC Voice,* February 1, 1988.
81. "Minnesota Alliance Against AIDS: Policy Statement on Closing of Bathhouses and Related Recreational Enterprises during the AIDS Health Crisis," 1986, folder Minnesota Alliance Against AIDS, Leo Treadway Papers, Minnesota Historical Society.
82. "Community Warning: Coyle Comes Out for Closing the Bathhouses," box 11, folder Bathhouse Ordinance, Brian J. Coyle Papers, Minnesota Historical Society.
83. Rob Hotakainen, "Coyle in Dilemma on Vote to Curb High-Risk Sex," *Star Tribune*, March 30, 1988; "MPLS. Health Commissioner Begins Anti-Tubs Campaign," *Twin Cities Gaze*, September 10, 1987.

84. Jim St. George in discussion with the author, March 2023.
85. Fladmark in discussion with the author, March 2023.
86. "'Bathhouses, Sexual Freedom, and the Law' Speech by Coyle."
87. "Dr. Strickland's Letter to Coyle," January 20, 1988, box 11, folder Bathhouse Ordinance, Brian J. Coyle Papers, Minnesota Historical Society.
88. "Olson Letter to Coyle," March 30, 1988, box 11, folder Bathhouse Ordinance, Brian J. Coyle Papers, Minnesota Historical Society.
89. "Gregg Riley Letter to Brian J. Coyle," February 24, 1988, box 11, folder Bathhouse Ordinance, Brian J. Coyle Papers, Minnesota Historical Society.
90. "Olson Letter to Coyle."
91. Craig Anderson and Douglas Federhart, "Opinion: Speaking on the Bathhouse Issue," *Equal Time*, December 16, 1987.
92. "Richard Notch Letter to Coyle," March 7, 1988, box 11, folder Bathhouse Ordinance, Brian J. Coyle Papers, Minnesota Historical Society.
93. Tom Webb, "DeMars: Bathhouse Plan Meant to Block Chain," *Star Tribune*, December 8, 1979; Tom Webb, "Some Gays Criticize DeMars's Bathhouse Plan," *Star Tribune*, December 7, 1979; Tim Campbell, "New Bathhouse Stirs Friction: Pesis Quells Mutiny," *GLC Voice*, January 1980.
94. Robert Halfhill and Claude Peck, "Opinion: Gay Meeting with Mayor and Chief Futile; A Message from Target City Coalition," *Minnesota Daily*, April 20, 1982, Box 8, Folder Minnesota Committee for Gay Rights (MCGR), Tretter Collection Information Files, 1938–2008, Tretter Collection.
95. Tim Campbell, "Bouza Warns of Hard Times Ahead for Gays," *GLC Voice*, September 21, 1981.
96. For an analysis of bathhouse closures in San Francisco and New York City, refer to Bérubé's "The History of Gay Bathhouses" and Woods's and Binson's *Gay Bathhouses and Public Health Policy*. For a broader history of gay bathhouses, see Serlin, "Bathhouses"; Chauncey, *Gay New York*, 207–25; Bayer, *Private Acts, Social Consequences*, 20–71.
97. Kate Parry, "Only Gay Bathhouse in Minneapolis Shuts Down," *Star Tribune*, March 30, 1988.
98. Brad Theissen, "How to Save the Gay Bathhouse," *Twin Cities Gaze*, March 24, 1988.
99. J. C. Ritter, "Goal at 315 Health Club Is Building New Social Image," *Equal Time*, October 30, 1985.
100. The steam room, however, was short-lived; management later shut it down citing HIV-prevention efforts.
101. Through these changes, the bathhouse management used architectural design to create an atmosphere of "moral cleanliness" in a space traditionally seen as unclean. In his analysis of mid-twentieth century London's queer public spaces, Matt Houlbrook notes a similar pattern, where homosexuality was associated with the unsanitary conditions of public urinals. This association helped reinforce the perception of homosexuality as a public health threat. Houlbrook, *Queer London*, 61–63; J. C. Ritter, "DeSilva Fired from 315 Health Club," *Equal Time*, December 18, 1985.
102. "Play It Safe!" ad, *Twin Cities Gaze*, January 1986, 39.

103. Ritter, "New Ordinance May Close Bathhouse."
104. Ritter, "New Ordinance May Close Bathhouse."
105. Ritter, "The Bathhouse and AIDS Question."
106. "315 Health Club" ad, *Twin Cities Gaze*, March 1986, 39.
107. Mark Kasel, "Minneapolis City Council Approves HIV Ordinance," *Twin Cities Gaze*, April 3, 1988.
108. Billund-Phibbs, "Steam Rooms."
109. "Restaurant May Go into Building That Housed Last Gay Bathhouse," *Star Tribune*, March 31, 1988; Parry, "Only Gay Bathhouse in Minneapolis Shuts Down."
110. Emphasis added. "Restaurant May Go into Building That Housed Last Gay Bathhouse."
111. Jim Schroeder, "Vice Squad Steps Up Activity," *Equal Time*, May 13, 1987.
112. Florida, *The Rise of the Creative Class*, 68–72, 77–80.
113. Alice Rainville, "Commentary: A Plan for Reclaiming Minneapolis' Prime Crime Corner," *Star Tribune*, September 8, 1987.
114. Smith, *The New Urban Frontier*, 44–47.
115. Rainville, "Commentary: A Plan for Reclaiming Minneapolis' Prime Crime Corner."
116. Hotakainen, "Coyle in Dilemma on Vote to Curb High-Risk Sex."
117. Hotakainen, "Coyle in Dilemma on Vote to Curb High-Risk Sex."
118. "Minnesota Alliance Against AIDS Press Release," 1988, box 32, folder Minnesota Alliance Against AIDS, Leo Treadway Papers, Minnesota Historical Society.
119. Hotakainen, "Coyle in Dilemma on Vote to Curb High-Risk Sex."
120. St. George in discussion with the author, March 2023.
121. "R. Carlson Letter to Coyle," April 3, 1988, box 11, folder Bathhouse Ordinance, Brian J. Coyle Papers, Minnesota Historical Society; "Letters: April Fool's Day and the Bathhouse," *Equal Time*, April 13, 1988.
122. "Stephen J. Lacanne Letter to Coyle," March 30, 1988, box 11, folder Bathhouse Ordinance, Brian J. Coyle Papers, Minnesota Historical Society.
123. *Doe v. City of Minneapolis*, 693 F. Supp. 774 (D. Minn. 1988).
124. Paul Gustafson, "Circuit Court Upholds Ban on Doors in Sex-Oriented Bookstore Booths," *Star Tribune*, March 3, 1990; *Doe v. City of Minneapolis*, 898 F.2d 612 (8th Cir. 1990).
125. Mark Kasel, "HIV Transmission Ordinance Debated at Community Forum," *Twin Cities Gaze*, February 25, 1988.
126. Ritter, "Should the Bathhouse Be Regulated"; Martin, "Coyle Says 'Bathhouse Must Go!'"
127. Hotakainen, "Coyle in Dilemma on Vote to Curb High-Risk Sex."
128. "Hillary Letter to City Council," April 1, 1988, box 11, folder Bathhouse Ordinance, Brian J. Coyle Papers, Minnesota Historical Society.
129. In a 1993 oral history, activist and historian Jean Nickolaus Tretter disclosed that he recorded conversations in which Coyle admitted to making a deal with the Minneapolis Police Department. According to Tretter, Coyle agreed to support the closure of bathhouses on health grounds in exchange for the police vice squad halting raids on bookstores. Scott Paulsen, "Interview with Jean-Nicholas Tretter," Twin

Cities Gay and Lesbian Community Oral History Project, November 20, 1993, https://media.mnhs.org/things/cms/10266/481/AV1994_173_7_M.pdf; Kasel, "Minneapolis City Council Approves HIV Ordinance."

130. "*Equal Time* Interview Request of Sayles Belton," July 9, 1993, folder Gay and Lesbian Issues, 1991–1993, Sharon Sayles Belton Papers, Minnesota Historical Society; *State v. Holmberg*, 527 N.W.2d 100 (1995).

131. John Townsend, "John 'Roy John Mehring II' Mehring: 1953–2018," *Lavender*, August 16, 2018.

132. Susan Du, "Does Minneapolis Have the Will to Bring Gay Bathhouses Back to the City?" *City Pages*, October 24, 2017.

133. Susan Du, "An Underground Sex Club Is Raided, and Minneapolis Is Forced to Face the Times," *City Pages*, May 3, 2017.

134. Delany, *Times Square Red, Times Square Blue*, 111.

135. Muñoz, *Cruising Utopia*, 34. According to Berlant and Warner, queer counterpublics function as sociocultural spaces where queer individuals gather to share experiences, express their identities, and cultivate a sense of belonging, all while challenging exclusionary bourgeois norms. See Berlant and Warner, "Sex in Public," 558; Warner, *Public and Counterpublics*, 57.

Chapter 6

1. Robert Whereatt, "Glen Anderson Offers Apologies for Sex Offenses," *Star Tribune*, September 9, 1989; Robert Whereatt and Kevin Diaz, "Glen Anderson Guilty of Sex Offenses, Withdraws Bid to Be Lottery Director," *Star Tribune*, September 8, 1989.

2. Kevin Diaz and Chuck Hags, "A Place to Cruise: Neighborhood Fights Gay Prostitution in Loring Park," *Star Tribune*, September 24, 1989.

3. Tim Campbell, "Park Cops Pushing for Sex, Arresting after Beating," *GLC Voice*, August 20, 1984.

4. Glen Warchol, "Loring Decoy Nights Are a Bust in More Ways Than One," 1989, box 1, folder Cruising Ordinance, 1991–1992, Dallas Drake Papers, 1950–2003, Tretter Collection.

5. Hubbard, *Cities and Sexualities*, 125. Also see Espinoza, *Cruising*, 32.

6. Hubbard, *Cities and Sexualities*, 111.

7. Foucault, "Of Other Spaces," 24. Cruising allowed men to use body language, spatial cues, and audio signals to create transient moments of sexual intimacy, embodying what Laud Humphreys refers to as "privacy in public." See Humphreys, *Tearoom Trade*, 11.

8. "Ghetto," undated, box 1, folder MCLU—Gay Task Force—Gay Rights, 1975–1993, MCLU Records, Tretter Collection.

9. Tom Burke, "The Changing Population of Gay Minneapolis," *The Gaily Planet*, November 12, 1980. By 1983, it was estimated that 17 percent of Minneapolis's population identified as LGBTQ. Tim Campbell, "Nontraditional Households Taking Over Minneapolis," *GLC Voice*, July 18, 1983.

10. "Minneapolis Neighborhood Population by Age Groups, 1980 and 1990," 1992, box 27, folder Minneapolis Neighborhood Population by Age Group, 1980 and

1990, Department of Community Planning and Economic Development (CPED) Records, Hennepin County Library.

11. "Letter from Garner to Daniels," February 25, 1993, box 21, folder Housing Problems—1993, CPED Records, Hennepin County Library; "Improving Housing Choices through the 1980s," January 1979, box 35, folder City of Minneapolis: Improving Housing Choices through the 1980s—1979, CPED Records, Hennepin County Library.

12. For a discussion on the liminal and erotic qualities of public parks, see Houlbrook, *Queer London*, 54–59.

13. Van Cleve, *Land of 10,000 Loves*, 233.

14. J. C. Ritter, "Suspect Held in Killing of Gay Minneapolis Man," *Equal Time*, October 2, 1985.

15. "Twin Cities Tear Down the Old to Make Room for the New," *Engineering News Record*, August 16, 1962, box 17, folder Engineering News Record: The Twin Cities Tear Down to Rebuild August 16, 1962, CPED Records, Hennepin County Library.

16. "Loring 100 Apartment: Final Environmental Impact Statement," undated, box 35, folder Loring 100 Apartment, CPED Records, Hennepin County Library.

17. Berlowe, "Brick, Brownstone and Grassroots."

18. Halfhill, "Loring's Gay and Lesbian Communities."

19. "'Toward a Loring Community' in *Picture* magazine," June 3, 1973, box 62, folder Loring Park neighborhood, 1970s–1990s, Tretter Collection Information Files, Tretter Collection.

20. "Loring Park Development District," undated, box 1, folder Irvin Projects: Loring Park Progress and Development, undated, 1972, 1973, 1975, 1980, Lawrence Irvin Papers, Hennepin County Library.

21. "Loring 100 Apartment: Final Environmental Impact Statement," undated, box 35, folder Loring 100 Apartment, CPED Records, Hennepin County Library.

22. "Loring 100 Apartment: Final Environmental Impact Statement."

23. "Loring 100 Apartment: Final Environmental Impact Statement."

24. John Kostouros, "Project to Put Plush Houses Downtown," *Minneapolis Tribune*, November 5, 1977.

25. When adjusted for inflation to 2025, the condos ranged in price from approximately $348,600 to $1.32 million. Trimble, *In the Shadow of the City*, 106.

26. Trimble, *In the Shadow of the City*, 105–6.

27. Robert T. Smith, "My Impression of Loring Park . . ." *Minneapolis Tribune*, April 18, 1979.

28. "Dramatic Loring Park Renewal Complete," *Downtown Profile*, February 1986, box 1, folder Downtown Profile November 1985–December 1987, CPED Records, Hennepin County Library.

29. Newman, *Defensible Space*, 3–4.

30. "Loring 100 Apartment: Final Environmental Impact Statement."

31. "Letter from Brucciani to Headquarters Precinct," March 20, 1979, box 11, folder MCGR—"No More Assault Project," 1979–1980, Leo Treadway Papers, Minnesota Historical Society.

32. "Loring Park Residents to Take Noise Complaints to City Officials," *The Gaily Planet*, August 27, 1980, 1.

33. Robert Halfhill, "Loring Park Residents Voice Complaints about Late Night Activities," *The Gaily Planet*, September 24, 1980, 5.

34. "Threat to Close 19 Bar," undated, box 8, folder Nineteen Bar (Minneapolis), Tretter Collection Information Files, 1938–2008, Tretter Collection.

35. "Update on Threat to Close 19 Bar," undated, box 8, folder Nineteen Bar (Minneapolis), Tretter Collection Information Files, 1938–2008, Tretter Collection.

36. "Amending Title 18, Chapter 466 of the Minneapolis Code of Ordinances Relating to Traffic Code," 1989, box 2, folder Cruising Ordinance, Minneapolis, 1980s, Tretter Collection Information Files, Tretter Collection.

37. Barbara Carlson, "Opinion: Heavy Traffic Is a Crime in Loring Park," *Star Tribune*, October 8, 1989.

38. Kevin Diaz and Chuck Hags, "A Place to Cruise: Neighborhood Fights Gay Prostitution in Loring Park," *Star Tribune*, September 24, 1989.

39. Diaz and Hags, "A Place to Cruise."

40. "Barbara Carlson Runs for Fourth Council Term," *The Surveyor*, October 1989.

41. Herbert Morgan, "Cruising Law Hotly Debated," *The Surveyor*, October 1989.

42. Neal Gendler, "Cruising Law Gets Mixed Reviews," *Star Tribune*, September 15, 1989.

43. David Anger, "Carlson Targets Loring Cruising after Complaints," *Equal Time*, September 13, 1989.

44. Dennis J. McGrath, "Gays, Lesbians Wielding Political Influence," *Star Tribune*, October 3, 1989; Gendler, "Cruising Law Gets Mixed Reviews"; Anger, "Carlson Targets Loring Cruising after Complaints."

45. Gendler, "Cruising Law Gets Mixed Reviews."

46. Diaz and Hags, "A Place to Cruise."

47. Tim Campbell, "Commentary: The Anticruising Ordinance Is Antigay on All Counts," *Star Tribune*, October 14, 1989.

48. Eric L. Shambach, "Letters: Rename Minneapolis New Johannesburg," *GLC Voice*, September 5, 1989.

49. Randolph Durbin, "Commentary: Cruising Law Won't Muffle Loring," *Star Tribune*, October 7, 1989.

50. Douglas Wilson, "Letters: Cruising," *The Surveyor*, October 1989.

51. Campbell, "Commentary: The Anticruising Ordinance Is Antigay on All Counts."

52. Robert Halfhill, "Letters: We Need Militants," *Equal Time*, October 25, 1989.

53. Anger, "Carlson Targets Loring Cruising after Complaints."

54. "Minutes of ACT UP Meeting," August 27, 1989, box 1, folder ACT UP, undated, Dallas Drake Papers, 1950–2003, Tretter Collection; "Gay Activists Form Political Action Group," *Twin Cities Gaze*, October 5, 1989; Robert Jacobson, "FAGS Protest Carlson's Proposed Anti-Cruising Ordinance," *Twin Cities Gaze*, October 5, 1989.

55. Richard Simon in discussion with the author, February 2023.

56. Gregor W. Pinney, "Council Shelves Anticruising Ordinance," *Star Tribune*, October 3, 1989.

57. Dean Asmundson in discussion with the author, March 2023.

58. "Campbell, Carlson File Complaints with Police over Scuffling Incident," *Star Tribune*, October 4, 1989.

59. Asmundson in discussion with the author, March 2023.

60. Robert Jacobson, "FAGS Protest Carlson's Proposed Anti-Cruising Ordinance," *Twin Cities Gaze*, October 5, 1989; Doug Grow, "You Can Call Campbell Gadfly, but Not a Spokesperson," *Star Tribune*, October 3, 1989.

61. Robert W. Peterson, "A Bruising over Cruising in Minneapolis," *City Pages*, December 5, 1989.

62. Mark Brunswick, "Gay Protests against Barbara Carlson Get Rowdy," *Star Tribune*, October 2, 1989; Jacobson, "FAGS Protest Carlson's Proposed Anti-Cruising Ordinance."

63. Jonathan Campbell, "Letters to the Editor," *Twin Cities Gaze*, October 19, 1989.

64. Bob Webster, "Letters: Improper Antics," *Star Tribune*, October 6, 1989.

65. Jean Taylor, "Letters," *Equal Time*, October 25, 1989.

66. Rick Bjorkman, "Former Loring Resident Supports Anti-Cruising Efforts," *Twin Cities Gaze*, October 5, 1989.

67. Taylor, "Letters."

68. Gordon Huser, "Letters: Loring Residents Need Residence," *Equal Time*, October 25, 1989.

69. Grow, "You Can Call Campbell Gadfly."

70. Peterson, "A Bruising over Cruising in Minneapolis."

71. Tim Campbell, "So What's the Big Deal about Cruising Loring Park?," *GLC Voice*, October 16, 1989.

72. "Joe K. and Pete S.," "Letters: Loring Park Cruising Not a Gay Issue," *Equal Time*, October 11, 1989.

73. "Joe K. and Pete S.," "Letters: Loring Park Cruising Not a Gay Issue."

74. Asmundson in discussion with the author, March 2023.

75. Grow, "You Can Call Campbell Gadfly."

76. "Meeting Minutes for the Public Health and Safety Committee," October 2, 1989, box 11, folder Public Health and Safety 8/21/89–10/16/89, Brian J. Coyle Papers, Minnesota Historical Society.

77. "Meeting Minutes for the Public Health and Safety Committee."

78. "Meeting Minutes for the Public Health and Safety Committee."

79. Robert Jacobson, "FAGS Protest Carlson's Proposed Anti-Cruising Ordinance," *Twin Cities Gaze*, October 5, 1989.

80. "Meeting Minutes for the Public Health and Safety Committee."

81. Campbell, "So What's the Big Deal about Cruising Loring Park?"

82. Jerry Fladmark in discussion with the author, March 2023.

83. J. C. Ritter, "The Month of August Is Hot for Gay Arrests," *Equal Time*, September 5, 1984.

84. Richard Osborne, "Letters: A Word to the 'Holier-Than-Thou,'" *Equal Time*, October 25, 1989.

85. Ken Darling in discussion with the author, February 2023.

86. Citizens for a Loring Park Community, "About CLPC," accessed January 7, 2022, https://loringpark.org/about-us/.

87. Yeros, *Queering Urbanism*, 95.

88. Wendy Webb, "Community: Loring Neighborhood Will Give Peace a Chance," *Skyway News*, June 27, 1991.

89. Webb, "Community: Loring Neighborhood Will Give Peace a Chance."

90. "Loring Park Protection Program Successfully Unites Citizens, Police in Cooperative Effort," *Twin Cities Gaze*, June 27, 1991.

91. "Citizens for a Loring Park Community Meeting Minutes," May 13, 1991, box 23, folder Citizens for a Loring Park Community, 1989–2001, John Yoakam Papers, Tretter Collection.

92. "Citizens for a Loring Park Community Meeting Minutes," June 10, 1991, box 23, folder CLPC, 1989–2001, John Yoakam Papers, Tretter Collection.

93. "Loring Park Protection Program Successfully Unites Citizens, Police in Cooperative Effort."

94. "CLPC Meeting Minutes," May 13, 1991, box 23, folder CLPC, 1989–2001, John Yoakam Papers, Tretter Collection.

95. "Citizens for a Loring Park Community Meeting Minutes," June 10, 1991; "Citizens for a Loring Park Community Meeting Minutes," July 8, 1991, box 23, folder CLPC, 1989–2001, John Yoakam Papers, Tretter Collection.

96. "Supplement #22 Statement of Kristy Taylor," Case Number MP-91-198777, Minneapolis Police Department.

97. Andy Birkey, "Turning Anti-Gay Hate into Love with a Loring Park Memorial to Joel Larson," *The Column*, June 16, 2014.

98. Mark Brunswick, "Man Is Shot, Killed at Loring Park in Apparent Robbery," *Star Tribune*, August 2, 1991.

99. Dan Eggen and Kathleen Brewer, "Life, Death in the Big City," *The Des Moines Register*, August 8, 1991.

100. Peter Leyden, "Shootings Shatter Serenity, Secrecy of Haven for Gays," *Star Tribune*, August 14, 1991.

101. Dennis J. McGrath and David Phelps, "Ex-Pension Chief Neither Hid nor Flaunted His Lifestyle," *Star Tribune*, August 13, 1991.

102. "Gay-Bashing Linked to Murders," *The Winona Daily News*, August 13, 1991.

103. "Letter from ACT UP/MN to the Twin Cities Anarchist Federation," January 27, 1992, box 18, folder Bathhouse "high risk sex" ordinance, Minneapolis, 1988, Tretter Collection Information Files, Tretter Collection.

104. "GAZE-TV. 1991–08–15, 1991–08–22," GAZE-TV: August 15, 1991 (Episode 9135) and August 22, 1991 (Episode 9136), Tretter Collection, https://umedia.lib.umn.edu/item/p16022coll100:212.

105. Asmundson in discussion with the author, March 2023.

106. "Police Must Work Hard to Stop Gay Killings," *Star Tribune*, August 15, 1991.

107. "GLCAC Press Release on Hate Crimes," March 6, 1991, box 38, folder Hate Crimes, Leo Treadway Papers.

108. "GAZE-TV. 1991–08–15, 1991–08–22," GAZE-TV: August 15, 1991 (Episode 9135) and August 22, 1991 (Episode 9136), Tretter Collection, accessed January 5, 2022, https://umedia.lib.umn.edu/item/p16022coll100:212.

109. Kevin Diaz, "500 Call for an End to Antigay Violence and 'Queer Bashing,'" *Star Tribune*, August 20, 1991.

110. "Marcus James" is a pseudonym used to protect the privacy of the individual, who was never formally charged or convicted in connection with the murders.

111. "GAZE-TV. 1991–12–05," GAZE-TV: December 5, 1991 (Episode 9149) and Raw Footage: Mona Smith Interview, Tretter Collection, https://umedia.lib.umn.edu/item/p16022coll100:146/.

112. Mark Brunswick, "Suspect Emerges in Larson Slaying," *Star Tribune*, November 27, 1991.

113. "#39—Supplementary Report by Sgts. Rorvick & Olson on 2/1/92," Case Number MP-91-198777, Minneapolis Police Department.

114. Mark Brunswick, "Police Comb Letter about Gay Killings," *Star Tribune*, February 6, 1992; Curt Brown, "Minneapolis Murders in 1990 Targeted Gays," *Star Tribune*, July 14, 2019.

115. "Hennepin County Social Workers Review Gay and Lesbian Hate Crime Studies and Phone Confessions by Alleged Killer of Three Gay Men," March 4, 1992, box 1, folder Gay Bashing, 1991–1992, Dallas Drake Papers, Tretter Collection.

116. "Supplement of Sgt. M. Smolley Made on 2–21–92 at 1710 hr. Sup #41" Case Number MP-91-198777, Minneapolis Police Department.

117. "Case Report with Supplements," Case Number MP-91-198777, Minneapolis Police Department, August 1991.

118. Neil Gendler, "Judge Denies Request to Lower Johnson's Bail," *Star Tribune*, February 28, 1992; David Southgate, "Court Orders HIV Test for Johnson," *Equal Time*, March 27–April 10, 1992; Brown, "Minneapolis Murders in 1990 Targeted Gays"; "#50. Supp. of Sgt. M. Rorvick on 2/26/92," Case Number MP-91-198777, Minneapolis Police Department.

119. The 700 Club was a conservative Christian television show hosted by evangelist Pat Robertson. *License to Kill*, directed by Arthur Dong (Deep Focus Productions, 1997).

120. Jill Hodges, "Roseville Man Held in Gay Killings," *Star Tribune*, February 22, 1992.

121. "Meeting Minutes for the Gay and Lesbian Police Community Task Force," February 9, 1993, folder Gay and Lesbian Issues, 1991–1993, Sharon Sayles Belton subject files, Minnesota Historical Society.

122. Glenn Howatt, "Lesbian Officer Looked Within, and Came Out," *Star Tribune*, January 10, 1993.

123. Howatt, "Lesbian Officer Looked within, and Came Out."

124. Darling in discussion with the author, February 2023.

125. Mark Brunswick, "Chief's Vow to Enforce Sodomy Law Angers Gays," *Star Tribune*, August 30, 1991; Chris Bull, "Minneapolis Activists Decry Police Chief's Sodomy-Law Support," *The Advocate*, October 8, 1991.

126. "Letter from Laux to Members of Gay and Lesbian Police-Community Task Force," January 24, 1993, folder Gay and Lesbian Police Community Task Force, 1987–1994, Sharon Sayles Belton subject files, Minnesota Historical Society.

127. "Police-Community Task Force on Gay and Lesbian Issues," October 1993, folder Gay and Lesbian Police Community Task Force, 1987–1994, Sharon Sayles Belton subject files, Minnesota Historical Society.

128. Reports claimed that both the MPD and paramedics hesitated to assist Larson as he bled to death, allegedly due to fears of HIV transmission. On the night of the shooting, Dean Asmundson and a friend were driving back from the Saloon when they saw Larson stumble out of Loring Park, clutching his chest, and collapse a few hundred feet away. Asmundson later recalled that none of the officers approached him as he lay dying, claiming that "the cops were so afraid of AIDS." Witnesses confirmed to *Equal Time* that Larson was still alive when police arrived but received no immediate medical attention. The incident gained further traction when a Minneapolis Park Police officer, the first uniformed responder on the scene, came forward after the MPD's official report, asserting that Larson was alive when help arrived. However, officials at Hennepin County Medical Center, including the ambulance manager, disputed this account, stating that both police and paramedics had followed protocol. The *Star Tribune* editorial board criticized members of the LGBTQ community for questioning the official account. Ken Darling, "Commentary: Police Must Do More to Build Bridges with Gays," *Star Tribune*, November 22, 1991; James Davies and Wizard Marks, "Reasons Remain to Question Police Care," *Star Tribune*, December 7, 1991; "Fear of AIDS and Joel Larson's Murder," *Star Tribune*, November 18, 1991; "GAZE-TV. 1991-12-05," GAZE-TV: December 5, 1991 (Episode 9149) and Raw Footage: Mona Smith Interview, Tretter Collection, https://umedia.lib.umn.edu/item/p16022coll100:146; Asmundson in discussion with the author, March 2023.

129. There is no public record verifying Chenoweth's HIV status, but given the circumstances of his death, it is likely that the MPD suspected he was HIV positive. "#26-Supplement of Sergeant Peter Jackson," August 21, 1991, Case Number MP-91-198777, Minneapolis Police Department.

130. "Gay and Lesbian Police Community Task Force Survey Responses," 1993–1994, folder Gay and Lesbian Police Community Task Force, 1987–1994, Sharon Sayles Belton subject files, Minnesota Historical Society.

131. Kimberly Hayes Taylor, "Gays Returned Green to Loring Park," *Star Tribune*, September 25, 1994.

132. Mark Brunswick, "Police Decoys Counter Cruising in Loring Park," *Star Tribune*, April 12, 1992.

133. Larry Oakes, "Police Seek to Halt Homosexual Activity in Shoreview Park," *Minneapolis Star and Tribune*, July 12, 1987.

134. Brunswick, "Police Decoys Counter Cruising in Loring Park."

135. Jill Hodges, "Loring Park Leader Quits over Police 'Sting,'" *Star Tribune*, April 14, 1992.

136. Darling in discussion with the author, February 2023.

137. Hodges, "Loring Park Leader Quits over Police 'Sting.'"

138. "The Loring News: CLPC Newsletter," Summer 1993, box 23, folder Citizens for a Loring Park Community, 1989–2001, John R. Yoakam Papers, 1956–2011, Tretter Collection; "Memorandum to Noise Safety Committee Members," February 5, 1993, box 23, folder CLPC, 1989–2001, John Yoakam Papers, Tretter Collection.

139. Jon Kerr, "Police, Residents Team Up in Loring Neighborhood," *Skyway News/Freeway News*, August 3–9, 1993.

140. "CLPC Newsletter," Summer 1993, box 23, folder CLPC, 1989–2001, John Yoakam Papers, Tretter Collection.

141. "Citizens for a Loring Park Community NRP Workshop Proposal," 1992, box 25, folder Loring Park Agreements, Action Plans, Neighborhood Revitalization Program Records, Hennepin County Library.

142. "CLPC Newsletter May 1996," box 23, folder, folder CLPC, 1989–2001, John Yoakam Papers, Tretter Collection.

143. "CLPC Newsletter November 1994," box 23, folder CLPC, 1989–2001, John Yoakam Papers, Tretter Collection. By the mid-1990s, parts of the LGBTQ community had embraced community-based policing. In 1994, LGBTQ activists in the Twin Cities launched the Queer Street Patrol to monitor Hennepin Avenue in downtown Minneapolis on weekend nights. One organizer explained that their focus was "dealing with violent crimes against people and property." The patrol coordinated closely with the MPD, attending officer roll calls and conducting joint patrols with the Community Crime Prevention-SAFE unit. Police welcomed their involvement, with the officer overseeing the downtown foot patrol saying, "We're more than happy to have another set of eyes and ears out there." Sgt. Sharon Lubinski also praised this effort, calling it a "complement to the kind of work we want to do." The Queer Street Patrol disbanded in the late 1990s, amid a period of economic revitalization in downtown Minneapolis. Pat Pheifer, "Fighting Back," *Star Tribune*, June 9, 1994; Van Cleve, *Land of 10,000 Loves*, 183–84.

144. "The Loring News: CLPC Newsletter," June 1995, box 23, folder CLPC, 1989–2001, John Yoakam Papers, Tretter Collection.

145. "Loring Park Neighborhood Action Plan," 1995, box 25, folder Loring Park Agreements, Action Plans, Neighborhood Revitalization Program Records, Hennepin County Library.

146. Dallas Drake in discussion with the author, February 2023; Asmundson in discussion with the author, March 2023.

147. Simon in discussion with the author, February 2023.

148. Erich L. Shambach, "Letters: Loring Citizen Harassment," *Gaze Magazine*, May 12, 1995.

149. Emphasis added. Jim Adams, "Group Protests Sweeps for Prostitutes," *Star Tribune*, November 14, 1997.

150. Anger, "Carlson Targets Loring Cruising after Complaints."

151. Peterson, "A Bruising over Cruising in Minneapolis."

152. Tim Campbell, "Barbara Carlson Courts Gays and Bigots," *GLC Voice*, September 5, 1989.

153. "Improving Housing Choices through the 1980s," January 1979, box 35, folder City of Minneapolis: Improving Housing Choices through the 1980s—1979, CPED Records, Hennepin County Library.

154. Tim Campbell, "'Un-Marriage' Proposal May Be Hot Point of Summer," *GLC Voice*, February 6, 1984.

155. "Letter from Coyle to Constituents," March 1, 1984, box 62, folder Brian Coyle—clippings and events, circa 1989, Tretter Collection Information Files, Tretter Collection.

156. Michele L. Norris, "City Looks at Rights of Unwed Couples," *Minnesota Daily*, January 1, 1984, box 1, folder MCLU—Homosexuals—Domestic Partnership Ordinance, MCLU Records, Tretter Collection.

157. Jim Parsons, "Domestic-Partners Ordinance Sponsor Is No Stranger to Strife," *Star Tribune*, July 30, 1990.

158. John Matthews, "Romance in a Questionable Health Environment," *Twin Cities Gaze*, January 1986.

159. Brad Theissen, "Labels Such as 'Gay Beach' Taint Society's Perception of a People," *Star Tribune*, August 31, 1991.

160. Andrew Gage, "Real Estate," *Twin Cities Gaze*, March 1986, 31.

161. Jon Jeter, "Minneapolis Council Appears Likely to Pass Domestic-Partner Ordinance," *Star Tribune*, January 15, 1991.

162. Neal Gendler, "Compromise on Domestic Partners," *Star Tribune* January 8, 1991.

163. Jeter, "Minneapolis Council Appears Likely to Pass Domestic-Partner Ordinance."

164. Jim St. George in discussion with the author, March 2023.

165. Fladmark in discussion with the author, March 2023.

166. Cynthia Scott, "In Memoriam," *Equal Time*, August 30–September 13, 1991.

167. Like Coyle, Shilts also passed away due to AIDS-related complications in 1994.

168. Lou Gelfand, "Readers Ask, 'Isn't an Obituary Written to Honor the Deceased?,'" *Star Tribune*, October 12, 1997.

169. Kevin Diaz, "Ruling Puts Struggle for Gay-Partner Rights Back to Square One," *Star Tribune*, June 13, 1994.

170. Gendler, "Compromise on Domestic Partners."

171. Schulman, *The Gentrification of the Mind*, 125.

172. Schulman, *The Gentrification of the Mind*, 155.

173. Schulman, *The Gentrification of the Mind*, 27–28.

174. Ghaziani, "Cultural Archipelagos," 4–7.

175. Cory Zurowski, "Finding Gay Suburbia Heaven in Golden Valley," *City Pages*, June 21–27, 2017.

176. Zurowski, "Finding Gay Suburbia Heaven in Golden Valley."

177. Van Cleve, *Land of 10,000 Loves*, 268.

178. "Quick Facts: Golden Valley City, Minnesota," United States Census Bureau, July 1, 2021, https://www.census.gov/quickfacts/goldenvalleycityminnesota.

179. Zurowski, "Finding Gay Suburbia Heaven in Golden Valley."

180. Shane Lueck, "A Tale of Two Prides," *Lavender Magazine*, May 26, 2016, https://lavendermagazine.com/our-affairs/a-tale-of-two-prides/; John Reinan, "Golden Valley Brings First Gay Pride Festival to Suburbia," *Star Tribune*, April 21, 2016; Gary J. Gates and Abigail M. Cooke, "Minnesota Census Snapshot: 2010," *The Williams Institute*, September 2011, https://williamsinstitute.law.ucla.edu/wp-content/uploads/2010-Census-Snapshot-MN-Sep-2011.pdf.

Epilogue

1. Muñoz, *The Sense of Brown*, xxxi.
2. For more on "radical care," see Kawehipuaakahaopulani Hobart and Kneese, "Radical Care," 2.
3. See Batza, *Before AIDS*, 46–52; Fernández, *The Young Lords*, 139–46; Nelson, *Body and Soul*, 77–82; Nelson, *Women of Color and the Reproductive Rights Movement*, 115–32.
4. Michael McConnell, "Michael McConnell: Married His Husband in 1971, Demands Equality for All," *Minneapolis Interview Project*, January 19, 2019, https://turtleroad.org/2019/01/19/michael-mcconnell-married-his-husband-in-1971-demands/.
5. "Gay House Newsletter," October 1975, box 1, folder Gay House—Associated Documents, 1973–1975, Gay House Records, 1971–1975, Tretter Collection; "Gay House Information Sheet," undated, box 1, folder Gay House—Associated Documents, 1973–1975, Gay House Records, 1971–1975, Tretter Collection.
6. Vaid, *Virtual Equality*, 87–88.
7. "Minnesota American Indian AIDS Task Force, 'Ganawenima,'" box 6, folder Minnesota American Indian AIDS Task Force, 1994–1999, undated, Two-Spirit Papers, Tretter Collection.
8. Day, Sharon, 2014-06-11, "Interview with Sharon Day," University of Minnesota Libraries, Jean-Nickolaus Tretter Collection in Gay, Lesbian, Bisexual and Transgender Studies, https://umedia.lib.umn.edu/item/p16022coll534:32.
9. "Services Provided at MAIATF," box 6, folder Minnesota American Indian AIDS Task Force, 1994–1999, undated, Two-Spirit Papers, Tretter Collection.
10. Mark Kasel, "American Indian Gays and Lesbians Open New Office with New Future," *Twin Cities Gaze*, no. 133 (January 1991).
11. The term "two-spirit" emerged in the early 1990s from a network of Indigenous queer individuals in North America who found the term "berdache" outdated and offensive, seeking a new way to describe their lived experiences. Being two-spirit involves challenging rigid Western notions of gender and sexuality by embracing a broader range of gender expressions and sexual orientations while also emphasizing the spiritual aspects of erotic desire. Morgensen, *Spaces between Us*, 86; MacDonald, "Two-Spirits Organizing," 151–52.
12. "The HIV Services Planning Project Update Number Three, September 1990," box 33, folder Minnesota Department of Health 1988–1994, Leo Treadway Papers, Minnesota Historical Society; "Men of Color Who Have Sex with Men," 1995, box 3, folder, Minnesota Men of Color (MMC) Records, Tretter Collection.
13. Nicholas Metcalf in conversation with the author, August 2021.
14. Edd Lee in conversation with the author, March 2023.
15. "Somos Familia Informational Pamphlet," box 23, folder Somos Familias, 1999–2003, MMC Records, Tretter Collection; "Ikĉé Wiĉáŝa Informational Pamphlet," 2003, box 1, folder MMC Records, Tretter Collection.
16. For further discussion on how professionalized nonprofit organizations and charity programs often promote a narrative of compassion that reinforces racist and classist cultural stereotypes about moral value, see Spade, *Mutual Aid*, 45–49; Beam,

Gay, Inc, 45–48. For more on the neoliberalization of nonprofits, refer to Rodríguez, "The Political Logic of the Non-Profit Industrial Complex," 21–22.

17. Roxanne "Rox" Anderson in conversation with the author, August 2021. MMC adopted a "decolonial queer praxis," a coalition-based health approach that frames illness and wellness within the broader contexts of racism, capitalism, and colonialism. This approach views health as more than simply "drugs into bodies," focusing instead on the importance of purposeful living. Unlike traditional nonprofits and charities that rely on hierarchies of moral worth to allocate resources, a decolonial queer praxis rejects racist and heteronormative metrics for determining who deserves care. Esparza, "'Qué Bonita Mi Tierra,'" 127.

18. "Talking Points Flyer," 2001, box 13, folder Minnesota Men of Color Internal Affairs, 2003, MMC Records, Tretter Collection.

19. "Welcome to Gender Girls! Flyer," box 21, folder Gender Girls, undated, 2002, MMC Records, Tretter Collection.

20. "Welcome to Gender Girls! Flyer."

21. Anderson in conversation with author, August 2021.

22. "Letter from MMC to GLBT Pride Twin Cities," July 11, 2000, box 22, folder Power to the People, MMC Records, Tretter Collection.

23. Anderson, Roxanne. 2015-09-30. "Interview with Roxanne Anderson." University of Minnesota Libraries, Jean-Nickolaus Tretter Collection in Gay, Lesbian, Bisexual and Transgender Studies, https://umedia.lib.umn.edu/item/p16022coll534:18.

24. Anderson in conversation with author, August 2021.

25. "Power to the People Plan," 2001, box, folder Power to the People, 2000–2003, MMC Records, Tretter Collection.

26. Cohen, "Punks, Bulldaggers, and Welfare Queens," 438.

27. Metcalf in conversation with author, August 2021.

28. Office of the Legislative Auditor, State of Minnesota, "Special Review: Minnesota Men of Color," October 30, 2003, https://www.auditor.leg.state.mn.us/fad/pdf/fad0357.pdf.

29. Office of the Legislative Auditor, "Special Review," 11.

30. "Audit Questions Money That Went to Nonprofit," *Star Tribune*, October 31, 2003.

31. Centers for Disease Control and Prevention, "HIV Surveillance Report," 2019, vol. 32, https://www.cdc.gov/hiv/library/reports/hiv-surveillance/vol-34/index.html, accessed March 2, 2022.

32. HIV/AIDS Surveillance System, "HIV/AIDS Statistics, 2021," *Minnesota Department of Health*, June 11, 2023, https://www.health.state.mn.us/diseases/hiv/stats/2021/index.html; "Quick Facts: Minnesota," *US Census Bureau*, accessed February 8, 2024, https://www.census.gov/quickfacts/fact/table/MN/PST045222.

33. Magnus et al., "Elevated HIV Prevalence despite Lower Rates of Sexual Risk Behaviors among Black Men in the District of Columbia Who Have Sex with Men," 619; Millett et al., "Explaining Disparities in HIV Infection among Black and White Men Who Have Sex with Men," 2087–89. For a discussion on the role of sexual networks in HIV transmission, see Maulsby et al., "Partner Characteristics and Undiagnosed HIV Seropositivity," 548–51.

Bibliography

Oral Histories by the Author

Dallas Drake, February 2023
Dean Asmundson, March 2023
Edd Lee, March 2023
Jerry Fladmark, March 2023
Jim St. George, March 2023
Ken Darling, February 2023
Nicholas Metcalf, August 2021
Richard Simon, February 2023
Roxanne "Rox" Anderson, August 2021
Scott Dibble, June 2023
Thomas Trisko, March 2023

Archival Sources

Minneapolis, MN
    City of Minneapolis
        Minneapolis Police Department Records
    Hennepin County Library
        Department of Community Planning and Economic Development (CPED) Records
        Lawrence Irvin Papers
    Jean Nickolaus Tretter Collection in GLBT Studies, University of Minnesota
        Allan Spear Papers
        Dallas Drake Papers
        Gay House Records
        James Eric Chalgren Papers
        John R. Yoakam Papers
        Michael McConnell Files
        Minnesota Civil Liberties Union Records
        Minnesota Gay and Lesbian Legal Assistance Records
        Minnesota Men of Color Records
        Tretter Collection Information Files
        Two-Spirit Papers
St. Paul, MN
    Minnesota Historical Society
        Brian J. Coyle Papers

Donald M. Fraser Papers
Governor's Task Force on Lesbian and Gay Minnesotans Records
Leo Treadway Papers
Minnesota Legislative Committee Hearings
Sharon Sayles Belton Papers
Thom Higgins Papers

Selected Newsletters, Newspapers, and Magazines

City Pages
Equal Time
Gaily Planet
GLC Voice
Lavender Magazine
Minneapolis Star
Minneapolis Tribune
Minnesota Daily
Positively Gay
Skyway News
Star Tribune
St. Paul Pioneer Press and Dispatch
Surveyor
Twin Cities Gaze
Twin Cities Reader

Moving Image Sources

The Daily Show with Jon Stewart, "Minneapolis Is the New Gay," aired May 9, 2011, on Comedy Central, https://www.cc.com/video/ys5uqo/the-daily-show-with-jon-stewart-minneapolis-is-the-new-gay.
Dong, Arthur, director. *License to Kill*. 1997; Deep Focus Productions.
Frontline, season 1986, episode 8, "AIDS: A National Inquiry," aired March 25, 1986, on WGBH and WCCO.

Secondary Sources

Adams, Thomas. "'New Life, New Vigor, and New Values': Privatization, Service Work, and the Rise of Neoliberal Urbanism in Postwar Southern California." In *Neoliberal Cities: The Remaking of Postwar Urban America*, edited by Andrew J. Diamond and Thomas J. Sugrue. New York: New York University Press, 2020.
Ahmed, Aziza, Catherine Hanssens, and Brook Kelly. "Protecting HIV-Positive Women's Human Rights: Recommendations for the United States National HIV/AIDS Strategy." *Reproductive Health Matters* 17, no. 34 (2009): 127–34.
"The AIDS Crisis Is Not Over," edited by Hobson, Emily K. and Dan Royles. Special Issue, *Radical History Review* 21, no. 2 (2001).
Armstrong, Elizabeth A. *Forging Gay Identities: Organizing Sexuality in San Francisco, 1950–1994*. Chicago: University of Chicago Press, 2002.
Atkins, Annette. *Creating Minnesota: A History from the Inside Out*. St. Paul: Minnesota Historical Society Press, 2007.
Bailey, Marlon M. *Butch Queens Up in Pumps: Gender, Performance, and Ballroom Culture in Detroit*. Ann Arbor: University of Michigan Press, 2013.
Batza, Katie. *Before AIDS: Gay Health Politics in the 1970s*. Philadelphia: University of Pennsylvania Press, 2018.

———. "Opening DOORWAYS and Closing Others: Tactical Deployments of Respectability, Religion, and Race in St. Louis Early-AIDS Response." In *Resist, Organize, Build: Feminist and Queer Activism in Britain and the United States during the Long 1980s*, edited by Sarah Crook and Charlie Jeffries. Albany: State University of New York Press, 2022.

Bayer, Ronald. *Private Acts, Social Consequences: AIDS and the Politics of Public Health.* New York: Free Press, 1989.

Beam, Myrl. *Gay, Inc.: The Nonprofitization of Queer Politics.* Minneapolis: University of Minnesota Press, 2018.

Bell, David, and Jon Binnie. "Authenticating Queer Space: Citizenship, Urbanism and Governance." *Urban Studies* 41, no. 9 (2004): 1807–20.

Bell, David, and Gill Valentine. *Mapping Desire: Geographies of Sexualities.* London: Routledge, 1995.

Berlant, Lauren, and Michael Warner. "Sex in Public." *Critical Inquiry* 24, no. 2 (1998): 547–66.

Berlowe, Burt. "Brick, Brownstone and Grassroots: A Political History of Loring Park." In *Reflections in Loring Pond: A Minneapolis Neighborhood Examines its First Century*, edited by Citizens for a Loring Park Community. Minneapolis: Citizens for a Loring Park Community, 1986.

Bérubé, Allan. "The History of Gay Bathhouses." In *Policing Public Sex: Queer Politics and the Future of AIDS Activism*, edited by Dangerous Bedfellows. Cambridge, MA: South End Press, 1996.

Billund-Phibbs, Myra. "Steam Rooms: A History of Public and Semi-Public Gay Sexual Space in 20th Century Minneapolis." Senior thesis, University of Minnesota, Twin Cities, 2018.

Biro Walters, Jordan. *Wide-Open Desert: A Queer History of New Mexico.* Seattle: University of Washington Press, 2023.

"The Black AIDS Epidemic," edited by Marlon M. Bailey and Darius Bost. Special Issue, *Souls* 21, no. 2–3 (2019).

Blade, Timothy Trent. "'Sodom on the Mississippi': The Homosexual Presence Shown in the Media." *Hennepin History* 52, no. 2 (1993): 4–34.

Blomley, Nicholas. "The Borrowed View: Privacy, Propriety, and the Entanglements of Property." *Law & Social Inquiry* 30, no. 4 (2005): 617–61.

Bonilla-Silva, Eduardo. *Racism without Racists: Color-Blind Racism and the Persistence of Racial Inequality in America.* 4th ed. New York: Rowman & Littlefield Publishers, Inc., 2014.

Bost, Darius. *Evidence of Being: The Black Gay Cultural Renaissance and the Politics of Violence.* Chicago: University of Chicago Press, 2019.

Brest, Paul, and Ann Vandenberg. "Politics, Feminism and the Constitution: The Anti-Pornography Movement in Minneapolis." *Stanford Law Review* 39, no. 3 (1987): 607–61.

Brier, Jennifer. "AIDS and Action (1980–1990s)." In *The Routledge History of Queer America*, edited by Don Romesburg. New York: Routledge, 2018.

———. *Infectious Ideas: U.S. Political Response to the AIDS Crisis.* Chapel Hill: University of North Carolina Press, 2009.

Briggs, Laura. *Reproducing Empire: Race, Sex, Science, and U.S. Imperialism in Puerto Rico*. Berkeley: University of California Press, 2002.

Bronson, Ken. *A Quest for Full Equality*. Minneapolis: Published by the author, 2004.

Brown, Wendy. *In the Ruins of Neoliberalism: The Rise of Antidemocratic Politics in the West*. New York: Columbia University Press, 2019.

Burris, Scott, and Edwin Cameron. "The Case against Criminalization of HIV Transmission." *Journal of the American Medical Association* 300, no. 5 (2008): 578–81.

Burt, Martha R. "Causes of the Growth of Homelessness during the 1980s." *Housing Policy Debate* 2, no. 3 (1991): 901–36.

Butler, Judith. *Frames of War: When Is Life Grievable?* New York: Verso, 2010.

Butler, Pamela. "Sex and the Cities: Re-Evaluating 1980s Feminist Politics in Minneapolis and St. Paul." In *Queer Twin Cities: Twin Cities GLBT Oral History Project*, edited by Kevin P. Murphy et al. Minneapolis: University of Minnesota Press, 2010.

Cacho, Lisa M. "'The People of California Are Suffering': The Ideology of White Injury in Discourses of Immigration." *Cultural Values* 4, no. 4 (2000): 389–418.

———. *Social Death: Racialized Rightlessness and the Criminalization of the Unprotected*. New York: New York University Press, 2012.

Canaday, Margot. *The Straight State: Sexuality and Citizenship in Twentieth-Century America*. Princeton, NJ: Princeton University Press, 2009.

Carroll, Tamar W. *Mobilizing New York: AIDS, Antipoverty, and Feminist Activism*. Chapel Hill: University of North Carolina Press, 2015.

Cartwright, Ryan Lee. *Peculiar Places: A Queer Crip History of White Rural Nonconformity*. Chicago: Chicago University Press, 2020.

Castells, Manuel. *The City and the Grassroots: A Cross-Cultural Theory of Urban Social Movements*. Berkeley: University of California Press, 1983.

Cayton, Andrew R. L., and Susan E. Gray, eds. *The American Midwest: Essays on Regional History*. Bloomington: Indiana University Press, 2001.

Cayton, Andrew R. L., and Peter S. Onuf, eds. *The Midwest and the Nation: Rethinking the History of an American Region*. Bloomington: Indiana University Press, 1990.

Chateauvert, Melinda. *Sex Workers Unite: A History of the Movement from Stonewall to Slutwalk*. Boston: Beacon Press, 2014.

Chauncey, George. *Gay New York: Gender, Urban Culture, and the Making of the Gay Male World 1890–1940*. New York: Basic Books, 1994.

Cheng, Jih-Fei, Alexandra Juhasz, and Nishant Shahani, eds. *AIDS and the Distribution of Crises*. Durham, NC: Duke University Press, 2020.

Child, Brenda J., and Karissa E. White. "'I've Done My Share': Ojibwe People and World War II." *Minnesota History* 61, no. 5 (2009): 196–207.

Chow, Rey. *The Protestant Ethnic and the Spirit of Capitalism*. New York: Columbia University Press, 2002.

Clendinen, Dudley, and Adam Nagourney. *Out for Good: The Struggle to Build a Gay Rights Movement in America*. New York: Touchstone, 1999.

Clumeck, Nathan, Marjorie Robert-Guroff, Philippe Van De Perre, Andrea Jennings, Jean Sibomana, Patrick Demol, Sophie Cran, and Robert C. Gallo.

"Seroepidemiological Studies of HTLV-III Antibody Prevalence among Selected Groups of Heterosexual Africans." *Journal of the American Medical Association* 254, no. 18 (1985): 2599–602.

Cohen, Cathy J. *The Boundaries of Blackness: AIDS and the Breakdown of Black Politics*. Chicago: University of Chicago Press, 1999.

———. "Punks, Bulldaggers, and Welfare Queens: The Radical Potential of Queer Politics?" *GLQ* 3 (1997): 437–65.

Cohen, Lizabeth. *Saving America's Cities: Ed Logue and the Struggle to Renew Urban America in the Suburban Age*. New York: Picador, 2019.

Cohen, Stanley. *Folk Devils and Moral Panics: The Creation of the Mods and Rockers*. New York: Routledge, 1972.

Colgrove, James. *Epidemic City: The Politics of Public Health in New York*. New York: Russell Sage Foundation, 2011.

Connolly, N. D. B. *A World More Concrete: Real Estate and the Remaking of Jim Crow South Florida*. Chicago: University of Chicago Press, 2014.

Cooper, Melinda. *Family Values: Between Neoliberalism and the New Social Conservatism*. Brooklyn, NY: Zone Books, 2017.

Craddock, Susan. *City of Plagues: Disease, Poverty, and Deviance in San Francisco*. Minneapolis: University of Minnesota Press, 2000.

Crimp, Douglas. *Melancholia and Moralism: Essays on AIDS and Queer Politics*. Cambridge, MA: MIT Press, 2002.

Delany, Samuel. *Times Square Red, Times Square Blue*. New York: New York University Press, 1999.

Delegard, Kirsten. "Contested Geography: The Campaign against Pornography and the Battle for Urban Space in Minneapolis." In *U.S. Women's History: Untangling The Threads of Sisterhood*, edited by Leslie Brown, Jacqueline Castledine, and Anne Valk. New Brunswick, NJ: Rutgers University Press, 2017.

D'Emilio, John. *Sexual Politics, Sexual Communities: The Making of a Homosexual Minority in the United States, 1940–1970*. 2nd ed. Chicago: University of Chicago Press, 1998.

De Orio, Scott. "The Invention of Bad Gay Sex: Texas and the Creation of a Criminal Underclass of Gay People." *Journal of the History of Sexuality* 26, no. 1 (2017): 53–87.

Diamond, Andrew J. *Chicago on the Make: Power and Inequality in a Modern City*. Oakland: University of California Press, 2017.

Diwas, KC. "Of Consciousness and Criticism: Identity in the Intersections of the Gay Liberation Front and the Young Lords Party." Sarah Lawrence College ProQuest Dissertations Publishing, 2005.

Drucker, Ernest. *A Plague of Prisons: The Epidemiology of Mass Incarceration in America*. New York: The New Press, 2011.

Duggan, Lisa. *The Twilight of Equality? Neoliberalism, Cultural Politics, and the Attack on Democracy*. Boston: Beacon Press, 2003.

Ehrman-Solberg, Kevin. "The Battle of the Bookstores and Gay Sexual Liberation in Minneapolis." *Middle West Review* 3, no. 1 (2016): 1–24.

Elias, Norbert. *The Civilizing Process: Sociogenetic and Psychogenetic Investigations*. Translated by Edmund Jephcott. Malden, MA: Blackwell, 1994.

Elifson, Kirk W., Jacqueline Boles, and Mike Sweat. "Risk Factors Associated with HIV Infection among Male Prostitutes." *American Journal of Public Health* 83, no. 1 (1993): 79–83.

Elifson, Kirk W., Jacqueline Boles, Mike Sweat, William Darrow, William Elsea, and R. Michael Green. "Seroprevalence of Immunodeficiency Virus among Male Prostitutes." *New England Journal of Medicine* 321 (1989): 832–33.

Endean, Steve. *Bringing Lesbian and Gay Rights into the Mainstream.* Edited by Vicki L. Eaklor. New York: Harrington Park Press, 2006.

Eng, David L. *The Feeling of Kinship: Queer Liberalism and the Racialization of Intimacy.* Durham, NC: Duke University Press, 2010.

Enke, Finn. *Finding the Movement: Sexuality, Contested Space, and Feminist Activism.* Durham, NC: Duke University Press, 2007.

Epstein, Steven. *Impure Science: AIDS, Activism, and the Politics of Knowledge.* Berkeley: University of California Press, 1996.

Eskridge, William N., Jr. *The Case for Same-Sex Marriage: From Sexual Liberty to Civilized Commitment.* New York: Free Press, 1996.

———. *Dishonorable Passions: Sodomy Laws in America, 1861–2003.* New York: Viking, 2008.

Esparza, René. "'Qué Bonita Mi Tierra': Latinx AIDS Activism and Decolonial Queer Praxis in 1980s New York and Puerto Rico." *Radical History Review* 140 (2021): 107–41.

———. "'We Lived as Do Spouses': AIDS, Neoliberalism, and Family-Based Apartment Succession Rights in 1980s New York City." *Journal of the History of Sexuality* 31, no. 1 (2022): 59–88.

Espinoza, Alex. *Cruising: An Intimate History of a Radical Pastime.* Los Angeles: Unnamed Press, 2019.

Faludi, Susan. *The Terror Dream: Fear and Fantasy in Post-9/11 America.* New York: Picador, 2007.

Ferguson, Roderick A. "Race-ing Homonormativity: Citizenship, Sociology, and Gay Identity." In *Black Queer Studies: A Critical Anthology*, edited by E. Patrick Johnson and Mae G. Henderson. Durham, NC: Duke University Press, 2005.

Fernández, Johanna. *The Young Lords: A Radical History.* Chapel Hill: University of North Carolina Press, 2020.

Florida, Richard. *The Rise of the Creative Class: And How It's Transforming Work, Leisure, Community, and Everyday Life.* New York: Basic Books, 2002.

Forstie, Clare. *Queering the Midwest: Forging LGBTQ Community.* New York: New York University Press, 2022.

Foucault, Michel. "Of Other Spaces," *Diacritics* 16, no. 1 (1986): 22–27.

Frank, Gillian. "'The Civil Rights of Parents': Race and Conservative Politics in Anita Bryant's Campaign against Gay Rights in 1970s Florida." *Journal of the History of Sexuality* 22, no. 1 (2013): 126–60.

Galletly, Carol L., and Steven D. Pinkerton. "Conflicting Messages: How Criminal HIV Disclosure Laws Undermine Public Health Efforts to Control the Spread of HIV." *AIDS and Behavior* 10 (2006): 451–61.

Gallup, George, Jr. *The 1986 Gallup Poll: Public Opinion*. Lanham, MA: Rowman & Littlefield, 1987.
Geary, Adam. *Antiblack Racism and the AIDS Epidemic: State Intimacies*. New York: Palgrave MacMillan, 2014.
Gerstle, Gary. *The Rise and Fall of the Neoliberal Order*. New York: Oxford University Press, 2022.
Ghaziani, Amin. "Cultural Archipelagos: New Directions in the Study of Sexuality and Space." *City & Community* 18, no. 1 (2019): 4–22.
Glass, Ruth. "Introduction: Aspects of Change." In *London: Aspects of Change*, edited by Centre for Urban Studies. London: MacKibbon and Kee, 1964.
Goluboff, Risa. *Vagrant Nation: Police Power, Constitutional Change, and the Making of the 1960s*. New York: Oxford University Press, 2016.
Gostin, Lawrence O. "The Isolation of HIV–Positive Patients Reply." *Journal of the American Medical Association* 262 (1989): 208–9.
Gould, Deborah. *Moving Politics: Emotion and ACT UP's Fight against AIDS*. Chicago: University of Chicago Press, 2009.
Gould, Peter. *The Slow Plague: A Geography of the AIDS Epidemic*. Cambridge, MA: Blackwell Publishers, 1993.
Gray, Mary L. *Out in the Country: Youth, Media, and Queer Visibility in Rural America*. New York: New York University Press, 2009.
Gray, Mary L., Colin R. Johnson, and Brian J. Gilley, eds. *Queering the Countryside: New Frontiers in Rural Queer Studies*. New York: New York University Press, 2016.
Gray Fischer, Anne. *The Streets Belong to Us: Sex, Race, and Police Power from Segregation to Gentrification*. Chapel Hill: University of North Carolina Press, 2022.
Gutterman, Lauren Jae. *Her Neighbor's Wife: A History of Lesbian Desire within Marriage*. Philadelphia: University of Pennsylvania Press, 2019.
Halberstam, Jack. *In a Queer Time and Place: Transgender Bodies, Subcultural Lives*. New York: New York University Press, 2005.
Halfhill, Robert. "Loring's Gay and Lesbian Communities." In *Reflections in Loring Pond: A Minneapolis Neighborhood Examines Its First Century*, edited by Citizens for a Loring Park Community. Minneapolis: Citizens for a Loring Park Community, 1986.
Hall, Stuart, Chas Critcher, Tony Jefferson, John Clarke, and Brian Roberts. *Policing the Crisis: Mugging, the State, and Law and Order*. London: Palgrave, 1978.
Halperin, David M. "Introduction: The War on Sex." In *The War on Sex*, edited by David M. Halperin and Trevor Hoppe. Durham, NC: Duke University Press, 2017.
Halverson, Britte E., and Joshua O. Reno. *Imagining the Heartland: White Supremacy and the American Midwest*. Oakland: University of California Press, 2022.
Hancock, Ange-Marie. *The Politics of Disgust: The Public Identity of the Welfare Queen*. New York: New York University Press, 2004.
Haney López, Ian. *Dog Whistle Politics: How Coded Racial Appeals Have Reinvented Racism and Wrecked the Middle Class*. New York: Oxford University Press, 2014.
Hanhardt, Christina B. *Safe Space: Gay Neighborhood History and the Politics of Violence*. Durham, NC: Duke University Press, 2013.

Hanson, Dan C. *History of the Minnesota Gay and Lesbian Legal Assistance (MnGALLA)*. Golden Valley, MN: Friends of the Bill of Rights Foundation, 2009.
Harcourt, Bernard E. "Neoliberal Penality: A Brief Genealogy." *Theoretical Criminology* 14, no. 1 (2010): 74–92.
Harris, Cheryl I. "Whiteness as Property." *Harvard Law Review* 106, no. 8 (1993): 1707–91.
Harvey, David. *A Brief History of Neoliberalism*. New York: Oxford University Press, 2005.
———. *The Condition of Postmodernity*. Malden, MA: Blackwell Publishing, 1990.
———. *The Limits to Capital*. Oxford: Basil Blackwell, 1982.
Herring, Scott. *Another Country: Queer Anti-Urbanism*. New York: New York University Press, 2010.
Hewetson, Dick. *History of the Gay Movement in Minnesota and the Role of the Minnesota Civil Liberties Union*. Minneapolis: Friends of the Bill of Rights Foundation, 2013.
Hickey, Georgina. "The Geography of Pornography: Neighborhood Feminism and the Battle against 'Dirty Bookstores' in Minneapolis." *Frontiers* 32, no. 1 (2001): 125–51.
Hinton, Elizabeth. *From the War on Poverty to the War on Crime: The Making of Mass Incarceration in America*. Cambridge, MA: Harvard University Press, 2017.
Hobson, Emily K. *Lavender and Red: Liberation and Solidarity in the Gay and Lesbian Left*. Oakland: University of California Press, 2016.
Hoganson, Kristin L. *The Heartland: An American History*. New York: Penguin Books, 2019.
Holmes, Kwamé. "The End of Queer Urban History?" In *The Routledge History of Queer America*, edited by Don Romesburg. New York: Routledge, 2018.
Holtzman, Benjamin. *The Long Crisis: New York City and the Path to Neoliberalism*. New York: Oxford University Press, 2021.
Hoppe, Trevor. *Punishing Disease: HIV and the Criminalization of Sickness*. Oakland: University of California Press, 2018.
Houlbrook, Matt. *Queer London: Perils and Pleasures in the Sexual Metropolis, 1918–1957*. Chicago: University of Chicago Press, 2005.
Howard, Clayton. *The Closet and the Cul-de-Sac: The Politics of Sexual Privacy in Northern California*. Philadelphia: University of Pennsylvania Press, 2019.
Howard, John. *Men Like That: A Southern Queer History*. Chicago: University of Chicago Press, 1999.
Hubbard, Phil. *Cities and Sexualities*. New York: Routledge, 2012.
Hugill, David. *Settler Colonial City: Racism and Inequity in Postwar Minneapolis*. Minneapolis: University of Minnesota Press, 2021.
Humphreys, Laud. *Tearoom Trade: Impersonal Sex in Public Places*. London: Routledge, 1970.
Humphries, Drew. *Crack Mothers: Pregnancy, Drugs, and the Media*. Columbus: The Ohio State University Press, 1999.
Janovy, C. J. *No Place Like Home: Lessons in Activism from LGBT Kansas*. Lawrence: University of Kansas Press, 2018.

Jansson, Maria. "An Economy of Protection: Agency, Responsibility and the Criminalization of HIV." *Women's Studies International Forum* 69 (2018): 171–79.
Johnson, Colin R. *Just Queer Folks: Gender and Sexuality in Rural America.* Philadelphia: Temple University Press, 2013.
Johnson, E. Patrick. *Sweet Tea: Black Gay Men of the South.* Chapel Hill: University of North Carolina Press, 2011.
Kawehipuaakahaopulani Hobart, Hiʻilei Julia and Tamara Kneese. "Radical Care: Survival Strategies for Uncertain Times." *Social Text* 38, no. 1 (2020): 1–16.
Kerr, Theodore (ted). "AIDS 1969: HIV, History, and Race." *Drain Magazine* 13, no. 2 (2016). https://drainmag.com/aids-1969-hiv-history-and-race/.
Kinsella, James. *Covering the Plague: AIDS and the American Media.* New Brunswick, NJ: Rutgers University Press, 1989.
Knopp, Lawrence. "Some Theoretical Implications of Gay Involvement in an Urban Land Market." *Political Geography Quarterly* 9, no. 4 (1990): 337–52.
Kohnen, Melanie. *Screening the Closet: Queer Representation, Visibility, and Race in American Film and Television.* New York: Taylor & Francis, 2017.
Lancaster, Roger N. "The New Pariahs: Sex, Crime, and Punishment in America." In *The War on Sex*, edited by David M. Halperin and Trevor Hoppe. Durham, NC: Duke University Press, 2017.
Lassiter, Matthew D., and Joseph Crespino. "Introduction: The End of Southern History." In *The Myth of Southern Exceptionalism*, edited by Matthew D. Lassiter and Joseph Crespino. London: Oxford University Press, 2009.
Leighton, Jared. "'All of Us Are Unapprehended Felons': Gay Liberation, the Black Panther Party, and Intercommunal Efforts against Police Brutality in the Bay Area." *Journal of Social History* 52, no. 3 (2019): 860–85.
Leonard, Arthur S. *Sexuality and the Law: An Encyclopedia of Major Legal Cases.* New York: Routledge, 1993.
Levine, Judith. "Sympathy for the Devil: Why Progressives Haven't Helped the Sex Offender, Why They Should, and How They Can." In *The War on Sex*, edited by David M. Halperin and Trevor Hoppe. Durham, NC: Duke University Press, 2017.
Lvosky, Anna. *Vice Patrol: Cops, Courts, and the Struggle over Urban Gay Life Before Stonewall.* Chicago: University of Chicago Press, 2021.
MacDonald, Megan L. "Two-Spirits Organizing: Indigenous Two-Spirit Identity in the Twin Cities Region." In *Queer Twin Cities: Twin Cities GLBT Oral History Project*, edited by Kevin P. Murphy et al. Minneapolis: University of Minnesota Press, 2010.
Macías-González, Víctor M. "Transnationalism and the Development of Domesticity in Mexico City's Homophile Community, 1920–1960." *Gender History* 23, no. 3 (2014): 519–44.
Mackenzie, Sonja. *Structural Intimacies: Sexual Stories in the Black AIDS Epidemic.* New Brunswick, NJ: Rutgers University Press, 2013.
Magnus, Manya, Irene Kuo, Gregory Phillips II, Katherine Shelley, Anthony Rawls, Luz Montanez, James Peterson, Tiffany West-Ojo, Shannon Hader, and Alan E. Greenberg. "Elevated HIV Prevalence despite Lower Rates of Sexual Risk Behaviors among Black Men in the District of Columbia Who Have Sex with Men." *AIDS Patient Care and STDs* 24, no. 10 (2010): 615–22.

Manalansan, Martin F., IV. *Global Divas: Filipino Gay Men in the Diaspora*. Durham, NC: Duke University Press, 2003.

———. "Race, Violence, and the Neoliberal Spatial Politics in the Global City." *Social Text* 23 (2005): 141–55.

Manalansan, Martin F., IV, Chantal Nadeau, Richard T. Rodríguez, and Siobhan B. Somerville. "Queering the Middle: Race, Region, and a Queer Midwest." *GLQ* 20, no. 1–2 (2014): 1–12.

Manuel, Jeffrey T., and Andrew Urban. "'You Can't Legislate the Heart': Minneapolis Mayor Charles Stenvig and the Politics of Law and Order." *American Studies* vol. 49, no. 3–4 (2008): 195–219.

Marx, Karl. *Capital: A Critique of Political Economy, Vol. 1*. Translated by Ben Fowkes. New York: Penguin Books, 1992.

Maulsby, Cathy, Frangiscos Sifakis, Danielle German, Colin P. Flynn, and David Holtgrave. "Partner Characteristics and Undiagnosed HIV Seropositivity among Men Who Have Sex with Men Only (MSMO) and Men Who Have Sex with Men and Women (MSMW) in Baltimore." *AIDS and Behavior* 16 (2012): 543–53.

McConnell, Michael, Jack Baker, and Gail Lander Karwoski. *The Wedding Heard 'round the World: America's First Gay Marriage*. Minneapolis: University of Minnesota Press, 2020.

McKay, Richard A. *Patient Zero and the Making of the AIDS Epidemic*. Chicago: University of Chicago Press, 2017.

Millett, Gregorio A., Stephen A. Flores, John L. Peterson, and Roger Bakeman. "Explaining Disparities in HIV Infection among Back and White Men Who Have Sex with Men: A Meta-Analysis of HIV Risk Behaviors." *AIDS* 21, no. 15 (2007): 2083–91.

Minkoff, Debra. *Organizing for Equality: The Evolution of Women's and Racial-Ethnic Organizations in America, 1955–1985*. New Brunswick, NJ: Rutgers University Press, 1995.

Mogul, Joey L., Andrea J. Ritchie, and Kay Whitlock. *Queer (In)Justice: The Criminalization of LGBT People in the United States*. Boston: Beacon Press, 2011.

Molina, Natalia. *Fit to Be Citizens? Public Health and Race in Los Angeles, 1879–1939*. Berkeley: University of California Press, 2006.

Montrie, Chad. *Whiteness in Plain View: A History of Racial Exclusion in Minnesota*. St. Paul: Minnesota Historical Society, 2022.

Moreton, Bethany. *To Serve God and Wal-Mart: The Making of Christian Free Enterprise*. Cambridge, MA: Harvard University Press, 2009.

Morgensen, Scott L. "Settler Homonationalism: Theorizing Settler Colonialism within Queer Modernities." *GLQ* 16, no. 1–2 (2010): 105–31.

———. *Spaces between Us: Queer Settler Colonialism and Indigenous Decolonization*. Minneapolis: University of Minnesota Press, 2011.

Muñoz, José Esteban. *The Sense of Brown*. Edited by Joshua Chambers-Letson and Tavia Nyong'o. Durham, NC: Duke University Press, 2020.

Muñoz, José Esteban. *Cruising Utopia: The Then and There of Queer Futurity*. New York: New York University Press, 2009.

———. *Disidentifications: Queers of Color and the Performance of Politics.* Minneapolis: University of Minnesota Press, 1999.

Murch, Donna. "The Color of War: Race, Neoliberalism, and Punishment in Late Twentieth Century Los Angeles." In *Neoliberal Cities: The Remaking of Postwar Urban America*, edited by Andrew J. Diamond and Thomas J. Sugrue. New York: New York University Press, 2020.

Murphy, Ryan P. *Deregulating Desire: Flight Attendant Activism, Family Politics, and Workplace Justice.* Philadelphia: Temple University Press, 2016.

Murphy, Ryan P., and Alex T. Urquhart. "Sexuality in the Headlines: Intimate Upheavals as Histories of the Twin Cities." In *Queer Twin Cities*, edited by Kevin P. Murphy et. al. Minneapolis: University of Minnesota Press, 2010.

Murray, Heather. *Not in This Family: Gays and the Meaning of Kinship in Postwar North America.* Philadelphia: University of Pennsylvania Press, 2012.

Myers, Samuel, Jr., and Inhyuck Ha. *Race Neutrality: Rationalizing Remedies to Racial Inequality.* Lanham, MD: Lexington Books, 2018.

Mykhalovskiy, Eric. "The Public Health Implications of HIV Criminalization: Past, Current, and Future Research Directions." *Critical Public Health* 25, no. 4 (2015): 373–85.

Nelson, Alondra. *Body and Soul: The Black Panther Party and the Fight against Medical Discrimination.* Minneapolis: University of Minnesota Press, 2011.

Nelson, Jennifer. *Women of Color and the Reproductive Rights Movement.* New York: New York University Press, 2003.

Nero, Charles I. "Why Are the Gay Ghettos White?" In *Black Queer Studies: A Critical Anthology*, edited by E. Patrick Johnson and Mae G. Henderson. Durham, NC: Duke University Press, 2005.

Newman, Oscar. *Defensible Space: Crime Prevention through Urban Design.* New York: Macmillan, 1972.

Paik, A. Naomi "Carceral Quarantine at Guantánamo: Legacies of US Imprisonment of Haitian Refugees, 1991–1994." *Radical History Review* 115 (2013): 142–68.

Painter, George. "History of Sodomy Laws." In *The Sensibilities of Our Fathers: The History of Sodomy Laws in the United States.* GLAPN: Gay & Lesbian Archives of the Pacific Northwest. Accessed May 10, 2022. https://www.glapn.org/sodomy laws/history/history.htm.

———. "Minnesota." In *The Sensibilities of Our Fathers: The History of Sodomy Laws in the United States.* GLAPN: Gay & Lesbian Archives of the Pacific Northwest. Accessed May 10, 2022. https://www.glapn.org/sodomylaws/sensibilities/minnesota.htm.

Pattillo, Mary. "Race, Poverty, and Neighborhood Planning in Chicago from the New Deal to Neoliberalism." In *Neoliberal Cities: The Remaking of Postwar Urban America*, edited by Andrew J. Diamond and Thomas J. Sugrue. New York: New York University Press, 2020.

Patton, Cindy. *Inventing AIDS.* New York: Routledge, 1990.

Perrow, Charles, and Mauro F. Guillén. *The AIDS Disaster: The Failure of Organizations in New York and the Nation.* New Haven, CT: Yale University Press, 1990.

Philipson, Thomas J., and Richard A. Posner. *Private Choices and Public Health: The AIDS Epidemic in an Economic Perspective.* Cambridge, MA: Harvard University Press, 1993.

Phillips-Fein, Kim. "The Politics of Austerity: The Moral Economy in 1970s New York." In *Neoliberal Cities: The Remaking of Postwar Urban America*, edited by Andrew J. Diamond and Thomas J. Sugrue. New York: New York University Press, 2020.

Plaster, Joseph. *Kids on the Street: Queer Kinship and Religion in San Francisco's Tenderloin.* Durham, NC: Duke University Press, 2023.

Pleck, Elizabeth H. *Not Just Roommates: Cohabitation after the Sexual Revolution.* Chicago: University of Chicago Press, 2012.

Puar, Jasbir K. *Terrorist Assemblages: Homonationalism in Queer Times.* Durham, NC: Duke University Press, 2007.

Queer Politics and the Future of AIDS Activism, edited by Dangerous Bedfellows. Cambridge, MA: South End Press, 1996.

Reddy, Chandan. "Home, Houses, Nonidentity: 'Paris Is Burning.'" In *Burning Down the House: Recycling Domesticity*, edited by Rosemary Marangoly George. Boulder, CO: Westview, 1997.

Redfield, Robert R., Phillip D. Markham, Syed Zaki Salahuddin, D. Craig Wright, M. G. Sarngadharan, and Robert C. Gallo. "Heterosexually Acquired HTLV-III/LAV Disease (AIDS-Related Complex and AIDS). Epidemiologic Evidence for Female-to-Male Transmission." *Journal of the American Medical Association* 254, no. 15 (1985): 2094–96.

Reeves, Jimmie L., and Richard Campbell. *Cracked Coverage: Television News, the Anti-Cocaine Crusade, and the Reagan Legacy.* Durham, NC: Duke University Press, 1994.

Reid, Debra A. "'The Whitest of Occupations'?: African Americans in the Rural Midwest, 1940–2010." In *The Rural Midwest since World War II*, edited by J. L. Anderson. Ithaca, NY: Cornell University Press, 2014.

Renfro, Paul M. *Stranger Danger: Family Values, Childhood, and the American Carceral State.* New York: Oxford University Press, 2020.

Rodríguez, Dylan. "The Political Logic of the Non-Profit Industrial Complex." In *The Revolution Will Not Be Funded: Beyond the Non-Profit Industrial Complex*, edited by Incite! Women of Color against Violence. Cambridge, MA: South End Press, 2007.

Rodríguez, Juana María. *Queer Latinidad: Identity Practices, Discursive Spaces.* New York: New York University Press, 2003.

Román, David. "Not-About-AIDS." *GLQ* 6, no. 1 (2000): 1–28.

Roque-Ramírez, Horacio N. "Claiming Queer Cultural Citizenship: Gay Latino (Im)Migrant Acts in San Francisco." In *Queer Migrations: Sexuality, U.S. Citizenship, and Border Crossings*, edited by Eithne Luibhéid and Lionel Cantú Jr. Minneapolis: University of Minnesota Press, 2005.

———. "Gay Latino Histories/Dying to Be Remembered: AIDS Obituaries, Public Memory, and the Queer Latino Archive." In *Beyond El Barrio: Everyday Life in*

Latina/o America, edited by Gina M. Pérez, Frank Guridy, and Adrian Burgos. New York: New York University Press, 2010.

Rothstein, Richard. *The Color of Law: A Forgotten History of How Our Government Segregated America*. New York: W. W. Norton, 2017.

Royles, Dan. *To Make the Wounded Whole: The African American Struggle against HIV/AIDS*. Chapel Hill: University of North Carolina Press, 2020.

Rubin, Gayle. "Thinking Sex: Notes for a Radical Theory of the Politics of Sexuality." In *The Lesbian and Gay Studies Reader*, edited by Henry Abelove, Michele Aina Barale, and David M. Halperin. New York: Routledge, 1993.

Rushbrook, Dereka. "Cities, Queer Space, and the Cosmopolitan Tourist." *GLQ* 8, no. 1–2 (2002): 183–206.

Satter, Beryl. *Family Properties: Race, Real Estate, and the Exploitation of Black Urban America*. New York: Metropolitan Books, 2009.

Schulman, Sarah. *The Gentrification of the Mind: Witness to a Lost Imagination*. Berkeley: University of California Press, 2013.

Scott, Damon. *The City Aroused: Queer Places and Urban Redevelopment in Postwar San Francisco*. Austin: University of Texas Press, 2023.

Sdunzik, Jennifer. *The Geography of Hate: The Great Migration through Small-Town America*. Urbana: University of Illinois Press, 2023.

Sears, Clare. *Arresting Dress: Cross-Dressing, Law, and Fascination in Nineteenth-Century San Francisco*. Durham, NC: Duke University Press, 2014.

Sears, James T. *Lonely Hunters: An Oral History of Lesbian and Gay Southern Life, 1948–1968*. New York: Basic Books, 1997.

Selik, Richard M., Kenneth G. Castro, and Marguerite Pappaioanou. "Racial/Ethnic Differences in the Risk of AIDS in the United States." *American Journal of Public Health* 78, no. 12 (1988): 1539–45.

Serlin, David. "Bathhouses." In *The Encyclopedia of American Lesbian, Gay, Bisexual, and Transgender History in America*, edited by Marc Stein. New York: Charles Scribner's Sons, 2004.

Shabazz, Rashad. *Spatializing Blackness: Architectures of Confinement and Black Masculinity in Chicago*. Urbana: University of Illinois Press, 2015.

Shah, Nayan. *Contagious Divides: Epidemics and Race in San Francisco's Chinatown*. Berkeley: University of California Press, 2001.

———. "Policing Privacy, Migrants, and the Limits of Freedom." *Social Text* 84–85, vol. 23, no. 3–4 (2005): 275–84.

Shevory, Thomas. *Notorious H.I.V.: The Media Spectacle of Nushawn Williams*. Minneapolis: University of Minnesota Press, 2004.

Shilts, Randy. *And the Band Played On: Politics, People, and the AIDS Epidemic*. New York: St. Martin's Press, 1987.

Shoemaker, Nancy. "Urban Indians and Ethnic Choices: American Indian Organizations in Minneapolis, 1920–1950." *Western Historical Quarterly* 19, no. 4 (1988): 431–47.

Sides, Josh. *Erotic City: Sexual Revolution and the Making of Modern San Francisco*. New York: Oxford University Press, 2009.

Simon, Patricia M., Edward V. Morse, Howard J. Osofsky, and Paul M. Balson. "HIV and Young Male Street Prostitutes: A Brief Report." *Journal of Adolescence* 17 (1994): 193–97.

Smith, Neil. *The New Urban Frontier: Gentrification and the Revanchist City.* New York: Routledge, 1996.

Snipp, C. Matthew. "American Indians and Alaska Natives in Urban Environments." In *Indigenous in the City: Contemporary Identities and Cultural Innovation*, edited by Evelyn Peters and Chris Andersen. Vancouver: University of British Columbia Press, 2013.

Somerville, Siobhan B. "Queer *Loving.*" *GLQ* 11, no. 3 (2005): 335–70.

Spade, Dean. *Mutual Aid: Building Solidarity during This Crisis (and the Next).* New York: Verso, 2020.

———. *Normal Life: Administrative Violence, Critical Trans Politics and the Limits of Law.* Brooklyn, NY: South End Press, 2011.

Spade, Dean, and Craig Willse. "Marriage Will Never Set Us Free." *Organizing Upgrade*. Last modified September 6, 2013. http://www.organizingupgrade.com/index.php/modules-menu/beyond-capitalism/item/1002-marriage-will-never-set-us-free.

Spear, Allan H. *Crossing the Boundaries: The Autobiography of Allan H. Spear.* Minneapolis: University of Minnesota Press, 2010.

Stein, Marc. *City of Sisterly and Brotherly Loves: Lesbian and Gay Philadelphia, 1945–1972.* Philadelphia: Temple University Press, 2004.

Stewart-Winter, Timothy. *Queer Clout: Chicago and the Rise of Gay Politics.* Philadelphia: University of Pennsylvania Press, 2016.

———. "Queer Law and Order: Sex, Criminality, and Policing in the Late Twentieth-Century United States." *Journal of American History* 102, no. 1 (2015): 61–72.

Strano, Andrea J. "Minnesota." In *Proud Heritage: People, Issues, and Documents of the LGBT Experience*, edited by Chuck Stewart. Santa Barbara, CA: ABC-CLIO, 2014.

Sugrue, Thomas J. *The Origins of the Urban Crisis: Race and Inequality in Postwar Detroit.* Princeton, NJ: Princeton University Press, 1996.

Taylor, Keeanga-Yamahtta. *Race for Profit: How Banks and the Real Estate Industry Undermined Black Homeownership.* Chapel Hill: University of North Carolina Press, 2019.

Tiemeyer, Phil. *Plane Queer: Labor, Sexuality, and AIDS in the History of Male Flight Attendants.* Berkeley: University of California Press, 2013.

Treichler, Paula A. *How to Have Theory in an Epidemic: Cultural Chronicles of AIDS.* Durham, NC: Duke University Press, 1999.

Trimble, Steve. *In the Shadow of the City: A History of the Loring Park Neighborhood.* Minneapolis: Minneapolis Community College Foundation, 1990.

Vaid, Urvashi. *Virtual Equality: The Mainstreaming of Gay & Lesbian Liberation.* New York: Anchor Books, 1995.

Van Cleve, Stewart. *Land of 10,000 Loves: A History of Queer Minnesota.* Minneapolis: University of Minnesota Press, 2012.

Venkatesh, Sudhir. *American Project: The Rise and Fall of a Modern Ghetto.* Cambridge, MA: Harvard University Press, 2000.

Vider, Stephen. "Public Disclosures of Private Realities: HIV/AIDS and the Domestic Archive." *The Public Historian* 41, no. 2 (2019): 163–89.

———. *The Queerness of Home: Gender, Sexuality, and the Politics of Domesticity after World War II.* Chicago: University of Chicago Press, 2021.

Walkowitz, Judith R. *Prostitution and Victorian Society: Women, Class, and the State.* Cambridge, UK: Cambridge University Press, 1982.

Wallace, Deborah, and Roderick Wallace. *A Plague on Your Houses: How New York Was Burned Down and National Public Health Crumbled.* New York: Verso, 1998.

Wallace, Roderick, Yi-Shan Huang, Peter Gould, and Deborah Wallace. "The Hierarchical Diffusion of AIDS and Violent Crime among U.S. Metropolitan Regions: Inner-City Decay, Stochastic Resonance and Reversal of the Mortality Transition." *Social Science & Medicine* 44, no. 7 (1997): 935–47.

Warner, Michael. *Publics and Counterpublics.* New York: Zone Books, 2005.

———. *The Trouble with Normal: Sex, Politics, and the Ethics of Queer Life.* Cambridge, MA: Harvard University Press, 1999.

Watkins-Hayes, Celeste. *Remaking a Life: How Women Living with HIV/AIDS Confront Inequality.* Berkeley: University of California Press, 2019.

Weston, Kath. "Get Thee to a Big City: Sexual Imaginary and the Great Gay Migration." *GLQ* 2, no. 3 (1995): 253–77.

White, Edmund. *States of Desire Revisited: Travels in Gay America.* Madison: University of Wisconsin Press, 2014.

Williamson, Terrion L., ed. *Black in the Middle: An Anthology of the Black Midwest.* Cleveland, OH: Belt Publishing, 2020.

Wilson Gilmore, Ruth. *Golden Gulag: Prisons, Surplus, Crisis, and Opposition in Globalizing California.* Berkeley: University of California Press, 2007.

Winunwe Rivers, Daniel. *Radical Relations: Lesbian Mothers, Gay Fathers, and Their Children in the United States since World War II.* Chapel Hill: University of North Carolina Press, 2013.

Wolf, Leslie E., and Richard Vezina. "Crime and Punishment: Is There a Role for Criminal Law in HIV Prevention Policy?" *Whittier Law Review* 25 (2004): 821–86.

Wolfe, Patrick. "Settler Colonialism and the Elimination of the Native." *Journal of Genocide Research* 8, no. 4 (2006): 387–409.

Woods, William J., and Diane Binson. *Gay Bathhouses and Public Health Policy.* New York: Harrington Park Press, 2003.

Yeros, Stathis G. *Queering Urbanism: Insurgent Spaces in the Fight for Justice.* Oakland: University of California Press, 2024.

Index

Italic page numbers refer to illustrations.

Abbott, Patti, 216, 217
accommodationism, 40, 123, 168; MCGR and, 56–57; resistance, 20, 28, 111. *See also* integrationism
ACLU (American Civil Liberties Union), 63; AIDS Projects, 139; Lesbian-Gay Rights Project, 64, 66, 67
activism: AIDS, 22, 24, 235; antiviolence, 92–93; "capturing the middle" strategy, 32; direct and confrontational approaches to, 37, 42, 55, 201, 215; "domestic," 12–13; gay, 35–36, 175–76; "gay liberation" vs. "gay civil rights," 31–32; and gay street patrols, 55; health, 233; integration vs. liberation, 34, 40, 61; radical, 8–9; radical farm movement, 162; radical to mainstream shift, 32–33
ACT UP/Minnesota, 58, 136, 151, 199–200, 211, 238
Ad Hoc Committee on Liberty, 64
adoption, 34–35, 64
adult bookstores, 49–50, 52–53, 82–83, 185, 186, 200
adultery laws, 66, 79, 86. *See also* sodomy laws
The Advocate (magazine), 1, 36, 74, 96
Agar, Tom, 148
age-of-consent laws, 65, 68, 70–71, 74–75, 258n60. *See also* minors
AIDS activism, 22, 24, 235
AIDS crisis: and antigay violence, 92, 95–99; criminalization and defamation of HIV positive people, 85, 124–27, 131, 133, 151; erasure of in public discourse, 11; gay men as "victims" of, 160–68; homecoming narratives, 163–65; Indigenous response to, 235–36; "innocent" vs. "guilty" binary, 130; media representations of heterosexual patients during, 129; and monogamy, 82, 228–31; and moral panic, 128, 129–30, 268n17; "non-compliant carrier" law (Minnesota), 138; overview and history of, 20–24; "Play It Safe" campaign, 109, *110*; quarantine and isolation orders during, 137–38; responses to, 11–12, 22; segregation, exclusion, and vulnerability during, 20; and sex workers, 127–36; and social service infrastructure, 234; and structural vulnerabilities, 23, 134, 270n52
AIDS epidemic: buddy caregiver programs, 98–99; contact tracing, 131–32; heterosexual transmission, 139–40; HIV awareness campaigns, 109; overview and history of, 61–62, 80–89; private caregiving in domestic spaces, 22–23; public health data, 20–21; and "risky behaviors," 23–24; and women of child-bearing age, 130–31. *See also* HIV (human immunodeficiency virus)
AIDS in the Heartland (Banaszynski), 163–68, *164*
Alexander, Ferris, 50, 182, 184–85
Alexander, Priscilla, 142

American Civil Liberties Union (ACLU), 63; AIDS Projects, 139; Lesbian-Gay Rights Project, 64, 66, 67
American Foundation for AIDS Research (amfAR), 140
American Indian Gays and Lesbians, 234–35
American Indian Movement (AIM), 55
American Law Institute (ALI), 66–67
American Society for the Prevention of Cruelty to Children, 72
amyl nitrite ("poppers"), 109–11
Anderson, Glen H., 189
Anderson, Jim, 112, 161
Anderson, Richard, 223
Anderson, Roxanne "Rox," 236, 290n17
Anderson, Wendell, 15–16, 31
And the Band Played On (Shilts), 168, 170–71, 172
Anishinaabe people, 17
antigay violence, 92; activism in response to, 92–93; history of, 95–96; House Judiciary Subcommittee hearings on, 121–22; increase in, 95–99; in Minneapolis, 93; NGLTF reports on, 95, 96; systemic nature of, 101–2
antipornography movement, 49
antiretroviral therapy (HAART), 150, 238, 239
Armstrong, Elizabeth, 10
Aryan Nations, 107
"ascendancy of whiteness," 15
Ashton, Mary Madonna, 136, 157–58, 171
Asmundson, Dean, 201, 211, 215, 223
Atkins, Annette, 8
AZT (first FDA-approved HIV treatment), 165

Backer, Howard, 161–62, 166
Baker, Jack, 29–31, 30, 32–34, 36–38
Banaszynski, Jacqui, 163, 166, 167; Aids in the Heartland, 163–68, 164
Banks, Darryl, 121, 267n79

bathhouses, 21, 39–40; antibathhouse ordinance, 186–88; Big Daddy's, 39, 41–42, 48, 169; closure of, 153–57, 169–72; as divisive issue, 46; as "gay space," 175–76; narratives of, 160–61; and "Play It Safe!" public service announcements, 179–81; rebranding and upgrading of, 179–81; as symbol of homophobia, 183; vice squad raids, 41–42, 43–44, 47–49; and zoning amendments, 178
Bathhouses, Sexual Freedom, and the Law (community forum), 173–74, 176–77, 185–86
Batza, Katie, 12
Belton, Sharon Sayles, 186
Benscoter, Les, 57–58, 95
Berean League, 81, 86
Berglin, Linda, 122–23
Bérubé, Allan, 39
Bias, Willie, 120
Big Daddy's bathhouse, 39, 41–42, 48, 169. *See also* bathhouses
Black Americans: and HIV infection inequities, 127–30, 133–35; racialized stereotypes of, 121, 127–28; urban migrants, 103–4
Black Panther Party, 9
blood transfusions and HIV transmission, 129
Bois Forte Band, Ojibwe, 234
Bonilla-Silva, Eduardo, 6
Bouza, Anthony, 47–48, 49–50, 52, 60, 98; community forum about violence, 118–20; and gay liaison, 119–20; and investigation of unsolved homicides, 104–5
Bowers v. Hardwick, 25, 63–68, 75, 88–89
Brandl, John, 138
Bridges, Fabian, 124, 126–27, 142–51, *143*
Brier, Jennifer, 12, 22
Britt, Harry, 21
Broadway Bookstore, 186
Brockway, Bruce, 20, 160

Brokaw, Tom, 128
A Brother's Touch Bookstore, 71
Brown, Howard, 33
Brown, Richard "Dick," 153, *154*, 156, 158–60, 168–69, 173, 177, 183, 206
Brown, Wendy, 22
Brucciani, Leonard, 195
Bryant, Anita, 37, 72
BSR Properties, 182
Buchanan v. Batchelor, 65
Buckley, William F., 148
Buns and Roses (bookstore), 186
Bureau of Criminal Apprehension (BCA), 70
Bureau of Indian Affairs, 17
Burger, Warren, 64
Burk, Dwight, 129
Bush, George H. W., 122
Butler, Judith, 101
Buttigieg, Pete, 232

Cacho, Lisa, 103
Campbell, Tim: on anticruising legislation, 199; on antisodomy legislation, 87; on bathhouse safety and regulation, 42, 46, 54, 174–75; on escort services, 98; on gay rights, 204–5; on gentrification, 204–5; and Hofstede 9, 41; and lawsuit against city of Minneapolis, 50; and liaison with police investigations, 118–19; liberationist approaches of, 34–36; on Loring Park, 56; and protest at Carlson's home, 201–3; and safety tips for gay men, 111; on sex workers, 136, 148–49; on "vampire theory," 71; and vice squads, 179
Canaday, Margot, 19
capitalism, 13
CARE (Comprehensive AIDS Resources Emergency) Act, 129, 139
Carlson, Arne, 36, 90, 214
Carlson, Barbara, 196, 197–99, 201–3, 202, 208
Castells, Manuel, 21

Castile, Philando, 23
Center for Media and Public Affairs, 129
"charmed circle," 77–78, 125
Chateauvert, Melinda, 130
Chauncey, George, 39
Chenoweth, John, 211, *213*, 215
Chicago, IL, 9
child custody cases, 64
Chow, Rey, 15
Christian Right, 72, 93
Churchill, Robert, 104, 120
Ciao! (magazine), 39
citizen patrols, 222, 223
Citizens Alert for Morality (CAM), 37
Citizens for a Loring Park Community (CLPC), 196–97, 207, 208–11, 220–22; Loring Park Neighborhood Action Plan, 222; Noise and Safety Committee, 221, 222
City Pages (newspaper), 224, 230
Clark, Karen, 52–53, 66, 77–79, 87–88, 122; and Minnesota Human Rights Act, 238; and "non-compliant carrier" law, 138
Classen, Julia, 78, 79, 87
Cleveland, OH, 144–45
Cloud 9 (gay bar), 98, 184
Club Baths (bathhouse), 178
Coalition of Concerned Gays, 34, 36
Cohen, Cathy J., 130, 149–50, 241n3
Cohen, Dan, 54
Community United Against Violence (CUAV), 92–93, 109, 214; and criminalization of "others," 112; and MAP, 111; on monogamy, 112; on punitive policing, 122; and "safe sex" PSAs, 112–18, *113*, *115*, *116*; San Francisco, 96; Violence Awareness Month (1986), 112–14
Concerned Women for America, 86
condom use, 83, 111, 181
conformity, 7
consent, 65, 68, 70–71, 74–75, 258n60
Conservative Digest (magazine), 88

Index   309

conservative fundamentalism, 96. *See also* religiosity
convict lease system, 126
Conyers, John, 121–22
Couch, Terry, 56
Coyle, Brian J.: and community forum about violence, 118–20; and domestic partnership ordinance, 224–25, 227–28; on domestic stability and homeownership, 226–27; on HIV-positive individuals, 85, 92–93; HIV status and health of, 97–98, 227; on Minneapolis protests, 64–65; on monogamous lifestyles, 189–90; on police budget increase, 107–8; political career and identity of, 51, 51–52; on punitive policing, 122; and "safe sex" messages, 111; on sexual morality, 106–7; on sodomy laws, 63; and 315 Health Club, 156, 157–58, 172–77; in town hall meeting, 147–48
COYOTE (Call Off Your Old Tired Ethics), 142
crack cocaine, 105–6; "crack houses," 155
Crespino, Joseph, 6–7
Crimp, Douglas, 128–29
Cronkite, Walter, 29
cruising: complaints about, 197–98, *198*; in gay culture, 207; and gentrification in Loring Park, 220–24; and HIV prevention, 203–4; and monogamous lifestyles, 224–28

Dahmer, Jeffrey, 210
The Daily Show with Jon Stewart (television series), 1–4, *2*, 232
Dakota people, 17
Darling, Ken, 209–10, 217, 220
Darrow, William W., 141
Dauphin, Erv, 41–42
Day, Sharon, 234
Dayton, Mark, 165
deindustrialization and migration, 102
Delany, Samuel, 187

DeMars, Lou, 42
Democratic-Farmer-Labor (DFL) Party, 31, 78, 162
Dobrotka, David, 211
Doe v. Ventura, 90–91
"domestic activism," 12–13
domestic partnerships, 177–78; domestic partnership ordinance, 224–28. *See also* same-sex marriage
Donahue, John Clark, 70–71
Downtown Profile (journal), 195
Drake, Dallas, 11, 58, 223
Draszt, Cord, 211
drug economy, 133–34; crack cocaine, 105–6, 155
Dugas, Gaëtan, 170
Duggan, Lisa, 2
Dworkin, Andrea, 49, 183, 225
Dwyer, Donald, 43, 45, 46, 48
Dziedzic, Walter, 107

Eagle Forum, 86
Elton John, 129
Endean, Steve, 31–36, 38–39, 80
Engstrom, Eric, 158
Enke, Finn, 5
Equal Time (newspaper): on AIDS as threat to gay community, 99; Backer profile, 161–62; on bathhouse ordinances, 158, 177, 184; on cruising culture, 204; on Loring Park, 192, 199; Osborne letter, 208; racist public service ad in, 158–59, *159*; Runyon profile, 161; on WCCO feature, 146, 147
Essence (magazine), 130
exceptionalism: gay, 61; Southern, 6

FAB (protest group), 36
F.A.G.S. (Friends Against Gay Suppression), 200–201, 205–7, *206*, 238
Fair Housing Act (1968), 17
Faludi, Susan, 129
Falwell, Jerry, 137
Farrell, Patrick, 107

310 Index

Federal Housing Administration (FHA), 17; mortgage guidelines and biases, 19
feminism, 49, 183, 225
Ferguson, Roderick, 101
Fight Repression of Erotic Expression (FREE), 29
Fischer, Mary, 132
Fladmark, Jerry, 53, 176, 207, 209, 220–21, 227
Florida, Richard, 24, 182
Floyd, George, 23
Foley, Tom, 57–58
fornication laws, 79
Foucault, Michel, 190
Fowler, Peter, 67
Fraser, Donald: on adult bookstores, 52; on antibathhouse ordinance, 183; fundraising for AIDS patients by, 165; and Gay Pride Day, 72; and Minneapolis Police Department, 43, 44, 47–48, 118–19, 179, 215; and war on drugs, 106
Fresh Fruit (radio series), 178
Frontline (television series), 124, 126–27, 142–50

"Ganawenima" (to take care of), 234
Gary, IN, 102
Gary Syndrome, 93–95, 102–3, 105–6, 112; and blame for crime, 125; and Fabian Bridges, 151; and criminalization of HIV, 142; and Larson and Chenoweth homicides, 215–16
Gateway Urban Renewal Plan, 18, 191
Gay Activists Alliance, 71
Gay and Lesbian Community Action Council (GLCAC), 173, 216, 217, 222
Gay and Lesbian Freedom Pac, 172–73
Gay and Lesbian Hate Crimes Awareness Day, 214
Gay and Lesbian Police Community Task Force, 217–18
Gay and Lesbian Pride Day, 72
"gayborhoods," 219, 221
Gay Community News (newspaper), 36

Gay Community Services, 56
"gay ghettos," 226
Gay House (community center), 31, 55, 233–34
gay identity: coastal-centric focus, 5; "flamboyant" vs. "straight-looking," 34–35; Midwestern, 183–84; of older gay men, 98–99; "old" vs. "new" gay, 1, 232; and "vampire theory" of homosexuality, 71, 72; "white habitus" and normative whiteness, 5–6, 9. *See also* identity formation
gay liberation vs. gay civil rights, 31–32
gay lifestyles: cruising culture, 190–91, 207; dating and monogamy, 111–14, 224–28; domestic partnerships and conservativism, 177–78; in inner-city neighborhoods, 19; promiscuity, 61, 89–90, 161, 162–63, 186; and risk, 97–99, 109
Gay Officers Action League (GOAL), 120
"gay panic" defense, 59, 92, 96, 125
gay populations: and antigay public sentiment, 37–38; closeted, 54–55, 68, 69, 98, 158, 177; and Minneapolis Police Department, 102–8; as targets of harassment, 54–55; and victimhood, 161–63, 165
Gay Pride Day, 41
Gay Rights Alliance of Minneapolis (GRAM), 147
Gay Rights Legislative Committee (GRLC), 32–33
gay rights movement: civil rights issue vs. sexual revolution, 204; history of in Minneapolis, 28–39; integrationism, 9–10, 87–88; national lobbying efforts for, 38
Gay Rights National Lobby (GRNL), 38
Gaze Magazine, 223
Gaze-TV, 215
Geary, Adam M., 19, 20
gender dysphoria, 100
Gender Girls program, 236

gender nonconformity, 100–101
gentrification, 155–56, 178–79, 196, 204–5, 219, 241nn8–9; "of the mind," 228
Gerlicher, Scott, 223
Gerstle, Gary, 13
Ghaziani, Amin, 230
Gilmore, Ruth Wilson, 126
Glaser, Elizabeth, 132
Glaser, Paul, 132
GLC Voice (newspaper): on bathhouses, 40, 42, 173, 175; Campbell's leadership of, 34, 87, 136, 179, 199, 204–5; on Olson case, 85; on sex workers and MPD, 136; on sodomy laws, 74
GLQ (journal), 7
Golden Valley neighborhood (Minneapolis), 230
Gonzalez, Carmen, 151
Goodspeed, Lyle, 54, 132
Governor's Task Force on Gay and Lesbian Minnesotans, 89, 90
Governor's Task Force on Prejudice and Violence, 107, 122
Gray, Richard Gordon, Jr., 72–75, 80
Great Gay Migration, 5
Greenfield, Lee, 78, 79, 83, 86
Greenway Gables, 193–94, *194*
GRID (gay-related immunodeficiency), 128
Griswold v. Connecticut, 65
guardian myth, 129–30

HAART (antiretroviral therapy), 150, 238, 239
Halberstam, Jack, 5
Halfhill, Robert, 74, 173, 175, 178, 192, 196–97, 200, 258n61
Halverson, Britt E., 15
Haney López, Ian, 102–3
Hanhardt, Christina B., 93–95
Hanson, Richard "Dick," 160, 162–68, *164*, 178
Hardwick, Michael, 63, 75
Harteau, Janeé, 23, 238

Harvey, David, 13
hate crimes, 96; Minnesota legislation on, 122–23. *See also* violence
Hate Crimes Statistics Act (1990), 122
heartland myth, 7, 15, 184
Heim, Clint, 153, *157*
hemophilia, 128–29
Hennepin Baths, 39, 169. *See also* bathhouses
Henningson, Bert, *164*, 165, 166, 167
"heterotopias," 190
Higgins, Thom, 34, 37
Hilary, Sandra, 169, 171, 185
Hill, Ray, 146
HIV (human immunodeficiency virus): hypothesis of transmission, 139–41; criminalization of, 124–27, 141, 150; ELISA test, 140; men infected by women, 139–40; prevention and anticruising legislation, 203–4; statistics, 239; testing, 81, 88, 89; transmission patterns, 139–40
Hofstede, Albert, 40–42, 43, 56–57
Hofstede 9, 41–42, 48
Hoganson, Kristin L., 7, 15
homecoming narratives, 163–65, 168
homelessness, 84–85, 90; transient populations, 104–5
homeownership, 17–18, 226
Homestead Act (1862), 17, 244n60
homonormativity, 171; as dominant lifestyle, 111; "new," 2
homophobia: internalized, 216–17; of New Right, 22; under Reagan administration, 61–62; and AIDS, 96
homosexuality, criminalization of, 19, 63–64
Hoppe, Trevor, 126
Houle, David R., 58–59
House Judiciary Subcommittee on Criminal Justice, 92
housing, affordable, 84–85
Housing Acts (1949 and 1954), 18
Housing and Urban Development (HUD), Department of, 84, 195

Howard, Clayton, 10
Howard, John, 6
Hubbard, Phil, 77, 190
Hudson, Rock, 163
Human Rights Campaign, 5; Human Rights Campaign Fund (HRCF), 38
Humphrey, Hubert, III, 74
Hunter, Nan D., 64, 67, 139

identity formation: in San Francisco, 10; identity-based advocacy, 10; Midwest as collective identity, 7. See also gay identity
Ikĉé Wiĉáša (Common Man) program, 235
Indian Relocation Act (1956), 17
Indian Removal, 17
Indigenous people, 17, 85, 234–35, 289n11; marginalization of, 101
Infectious Ideas (Brier), 12
"innocence": protection of, 144; white, 7
integrationism, 49–54, 160; and middleness, 9–10; Minneapolis vice squad encounters (pre-AIDS), 52, 54; and monogamy, 147–48; and private space, 21–22. See also accommodationism
intersectionality: and queer Indigenous people, 234–35, 261n114, 289n11; of race and sexuality, 9, 20, 23, 85, 90, 246n88
Iowa Supreme Court, 80

Jackson, MS, 127
James, Marcus, 215–16
Jet (magazine), 130
Johnson, Earvin "Magic," 130
Johnson, Jay, 216–17
Johnson, Thomas L., 45, 46, 59, 135
Jones, Jason, 1–3, 2
Jones, William, 210

Kahn, Phyllis, 52–53
Kastner, Lyle E., 96–97
Keate, Ken, 49–50

Kieley, John J., 96–97
Kissling, Gerald, 57
Knudsen, Terry, 56–57, 59, 95
Krim, Mathilde, 140–41

LaFortune, Richard, 234–35
Lambda Legal Defense and Education Fund, 66, 67, 69, 75
Lambda Squad, 55
Larson, Joel, 210–11, 213, 215, 286n128
Lassiter, Matthew D., 6–7
Latimer, George, 165
Laux, John, 211, 215, 217, 219
Lawrence v. Texas, 91
Lee, Edd, 235
Lesbian Feminist Organizing Committee (LFOC), 53
LGBTQ populations: closeted lifestyles of, 69; diversity of in Midwest, 8; oppression of, 40–41; as parents, 64; and public space, 21; use of terms, 241n3; violence against, 55–58, 107–8. See also gay populations
Locke, John, 41–42
Locker Room bathhouse, 39–40, 43–44; raids and charges from, 44–47. See also 315 Health Club (bathhouse)
Loring Community Oriented Policing Program (L-COPP), 222
Loring Park Development District (LPDD), 191, 193, 195
Loring Park neighborhood (Minneapolis), 19; anticruising legislation in, 197–208; citizen patrols in, 222, 223; Citizens for a Loring Park Community (CLPC), 208–11; gentrification of, 219–24, 229; history and overview of, 190–92; Laurel Village, 182; "livability" and street noise in, 209–10; murders, 210–17, 213, 214; and sex workers, 59–60, 69, 75–76; sting operations in, 189; urban renewal in, 192–97; violence in, 56, 58–59
Loring Park Neighborhood Action Plan, 221–22

Index   313

Loring Park Shelter Building, 196
Lubinski, Sharon, 217, 221
Lurie, David, 169, 171
Lutheran Social Services, 31

MacKinnon, Catherine, 49, 183, 225
Manalansan, Martin, 2, 7
"man/boy love," 71. *See also* North American Man/Boy Love Association (NAMBLA)
Marion County, IN, 169
Marx, Karl, 126
The Mary Tyler Moore Show (television series), 104
mass incarceration, 13, 126–27
Matthews, Tyrone, 127, 131, 267n12
McArthur, James, 191
McCarthy, Jack, 100, 102, 105, 118–19, 121
McClellan, Stephen, 66, 74
McConnell, Michael, 29, 31, 233
Mehring, John, 186–87
mental health institutions, 84
Metcalf, Nick, 235, 237
"Metro Center '85" plan, 193
"metronormativity," 5
middleness: and AIDS, 21; as analytical tool, 10–11; concept of, 3; and exclusion, 14–20; Midwest embodiment of, 7–8; and neoliberalism, 11–14; and sympathy for white gay men, 168
Midwest: and AIDS crisis, 11–12; collective identity of, 7; definitions and boundaries of, 4–5; gay life in, 2–3; "middleness" of, 3; stereotypes of, 2, 15, 183–84
Miller, Dennis, 46
Miller, Mark, 57–58
Miller-Schroeder Municipals, Inc., 42
Minkoff, Debra, 61
Minneapolis, MN: antibathhouse ordinance in, 186–88; anticruising ordinance in, 191–92; demographics of, 102, 190; Department of Community Planning and Economic Development, 193; downtown development in, 42–43; Gateway Urban Renewal Plan, 18; gay rights in, 28–39; Golden Valley neighborhood, 230; Greenway Gables, 193–94, *194*; Hennepin Avenue, 19; "High Risk Sexual Conduct" ordinance, 183; "Metro Center '85" development plan, 193; Mississippi River Flats, 211; Neighborhood Revitalization Program (NRP), 221; as "new" gay city, 1–4, *2*; Nicollet Mall, 193; Police-Community Relations Task Force, 50; Powderhorn neighborhood, 53; urban renewal in, 9–10, 18–19. *See also* Loring Park neighborhood (Minneapolis)
Minneapolis City Council, 33
Minneapolis Commission on Civil Rights, 44, 64, 118; domestic partnership ordinance, 225
Minneapolis Community and Technical College (MCTC), 193
Minneapolis Men (escort agency), 135
Minneapolis Planning Commission, 42, 54
Minneapolis Police Academy, 50
Minneapolis Police Department (MPD): and AIDS crisis, 82–83; and antigay violence, 93–95; Bouza's leadership of, 47–48, 53–54; budget increase, 107–8; corruption in, 43; and gay communities, 102–21, 264n38; and gay liaison, 119–20; gay officers in, 217–18; and homicides, 96–98, 104–5; and lawsuits by sex establishments, 50–51; liaison with GLCAC, 217; patrol initiative in Loring Park, 210; vice squad, 40–43, 47–48, 53–54, 179
Minneapolis Tribune (newspaper), 37–38
Minneapolis Tribune Picture Magazine, 192

Minnesota: Gay Rights Legislative Committee (GRLC), 32–33; House Judiciary Committee, 86; racial disparities in, 15–16; racial history of, 17; same-sex marriage legalization in, 5; Senate Judiciary Committee, 86; sodomy laws in, 67
Minnesota AIDS Project (MAP), 109, 156, 158, 181, 211; and CUAV, 111; Human Rights Committee, 87
Minnesota Alliance Against AIDS (MAAA), 87, 138, 148, 173, 175
Minnesota American Indian AIDS Task Force (MAIATF), 234–35
Minnesota Citizens Concerned for Life, 86
Minnesota Civil Liberties Union (MCLU), 66, 74, 138, 174
Minnesota Coalition for Privacy, 78, 79–80, 90
Minnesota Committee for Gay and Lesbian Rights (MCGLR), 38, 87, 178, 214
Minnesota Committee on Gay Rights (MCGR), 32–33, 46, 56–57, 63
Minnesota Department of Health (MDH), 131–32
Minnesota Gay and Lesbian Legal Assistance, 138
Minnesota Gay Defense Fund, 46, 71
Minnesota Gender Identity Association, 34
Minnesota Human Rights Act, 90, 238
Minnesota Mattachine Society, 54
Minnesota Men of Color (MMC), 235–38
Minnesota Miracle, 16, 18
Minnesota Nice, 8; and exclusion, 14–16; and middle-class ideals, 100–101; and racial attitudes, 103, 107
Minnesota Paradox, 15, 17–18
Minnesota Public Health Association (MPHA), 81–82
minors, 65, 68, 70–71, 74–75, 258n60. *See also* age-of-consent laws

Mississippi River Flats, 211
Model Penal Code (American Law Institute), 66–67
modesty, 8
monogamy: casual sex and violence, 118–19; monogamous lifestyles, 111–14, 224–28; prevalence and promotion of, 61–62, 160. *See also* integrationism
"moral geographies," 77
Moral Majority Report (Falwell), 137
Morbidity and Mortality Weekly Report (CDC), 141
Municipal Equality Index (MEI), 5
Muñoz, José Esteban, 187, 233
Myers, Samuel L., 15

Nadeau, Chantal, 7
Nadler, Mark, 165
National Children with AIDS Awareness Day, 133
National Farmers Organization, 162
National Gay and Lesbian Task Force (NGLTF), 95, 96; Violence Project, 92
National Gay Rights Advocates, 69
National Gay Task Force, 33
Neighborhood Revitalization Program (NRP), 221
Neoliberal Cities (Diamond and Sugrue), 18
neoliberalism, 124; and carceral aims, 126; and "disposable" populations, 126; and health care, 13; and health crisis, 13–14; and homonormativity, 2; and "middleness," 11–14; and privatization of social welfare, 22–23; and urban space restructuring, 178; values of, 3, 89
neo-Nazis, 107
Nevada: mandatory HIV testing in, 138–39; murder charges for sex workers in, 139
New Hampshire Supreme Court, 64
New Right, 22

Index 315

No More Assault Project (NMAP), 55–56
Nordlund, Elmer, 42, 43, 56–57
North American Man/Boy Love Association (NAMBLA), 71–72, 74
Northland Companion (newspaper), 20

Ojibwe people, 234
Olhoft, Wayne, 86
Olson, Phyllis, 85, 99–101, 121, 131, 261n110, 261n114
Orth, Carrie, 174
Osborne, Richard, 207–8
Osterholm, Michael, 134

Parents and Friends of Lesbians and Gays, 87
patriarchal structures, 105, 130, 165, 232
Patterson, James, 59
Pattillo, Mary, 13
Peck, Claude, 178
Pediatric AIDS Foundation, 132
pedophilia, 37, 60, 68, 70–72
Perpich, Rudy, 89, 165
Peterson, Donna, 78–79, 80, 83
Philadelphia, PA, 9
Phillipson, Tomas, 89–90
pie throwing, 37
"Play It Safe!" campaign, 92–93, *94*, 109, *110*
"poppers" (amyl nitrite), 109–11
pornography, 49
Positively Gay (newspaper), 42, 58, 160
Posner, Richard, 89–90
poverty: and crime, 104–5; and migration from Rust Belt, 102; neoliberal views of, 103; and victimization, 95
PrEP (pre-exposure prophylaxis), 150
Presidential Commission on the HIV Epidemic, 139
Preston, John, 31, 233
privacy: and court decisions, 68–76; and HIV testing, 89–90; right to, 46, 64–65; sexual, 10; and unhoused persons, 90

private space: and consensual sex, 63; legal definitions of, 77–78; politicization of, 12–13; and public space, 48; "zone of privacy," 46, 75, 185. *See also* public space
privatization, economic, 22–23
promiscuity, 61, 89–90, 161, 162–63, 186
prostitution. *See* sex workers
Puar, Jasbir, 15
public health: and decriminalization of sodomy, 86–87; gay sex and AIDS, 81
Public Health Advisory Committee, 172
public space: during AIDS crisis, 21–22; and communal care, 187–88; criminalization of sex in, 84; desexualization of, 21; loss of for LGBTQ people, 21; public vs. private sex, 2, 77–78, 101, 274n19. *See also* private space

quarantine: bathhouse closure as, 169–72; quarantine orders, 127–36
Queer Nation, 200
queer of color critique, 4, 12, 23, 90
Queer Street Patrol, 287n143

Rachner, Mary Jane, 82
racial issues: cross-racial alliances, 9; George Floyd murder, 23; health inequities, 239; housing, 17–18; in Minnesota, 17; racial disparities, 15–16; in Twin Cities, 16–17; white gay men and Gary Syndrome, 93–95
racism: and Black sexuality, 133–35; and "Black underclass," 105–7; and criminalization of "others," 112; and *Equal Time* "public service" ad, 158–59, *159*; and neoliberal policies, 124; and racially coded language, 102–3, 112; white vs. Black sex workers, 133–36
"radical care," 26, 233, 239
Rainville, Alice, 54, 169, 182
Rand, Rebecca, 41, 141–42
Rankila, Gary, 64, 147–48

Ray, Randy, 129
Ray, Robert, 129
Rayford, Robert, 276n58
Reagan, Ronald, 38, 139; budget cuts, 84. *See also* Reagan administration
Reagan administration, 61, 102–3; and AIDS, 170
Red Door Clinic, 135, 187
redistributive politics, 10
religiosity: Midwest vs. South, 6; religious conservatives, 88, 96
Renfro, Paul M., 70
Reno, Joshua O., 15
Reynolds, Scott, 135–36, 139
Riga, Fred, 99–101
Ritter, J. C., 99
Rittman, John, 62
Robertson, Pat, 217
Rodríguez, Juana María, 27
Rodriguez, Richard T., 7
Rubenfeld, Abby, 75
Rubin, Gayle, 77–78, 125
Runyon, Bill, 161
Rust Belt cities, 16, 102
Ryan White Comprehensive AIDS Resources Emergency Act, 129, 139
Rybak, R. T., 5

"safe sex" messages, 111, 112–14, *113*, 179–81
Saloon (gay bar), 112, 161
same-sex marriage, 228–31, 238; Jack Baker and Michael McConnell, 29–31; legalization of in Minnesota, 5, 23. *See also* domestic partnerships
San Francisco, CA, 232; Community United Against Violence, 92, 96; gay identity in, 10; Gay Men's Chorus, 1, 11; as "old gay" city, 1
Satterfield, Sharon, 79
"Save Our Children" campaign, 72
Sawina, Tom, 199, 219, 220
Schlafly, Phyllis, 86
Schroeder, Dennis, 41, 42
Schulman, Sarah M., 20, 228–29

Schwartz, Patrick, 42, 48
Seelig, Tim, 1, 11
self-defense classes, 58
self-esteem, 117–18
Sero Project, 150
Severson, Dean, 171
sexuality: casual sex, 93–95, 98–99; liberation and expression of, 161
sex workers, 41–42, 43; and Black populations, 125, 134–36; and heterosexual HIV transmission, 139–41; and "high-risk gays," 99–101; HIV status of, 127–36, 137–42; HIV testing of, 138–39; and Loring Park neighborhood, 59–60, 69, 75–76; proactive efforts by, 141–42; stigmatization of, 85–86; targeting of in anticruising legislation, 205; US PROStitutes Collective, 139
Shambach, Eric, 173, 200, 223
Shilts, Randy, 140, 168, 170–71, 172, 276n55
Simon, Nancy, 133
Simon, Richard, 200–201, *214*, 223
Smith, Greg, 59, 255n177
Smith, Neil, 182
sodomy laws, 45, 208; and AIDS and public health, 81–89; and *Bowers v. Hardwick*, 63–68; and *Buchanan v. Batchelor*, 65; constitutionality of, 90; and decriminalization and public health, 86–87; in *Gray* case, 74–76; and *Griswold v. Connecticut*, 65; and GRLC, 32; and heterosexual couples, 78–79; and post-*Bowers* decision, 73; prevalence of, 67; repeal of, 63, 66, 88–89, 118, 238
Somerville, Siobhan, 7
Somos Familias (We Are Families) program, 235
Soul Force, 55
"Southern exceptionalism," 6–7
spaces: bathhouses as "gay space," 175–76; "brown commons," 233. *See also* private space; public space

Index   317

Spade, Dean, 88
"spatial fixes," 13–14, 62, 93, 125–26, 238
Spear, Allan H.: on antigay violence, 215; background of and approach to "equality," 33–36, 38; community forum on sodomy law, 66, 79; and gay rights legislation, 87; on HIV testing, 81; on integrationism, 52–53; and Minnesota Human Rights Act, 238; and "non-compliant carrier" law, 138; on privacy and sodomy repeal, 118; and Senate Judiciary Committee, 86; on sodomy laws, 77, 78–79; on Winton's case, 69
Staples, Lee, 234–35
Stark, Matthew, 74, 87
Star Tribune (newspaper), 104, 131, 132–33
State v. Gray, 74
State v. Nelson, 68
State v. Price, 80
Stein, Marc, 9
Stenvig, Charles, 40–41
stereotypes: AIDS and gay men, 81, 88, 177; Black criminality, 121; Black sexuality, 133–35; gay male promiscuity, 61, 89–90, 161, 162–63, 186; Midwest, 2, 15, 183–84; pedophilia among gay men, 37, 60, 68, 70–72, 74; "queer criminal archetype," 100–101
Stewart-Winter, Timothy, 9, 108
St. George, Jim, 109, *110*, 156, 158, 176, 184, 227
Stoddard, Thomas, 67
St. Paul, MN, 37
St. Paul Pioneer Press Dispatch (newspaper), 86–87, 102, 104, 163, 165, 173
street theater, 37, 42, 201, 215. *See also* activism
Strickland, Scott, 176
"structural vulnerabilities," 23, 134, 270n52
Sugrue, Thomas J., 16
Sullivan, Gene, 72

Take Back the Night marches, 58
Target City Coalition (TCC), 37, 178, 238
Taylor, Robert Allan, 58–59, 95
Theissen, Brad, 179, 225–26
Thorstad, David, 71–72
315 Health Club (bathhouse), 153, *154*, 156–58, *157*, 166, 169, 172, *180*; closure of, 181–82; "Play It Safe!" public service announcements in, 179–81; public efforts to close, 172–78. *See also* bathhouses
Tiggas, Jon, 98–99
Time (magazine), 15–16, 102
transgender advocacy, 34, 261n110
transgender people, 85, 236; in gay rights legislation, 87
"transvestites," 34–35, 85
Trisko, Thomas, 61–62
Twin Cities: contemporary economy of, 16; demographics of, 16–17; housing in, 84–85; immigration to, 244n55; overview of, 4–5; police crackdown and brutality in, 67–68; social service infrastructure in, 234. *See also* Minneapolis, MN; St. Paul, MN
Twin Cities Gay and Lesbian Pride Festival, 222
Twin Cities Gaze (newspaper), 109, 175, 179, 203–4, 209, 225–26
Twin Cities Pride (TCP), 230; Power to the People tent, 236–37
Twin Cities Transsexuals, 34
"two-spirit" people, 289n11

unhoused persons. *See* homelessness
United Farm Workers, 9
University of Minnesota: Fight Repression of Erotic Expression (FREE), 29; Human Sexuality Program, 79; Minnesota Student Association, 29
urban development: in Loring Park, 192–97; "revanchist urbanism," 182; urban renewal, 18–19, 182–83, 191. *See also* gentrification
"urban ghettos," 84–85

urban-rural divide, 11–12
US Congress, 92
US PROStitutes Collective (US PROS), 139
US Supreme Court, 90

vagrancy laws, 40, 66–67
Vaid, Urvashi, 61
"vampire theory" of homosexuality, 71, 72
vice squads, 40–41, 252n123; brutality of, 50–51; and public health risks, 82–83. *See also* Minneapolis Police Department (MPD)
victimhood narratives, 161–63, 165
Victor, Douglas, 45–46, 48
Vider, Stephen, 12
Vietnam Veterans Against the War, 31
violence: bias-motivated, 122; homicide, 96–98, 104–5; House Subcommittee on, 92; against LGBTQ populations, 55–58; and police, 60–61. *See also* hate crimes

Wallace, George, 40
Wallace, Roderick, 20

Walter Reed Army Medical Center, 139
The Warehouse (sex club), 186–87
WCCO-TV, Minneapolis, 124, 135, 143–46, 147–48, 151
White, Edmund, 28, 38, 61
White, Ryan, 129–130
whiteness: "ascendancy of," 15; South vs. upper Midwest, 6–7; "white habitus," 6; "white injury," 103; white supremacy, 107
Williams, Brenda, 131–36, 139, 141, 269n37
Willse, Craig, 88
Winton, Crane, Jr., 68–69, 71
Wolf, Wolfgang, 201, 206–7
women: AIDS cases, 130–31; in anti-pornography movement, 49
Woodruff, Judy, 147
Woodward, Kerry, 37, 55

Yeros, Stathis, 21, 209
Young Lords, 9

"zone of privacy," 46, 75, 185. *See also* private space

www.ingramcontent.com/pod-product-compliance
Lightning Source LLC
Chambersburg PA
CBHW030128240426
43672CB00005B/60